A Great and Rising Nation

AMERICAN BEGINNINGS, 1500–1900

A Series Edited by Hannah Farber, Edward Gray, Stephen Mihm, and Mark Peterson

Also in the series:

Trading Freedom: How Trade with China Defined Early America
by Dael A. Norwood

Accidental Pluralism: America and the Religious Politics of English Expansion, 1497–1662
by Evan Haefeli

Wives Not Slaves: Patriarchy and Modernity in the Age of Revolutions
by Kirsten Sword

The Province of Affliction: Illness and the Making of Early New England
by Ben Mutschler

Puritan Spirits in the Abolitionist Imagination
by Kenyon Gradert

Trading Spaces: The Colonial Marketplace and the Foundations of American Capitalism
by Emma Hart

Urban Dreams, Rural Commonwealth: The Rise of Plantation Society in the Chesapeake
by Paul Musselwhite

Building a Revolutionary State: The Legal Transformation of New York, 1776–1783
by Howard Pashman

Sovereign of the Market: The Money Question in Early America
by Jeffrey Sklansky

National Duties: Custom Houses and the Making of the American State
by Gautham Rao

Liberty Power: Antislavery Third Parties and the Transformation of American Politics
by Corey M. Brooks

The Making of Tocqueville's America: Law and Association in the Early United States
by Kevin Butterfield

A complete list of series titles is available on the University of Chicago Press website.

∴

A Great and Rising Nation

∵

NAVAL EXPLORATION AND
GLOBAL EMPIRE IN
THE EARLY US REPUBLIC

Michael A. Verney

THE UNIVERSITY OF CHICAGO PRESS
CHICAGO AND LONDON

PUBLICATION OF THIS BOOK HAS BEEN AIDED BY
A GRANT FROM THE BEVINGTON FUND.

The University of Chicago Press, Chicago 60637
The University of Chicago Press, Ltd., London
© 2022 by The University of Chicago
Published 2022
Printed in the United States of America

31 30 29 28 27 26 25 24 23 22   1 2 3 4 5

ISBN-13: 978-0-226-81838-2   (cloth)
ISBN-13: 978-0-226-81992-1   (paper)
ISBN-13: 978-0-226-81837-5   (e-book)
DOI: https://doi.org/10.7208/chicago/9780226818375.001.0001

Library of Congress Cataloging-in-Publication Data
Names: Verney, Michael A., author.
Title: A great and rising nation : naval exploration and global empire
    in the early US Republic / Michael A. Verney.
Other titles: American beginnings, 1500–1900.
Description: Chicago : The University of Chicago Press, 2022. |
    Series: American beginnings, 1500–1900 | Includes bibliographical
    references and index.
Identifiers: LCCN 2022001051 | ISBN 9780226818382 (cloth) |
    ISBN 9780226819921 (paperback) | ISBN 9780226818375 (ebook)
Subjects: LCSH: Sea-power—United States—History—19th
    century. | Imperialism—History—19th century. | United States—
    History, Naval—19th century. | United States—History—1815–1861.
Classification: LCC E182 .V47 2022 | DDC 359.00973—dc23/eng/
    20220120
LC record available at https://lccn.loc.gov/2022001051

♾ This paper meets the requirements of ANSI/NISO Z39.48-1992
(Permanence of Paper).

For my parents, Steve and Kay Verney, and especially for my beloved wife, Blair Bailey Verney, whose love and support enabled me to write this book

Contents

Introduction

David Porter was restless. A veteran captain in the United States Navy, he had been appointed one of three founding members of the Board of Navy Commissioners in early 1815.[1] Despite the honor, Porter found paperwork tedious and dull. He was used to more exciting fare. The War of 1812 against Great Britain had ended in February 1815, leaving him and his fellow commissioners to advise the Navy Department on the transition to peace. It was a far cry from Porter's wartime command of the frigate *Essex*, when he had scuttled the British whaling fleet in the eastern Pacific, claimed the Marquesan island of Nuku Hiva for the United States, conquered two of its tribes, and endured a bloody sea battle with the Royal Navy at Valparaiso, Chile.[2] By late October, Porter again felt the lure of the sea—and of empire. Taking a page, he began writing a proposal for President James Madison.

"Prompted by a desire of serving my country, and of using every effort for her honor and glory," Porter offered to lead a naval exploring expedition into the Pacific Ocean. He promised Madison that the Pacific still harbored many secrets, including peoples wholly unknown to the Western world. Recounting the names of famous European navigators like Captain James Cook, George Vancouver, and the Comte de la Pérouse, Porter bemoaned that "every nation has successively contributed in this way but us." US citizens had "profited by their labours" without making any "efforts of our own." By launching a national voyage of discovery, the United States would pay its cultural debt to European powers, establish valuable lines of trade with Pacific islanders, "enlarg[e] the bounds of science," and contribute "to the knowledge of men, and to the fame of the Nation." A well-conducted mission might even increase trade with China and convince Japan to further open its ports. Above all, it would place the United States on a more equal footing with the major European powers: "We, Sir, are a great and rising nation," Porter reminded Madison—it was time to put the United States "on an eminence with others."[3]

Although it took several more decades, the United States would eventually realize Porter's imperial ambitions and more. Between 1838 and 1860, the US Navy sent or contributed men and resources to at least seventeen exploring expeditions around the world. True to Porter's original vision, two squadrons surveyed and charted the Pacific World. A third Pacific mission, led by Commodore Matthew Calbraith Perry, fulfilled Porter's fantasy of widening US commercial access to Japan, though it was not technically an exploring expedition. Other expeditions sailed to portions of the globe that Porter had failed to anticipate and for purposes that he never imagined; in the 1840s and 1850s, the Navy Department dispatched officers and men to prove the veracity of the Bible in the Holy Land, conduct astronomical science in Chile, probe for new slave territories in South America, extend free Black colonization in Africa, plumb the bottom of the Atlantic Ocean, discover a canal route in Panama, and rescue imperiled British explorers in the Arctic. The duties of naval explorers continued when they returned home; in the 1840s and 1850s, it was not uncommon for the Navy Department to direct commanders to compose narrative and scientific accounts of their voyages. In 1843, Congress entrusted the management of the nation's first federally funded museum of natural history to a naval officer.[4]

The exploring expeditions of the antebellum US Navy had strong echoes of European imperialism. As with societies in Asia, North Africa, and Oceania, European polities had long relied on maritime exploration as a powerful tool for imperial aggrandizement. That trend accelerated in the fifteenth century, when early modern European vessels began sailing to geographies, resources, and ecologies outside European and Mediterranean waters.[5] In addition to power and wealth, such voyages amassed prestige. As the Maryland House of Representatives declared in early 1828, European exploring expeditions had not only "opened new channels for commercial enterprise," but also "acquired reputation" for the countries that dispatched them.[6] They were one of those things, explained a congressman, "that elevates and dignifies the character of a nation."[7]

Acquiring a "reputation" or "character" in Europe was very much what many white antebellum US citizens wanted.[8] Since colonial days, white denizens of what would become the United States had felt impoverished when it came to European culture, especially the fine arts, literature, science, and fashion.[9] Though they practically invented the modern nation-state with their revolution, white US citizens still suffered from an inferiority complex when faced with the refined grandeur of the Great Powers of Europe.[10] Indeed, scholars have suggested that the overblown patriotism of many ordinary white US citizens was the result of diffidence, not confidence.[11] Postcolonial anxiety was a fact of life for governing elites as well, with US statesmen and diplomats in the early republic worrying about making the United States into a "treaty-worthy" nation, to borrow Eliga Gould's phrase.[12] Seen in this light, independence was a process, not a single event.[13] In the words of the Declaration of Independence, the goal of the Revolution was "to assume among the powers of the earth, the separate and equal station to which the Laws of Nature and of Nature's God entitle them." It was thus a combination of home rule and equal international standing, especially in European circles. It was for this reason that Benjamin Franklin, while serving as the revolutionary ambassador to France, ordered all US fighting vessels not to molest Cook's discovery ships in 1779: by demonstrating the revolutionaries' respect for scientific expeditions, he was laying an early claim to his nascent country's gentility.[14]

Citizens like Franklin and Porter were "explorationists." They believed that partaking in European-style voyages of discovery would win them the international respect they coveted. Their sense of honor was highly European, even aristocratic; they were convinced that the "empire of science" was something that all civilized nations had an obligation to contribute to, and they spoke passionately about US failures to repay those cultural debts. Unsurprisingly, explorationists largely came from the middle and upper classes of white US society. Some, like David Porter, were naval officers—individuals who were already steeped in a culture of genteel honor.[15] Others were statesmen and diplomats, while still others were private middle-class citizens who aspired to fame, glory, and adventure. Whatever their background, they agreed on two main principles: one, that naval exploration was glorious and useful, and two, that it had to be a state enterprise. This put them at odds with those merchant mariners who saw themselves as republicanized versions of the enlightened naval explorers of Europe.[16] Explorationists didn't buy it; they doubted that private actors had the means or the motives to produce accurate charts or pursue scientific discovery. Private expeditions, after all, had to worry about the bottom line. Nor could they be, as one congressman put it, "stamp[ed] . . . with a national character."[17]

Explorationists understood that there were three overlapping components to being a great imperial nation in the late eighteenth and early nineteenth centuries. The first was developmental strength, or possessing raw economic and military vigor. The second was civilizational maturity, meaning cultural sophistication according to European standards, and the third was diplomatic recognition as a Great Power by one of the other Great Powers.[18] This last honor often came with the expectation of managing the balance of power in Europe and the Mediterranean world.[19] White US citizens were suspicious of large standing militaries and had little appetite for intervening directly in European or Ottoman affairs, but they wanted the respect that the Great Powers of Europe afforded to each other. In essence, they sought European recognition as a "great power" without having to act on some of the chief requirements of Great Power–hood—especially an expensive military machine and extensive diplomatic (and often belligerent) engagements in Europe and its environs.

Such restrictions made it hard for explorationists to argue that the federal government ought to replicate a key aspect of European global imperialism. When Madison scrapped plans for Porter's expedition in 1816, he reflected white public opinion.[20] In the 1810s and 1820s, most white citizens rejected the notion that the federal government ought to embark in grand, European-style voyages of discovery. Such expeditions smacked of monarchism and aristocracy. They seemed elitist, often profligate, and impractical. They might require new taxes, uplift some men over others, and unnecessarily strengthen the powers of the federal government.[21] At worst, they would concentrate too much power in the central government and thereby undermine liberty for whites and slavery for Blacks. If any voyages of discovery were to be undertaken at all, most white citizens thought they should follow the route of the Lewis and Clark Expedition up the Missouri River in 1804–1806 or Major Stephen Harriman Long's overland mission to the Rocky Mountains in 1820.[22] European respect was valuable, but not so precious as to risk liberty for white men.

Explorationists, then, had the difficult task of persuading their countrymen to join them in a global imperial venture that seemed to imperil their most cherished political and social values. The plethora of exploring expeditions in the 1850s is proof that they succeeded. Indeed, some of these missions were on a mammoth scale; when the North Pacific Exploring Expedition set off from Hampton Roads, Virginia, in 1853, it counted five ships and four hundred officers and men. It was not only monstrously larger than most contemporary European expeditions (which tended to comprise just one or two vessels), but it appears to have been the largest Western voyage of discovery ever undertaken up to that time.[23] How did this happen? What had changed between 1816 and 1853?

Simply put, naval exploration had become more popular. The United States embraced a European strategy for global imperialism because explorationists made it more desirable. They learned to translate their aristocratic, European-style vision into a utilitarian, republicanized one. They recognized that although global exploring expeditions could be massively expensive, they did not have to be; indeed, some of the expeditions covered in this book were actually quite small (and therefore cheap). Others were the product of public-private partnerships, thereby diminishing their cost. And while one navy expedition did sail to the Ottoman Empire, the rest were projections of power far beyond Europe and western Asia—thereby avoiding entanglements with the Great Powers in their immediate neighborhoods. The dream of achieving European respect would remain, but gradually explorationists came to understand the importance of emphasizing how the most influential segments of white US society would benefit directly from naval exploration. The turning of the United States toward a form of European imperialism is therefore a story about coalition building. As new groups bought into the explorationist vision, they imported their own imperial interests and aspirations. The movement changed, and its scope broadened. Naval exploration became a tool for achieving diplomatic prestige and many other things besides. What had once seemed an unnecessary expense and even a dangerous undertaking had been transformed into a popular instrument of imperial power.

This book is about that process of imperialization. Each chapter of *A Great and Rising Nation* examines either the conversion of a particular interest group and its ramifications or the implications of failure. Chapter 1 describes how the Europeanized, glory-drenched vision of early explorationists crashed and burned in the late 1820s. Proponents quickly realized that they had to couch their proposals in republican terms and appeal to concrete imperial interests—things like capitalism, class, religion, race, and US–UK rapprochement. Chapter 2 explains how Jacksonian Democrats, once opposed to Adams's proposal for a voyage of discovery to the Pacific, ended up embracing it. They championed the United States Exploring Expedition of 1838–1842 because they came to believe that US economic interests were threatened by Oceanic Islanders, unruly sailors, and insufficient cartography. Their investment helped forge an empire of commerce in the Pacific World. Chapter 3 follows the United States Exploring Expedition back home. It shows how explorationists used the expedition's publications and specimens to sell global imperialism to white, middle-class citizens. They succeeded wildly; white readers devoured expeditionary narratives and thronged the National Gallery in Washington, DC, eager to see the mission's specimens and curiosities firsthand. The imperial products of the expedition reinforced domestic hierarchies, especially in terms of class, culture, and race.

Chapter 4 enters the Islamic world with an examination of the US Expedition to the River Jordan and the Dead Sea of 1847–1848. It demonstrates that the mission was dispatched to bolster conservative Protestant Christianity against Catholic immigrants, morally suspect western pioneers, and liberal biblical skeptics. Faith was power, and the expedition's evangelical commander, William Francis Lynch, wanted the United States to amass as much spiritual power as possible. The fact that Lynch's expedition relied so heavily on Muslim actors is one of more interesting twists of that story. Chapter 5 turns to slavery. It details how, in the turbulent 1850s, proslavery expansionists seized on naval exploration as a means of expanding US slaveholding territory into the teeming river valleys of South America. Though no US colonies emerged in the South Atlantic, the navy's explorations demonstrated that naval reconnaissance could serve the interests of slaveholders. Chapter 6 returns to the seminal issue of European acclaim. When a famed British explorer, Sir John Franklin, went missing with his men in the Arctic in the late 1840s, his wife, Lady Jane Franklin, asked President Zachary Taylor for help. The US Navy responded to the call by partnering with a New York City merchant named Henry Grinnell. The expeditions named in his honor garnered unprecedented British praise and led to a forgotten era of imperial rapprochement along racial and gendered lines.

Like all studies, this one has limits. It does not cover all seventeen of the antebellum US Navy's exploring expeditions, but has instead selected seven. Each embodies a specific form of US global imperialism in the antebellum era—especially empires of knowledge, commerce, religion, slavery, and diplomatic prestige. As most of the seventeen missions were commercial, I felt there was no need to replicate commercial imperialism beyond the United States Exploring Expedition. The selected expeditions were also the most popular ones. They offer, therefore, the best opportunity to study empire building as a domestic political process. Crucially, this book does not claim that every member of a newly persuaded constituency remained forever wedded to the explorationist program. Such an explanation would be too facile, and it would ignore the ways in which imperial impulses can compete.[24] Instead, it suggests that the use of naval exploration to address a constituency's core concern made the strategy itself more appealing to members of that constituency. Having experienced its benefits firsthand, the white, well-to-do US citizens of a "converted" interest group were more inclined to view similar projects favorably, even when applied to other purposes and imperial contexts.

A central contention of this book is that the United States was neither wholly exceptional nor unexceptional as an imperial power. Instead, it was both.[25] As explorationists' infatuation with European navigational feats makes clear, the nation lived and breathed in a transimperial world.[26] The explorationist vision, at its core, was not unique because it sought to replicate precisely what European nations had been doing for a long time. On the other hand, that European spark had to be kept alive and nourished in a US context. Many of the navy's exploring expeditions bore the unmistakable marks of US, not contemporary European, imperialism. The proslavery surveys of South America are a case in point; so, too, is the Dead

Sea expedition. Though the British had tried to do virtually the same feat as Lynch and his party (i.e., descend the Jordan River in small boats from the Sea of Galilee to the Dead Sea), they did so primarily to resolve a stubborn geographical mystery. Their goal was to seize the honor of determining the level of the Dead Sea, not to buttress a particular interpretation of Protestant Christianity.[27]

Another key argument of this book is that antebellum US imperialism was multidimensional. While early national leaders liked to think of the United States as a young Hercules, it was actually more like a kraken.[28] The head of this antebellum US empire was the upper- and middle-class white body politic. This was a racially and economically exclusive community bounded by a common adherence to republicanism, capitalism, Protestantism, white supremacy, traditional gender roles, and imperial expansion.[29] Its tentacles were the varied imperial impulses of the antebellum period: naval expeditions across the world, but also state and nonstate imperial projects in the North American West, Latin America and the Caribbean, the Pacific World, West Africa, and at home. Indeed, the coils of empire nearly always reached back to the metropole, often fortifying the same principles that had dispatched them. Not all these tentacles were in harmony; they got in each other's way at times, and sometimes even struggled against each other. The US Civil War was the result of one of these clashes. As the naval lieutenant and explorationist Matthew Fontaine Maury put it, the contest over the expansion of slavery was "a question of Empire."[30] In 1860–1861, the monster split, and one devoured the other. Before that crisis, various groups—including white and Black abolitionists, free-thought advocates, first-wave feminists, pacifists, missionaries, North American Indians, and even some working-class sailors—tugged valiantly at the nation's conscience in the antebellum era. Their objections were largely ignored. The beast stretched on.

Like the mythological sea monster itself, the antebellum United States was an organic whole, a single nation. As the experience of the twenty-first-century United States attests, nations can have divisions and continue to be what Benedict Anderson has called an "imagined community."[31] Much has been made in the scholarly literature about the actual site of this US ethnogenesis. Western historians since Theodore Roosevelt and Frederick Jackson Turner have proclaimed that US national identity was forged on the frontier. More recently, maritime historians have claimed that the eastward, oceanic frontier was more important than the North American West in the making of a national identity, especially in the early years. The work of other scholars has allowed us to transcend this question. The communication, transportation, and print revolutions connected the corners of the nation and even beyond in the antebellum period.[32] With their construction, there were very little practical boundaries among the regions of the United States—and even less in the imaginations of white citizens. This connectivity undermines the issue of where the nation was made, because the nation, as an imagined community, extended wherever its citizens and their imaginations spread. It followed them, even if they passed national boundaries.[33] To the perennial question of where the US nation was made, neither borderlands nor maritime historians are wholly correct because the answer lies with both: US national identity was made at sea and in the North American North, South, East, and West, across the globe, and in its heartlands. It was the product of the entire national experience, which was unfolding simultaneously in all of these spaces during the era of the early US republic.

An example may illustrate this fact. William Francis Lynch, the commander of the Dead Sea expedition, understood his encounters with Bedouin Arabs in light of stereotypes of Native North Americans. I say "stereotypes" because there is no evidence that Lynch ever met an Indigenous North American; the closest that he appears to have come was through the midnight stories of a frontiersman during a western steamboat ride.[34] Nonetheless, he believed he "*knew*" Indigenous Americans, and brought this metropolitan and cultural "knowledge" with him to western Asia. He did this literally, giving the Ottoman sultan handsome folios on Indigenous North American life as a way to win Ottoman permission for his survey of the Dead Sea.[35] Afterward, when Lynch composed a narrative account of his odyssey in the Holy Land, he fashioned himself an expert on how Indigenous Americans compared to Bedouin Arabs.[36] One of the readers of his book was an army officer stationed at Fort Gratiot, Michigan.[37] We do not know exactly what Colonel Keeney thought about Lynch's narrative, but the naval officer's anthropological and cultural descriptions may have informed Keeney's ideas about how to deal with the Indigenous North Americans he encountered as an army officer. In this way, the pathways of nineteenth-century communication, transportation, and print technologies created a national network that surpassed national boundaries. They amalgamated western borderlands, the globe, and metropole into a single nationalized space.

In addition to being a nation, the antebellum United States was a globally informed imperial society. The narratives and scientific findings of US naval exploration helped create a vertical and hierarchical society based on race, class, and gender. A visit to the National Gallery in Washington, DC, left white visitors feeling assured of their (supposed) social, racial, cultural, and national superiority to peoples at home and abroad. Likewise, proslavery defenders used both the skulls and naval accounts of Oceanic Islanders to argue in favor of Black bondage. Evangelicals pointed to Lynch's federal survey of the Dead Sea region to contend that the Bible was fact and not subject to disbelief or literary criticism. This kind of thinking contributed to state antiblasphemy laws and created a legal hierarchy of conscience.[38] Gender traditionalists, meanwhile, could pedestal Lady Jane Franklin, the wife of lost British explorer Sir John Franklin, as an ideal picture of what a "noble and devoted wife" should look like.[39] Similarly, Lady Franklin's friend and ally, Elisha Kent Kane, was fêted for demonstrating white male strength and chivalric patriarchy in his quest to restore Sir John to his wife and daughter. Cosmopolitanism, for all its virtues, could also sometimes be a mechanism of oppression and restriction at home.

Lastly, the antebellum United States was a global empire as well as a single nation and an imperial society. Early US nationals described the United States as an empire, but they used the word with far less precision than we do today. For them, *empire* could mean any vast field (whether spatially or culturally) of domination or significant mastery. Thus, an empire could be private or public, national or transnational, or even natural—the "empire of desolation," for instance.[40] A human empire might be territorial, as in the British or Japanese Empires, or it could be commercial, as in "the empire of commerce."[41] Scientists spoke of "the Republic of Science" in imperial terms, while Christians sought to expand "the great Saviour's empire."[42] When Jefferson looked west, he saw a federated, political "empire of liberty." Others used *empire* to refer to military strength, as when George Washington fantasized about the United States eventually having "some weight in the scale of empires."[43] This book combines these fluid, often positive eighteenth- and nineteenth-century definitions of empire with our more modern, anti-imperial sensibilities. It defines *empire* as a field of cultural domination or spatial governance where power, knowledge, and/or access to resources is structured hierarchically. In this sense, the National Gallery was the site of both a national and transimperial empire of science. Beyond US borders, the global aspect of the US antebellum empire can be seen most clearly in the Pacific. It was there, as chapter 2 relates, that the navy and its explorers forced US capitalistic governance on Oceanic Islanders and ordinary seamen through treaties, the exercise of legal and judicial power, and state violence.

The creation of this global US empire was mainly a state enterprise. While some early secretaries of the navy tried the extinguish the explorationist vision, others championed it. Under Secretary John Pendleton Kennedy in the early 1850s, the Navy Department came to look much like the British Admiralty: an unprecedented locus of imperial activism and power, the very heart of the kraken. Yet even Kennedy did not act alone; the making of a global empire and the raising of an imperial society was the work of many hands. Private citizens, enlisted seamen, Ottoman statesmen, Bedouin Arabs, South American elites, Manhattan merchants, British noblewomen, and Greenland Inuits all lent their assistance to the US imperial project in the early republic. In many ways, we are still living with the edifice that they helped to erect. This is—at least, in part—their story, too.[44]

CHAPTER 1

Jeremiah Reynolds and the Empire of Knowledge

The rain chased them back down the mountainside. Spurred on by the wet pelting of the storm, Jeremiah Reynolds and his companions scurried back to their headquarters, a meager outpost that guarded the pass of Antuco, Chile, from bandits and outlaws. There they joined the fort's small contingent of soldiers and watched as the ripening gale approached the volcano from the north. As evening fell, "the wind began to blow powerfully," Reynolds later remembered, "and a scene occurred which can never be erased from our memory." What followed was a "violent conflict of the elements," in which the "tempest expended itself in drifting snow and hail" upon the mountain, while "lightning issued in one tireless flash, from a cloud that seemed to gather, concentrate, and repose, on the apex of the volcano. The peals of thunder were fierce and deafening, as they reverberated along those everlasting collonades [*sic*] of rock." At times, the "flames of the volcano might be seen' [*sic*] though generally they were veiled by the drifting snow," while, further down, swollen streams "bearded the mountain with foam."[1]

Learned, gifted, and with seemingly boundless energy and confidence, Reynolds possessed ambitions almost as fiery as the volcano he hoped to summit. A former schoolteacher and newspaper editor from Ohio, he had become enthralled with maritime exploration and the possibility of adventure and fame that it offered. By the time of his arrival at Antuco in the fall of 1830, he had devoted four years of his life to convincing his countrymen to dispatch a national exploring expedition. He had found ready allies in President John Quincy Adams and Adams's secretary of the navy, Samuel Southard. Like Reynolds, both men viewed naval exploration as a potent tool for advancing US honor in European eyes. And while all three were deeply committed to bolstering the US commercial empire in the South Pacific, they believed that knowledge, not commerce, would garner the greatest laurels. Fired by visions of grandeur, they had assembled a formidable coalition of elites to aid them. These included state actors—especially naval officers and "Adams men" in state legislatures and Congress—but also private citizens like scientists and sea captains. United by mutual interests, this broad coalition arose to clamor for a national voyage of discovery to the South Pacific.

Their dreams came to shambles. While two explorationist bills passed the House, a powerful senator from South Carolina, Robert Young Hayne, arose to deny Reynolds his campaign for glory. A strong republican and chairman of the Senate's Naval Affairs Committee, Hayne's preference was for an empire of commerce in the Pacific, not an empire of knowledge. And herein lay the source of his opposition: he was frightened by the sweeping, Europeanized, sentimental vision that Reynolds and his allies had brought to his committee. If acted upon, Hayne feared, the United States would embark on an endless series of voyages of discovery, all in pursuit of knowledge. These would entail an enormous expansion of federal power, at great expense, and possibly even result in overseas colonies. Perhaps worst of all, it would Europeanize the United States. A voyage for commercial security made sense to him, but a voyage for knowledge appeared to threaten the empire of liberty—at least for white men.

Stymied by Hayne, the project collapsed. Reynolds sailed south on his own. Capitalizing on contacts he had made during the preparation for the original national exploring expedition, he cofounded the South Sea Fur Company and Exploring Expedition in New York in March 1829.[2] Sealers, not the US Navy, had carried him to the Southern Hemisphere.

That autumn night, gazing up at the contest of the elements above him, Reynolds may have seen a metaphor for his own political fortunes. His fiery ambitions would remain—they were at the core of who he was—but he would have to translate them into new political languages. He would have to be especially sensitive to republican anxieties; when it came to winning over politicians, he had learned that rhetoric mattered. The phoenix may have crashed, but it would not remain so for long. Reynolds knew that he and his allies had ignited serious enthusiasm for naval exploration in elite circles. Their failed crusade had been an exploration in itself, charting the nation's conflicted feelings over global imperialism in the late 1820s. The measure's near success had demonstrated a deep craving for European esteem among US citizens and politicians alike. It also revealed that significant numbers of US politicians were warm to maritime discovery, so long as they were framed in limited, practical rhetoric. An empire of commerce, not an empire of knowledge, would have to be his path forward.

That was, if he ever got back to the United States. Reynolds turned aside. Cold and wet, with stormwater rushing through the leaky fort, he and his companions settled in for a long and sleepless night. Come morning, they hoped they could complete their mission and ascend the volcano itself. For now, only the dawn could enlighten their prospects.

JEREMIAH REYNOLDS

Jeremiah Reynolds was a striver in a nation of strivers. Born in Pennsylvania in 1799, he moved to Wilmington, Ohio, with his mother, new stepfather, and stepbrother, in 1808.[3] Wilmington was a new town then, having recently been carved out of deep forest.[4] Though most of the town's buildings were composed of log cabins, it was well laid out, with 128 plots and six streets.[5] Larger frame and even brick buildings soon followed, such that Wilmington became the county seat in 1810.[6] It may have been here that Reynolds acquired an attachment to the masculine ethos that would guide his life. After all, Wilmington was a hard-drinking, rough place. It was a rare Saturday afternoon that passed without fisticuffs downtown.[7] Reynolds's physical size may have helped him fit in; contemporaries described him as "large of his age," and that later he grew up to be "a firmly built man, of medium stature, with a short nose, and a somewhat broad face."[8]

Throughout his adult life, Reynolds would value a brawny masculinity. He later described himself as being "inured to hardy culture, and self-relying from my boyhood."[9] When trying to organize the Adams administration's expedition in 1828, he proclaimed that "these are times and circumstances under which I would not hesitate to assume almost any responsibility.—No Man ever deserved greatness, or was in reality great who would not."[10] That same year, he wrote a patron that he had "contended manfully" while trying to convince Virginians to join him in his explorationist campaign.[11] Later, when faced with his greatest opponent, Secretary of the Navy Mahlon Dickerson, Reynolds questioned the secretary's masculinity, challenging him "to point out a single manly expression in anything [he had] written connected with the enterprise."[12]

Yet Reynolds also wanted to be something more than a tough farm boy from Ohio. An anecdote about a community log-rolling event is revealing in this regard. He and his stepbrother were known locally as "Job's oxen," after Job Jeffries, Reynolds's stepfather. When Reynolds broke down under his share of a load, a wag "remarked that one of Job's oxen was a calf." Laughter rang out. Reynolds picked himself up, mounted a fence, and addressed his neighbors "in the most stately attitude": "Gentlemen," he began, "I have no father to guide and protect me in life, and you have had your fun with me to-day. Many of you are old enough to be ashamed of thus rallying a young and unprotected boy; but, gentlemen, you know little about him of whom you are making fun to-day, for I assure you the time is coming when you will feel proud that you ever rolled logs with Jeremiah N. Reynolds."[13]

Of course, Reynolds was not the only ambitious young man in the United States. He came of age in a culture that was obsessed with what one scholar has called "the gospel of ascent."[14] As economic growth increased opportunities for social mobility, US society came to champion qualities associated with economic success.[15] In 1840, the celebrated French traveler, Alexis de Tocqueville, commented that "ambition is the universal feeling" in the United States.[16] Reynolds's countrymen loved the phrases *go ahead* and the *go-ahead principle*, and they invoked them regularly.[17] "Self-respect in America," Scott Sandage claims, "depended on approaching life with a sense of perpetual ambition."[18] Reynolds's Ohio was part of these economic and cultural trajectories. Far from a provincial backwater in the early 1800s, Ohio had long been subject to the capitalist forces that were then transforming the United States.[19]

Yet even by the standards of the day, Reynolds's ambitions were unusually grand. He did not merely want a decent law career, his own land, or a rich family life. He wanted something more; he wanted to be remembered as a great man, and to be remembered forever. As he proclaimed to a patron in 1827, "I am not great yet, but will be & glorious!—"[20] The following year, he urged the Navy Department to "give me latitude and I will strike bold for Immortality."[21] At the end of one of his letters, he penned a small ditty: "Higher, higher let us rise, / up the steps of glory, / that our names may [be listed] this time, / in our countrys story."[22] If antebellum US citizens harkened to the "gospel of ascent," Reynolds was one of its high priests. No wonder his enemies pegged him—with not a little justice—as a monomaniac.[23]

Where did such limitless ambition come from? His lack of a father may have played a role, but his education may have, too. Jeffries did not value book learning, so Reynolds had to work mornings, evenings, and Saturdays to pay tuition at his local school. When particularly low on funds, he was "known to have gone to the prairies of Clark County and engaged in ditching."[24] By 1816, he had learned enough to become a teacher himself.[25] Like many of his countrymen, Reynolds was enchanted with Greek and Roman authors. Between 1819 and 1822, he attended Ohio University in Athens, where he was an active member of the Athenian Literary Society and the university debate club, and a founder of the Philomathean Society.[26] Whether he graduated or not is unclear, but by the summer of 1822 he had become a pupil of Francis Glass, a teacher of classical languages from the eastern states.[27] From Glass and other sources, Reynolds may have ingested classical authors' emphasis on fame and reputation. He admired the legend of Jason and the Golden Fleece, for instance, and in the 1830s he chided his opponents to think what "the future Plutarch of our republic may inquire" about their actions.[28] When Mahlon Dickerson charged him with seeking to be "Palenurus [*sic*] of the [exploring] squadron,"[29] Reynolds did not refute the charge. In fact, he probably wished that Dickerson had compared him to Aeneas himself, and not merely to his helmsman.

Another likely and major source for Reynolds's ambitions were the romantic descriptions of voyages of discovery that he pored over as a boy. We don't know exactly what he read as a youth, but he confessed to having, "at an early period of my life[,] . . . imbibed a relish . . . for books of voyages and travels, when I had not yet seen the ocean."[30] Perhaps, like Washington Irving, he smuggled accounts of exploration with him to school, "where he slyly read them instead of working at his lessons."[31] However Reynolds encountered them, accounts of nautical voyages and foreign travel convinced him "that the maritime enterprise of our ancestors was an important element in the foundation of our subsequent power."[32] The near-hagiographic celebration of explorers may have played a formative role in his personality. Strong and smart but emotionally isolated, Reynolds may have burrowed himself in books, looking for role models in the stern, imposing faces of men like Christopher Columbus. Columbus's star was indeed rising in this period; it was no coincidence, in fact, that while Reynolds was seeking to convince his countrymen to support the US Navy's first voyage of discovery, Washington Irving was in Madrid, laboring over a romanticized, heroic biography of Columbus.[33]

What we do know for certain is that one of Reynolds's heroes was Alexander von Humboldt. It was a relationship that spoke volumes about Reynolds and who he sought to become. Humboldt was a Prussian baron who had embarked on an epic trek through the South American continent between 1799 and 1803. He wrote prolifically after his return, publishing scientific volumes that proved hugely popular on both sides of the Atlantic. Translations of *Vues des Cordilleres* and *Political Essays on the Kingdom of New Spain* were affordable and readily available in the English-speaking world.[34] Part of Humboldt's appeal was that he combined the best traditions of Enlightenment science with the rising, stirring sentiments of Romanticism. He gathered reams of data on every conceivable subject in natural history, but he also wrote passionately and poetically—almost rhapsodically—about nature. In South America, he was awestruck at the feeling of being part of a larger, organic, and interconnected whole. In later works, he would call this sense of the universe "cosmos."[35] Indeed, it was Humboldt who developed the modern field of ecology, or the study of the relationships among communities of organisms and their environments.[36]

Figure 1.1 Julius Schrader, *Baron Alexander von Humboldt*, 1859. In the background is the volcano of Chimborazo, modern-day Ecuador. Humboldt was a perennial source of inspiration for US explorationists like Jeremiah Reynolds. They hoped the United States would eventually acquire the kind of European-style gentility that Humboldt embodied. (Courtesy of Metropolitan Museum of Art, New York; https://www.metmuseum.org/. Gift of H. O. Havemeyer, 1889, 89.20.)

In recent decades, historians and journalists have chronicled Humboldt's enormous influence on Anglophonic writers, scientists, explorers, and early environmentalists.[37] Among his admirers was Reynolds. Like Humboldt, Reynolds was a gifted writer, an inveterate Romantic, and an insatiable adventurer. His theories, methods, and travels, in fact, were very much inspired by the Prussian scientist.[38] His sojourns through South America, for instance, and especially his obsession with mounting volcanoes, were partly undertaken in tribute to the man he called "the learned Humboldt."[39] Reynolds's later lectures, travels, publications, and focus on networking were also reminiscent of Humboldt's own tireless strategies for disseminating his theories and knowledge.

On the surface, Reynolds's identification with the esteemed Humboldt seems odd. How could a classically trained schoolteacher in Ohio with virtually no scientific credentials compare himself with a European aristocrat and one of the world's greatest scientific luminaries? The answer lies in the evolution of Western knowledge. In the early 1800s, science was only gradually evolving as a distinctive profession; for most of the Enlightenment, it had been a pastime or hobby for gentlemen who could afford to devote themselves to it. The term *scientist*, in fact, would not even emerge until the 1830s;[40] before then, writers used the term *scientific* as an adjective, as in "scientific men" or "scientific corps."[41] *Naturalist, natural philosopher*, and *experimental philosopher* were also preferred by many who would be subsequently dubbed *scientists*.[42] The early 1800s witnessed the creation of a growing coterie of these men. Unlike their Enlightenment-era predecessors, these were not individuals whose fortunes were already made, but those who earned their living through science. In the United States, they competed for authority with more democratically inclined citizen naturalists. In the words of one historian, "an empire of reason" jousted with a "democracy of facts."[43] This phenomenon played out at sea as well as on land, with professionalized astronomers, hydrographers, and meteorologists competing with mariners and their "folkloric" and "vocational" knowledge of the marine environment.[44]

Rough know-how and professional science combined in what might be called an "empire of knowledge." This was an expansive field of diverse (and often contested) facts and methodologies about the natural world. Professional scientists merely played a part in this empire, albeit an increasingly important one. As Cameron Strang has recently argued, the term *knowledge* is more inclusive than *science*, allowing US historians to study Black, Indigenous, and working-class comprehensions of the natural world.[45] And knowledge in the early US republic was still something fairly democratic, at least for whites; it could be acquired through reading, observation, and direct experience in addition to formal training. Reynolds may not have been a "naturalist" or a "scientifick" per se, but he was a learned man for his time and country, and he was willing to experience the natural world personally, forcefully, and directly. While a few rivals questioned his authority, on the whole these qualities made it possible for him to be an active mover and shaker in the US empire of knowledge.[46]

Even so, Reynolds might never have become an explorer had it not been for a veteran army officer and fellow Ohioan named John Cleves Symmes. Like Reynolds, Symmes had become infatuated with Humboldtian exploration. Having earned a reputation for his service as an army lieutenant during the War of 1812, Symmes now turned an eye toward scientific and geographical conquest. After reading Humboldt's works, he developed a theory that the world was hollow and that it contained other spheres, "each maintaining highly specialized life-forms, and each, because of the way it turned on its central axis, accepting a tremendous flow of water at its poles, which then cycled back through desalinating tunnels to burst forth again as equatorial springs and sources for mighty rivers like the Nile and Amazon."[47] The entrance to these fruitful subterranean worlds, Symmes believed, would be found in the North and South Poles. He viewed exploration as glorious and potentially lucrative, and contended that the reputation of the United States in Europe would soar if it discovered the rich inner worlds that lurked below.[48]

Infatuated with this theory, Symmes crisscrossed Ohio, speaking to packed lecture halls across the state. Before intrigued audiences, the ex-soldier demonstrated scientific principles using a set of homemade rotating globes, magnets, and iron filings. He mixed his presentations with passionate nationalistic calls for an exploring expedition to the North Pole to locate entrances to interior worlds.[49] It was during one of these performances sometime around 1824 that Reynolds first encountered Symmes.[50] Reynolds was serving as the editor for the *Wilmington Speculator*, and was deeply immersed in election-year politics.[51] During Symmes's lecture, however, he found himself transfixed. Here was an older, grizzled man with knowledge, calling for the kinds of expeditions that he had worshiped since his boyhood. To Reynolds, Symmes may have seemed his ticket out of Wilmington and to the greater career that he craved. He may have seen the old veteran as a masculine role model, describing him later as "a gallant soldier and an estimable man."[52] Even if Reynolds harbored some concerns about the soundness of Symmes's intellect, he admired the elder man's quest for personal and national glory.[53] In a heartbeat, Reynolds abandoned the *Speculator*, became Symmes's disciple, and joined him on his lecture circuit.[54]

Neither Symmes nor Reynolds were alone in aching for European approval and esteem. Early US nationalism was intensely partisan and heady, but also profoundly insecure when it came to European opinion.[55] While US citizens were proud of their booming economy and vaunted their political system, many fretted over their lack of cultural attainments. Their limited contributions to the empire of knowledge were especially embarrassing. When Abbé Guillaume Raynal commented disparagingly how "astonishing" it was "that America has not yet produced a single good poet, an able mathematician, a man of genius in a single art, or a single science," or when the British minister Sydney Smith asked who read a US book or learned of a US chemist, patriots in the United States felt compelled to vindicate their country.[56] Recognition was therefore not solely an individual matter, but a national concern; many elite white US citizens believed they had to prove themselves capable of producing the kinds of art, science, and culture that Europe had for centuries. In this sense, the youthful, ambitious Reynolds was a microcosm of the nation in the larger Atlantic World. No wonder, then, that when Reynolds learned of the ambition of his former mentor, Francis Glass, to compose a life of Washington in Latin, he underwrote the project. His goal, he explained, was to preserve "every memorial of [US] intellectual superiority" in order to "reflect honor on our native genius."[57]

JOHN QUINCY ADAMS

One of the most prominent areas in which US citizens felt the dearth of their achievements was in geographical knowledge. When the US diplomat Caleb Cushing visited Madrid, he met Don Martín Fernández de Navarrete, a chronicler of Spanish exploration and the director of Spain's national office of cartography. While giving Cushing a tour of the facility, Navarrete "expressed his regret and surprise that the United States, a nation so opulent, and possessed of such extensive commerce, was so totally neglectful of its duty to science, to itself, and to the world, in this matter." Cowed, Cushing "could not but feel the force of his reproaches."[58] Even US exploration of North America had suffered several embarrassing episodes. The much-celebrated Lewis and Clark Expedition of 1804–1806, for example, was partially a failure from a scientific point of view. In European eyes, the embarkation of an exploring expedition was only half the battle; the other half was describing specimens and publishing scientific volumes and a historical narrative of the venture. One of Thomas Jefferson's enduring disappointments with his presidency was that Meriwether Lewis never wrote up the expedition's findings. A correspondent of Humboldt, Jefferson felt compelled to write to the distinguished man and apologize for his country's failure to publish the mission's results.[59] The public had to wait until 1814 to peruse the journals of that expedition, and even those were heavily edited.[60] Another glaring shortcoming was the US Coast Survey. Legally established in 1807 to chart the Atlantic coast, the survey was racked by poor Congressional oversight and shifting political priorities. Congress, frustrated by the Survey's slow pace, cancelled it in 1818. In its place, congressmen and the Navy Department authorized army and navy officers to chart specific portions of the Atlantic seaboard.[61]

No US citizen was more painfully conscious of his country's lackluster contributions to geography than President John Quincy Adams. While his parents, John and Abigail Adams, had raised their son with the strict expectation that he would be a public servant, it was knowledge, not politics, that had always been his primary passion.[62] Throughout his long career as a diplomat and statesman, Adams sought refuge from the ravages of public life in nature and in science. And never was he more satisfied than when he managed to converge natural history and public service. But the juncture of these was more than simply passion; as Charles Edel has argued, Adams was an ingenious grand strategist who understood that the path to national greatness entailed successive development through military, political, cultural, and moral power. Indeed, more than any other living US citizen, Adams had been the primary architect of the country's expansionism in the early nineteenth century. He had played a critical role in the Treaty of Ghent ending the War of 1812, in the Adams–Onís Treaty of 1819, and in the formation of the Monroe Doctrine in 1823. These diplomatic achievements had been designed to insulate the United States from Europe and to provide for its territorial growth. Now, as president, Adams sought to achieve the next phases of US development. That meant fostering prosperity through internal improvements and by promoting scientific and cultural attainments. In Adams's mind, great nations were like great men: strong and independent, but also aesthetically and scientifically sophisticated.[63]

As he surveyed the country's relationship with geographical knowledge, Adams could at least take some comfort from recent army surveys of the North American West. In his inaugural address in March 1825, he told attendees that "progress [had] been made . . . in exploring the interior regions of the Union, and in preparing by scientific researches and surveys for the further application of our national resources to the internal improvement of our country."[64] Here he was likely referring to Major Stephen H. Long's various expeditions in the West between 1819 and 1823, which combined military, commercial, and scientific objectives. In his mission from 1819, Long's primary orders were to site a fort at the convergence of the Missouri and Yellowstone Rivers.[65] As a former mathematics instructor at West Point who valued Humboldtian science, however, Long ensured that his exploration would enhance US scientific as well as territorial empire. His journey up the Missouri River in 1819 was the earliest federal expedition to rely on professional scientists to collect specimens of natural history and ethnographic information of western Native nations.[66] Impressed by Long's findings, Adams tasked the Army Corps of Engineers with further exploration. As a result, their surveying duties skyrocketed during his administration.[67]

As a grand strategist, Adams knew that army explorations like Long's increased the power of the United States by enlarging its boundaries and expanding its settlements. As the *Daily National Journal* asserted in 1827, "The enterprising settler is ready to follow the path of the explorer, and almost to tread upon his heels."[68] It was for this reason that John Charles Frémont, one of the most renowned army explorers of the West, would earn the monikers "Pathfinder" and "the Columbus of the Plains."[69] In the West, at least, settlement and Indigenous dispossession followed the flag.

In the Pacific, however, the sequence was largely reversed: James Monroe established the Pacific Squadron in 1822 only because a booming US commerce demanded it.[70] To further protect this commerce, Adams decided that the navy could explore as well as the army. For models, he looked east. Across the Atlantic, European powers had been fitting out maritime exploring expeditions for centuries. Before the Enlightenment, these activities had been largely pragmatic—quests for territorial and economic aggrandizement as well as religious and monarchical glory. With the advent of the scientific revolution, however, discovery was no longer perceived solely as a royal, national, or religious achievement, but a heroic contribution to Western science. This scientific veneer made exploration especially compelling to upper-class elites in Britain and beyond.[71]

No European navigator looked more heroic in this regard than Captain James Cook. Between 1768 and his death in Hawaii in 1779, Cook led three famous voyages of discovery around the world. Like Humboldt in the early nineteenth century, Cook epitomized the Western world's image of the bold agent of science in the eighteenth century. Adams was among his admirers.[72] So was the Second Secretary of the British Admiralty, John Barrow. Lobbied constantly for assignments by thousands of bored, dispirited British naval officers in the wake of the Napoleonic Wars, Barrow argued that the Royal Navy ought to expand on Cook's voyages and embark its officers and men on exploring expeditions.[73] He believed these missions would increase scientific knowledge, train future generations of naval officers, promote Britain's expansionist aims, and bolster Britannic pride.[74] Accordingly, the Admiralty Office dispatched dozens of exploring expeditions across the globe in the early nineteenth century, from the quest for the source of the Niger River in the Sahara Desert to Mesopotamia, the Pacific, Antarctica, and the North Pole.[75] In fact, the Royal Navy was the primary instrument of Western global exploration until the middle of the nineteenth century, at which point so many of the world's oceans and major rivers had been surveyed that only the interiors of major continents like Africa and Australia remained relatively unknown to the Western world.[76]

Inspired by Cook and his heirs, Adams sought to arouse his countrymen to join the Royal Navy in pursuing an empire of knowledge. He used his first annual message to Congress to do so. Delivered to the Capitol on December 6, 1825, Adams's manifesto began by shaming legislators about how little the country had contributed to astronomy and coastal geography: "In assuming her station among the civilized nations of the earth," Adams contended, the United States had an obligation "to the improvement of those parts of knowledge which lie beyond the reach of individual acquisition." Noting the examples of Great Britain, France, and Russia, he asked legislators whether US citizens were "not bound by obligations of a high and honorable character to contribute our portion of energy and exertion to the common stock?" He portrayed the discovery voyages of European navies as "heroic enterprises" that "have not only redounded to their glory, but to the improvement of human knowledge." Anticipating criticism, the president acknowledged that a circumnavigation of the globe would be impractical and that the United States had "objects of useful investigation nearer home." He observed that the Pacific coast of North America, "though much frequented by our spirited commercial navigators, [had] been barely visited by our public ships." Renewing an earlier call by James Monroe for the establishment of a fort on the Columbia River, Adams pressed Congress to fund and authorize the "equipment of a public ship for the exploration of the whole northwest coast of this continent."[77]

The president's message ignited a fierce political battle over the scope of US imperialism and federal power. That the United States would be an empire was a settled opinion among its statesmen and elite citizens, but the real question was what kind of empire it would be. Reynolds, Adams, and Symmes desired the United States to be an empire of knowledge in addition to an empire of liberty and commerce. Others disagreed; they resented the president's view that the United States was indebted to aristocratic Europeans. In Virginia, the editor of the *Richmond Enquirer* ridiculed the president by clarifying who was indebted to whom: "If we are in *debt* to Europe for her scientific discoveries," the editor wrote, "how much does she *owe* us for the *splendid* example we have furnished of a *free* government[?]"[78] He saw little reason for "entering into competition with the governments of Europe, in the building of castles in the air."[79] Other citizens concurred; writing in the 1840s, the proslavery apologist Matthew Estes admitted that the United States did not have "the polish and glitter of European society," but "nor do we desire these"; instead, "we are in the possession of those physical energies which will ultimately work out for our country a destiny more glorious than Europe ever dreamed of."[80] The message was clear: the United States should let Europe stay decadent, effeminate, and corrupt. The nation had a far greater obligation to develop itself as an "empire of liberty"—at least for white men.

The debate that unfolded in the House of Representatives shortly after Adams's message reflected the divisions on the future of the US empire. On December 16, Congressman Francis Baylies of Massachusetts introduced a resolution asking the navy secretary to inform the House whether or not a ship was available to explore the Northwest Coast. Lemuel Sawyer of North Carolina, a friend of Adams, immediately attached an amendment to explore the polar North. "The time has come," he proclaimed, "when this nation should likewise enter into this glorious career of discovery and human improvement. . . . Will not but kings enlist in the cause of science?"[81] Baylies responded with an emphatic no. Citing British precedents, he believed that a single vessel was unprepared to explore the Arctic on its own. Sawyer's rider would necessitate additional ships and costly expense. Besides, Baylies added, the president himself had not mentioned the Arctic and had asked only for a survey of the coastal Pacific Northwest. Sawyer countered that such a restricted survey would be a "lame and impotent one," adding that the president's language hinted at something far grander. Furthermore, expense was nothing "when weighted with the great importance of the object to be gained—the elevation of the national character . . . at home and abroad." Appalled, the House rejected Sawyer's amendment, preferring Baylies's original resolution.[82] In the House of Representatives at least, the empire of commerce continued to hold sway over the empire of knowledge.

Sawyer's suggestion of extending the mission to the Arctic was likely due to Symmes's influence. Symmes had sent his very first memorials for a polar exploring expedition to Congress back in 1822.[83] Since then, his lectures and letters to the editor in major national newspapers had resulted in the arrival of more and more petitions in Washington. These mostly came from Ohio, but some arrived from neighboring states like Pennsylvania and even South Carolina.[84] Yet, by 1825, Symmes's influence was waning. Even Reynolds was growing restless. Bored of Ohio, he convinced Symmes to move east in September 1825 and barnstorm the lecture halls of major East Coast cities. On the road, their relationship fell apart. Symmes grew jealous of his protégé's lecturing skills and resented Reynolds's increasing insistence on searching for warm polar seas instead of subterranean worlds. Rankled, the pair split, lecturing in different venues. In August 1826, Symmes went so far as to contemplate challenging Reynolds to a duel.[85] By then, however, Reynolds had transcended Symmes and appears to have simply ignored the summons, if any actually came. The weakened veteran returned to Ohio, where he died in 1829.[86] Over his grave, his supporters raised "a monument bearing a hollow globe."[87]

With Symmes gone, Reynolds lost no time in distancing himself from his mentor's hypotheses, which had become a general object of ridicule. Even Reynolds's hero Humboldt, who was normally generous to fellow scientists, publicly scoffed at "Symmes's Holes."[88] Instead, Reynolds began emphasizing a notion with more currency and older roots: that warmer polar seas existed where Symmes believed there to be holes, and that they were full of vibrant animal life—including seals and whales.[89] Whereas Symmes had envisioned himself garnering glory in the Arctic, Reynolds now proposed a voyage to the "South Seas," as US citizens then called the South Pacific.[90] There, he hoped to unfurl the national flag "on the point where all the meridians terminate"[91] and "to have the pleasure of drinking a cup of tea, procured in exchange for, furs taken, within the Antarctic circle."[92]

As Reynolds's fantasy suggests, the China trade was a major influence on his plans. Indeed, the search for marketable commodities to exchange for tea and porcelain in Canton (modern-day Guangzhou) had long been a driving factor in US expansion, both within North America and beyond. That process began in 1783, when a US traveler named John Ledyard had published an account of Cook's third voyage in the United States. Ledyard, who had served on the expedition, recounted how Cook's men had fetched fabulously high profits by selling sea otter pelts in Canton, China.[93] Thus began a highly lucrative industry in which Massachusetts supercargoes bartered for sea otter skins from the Northwest Coast to bring to China.[94] Further south, crews from Connecticut and elsewhere began killing fur seals, whose thick pelts were easily skinned, dried, and sold to Chinese furriers. As a result, the marine mammals' geographic range—mostly along eastern Pacific coastlines and within the Antarctic Circle—became extermination fields.[95] The lure of Chinese goods had even promoted continental exploration; Jefferson's instructions to Meriwether Lewis, for example, envisioned Lewis discovering a route from the Missouri River to the Pacific Ocean that would link the fur trade of the trans-Mississippi West with Canton.[96]

Whalers, too, were swarming the Pacific by the 1820s. Since colonial times, the sperm whale fishery had been especially lucrative on account of spermaceti, the white fluid stored in the head casks of sperm whales. When used as candles, it produced a particularly white and clear light.[97] By the late eighteenth century, however, the fishing pressure on the Atlantic sperm whale population was so intense that whalers began searching for new grounds in the Pacific. The first Nantucket whaleship rounded Cape Horn in 1791.[98] The extra mileage paid off, and the US Pacific whale fishery expanded accordingly. By 1819, Yankee whalers were sailing as far as Japan in search of prey. In 1820, they moved west of South America and opened the offshore ground, a massive oceanic territory twice the size of Texas.[99] By 1828, they were hunting whales in the Indian Ocean.[100]

To Reynolds, US commercial activity had made the South Seas "our field of fame."[101] This was more than just an empire of commerce; it was also a working-class, masculine empire of knowledge.[102] Reynolds translated Europe's elitist empire of science into a more democratic, US form. In his telling, the South Seas was a heroic realm where brave and hardy men enriched themselves through the pursuit of dangerous marine life. He had a special penchant for the figure of the manly mariner, who may have reminded him of the rough, brawling men of his Ohio youth. He even once directly compared the sealer and whaler to the "sturdy backwoodsman," who also chased wild animals "with so much vigor . . . to more remote regions."[103] In this sense, Reynolds imagined the South Seas as an extension of the North American West. As Jimmy Bryan has argued, romantic-minded white men in the 1820s and 1830s went west for adventure and to forge a racially exclusive, masculine sense of themselves. Reynolds's writings and experience suggest that this destructive orientation was not simply west but also south—and salty to boot.[104]

Nowhere was Reynolds's admiration for US mariners more evident than in his story "Mocha-Dick." First published as a short piece in a New York magazine in May 1839, "Mocha Dick" recounts the pursuit and grisly death of a white, aggressive sperm whale bull off the South American coast.[105] It was a tale that would later serve as a primary inspiration for Herman Melville's *Moby-Dick*.[106] Reynolds claimed to have heard the story straight from the lips of the first mate who had harpooned the beast. In his telling, the mate was a muscular and democratic superman whose enormous bravery and skill had allowed him to conquer "the monarch of the seas."[107] Like Mocha Dick, the first mate himself was a "*lusus naturae*," a freak of nature whose "overhanging shoulders" and long, "loose, dangling arms" gave his "muscular frame an air of grotesque awkwardness."[108] The mate's attempt to slay the whale, or "to try the muscle of this doughty champion," was a rousing contest of nerve and strength.[109] When, during one pursuit, Mocha Dick turned and charged the mate's whaleboat, the "sinewy arm" of the regular harpooner "wavered" before the white whale's frothy onslaught.[110] From here the first mate intervened, leading a second chase and spearing the whale to its bloody destruction. In the story's closing passage, Reynolds claimed that the tale "may be regarded as a fair specimen . . . of the romance of a whaler's life." In his mind, the Pacific was a "vast expanse" where "scenes of toil" and "unparalleled industry and daring enterprise" unfolded.[111]

ALLIES AND PATRONS

Reynolds's celebration of US fisheries in the South Pacific led him to political conclusions. He especially believed that the federal government had a responsibility to reinforce and extend this democratic empire of skill and knowledge. In other words, it should do in the Pacific what it had long done in the North American West: invest in expansion through exploration and cartography. Reynolds was therefore not unlike Henry Clay and Abraham Lincoln—other western men who believed that a powerful, active federal government could do wonders for the common man. Indeed, Reynolds was a firm Clay supporter in 1824 and would remain a strong Whig throughout his life.[112] He agreed fully with Adams's portrayal of oceanic exploration as an "enlarged" form of internal improvements—in this case, what one scholar has called "external improvements," or developments for the benefits of commercial expansion.[113]

Persuading the federal government—especially Congress—meant finding friends in high places. And herein lay one of the profound contradictions of Reynolds's movement: while he deeply admired the working-class sailors who worked the South Seas, he knew that governing and social elites, not tars, would launch his explorationist career. What was more, his pursuit of immortality was fundamentally an elitist one. It is indeed telling that his great hero was the noble (though republicanized) Humboldt. Though a man of humble beginnings, Reynolds wanted admission to the highest rungs of national and international society. Like the Continental naval officer John Paul Jones and the explorer John Ledyard, Reynolds knew that hobnobbing with elites could get him there. Like them, he set out to cultivate patrons at the highest levels of US society. His bid for patronage therefore replicated well-established patterns of political sociability that had proven so successful to generations of aspiring young men in the Atlantic World.[114]

He began by winning the patronage of the Adams administration. As it was customary for newspapers to publish huge swaths of official political proceedings, the former journalist would have been well aware of the president's first annual message. He must have trembled while reading it—here was a Chief Executive who, like him, prized glory, and who believed that it was time for the United States to claim "her station among the civilized nations of the earth" by partaking in a voyage of discovery.[115] Like Lemuel

Sawyer, he could read between the lines: Adams cared more about the actual dispatch of an expedition than its destination. Reynolds was confident that he could steer Adams into embracing a voyage to the South Pole in lieu of one to the Northwest Coast.

Accordingly, Reynolds moved his operations to the nation's capital in order to enlist members of the administration in his crusade for personal and national grandeur in the Southern Hemisphere. Once there, he wasted little time in charming members of the Adams administration. In August 1826, he penned a letter to Samuel Southard, Adams's secretary of the navy. "The object of my visit to the City," he informed the navy secretary, "is Respectfully to lay before the Heads of the several departments, the plans of a contemplated voyage to the unexplored seas to the south—for the sake of discovery on the broad and liberal principles of science." Noting that he would be lecturing in the city that evening, Reynolds invited Southard to attend.[116]

Though the secretary's reply (if he ever gave one) has been lost, Reynolds would soon find Southard to be a welcome and eager patron. One of New Jersey's most distinguished men, Southard had served as navy secretary since 1823, first under James Monroe and then under Adams.[117] While he had once been allied with John C. Calhoun, he had lately become a close ally of Adams and Henry Clay.[118] Like Adams, he was a great patron of the sciences.[119] And like him, too, he was a strong navalist who repeatedly urged lawmakers to make the United States, in Adams's words, "a great naval power."[120] Most important for Reynolds, Southard believed in using the navy aggressively to safeguard commerce. In 1826, he ordered the commander of the Pacific Squadron to survey Pacific islands and make diplomatic arrangements with Oceanian leaders with a view toward protecting US vessels.[121] Captain Thomas ap Catesby Jones fulfilled this directive between 1826 and 1827.[122] When he returned, both Adams and Southard read his report with interest.[123]

Southard was further inclined to welcome Reynolds because the administration desperately needed friends. Adams had come to the executive mansion after one of the most controversial elections in the young republic's history. Longstanding factional divisions within the National Republican Party had erupted in 1824, with five party leaders vying to replace the outgoing President, James Monroe. Adams, Clay, and Calhoun ran as Monrovian National Republicans, while William H. Crawford of Georgia represented the Old Republican wing of the party, which held fast to the conservative faith originally prescribed by Jefferson in the 1790s.[124]

Then there was General Andrew Jackson. Lionized for winning the Battle of New Orleans near the end of the War of 1812, Jackson ran primarily as a military chieftain and Indian fighter. He remained relatively mute on the great questions of the day, especially internal improvements. The strategy nearly worked: Jackson won the popular vote and the most ballots in the Electoral College. However, because he did not achieve a clear majority in the latter body, the election went to the House of Representatives. When Clay realized he could not be president himself, he embraced his role as kingmaker. After conferring with Adams, he threw his support behind the Massachusetts candidate and won him the presidency. When Adams turned around and nominated Clay as his secretary of state, a regular stepping-stone to the presidency, his opponents cried foul.[125] "The Judas of the West has closed the contract," Jackson fumed, "and will receive the thirty pieces of silver."[126]

Denouncing the "corrupt bargain" between Adams and Clay, Jackson and his allies set out to undermine the Adams administration and prepare for vengeance in 1828. Lingering anger over the manner of Adams's election handed both houses of Congress to the Jacksonians in the midterm elections of 1826 and fueled a furious resistance to his agenda.[127] The president's first annual message, with its visionary program of federal internal and external improvements, fanned the flames even further. By May 1828, Adams described Congress as a "mass . . . of every material of factious opposition" and animated "by one Spirit of bitter, unrelenting, prosecuting malice against me."[128] His unpopularity on Capitol Hill doomed his chances at shepherding his legislative agenda through Congress. If the explorationist cause was to flourish, the administration needed a popular public advocate.

In this, Reynolds's status as a private actor was actually an advantage. It was much easier to rail at a corrupt Adams man in public office than a committed citizen. Whereas previous historians saw the nineteenth-century federal government as weak, we now recognize that its willingness to partner with private entities made it anything but. Instead, the federal government's postal system, its custom houses, and its ability to shape US law, commerce, and society in subterranean ways is proof of an exceptionally competent, durable structure of power. Private-public alliances like the one between Reynolds and the Adams administration was a pillar of that strength; they helped make US governance invisible to ordinary US citizens, whose republican hackles might have been raised had the government tried to enforce its authority through more traditional, overt means.[129] Considering the national outcry over Adams's first annual message, finding a talented, passionate volunteer to advocate for one of the president's proposals was good policy. And a volunteer was all Reynolds was; while Adams and Southard valued his opinion and described him as a navy agent, Reynolds had to underwrite the explorationist campaign himself. A man of deep feeling and a brilliant orator, he nonetheless proved a poor businessman—by November 1828, he was sufficiently broke that he could not even afford a ferry ticket to Brooklyn.[130]

In this larger political context, Adams and Southard happily embraced Reynolds as the administration's public messenger on naval exploration. One of Southard's earliest surviving letters to Reynolds, dated July 11, 1827, struck an encouraging note: "Altho' no advocate of M^r. Symmes Theory, I feel deep solicitude for the promotion of an enterprise which if successful, cannot fail to add largely to our stock of knowledge, & to promote the interest & glory of our country."[131]

Now the younger man's challenge would be to convince Congress to support the navy's exploration of the Southern Hemisphere. Having won the blessing of the Executive branch, Reynolds determined that the best way to overcome congressional deadlock was by gathering other elites across the nation. He therefore embarked on a grand lecture tour of major East Coast cities, engaging in what one critic called "electioneering."[132] The goal, as Reynolds explained to Southard, was "to concentrate the force of public opinion, and to attack the peoples men, by the will of their Masters the sovereign people."[133] Overall he spent less time in the West, because he knew that statesmen in Ohio and other western states would support his cause. Ohioans were already quite familiar with explorationist schemes thanks to Symmes, and they had gotten to appreciate Reynolds's talents while the younger man had still been an ally of the elder. As Reynolds became a national figure in the East, Ohioans and other westerners embraced him with pride as a native son. Later, when Reynolds's inclusion among the crew of the United States Exploring Expedition seemed in doubt, congressmen from Ohio and other western states demanded, "in the name of the people of the West," that he be kept on.[134] For these reasons, Reynolds would tell Southard in November 1827 that they "may rely on being backed by Ohio—and I trust Kentucky."[135]

Instead, Reynolds focused most of his early attention on the South. Knowing that the region was a hotbed of Old Republicanism and pro-Jackson sentiment, he wanted to reduce Southern opposition as quickly as possible. Believing that only a personal touch would do the trick, he set out on an odyssey through the South in January 1827. "Indeed the great object of my visit south," he later explained to Southard, "is not so much to collect more ays as to render prejudice and enlist a southern feeling in behalf of planting our colours on the 90°."[136]

The white (and perhaps some Black) Southerners who would hear Reynolds speak were in for a treat. Later observers thought his lecturing style "monotonous" and "very sad, as though some great sorrow lay upon his heart," but this was long after his explorationist hopes had been crushed.[137] As a younger man, Reynolds was passionate, entertaining, and persuasive. He had modeled himself on Symmes's presentations, who in turn had replicated their mutual hero, Humboldt. An accomplished public speaker and writer, Humboldt lived by the motto that "an author must ring bells in order to get attention."[138] Judging by his rhetorical successes, Reynolds appears to have done so in spades. In 1827, he may still have had props from his days with Symmes, or he may have acquired new ones—maps, wooden globes, or perhaps portraits of the famous explorers he referenced in his lectures. What is clear is that he valued powerful language. "There is a great deal in telling a story well," he told Southard.[139] Quoting the pre-Romantic British poet Thomas Gray, Reynolds said his aim had always been to write and speak "in thoughts that breathe and words that burn."[140]

Upper-class white Southerners appear to have been burned badly. The first to find themselves enflamed were the state legislators of Maryland. Since state legislatures elected each state's federal senators until the ratification of the Seventeenth Amendment in 1913, Reynolds hoped their support would bring additional pressure to bear on senators in Washington. On January 23, 1827, he sent a hasty but victorious note to Southard from Annapolis, reporting that the "enclosed resolution, passed almost unanimously today" in the state legislature. In Charleston, too, Reynolds sought out and cultivated leading citizens. Within a week of his arrival in May 1827, he had given his first public lecture "to a highly respectable audience." In a private meeting with a local aristocrat and congressman, Colonel James Hamilton Jr., Reynolds promised him that Southard would distribute naval patronage in exchange for his support. Hamilton immediately pledged to aid the expedition in Congress. Reynolds was ecstatic: "This community will be with us," he promised Southard.[141]

From Charleston, Reynolds moved to the Upper South. By December 1827, he had reaped enough success in Raleigh, North Carolina, to feel like Julius Caesar: "Veni, Vidi Vici," he penned Southard.[142] By January 1828, the self-styled conqueror had crossed into Virginia. Entering a crowded Hall of Delegates in Richmond, he challenged Old Republicanism on its home turf. "You would be amused to hear me expound the Constitution," he later recollected in a letter to Southard. "I maintained lustily, that this expedition did not encroach on the 'few remaining rights of the states.'" Reynolds brushed aside concerns that the expedition was unconstitutional or that it would "take 'money out of one mans pocket and put it into another's.'" He declared that maritime exploration was a national concern, as it was far beyond the capabilities of any single state. For legal backing, he summoned the Louisiana Purchase and pointed to the Lewis and Clark Expedition as a precedent. He also reminded Virginians of their own expansionist history, from the Louisiana Purchase to Congressman John Floyd's arguments in favor of annexing Oregon Country. "I have contended manfully," he boasted to Southard. "No active opposition need be apprehended from this quarter."[143]

Reynolds cultivated Northern elites as well. From Hagerstown, Maryland, he reported to a friend that "the citizens were very spirited—even the ladies raised upwards of *fifty dollars* in half an hour." One wealthy New Yorker pledged $15,000 to the exploring expedition in exchange for a berth aboard ship.[144] Further north, Reynolds had little trouble securing the fealty of Yankee sea captains. They knew where their interests lay. In February 1828, the citizens of Nantucket composed a memorial begging Congress to secure the whaling trade through naval cartography. They specifically urged the navy to visit unknown islands and rescue castaways who had survived shipwreck. "Many of our fearless navigators are now, probably, wasting a wretched existence on some desolate island in these immense seas," they wrote.[145] New England newspapers agreed; throughout the late 1820s, they reported extensively on Reynolds's operations and on the politics of naval exploration in Washington. Among these papers was the *New-Bedford Mercury* of New Bedford, Massachusetts, which was one of the largest whaling ports in the country and among the wealthiest cities in the United States.[146] Unsurprisingly, most of the federal legislators who introduced bills in favor of naval exploration in the late 1820s hailed from New England.[147]

A more geographically diverse set of elites was the naval officer corps. While not all naval officers came from leading families, the profession itself was considered "gentlemanly and honourable" in US society.[148] Because the navy had a limited number of command positions available, many officers suffered agonizingly long waits before getting an assignment.[149] Eyeing the way the Royal Navy had been employing its servicemen during peacetime, naval officers hungered for similar orders. Exploration would lay out another avenue for adventure, promotion, and fame for shorebound officers.[150] When Reynolds asked Captain Thomas ap Catesby Jones his opinion on the matter in February 1828, Jones responded with a glowing endorsement: "Such a voyage as you contemplate," he wrote, "would open to our commercial, and of course, national interests, sources of great wealth."[151]

Scientists, too, were eager to be of service. Aside from the few jobs available as instructors at West Point, through army surveys, and in the US Coast Survey, federal patronage for scientific men was minuscule before the establishment of the Smithsonian Institution in 1846. Instead, gentlemen of science and their supporters found employment in colleges and universities, as private tutors, and through state geological surveys. They also collaborated through private natural history societies such as New York's Lyceum of Natural History and the American Philosophical Society in Philadelphia. Even so, many scientists still felt shunned by their fellow citizens; as one explained to Southard in May 1829, "Science is yet a bad trade in this country."[152] Unsurprisingly, therefore, scientific men were "not far behind the maritime community in urging exploration."[153] Like naval officers, US scientists yearned for the opportunities available to their British and French colleagues, who were occasionally employed as naturalists on voyages of discovery. In July 1828, for instance, Reynolds reported to Southard that the noted zoologist James Ellsworth De Kay was thinking "of devoting himself . . . to the naval service of the country—believing, that cruising in any part of the world, in our public vessels, will afford him a fine opportunity to indulge his favorite study of natural history."[154]

This coalition of naval officers, scientists, and sea captains mattered because they often had special influence on members of Congress. Many naval officers were already well known to the political elite. After all, midshipmen typically received their warrants from the executive branch because a congressman had written a personal letter of recommendation on their behalf.[155] Given the shortage of active-duty assignments, many officers also learned that having friends in high places amplified their chances of sea service and promotion, which had to be approved by the Senate.[156] As Harold Langley writes, "It was a well-known maxim in the navy that a cruise in Washington was worth two around Cape Horn."[157] Likewise, most scientific men and merchants in the early republic hailed from the elite rungs of US society, which added weight to their memorials. The "respectability" of signees for these petitions mattered to congressmen; Representatives Thomas C. Worthington of Maryland and James Buchanan of Pennsylvania were among those who argued that explorationist memorials deserved "proper attention" on account of the "character and standing of these memorialists."[158]

Reynolds's coalition was a motley one, but it represented the broad range of actors in the empire of knowledge. To greater or lesser degrees, working-class seafarers, wealthy gentlemen, naval officers, leading scientists, and merchant captains all operated within its orbit. At first glance, seamen might seem to fit better into the category of commercial imperialists. To some extent, this is correct; however, mariners also knew that knowledge was critical to commerce—both in terms of acquiring accurate cartography and learning of new trading opportunities and resources.

Southard struck this note clearly when, in a letter to the chairman of the House Committee on Naval Affairs in April 1828, he explained that a voyage of discovery would "search for new and profitable fountains of trade."[159] In Massachusetts, The *Newburyport Herald* concurred, describing the South Pacific as "a vast expanse of waters" that urged nations "to investigate the islands or continents—the fisheries of [*sic*] other treasures, which may be contained within its unknown boundaries."[160] As always, Reynolds summed it up best: "There is an intimate connexion between sealing and discovery," he told John Quincy Adams in 1829, "the highest latitudes South affording the finest and richest furs."[161]

Was Reynolds aware that his labors would promote environmental catastrophe in the South Seas? Unfortunately, yes. Unlike Melville, Reynolds knew that marine mammal populations were limited.[162] He explained to a congressional leader, "The hunting of the whale and seal . . . has produced the natural and necessary consequence of rendering those animals more timid, and fewer in number, by their destruction." The demand for fur seal skins, he added, was "increasing in this country, as the seals are diminishing in the Pacific."[163] Privately, Reynolds expressed disgust with the cruelty of sealing: "'Tis most barbarous to peel the fine skins off those poor Animals," he wrote Southard in June 1829.[164] Here was a paradox: Reynolds simultaneously celebrated the "hardy navigators" who hunted pinnipeds and cetaceans in the South Seas while secretly decrying the animals' destruction.[165] "What place is exempt, what creature safe, from the intrusion of man!" he once bemoaned.[166] Nonetheless, as Aaron Sachs writes, "Reynolds's own efforts to spur exploration exacerbated the slaughter of animals and facilitated humanity's general pillaging of the natural world."[167] Reynolds may have been somewhat conflicted, but in the end he willingly embraced the hunt for marine mammals if it carried him and his nation to their explorationist destinies in the South Seas.

Environmental concerns aside, Reynolds's cultivation of elites paid off. When he had sent Southard his memorial from Charleston, he had promised that the petition was "merely as the dew drops before a copious shower, compared, with what you may see by October next."[168] His words were prophetic—as Reynolds lectured and labored across the country, more and more memorials from state legislatures and elite citizens poured into Southard's lap in Washington and into the Capitol.[169] "I think we may now take high ground," Reynolds told Southard in October 1827, "and threaten the people's men, with the people."[170] The following month, he wrote the Navy Department from Boston and reveled in his success: "The public feeling is with us," he declared to Southard. "I will soon send you a memorial from <u>here</u>—and from <u>Trenton N.J.</u> . . . with these and other forces," he mused, "I trust Congress will act at once."[171]

ORGANIZING AN EXPEDITION

As Reynolds had hoped, public pressure and persuasive rhetoric resulted in legislative action. On May 21, 1828, the House voted on a bill that granted the president the authority to send "one of our small public vessels . . . to the Pacific ocean and South seas to examine the coasts, islands, harbors, shoals, and reefs" of the region, provided that it could be "done without further appropriations during the present year."[172] While it was not as grandiose as Adams would have wished, the president was nonetheless pleased. When he met Reynolds for dinner in February 1829, he told him that "nothing during the past session had given him more pleasure than that resolution."[173]

Adams's relish aside, a clerical error would hamstring the legal justification for the expedition: when the House had failed to send the bill to the Senate by May 26, 1828, when the First Session of the 20th Congress closed for summer recess. Because the second session would not begin until December 1, there would be little time for the Senate to take up the measure before the annual deadline stipulated in the House bill. Adams and Southard therefore made a risky decision: they would prepare for the expedition anyway, even without Senate approval.[174] They justified their decision because they believed that the ends warranted the means—and they believed that time was against them. In a July meeting with Southard and Commodore John Rodgers, Adams expressed his "deep anxiety that this expedition Should be undertaken, and as far as possible executed under the present Administration." He further "observed that the next year we might not . . . have the opportunity."[175]

Their decision underscored a great irony in the explorationist campaign of the 1820s: while Reynolds, Adams, Southard and others were anxious to prove to European powers that a republic could also undertake liberal voyages of discovery, in practice they actually skirted republican governance. Reynolds's "soul" might "burn" at the prospect of dispatching "the first American expedition of discovery . . . and first from any Republican Government, of all past time, or present," but privately he scoffed at the people's slow-moving representatives in Congress.[176] A favorite adjective for him was "little," as in, "We only wait the passage of that <u>little bill</u>," and "the little politicians wish it deferd [*sic*]."[177] Adams and Southard, for their part, engaged in creative accounting in order that their expedition might sail.[178] In time, this arrogant approach to policy would come back to haunt them.

In the interim, however, planning for the expedition stoked the enthusiasm of Reynolds's coalition. Several New England congressmen wrote Southard and recommended native sons for the expedition's officer corps.[179] "There are already many applicants," an exhausted navy clerk wrote in reply. "When the time of selection arrives," he promised, "their respective claims will be duly considered."[180] Elsewhere, as William Stanton observes, "experienced sailing captains coveted the posts of pilot and navigator, others offered their ships, artists sought appointments as draughtsman, medical doctors begged to be taken along as surgeons."[181] Even Nathaniel Hawthorne angled to replace Reynolds as the mission's official historian.[182] And, of course, "scientists of every description asked to go."[183] Elite excitement affected the larger public; newspapers followed expeditionary appointments closely. They praised the role of the "father protector to the Expedition,"[184] "the persevering and meritorious J. N. Reynolds,"[185] who had now assumed the role of recruiting agent for naval officers and scientists.[186] When, in September 1828, the navy launched the sloop of war *Peacock* as a discovery vessel, cannons saluted the historic occasion and a great crowd turned out to cheer the *Peacock*'s thunderous slide into the sea.[187]

As the planning process unfolded, the Navy Department continued to rely on Reynolds. On June 27, 1828, Southard proposed to send the young man on a fact-finding mission to New England, with the goal to ascertain the state of navigational knowledge among the region's whaling captains. Adams readily assented.[188] Reynolds was enormously grateful: "I can and will do all you require," he wrote Southard after receiving his orders.[189]

Reynolds's visit north deepened his appreciation for mariners' knowledge of the South Seas. In early July, Reynolds sent a series of cartographic questions to Yankee sea captains in preparation for his visit. By early August he was in Nantucket, striding the town's wooden docks and quays and interviewing its Quaker whaling captains. "I am now in the region of romance," he gushed to Southard. His ecstasy stemmed from the shear breadth of his new navigational knowledge and his physical proximity to the rugged salts he so admired: "I have now in my possession more knowledge of the south seas and Pacific Ocean, by ten times, than the British Expeditions will have when they return," he told Southard proudly. "I have met with Captains just off a whaling voyage, who are more than 70 years of age—Doubled Cape Horn 20 times, taken 30 thousand barrel of oil, and traversed more than one million miles by the sea." Reynolds's final report, dated September 24, 1828, asserted that the South Seas were indeed a brave new field for discovery. A detailed synopsis of the state of US navigational knowledge in the South Pacific, it offered the best-known information regarding almost two hundred uncharted reefs, shoals, and islands. Southard was duly impressed; as he later told senators, Reynolds's report "ought to be published for the benefit of our seafaring people."[190]

Reynolds was especially taken with the sealing barons of Stonington, Connecticut. Though reticent at first, they soon warmed to him, sharing snippets of "their adventurous exploits" near the Antarctic Circle.[191] Edmund Fanning, whom Reynolds described as "the Father of all sealers," probably shared that he had been instrumental in convincing James Madison to equip an exploring expedition before the War of 1812 had intervened.[192] Now, with Reynolds before him, Fanning recommended that he talk with a junior colleague, Captain Benjamin Pendleton.[193] When Reynolds tracked down Pendleton, he was again awestruck. Like the mate who speared Mocha Dick, Pendleton personified Reynolds's ideal of the masculine, democratic shaker of the empire of knowledge. Reynolds admired "his rugged and weather beaten check," and delighted in hearing of his "many wild adventures."[194] Calling him "the Scoresby of America," Reynolds claimed that the captain had more knowledge of the seas from the "Equator, to the high and rugged region South, than any man in Europe or in America." He urged Southard to hire Pendleton as the pilot of the expedition.[195]

Southard assented, but by the early fall of 1828, he was growing increasingly distracted by the upcoming election. Supporters of Andrew Jackson were waging a pitched battle to put "Old Hickory" in the executive mansion. Soon enough, the election returns were clear: Jackson had won. Explorationists were crestfallen. "I have only to submit to it with resignation," Adams confided in his diary. "The Sun of my political life sets in the deepest gloom. But that of my Country shines, unclouded."[196] Reynolds was less sure about his own future. As he told Southard, he had hoped that the expedition would return to the United States "during your administration of the marine," but alas, "this is not to be my good fortune." Instead, "I shall fall into other hands, and will have to fight my way through them."[197]

Glum as they were, Reynolds and his allies pressed on. When Congress opened in December, Adams urged lawmakers to provide funds for the May 19 bill. He hoped an appropriation would allow them to purchase an additional vessel to use as a supply ship, which Reynolds had urged as a common practice for many Royal Navy expeditions.[198] For his part, Reynolds lobbied and worked constantly—attending Congressional committee meetings, writing editorials to major newspapers, even pledging appointments on the expedition in exchange for votes.[199] On January 15, 1829, his efforts bore fruit: the House appropriated $50,000 for a store ship and other expenses.[200] At last, Reynolds's great ambitions were closer than ever before.

SENATORIAL CHECKMATE

This time, the House bill went to the Senate. On January 19, the Senate referred it to the Naval Affairs Committee, chaired by Senator Robert Hayne of South Carolina. In 1829, both Hayne and his native South Carolina were in the midst of a profound political transformation. While South Carolina's metamorphosis into an Old Republican and states' rights enclave were well underway by the late 1820s, the state had once been a Federalist stronghold. Even more recently, it had leaned toward the activist National Republicanism of Monroe, Adams, and Clay. John C. Calhoun, Adams's vice president and Hayne's mentor and patron, exemplified this trend; until recently, Calhoun had been an avid pro–internal improvements National Republican. His activist ideology had allowed him to develop a close political partnership with Southard in the early 1820s. Ironically enough, Calhoun had even feuded viciously with strict constructionist rivals within his home state. These included William Smith, an early states' righter who had won election to the Senate in 1816.[201] In 1822, Calhoun managed to replace Smith with his protégé Hayne.[202] Coordinating with his mentor from the Senate, Hayne supported a powerful federal government in the early 1820s.[203] At the time, he would have agreed with the sentiments of A. P. Butler, a South Carolina state legislator who declared that the United States was "a government operating on one common people, composing one entire Empire."[204]

Hayne brought his vision of an empowered federal government to the Senate's Naval Affairs Committee. He assumed his post in 1823, the same year Southard became secretary of the navy.[205] Calhoun soon managed to elevate Hayne to the chairmanship of the committee.[206] There, he demonstrated an Adams-like penchant for navalism and naval reform.[207] He supported efforts to increase the pay of the surgeon corps, was an avid naval expansionist, and even wrote a spirited history of the navy in the November 1828 issue of the *Southern Review*.[208] He also had great esteem for Southard. They frequently dined together, and they cooperated extensively over naval affairs.[209] "However we may be seperated [*sic*] . . . on political questions," Hayne wrote the navy secretary just before the election, "I trust we shall always think and feel alike on all national points connected with the naval establishment."[210]

That was not to be the case with naval exploration. Why? The ever-suspicious Adams believed that Hayne rejected the bill because he had been "swallowed up by the passions of party."[211] Southard's most recent biographer agrees, describing Hayne's opposition to the exploring bill as "partisan naysaying."[212] At first glance, the partisan explanation seems reasonable. Indeed, by the time the January bill reached Hayne's desk, political circumstances had changed. Though Hayne's relationship with the administration stayed cordial, his patron, Vice President John Calhoun, had turned on Adams long ago. Calhoun was alarmed by Adams's first annual message, declaring in a letter to Andrew Jackson in 1826 that "liberty was never in greater danger."[213] He forged a political alliance with Jackson for the upcoming 1828 election.[214] Federal tariff policy further convinced Calhoun that the states had to jealously guard their own interests. In domestic policy at least, Calhoun became precisely the kind of strict constructionist he had battled against so viciously in his early career. Privately, he began urging the Senate to ignore or cripple Adams' legislative agenda.[215] Gradually, the affable Hayne reflected more and more of his mentor's views. Perhaps most tellingly, Hayne's spotlight moment would come later that year, in December 1829, when Calhoun nudged him into a rhetorical battle with Daniel Webster over the nature of the Union and states' rights.[216]

A closer reading of Hayne's reports, though, reveals a different story. In this one case, at least, Hayne was a principled republican, not a partisan. His first objection was that by circumventing the Senate and acting on the House resolution from May 1828, the administration had tried to assume unprecedented power. And power for good republicans was a thing very much to be feared—especially in an ambitious executive. Accordingly, on February 5, Hayne demanded that the president submit a full account of Southard's activities on behalf of the Pacific survey. "The importance of the exploring expedition," Hayne told his colleagues, "was nothing, in comparison with the question of the power assumed by the Executive to transfer, at pleasure, appropriations made by law to certain objects, to another and distinct object, not having the sanction of Congress."[217] On February 13, Southard provided a lengthy accounting of expenditures on the exploring expedition, claiming that all of them had fallen into categories already approved by Congress. He then justified Hayne's fears by arguing that presidents could, in fact, "direct a transfer from one appropriation to another."[218] Hayne was alarmed. In his final committee report, he slammed the administration for organizing "an expedition of such an extraordinary character" without Senate approval.[219]

Hayne's other objection was cost. He asked Southard whether the expedition intended only "to examine any Known coasts, islands, harbors, shoals,—and reefs in order to ascertain their true situation and description or whether 'The Pacific Ocean and South Seas' are to be 'explored' in the view of the discovery of unknown regions."[220] When Southard responded that "the coasts, islands, &c. both 'known' and 'unknown' will fall under observation," Hayne felt his worst fears realized.[221] In light of the immensity of the South Seas, he reasoned that no single expedition could possibly chart it. Therefore, "the proposed expedition [could] only be considered as the first of a series of explorations."[222] He estimated that Southard's plan for a voyage of discovery would cost nearly half a million dollars, and that successive expeditions would draw similar sums from the public treasury.[223] Such an expensive global campaign would have to be paid for through either direct taxation or tariffs, or possibly raising the price of public lands. South Carolinians were deeply opposed to all three. In fact, Hayne's epic clash with Webster over the Union later that year would begin with a debate over the pricing and sale of western territory.[224] If enacted, Southard's proposal would force white Southerners to pay exorbitant taxes in order to secure northern mariners in the South Seas.

In making his committee's opposition clear on fiscal grounds, Hayne was tapping into republican concerns that expensive military machines threatened freedom.[225] He especially feared that the pursuit of an empire of knowledge would jeopardize the empire of liberty for white men. He had heard Reynolds speak during the latter's visit to Charleston in 1827, and had been dismayed by the younger man's zest for national glory through oceanic discovery. Reynolds himself embodied the "spirit of adventure" that would coax the United States into pursuing imperial aggrandizement far beyond its neighborhood. Haynes worried that "the discovery of countless islands, even of new continents" would incite "visionary hopes" among US citizens, encouraging them to colonize overseas territories. Protecting such possessions not only would be expensive, but would form a "departure from those wise and prudent maxims which have hitherto restrained us from forming unnecessary connections abroad."[226] History had taught him that liberty had too often been sacrificed on the altar of imperial aggrandizement and defense. Now he worried that an explorationist career would take the United States off the noninterventionist path prescribed by George Washington and James Monroe. Peering into the future, Haynes foresaw republican ruin: if the Senate permitted this voyage of discovery, the United States might crumble through excessive taxation, foreign colonization, and protectionist wars with expansionist European empires.[227]

Of course, another fear animated Hayne and Calhoun by 1829: the fear of federally directed emancipation. Here was the irony of championing an empire of liberty at all, because it was also, for millions of US residents of color, an empire of slavery. Hayne may have been a good republican, but he was also a major slaveholder in South Carolina. And many slaveholders

feared that centralized state power—especially in the hands of closet abolitionists like Adams—would result in emancipation. "If Congress can make
canals," warned Nathaniel Macon, a leading Old Republican, "they can
with more propriety emancipate."[228]

Struggling to reconcile his navalism, republican principles, and slaveholding, Hayne conjured an alternative vision. He was not opposed to
naval exploration per se, but believed that a limited surveying expedition
would be much more in line with white republican values. Supporting an
empire of commerce, in his mind, was far more preferable than an empire
of knowledge. Reynolds's efforts to Americanize Europe's empire of science by infusing it with a democratic masculinity had failed to appeal to
Hayne. The South Carolinian therefore recommended that the expedition
be downsized, stripped of its scientific pretensions, and strictly held "to
the examination and survey of the islands, reefs, and shoals which lie in the
track of our vessels" in the South Pacific. He ended his report by introduc-
ing a bill to do just that.[229]

The bill went nowhere; nor did a last-ditch attempt to resolve the im-
passe in the Senate two days before Jackson's inauguration.[230] The general's
triumphant entrance into Washington City marked the death knell of the
first legislative push for a national exploring expedition. In his inaugural address on March 4, 1829, Jackson promised federal frugality, the extinguish-
ment of the federal debt, and checks on the growth of the army and navy.[231]
"In time of peace," he told congressmen in December 1829, "we have need
of no more ships of war than are requisite to the protection of our commerce."[232] Acting on his archrival's proposal for an expensive exploring expedition in a distant ocean was not high on Jackson's agenda—at least, not
at the start of his administration. Recognizing that the political winds had
changed, Reynolds submitted his New England report to the Navy Department, "where I suppose it belongs," he sighed, "as a public document."[233]

"A PROPHET IS NEVER HONORED IN HIS OWN COUNTRY"

Disgusted with Washington, Reynolds turned back to the hardy mariners
who had so impressed him originally. In New York in the spring of 1829, he
joined with Fanning and Pendleton in founding the South Sea Fur Company and Exploring Expedition.[234] The new company maintained the old
coalition's alliance with scientists, with the Lyceum of Natural History in
New York composing the scientific orders that Reynolds and his surgeon-
naturalist would follow.[235] The expedition left the city in 1829, bound for
the South Seas on a private voyage for seal pelts and scientific discovery.

Reynolds later wrote, "We sought adventure . . . without the aid or patronage of government."[236]

It was a disaster. Caught between Reynolds's quest for scientific discovery and the sealers' need for profits, the empire of knowledge fractured. Reynolds was bitterly disappointed. He wrote Southard in October 1830: "I have a hard task to inspire these men, with the feeling that there is something worth living for, besides money." Their preference for Mammon over "the attainment of glory" in particular represented a "total want of manly daring."[237] Reynolds's admiration for rugged, adventurous working-class men would endure—as the tale of "Mocha Dick" indicates—but it sustained a heavy blow.

Tired of trying to rouse sealers to look for anything other than seals, Reynolds quit; in April 1830, he left the company's vessels in Valparaiso, Chile, and set off on foot, determined not to miss his own personal opportunity for discovery.[238] If he could not be Cook, then, by God, he could be Humboldt. This was fitting enough; it had been Reynolds's infatuation with Humboldt that had inspired his explorationist efforts and then led him to the volcano of Antuco. Indeed, one of the most sublime and moving of Humboldt's South American adventures had been his summiting of the volcano of Chimborazo, in modern-day Ecuador, in 1802.[239] Now Reynolds aspired to replicate his hero's achievement. He hoped, he told Adams, to summit two Chilean volcanoes and "plant the American colours, on the top of their burning craters."[240]

By October 22, 1830, his party was dry, rested, and resupplied. They were ready to attempt the volcano once again. After lunching with the Chilean soldiers at the old mountain fort, they restarted their ascent. The depth of the snow hindered their progress, but by nightfall they were within reach of the smoldering crater. In the predawn darkness of the 23rd, they resumed their quest. As the sun rose, "the difficulties of the ascent multiplied at every step." The party resorted to pulling themselves up the steep, sharp summit. The stones they stepped on were so hot that they "crisped the soles of [their] shoes." Beside them, the volcano breathed every few minutes, "discharging vast quantities of stones and ashes." The temperature seemed to increase with every step. Finally, they reached the top. They stood there, dizzy with exhaustion, heat, and thin air. Swirling vapor obscured the volcano's mouth, but they were satisfied nonetheless. Unfurling a US flag, Reynolds and his men planted it in a fissure "at the highest point attained, very near the edge of the crater."[241]

There it would soar above the fumes of Antuco, one of the few physical remnants of the failed explorationist campaign of the 1820s. Reynolds was still embittered ("a prophet is never honored in his own country," he complained to Southard), but he was nonetheless a wiser man for his failure.[242] For one, he had learned that the empire of knowledge had its limits as a rallying cry in the United States; US republicans needed something more compelling and practical than European-style glory. Even Reynolds's attempts to couch empire in terms of nautical masculinity was insufficient. Hayne's cautious support for an empire of commerce suggested a more promising course for a republican nation. In retrospect, Reynolds may have also thought that the alliance with Adams had been a mistake. If he was to realize the explorationist vision, he needed the backing of a popular president—someone of Thomas Jefferson's stature at the time of the Lewis and Clark Expedition. If only Andrew Jackson and his followers had been converted, Reynolds might have triumphed.

CHAPTER 2

The United States Exploring Expedition as Jacksonian Capitalism

The residents of Kuala Batu, Sumatra, were feeling increasingly desperate. The price of their pepper exports—the economic lifeblood of their community—had dropped precipitously in early 1830. The townsfolk fell on hard times.[1] Many blamed the downturn on the greed of the Salem shipmasters who had dominated the global pepper trade. Since distrust and deceit had long characterized relations between US and Sumatran merchants, it was an easy conclusion to reach.[2] Growing poverty and a sense of economic dependence nourished a quiet rage. Kuala Batu's moment of revolution finally came on February 7, 1831, when a group of villagers boarded the Salem pepper ship *Friendship*, anchored just offshore. There they unleashed their fury, killing three sailors and driving the rest into the water. In town, other Sumatrans tried to catch Captain Charles Endicott and his companions. They were busily overseeing the weighing of the pepper cargo when their work came to a startling halt with the commotion on the *Friendship*. Spooked, the Yankees jumped into the ship's launch and escaped.[3]

Still, the denizens of Kuala Batu reveled in their success. Not only had they acquired $12,000 of silver, twelve crates of opium, and everything else of value on board the *Friendship*, but they had also restored a sense of pride for themselves and for all Sumatrans living on the island's southwestern coast.[4] When the fugitive mariners landed at a nearby town, its villagers taunted them through the streets. "Who great men now Malay or America!" they shouted.[5] The Yankees were furious. "May the mistake under which they rest, that the Americans have not power to chastise them, be corrected with all convenient dispatch," Captain Endicott prayed in a letter to the Navy Department.[6]

His letter did not go unheeded. Nearly one year later, the United States heavy frigate *Potomac* arrived off the Sumatran coast. Though Captain John Downes had orders to negotiate first and use force as a last resort, he had already decided to fight.[7] On the morning of February 6, 1832, he began

Figure 2.1 *Action of Quallah Batto, as Seen from the Potomac at Anchor in the Offing,*
J. Downes, ESQ. Commander, February 5, 1832, from Jeremiah N. Reynolds, *Voyage of*
the United States Frigate Potomac (New York: Harper & Brothers, 1835), 120. (Courtesy
of Biodiversity Heritage Library, contributed by Smithsonian Libraries)

landing his troops. In Kuala Batu, a lookout roused his countrymen from
slumber: white men were massing on shore. The townsmen shouldered
their weapons, dashed to the town's five forts, and peered out at the advancing US lines.[8] When the *Potomac*'s divisions began surrounding their
strongholds, the Sumatrans opened fire. They killed two US servicemen
and wounded eleven.[9] Outraged, the landing force erupted, smashing pali-
sades, chopping down gates, shooting and stabbing defenders, and torch-
ing the forts. As their vengeance raged, the fire spread. Private homes burst
into flames. After nearly three hours of bloody fighting, Kuala Batu was
silenced. Exultant, the Yankees raised the stars and stripes over the town's
main fortress. Beneath it lay the burned and bloodied bodies of a hundred
and fifty Sumatran men and an unknown number of women and children.[10]

The navy's ferocious response to the assault on the *Friendship* heralded
a new phase of US expansionism in the greater Pacific World. Presidential
administrations since Washington had zealously worked to bolster a global
US empire of commerce.[11] Among them, Andrew Jackson and Martin Van
Buren pursued commercial treaties, dispatched consuls around the world,
sent the navy to show guns and the flag in distant seas, and invested in harbor and lighthouse improvements. Jacksonian commercial policy, however, differed in tone and strategy. Like the capitalist system that unfolded

within the United States and its borderlands, Jacksonian commercialism was highly legalistic, militant, and dedicated to the doctrine of white supremacy. The massacre at Kuala Batu reflected these qualities. Jacksonian Democrats would go to great—sometimes inhuman—lengths to bolster US capitalism at sea against all challengers. In Democratic eyes, Indigenous polities, mutinous sailors, and even the subaqueous terrain of the Pacific World were threats to be managed for the benefit of the US economy.

The United States Exploring Expedition of 1838–1842 was the largest and most important manifestation of this Jacksonian commitment to US capitalism overseas. Composed of six vessels and 246 officers and men, the "Ex Ex" (as contemporaries called it) was one of the largest economic investments ever made by the antebellum United States.[12] For nearly four years, it crisscrossed the Pacific, charting, fighting, and negotiating with Islanders. By the time the Ex Ex had returned home in the summer of 1842, it had cost taxpayers close to a million dollars—$928,183.62, to be precise.[13] If one includes the cost of the failed 1820s push, that figure rises to $995,264.38.[14] And if one further adds the production costs for the 180 charts, the four-volume narrative, and the fourteen published scientific volumes that followed the expedition's return,[15] the total cost of the Ex Ex was $1,355,099.38.[16] And even this figure is not fully accurate, as it fails to include all the expenditures for the National Gallery, the nation's first national museum and the caretaker of the Ex Ex collections. Since these specimens continue to form the historic nucleus of the Smithsonian Institution, in some ways US taxpayers are still paying for the preservation of the expedition's results. For a Democratic Party that prided itself on having "some old-fashioned notions of economy," in one politician's words, this was a remarkable investment.[17]

How did this come to be? In a phrase, capital required it. As Richard Hofstadter argued long ago, the underlying principle of Jacksonianism was not so much democracy as capitalism.[18] He was right; while Jackson continues to receive credit for expanding white male democracy in popular memory, he deserves little of it. After all, most of the states had already expanded suffrage rights by his second run for the presidency in 1828. Jackson was thus the manifestation of the democracy that bears his name, not its genesis.[19] What Jacksonians did impact, however, was the process by which the national and state governments replaced old mercantilist holdovers with free-market policies. Jacksonian Democrats were popular, in large part, because they pursued the economic agenda that many striving white men wanted. Primary among those was creating the impression of a fair shot in the marketplace. Indeed, the entire Jacksonian economic program was about evening opportunities for commercial success among all classes of white men. Jacksonian courts and legislatures struck down barriers to economic mobility for white males at home, while the chief magistrate himself made war on the Second Bank of the United States, which he saw as a nest of special privilege and corruption.[20]

As with class, the racial dimension of Jacksonian capitalism was central. These were policies designed to benefit white men—often at the expense of Black and brown communities.[21] At home, Jacksonians forced Indigenous removal, championed slavery and capitalist slaveholders, backed white Southern officials who destroyed abolitionist mailings, and imprisoned free Black sailors stopping in Southern ports.[22] What people of color lost, white men gained—especially freedom, land, and increased social mobility. They further benefited from new legal regimes that encouraged risk, protected them creditors, and forbade government monopolies at the state and federal levels. The two most famous decisions of Jackson's nominee to the Supreme Court, Chief Justice Roger Taney, exemplify the white working-class supremacy of Jacksonian economic policy: in the Charles River Bridge case in 1837, Taney declared that government-granted monopolies were unconstitutional and against the public interest.[23] In the infamous Dred Scott decision of 1857, Taney asserted that only whites could enjoy the rights of life, liberty, and the pursuit of capital.

Yet even as white men acquired greater opportunities at home, their fortunes in the Pacific Ocean remained fraught with risk. As more and more merchants, mariners, and especially whalers swarmed the Pacific, they confronted greater and greater challenges to amassing capital easily and safely. Oceanians challenged US notions of free trade and free whales; ordinary US sailors and violent, ill-tempered shipmasters threatened the smooth production of wealth; and, lastly, imperfect cartographic knowledge of the Pacific World flummoxed even the most experienced sea captains. In Jacksonian eyes, such maritime threats appeared as dangerous to white male capitalism abroad as their classic enemies at home—federal internal improvements, state-sanctioned monopolies, Black and white abolitionists, and sovereign Native polities. Eager to secure a safe and profitable marketplace for white citizens overseas, the Jackson and Van Buren administrations cast about for some means of extending their protective policies into the South Pacific. They found it in the ideas of their old foes: they would send the navy on an exploring expedition. Jeremiah Reynolds, Samuel Southard, and even John Quincy Adams himself returned to help them. The new coalition succeeded where the old one had failed. With the sailing of the Ex Ex, the tentacle of state power thrust out into the Pacific World. The result was twofold: in the Pacific, a federal empire of commerce; at home, an expanded imperial alliance.

AN EMPIRE OF COMMERCE BESIEGED

In the first few decades of the nineteenth century, the siren song of profits drew increasing numbers of US mariners further into the Pacific World. Among them were China traders. When otter and fur seal populations in the eastern Pacific plummeted in the early 1820s, US supercargoes sailed west to look for supplemental goods to convey to Canton.[24] They found them in Oceania, where sheltered groves of sandalwood and large colonies of sea cucumbers abounded. Sea cucumbers, also known as bêche-de-mer, are slimy echinoderms that inhabit the sharp nooks and crannies of Pacific reefs.[25] The Chinese valued sandalwood and sea cucumbers highly, fashioning the former into incense and aromatic furniture and enjoying the latter as delicacies, aphrodisiacs, and a form of medicine.[26] While the populations of sea cucumbers proved far more durable, sandalwood forests melted before the axes of Indigenous workers hired by US merchants.[27] The forests of Fiji especially suffered; previously known to mariners as the Sandalwood Islands on account of their ample supply, Fiji witnessed such deforestation in the early nineteenth century that Fijians began fighting for the few trees that remained.[28]

Other US industries in the Pacific were important, too. Salem's Indonesian pepper trade was just one example, as was a lucrative exchange of cattle hides from Mexican *rancheros* on the West Coast of North America. In fact, one of the most classic and enduring accounts of seafaring, Richard Henry Dana Jr.'s *Two Years before the Mast* (1840), emerged out of the California hide trade. Finally, US exports nearly doubled between 1828 and 1836, leading more and more farmers to ponder whether they could ship surplus crops to Asia.[29]

Looming over all these industries, however, was the leviathan of the Yankee whale fishery. Whale oil was in high demand as a light source and industrial lubricant. Consumers especially prized spermaceti, the bright-burning, mild-smelling liquid excavated from the head cavity of the sperm whale. The US whaling fleet responded to these market pressures, experiencing frightening growth between its Pacific debut in the 1790s and the start of Andrew Jackson's presidency in 1829. One estimate puts the number of sperm whales killed in the 1830s at approximately six thousand per year.[30] By the early 1830s, whalers had mined their existing grounds in the South Pacific so extensively that they opened a new one off the Northwest Coast of North America.[31] In 1835, the US whaling fleet counted over 450 vessels—almost a tenth of all the nation's tonnage.[32] Jeremiah Reynolds estimated that the mere value of the vessels alone was worth $18.4 million, that the fishery employed twelve thousand seamen, and had reaped a profit of $1,165,999. "There is no branch of business more important to a nation," he concluded, "than such an investment of its capital."[33]

Jacksonians valued this capital greatly. Like previous generations of US citizens, they were adamantly committed to the principle of free trade. Originating with the theories of the Dutch jurist Hugo Grotius, free trade was later adopted by enlightened French *philosophes* and US Jeffersonians, who saw it as a cure-all for wars and international tensions.[34] With the advent of the Second Great Awakening, white Christians in the United States also began to portray free trade as having divine sanction.[35] US citizens and statesmen alike celebrated the extension of oceangoing commerce, such that nearly every major public address included an obligatory paean to US maritime enterprise.[36] As John Quincy Adams told listeners at his inaugural address in 1825, "Our commerce has whitened every ocean."[37] Like the Dutch of the seventeenth century, US policymakers supported free trade for practical reasons. After Great Britain, the United States had the world's largest commercial fleet in the early nineteenth century. Unsurprisingly, therefore, both powers championed free trade, for it was they who had the most to benefit.[38]

Jacksonians took a special interest in extending US commercial capitalism across the globe. Like previous administrations, they worked to expand and reform the US Consular Service, an extensive transimperial network of agents in major port cities who were tasked with assisting US merchants and sailors in distress. By 1834, there were over 150 consuls across the globe.[39] In addition, they pursued new markets and commercial treaties with vigor. Taking advantage of the new British penchant for free trade, for example, Democratic diplomats managed to reopen the British West Indies to US shipping.[40] Further afield, they also negotiated valuable commercial treaties with Turkey and Russia.[41] And beyond them, Jackson pursued markets in eastern Asia, dispatching an agent to acquire intelligence and treat with royal courts in Vietnam, Oman, Japan, and Siam.[42] In 1834–1835, Jackson nearly led the country to war with France for that country's failure to compensate US merchants for vessels seized by Napoleon.[43] At home, meanwhile, Democrats did an about-face on their usual ideological opposition to internal improvements, investing heavily in such "external improvements" as the deepening of harbors and the establishment of lighthouses.[44] Jackson also restarted the United States Coast Survey and raised a small astronomical observatory to help the navy produce knowledge for celestial navigation.[45]

Jackson and his allies championed global US commerce at least in part because of its precarious standing. That commerce was especially endangered than in the Pacific World. The often violent, destabilizing relations between US sailors and Oceanians were a major area of concern. Indeed, US mariners' interactions with Indigenous peoples was extensive in the antebellum era. Just as enslaved men, women, and children helped build the domestic economy, Indigenous hands helped power US commerce abroad: Indonesians grew and packed pepper and other spices, delivering them to Salem and Boston vessels; Oceanian divers plucked sea cucumbers, sea turtles, and pearl-growing oysters from the sea and processed them ashore; Fijian and Hawaiian men harvested sandalwood trees and bore their trunks to Yankee ships; while Maoris, Tahitians, and Hawaiians hauled lines and harpooned cetaceans in the whale fishery. There they sweated alongside Native North Americans—men who had escaped impoverished reservations in Southeastern New England for better economic chances on the high seas and who formed the real-life model behind Melville's character Tashtego in *Moby-Dick*.[46] Melville's Queequeg, from the fictional island of Rokovoko, had real antecedents as well: Islanders frequently signed on to Western vessels in order to become global travelers themselves.[47] By the middle of the 1830s, nearly three thousand Hawaiians were working on US whalers.[48]

Not all these interactions were pleasant. Many white sailors viewed encounters with Oceanians and their nonwhite shipmates through the lens of white supremacy.[49] White racism and the clash of cultures in the Pacific made for a frontier of violence. Some white US citizens shot at Islanders simply for sport; at least one even memorialized the occasion with a silver engraving on his musket.[50] In the semiautobiographical novel *Omoo*, Melville drew on his experiences as a South Seas whaler and bemoaned that "wanton acts of cruelty . . . are not unusual on the part of sea captains landing at islands comparatively unknown."[51] White supremacist capitalism drove mariners not only to chase whales wherever they could be found, but also encouraged them to loot an island's water, wood, and animal life without compensating its human inhabitants. When Lieutenant Thomas ap Catesby Jones visited the Marquesas Islands aboard the USS *Peacock* in 1826, the natives complained of precisely this activity, adding that "there had been times when chiefs requested payment for the goods and ship masters had them bound and flogged for their supposed impertinence."[52] As Samuel Eliot Morison noted nearly a century ago, "'Paying with the foretopsail' (sailing away without paying for goods and services) was frequently practiced on Pacific islanders who had furnished supplies."[53]

Violence begat violence in the Pacific World. One vessel's cruelty or mistreatment often resulted in distrustful or hostile receptions for the next one. As on the Northwest Coast in the early 1800s, some Oceanian peoples saw all Western seafarers as members of a single nation, permitting retaliation on an innocent crew for those of another nation's guilty crimes.[54] Throughout the Ex Ex, for instance, officers and crew attributed Indigenous resistance to the Islanders having "been visited & badly treated by the Whites."[55] Of course, US writers may have overlooked the possibility that Oceanians simply did not want them around—whether they had had good or bad experiences with them.[56] At other times, Indigenous cultural traditions appear to have prompted violence; Fijians believed, for instance, that their gods demanded the sacrifice of shipwrecked vessels and crews.[57] There may have been human as well as divine judgment here: since Fijians were expert navigators and boat builders, they may have looked down on whites' inabilities to navigate their waters.[58] Elsewhere, basic human covetousness and different cultural notions of property may have led to clashes.[59]

Unruly white sailors posed another danger to US capitalistic expansion in the Pacific World. While US actors preferred to blame British seamen for most shipboard disturbances, there were plenty of US seamen who pursued their own interests at the expense of their employers.[60] In 1824, for example, mariners on the Nantucket whaleship *Globe* rose up, killed their officers, and directed the vessel to the Mulgrave (present-day Marshall) Islands. Such a blatant challenge to property and the class hierarchy of capitalism could not go unpunished; the navy dispatched one of its most vicious commanders, Captain "Mad Jack" Percival, to retrieve the mutineers and bring them to justice.[61] Desertion was another means by which ordinary sailors could throw a wrench into the smooth functioning of capitalism. While preparing to sail from Hawaii in March 1826, Percival received a letter from over a dozen whaling captains pleading with him to stay. Noting that, between them, they were responsible for "Property to the Amount of a Million of Dollars," the captains argued that Percival's presence "would prevent the desertion of our Crews and tend to the protection of property."[62] In addition to their mutinies and desertions, disaffected whalers also rioted. After the death of a sailor in Honolulu in November 1852, nearly four thousand sailors ripped through the town, smashing businesses and targeting symbols of authority.[63] Mariners may not have had the kind of class consciousness of later industrial workers, but they did have a shared sense of vocational identity. When things were not breaking their way, they knew who to blame.

Whalers' violence can be partly attributed to the dirty, dangerous, exploitative conditions in which they labored. Maritime writers like Melville and Dana frequently used such adjectives as "slatternly," "dingy," "slovenly," "oily," and "rough" to describe whaleships.[64] Whalers themselves were "uncombed," "dirty," "wild," and "haggard-looking."[65] Their jobs were boring, ill paying, and enormously dangerous. To make matters worse, the masters of whaling ships were infamous for their abusiveness. Samuel Eliot Morison described whaling captains as the most "tight-fisted, cruel and ruthless a set of exploiters as you can find in American history."[66] Since deserting sailors abandoned any claims to their "lay," or percentage of the voyage's profits, some sailors suspected that violence was a way of increasing the capital returns of a voyage.[67] Melville compared whalers to slaves and cast Ahab as an angry Old Testament ruler; as the mad captain roared at his first mate, "There is one God that is Lord over the earth, and one Captain that is Lord over the Pequod."[68] Ahab was right—US maritime law invested sea captains with enormous power. Federal legal regimes protected the rights of officers to beat sailors for disciplinary purposes, and, in the navy, even allowed officers to try and hang seamen at sea.[69] During Percival's stopover in Hawaii, one tar made the mistake of smirking at him. In response, "Mad Jack" beat him to within an inch of his life.[70]

Finally, and perhaps most important, one of the most basic and fearsome challenges to the United States' burgeoning commercial empire in the Pacific World was the lack of accurate Western charts. Despite advances by Cook and other European explorers, vast swathes of the Pacific Ocean remained uncharted by Westerners in the first decades of the new century. At thirty-nine million square kilometers, Oceania far outstrips the continent of Africa in size and scope.[71] While Oceanians developed complex and elaborate means of navigating Pacific waters, or wayfinding, Western navigational techniques were most effective when paired with Western-style charts.[72] For European and US mariners, hundreds of unmarked coral islands, reefs, and shoals made navigating the South Pacific a perilous business. While shipwrecks most commonly occurred during storms, even windless days could prove dangerous, when the lack of foaming breakers often masked the presence of subaqueous features.[73] Nighttime was especially hazardous, with lookouts straining in the darkness for sights and sounds that could herald disaster. For hundreds of mariners in the Age of Sail, the sudden crash of their ship's keel on a reef at night proved their death knell. For striving men who felt the call of the sea, the uncharted dangers of the deep posed a special threat to life, limb, and property.

A RENEWED PUSH FOR EXPLORATION

The multiplying threats to US capitalism in the Pacific forced Jacksonian Democrats to give naval exploration another look. As before, Jeremiah Reynolds played a key role in congressional politics. While he never fully abandoned the empire of knowledge, his public career in the 1830s reflected the rise of violent Jacksonian capitalism. Reynolds's private explorations of South America came to an end when, in October 1832, he signed onto the *Potomac* as Captain Downes's private secretary in Valparaiso, Chile, for the homeward voyage.[74] Once aboard the *Potomac*, he sensed the winds of change and trimmed his sails accordingly. By the time he arrived in Boston in May 1834, Reynolds had become a converted gunboat diplomat.[75] It was a dramatic change for a man who had once balked at skinning seals.[76] Nonetheless, the new, militarized Reynolds maintained his old explorationist ambitions; as soon as the *Potomac* docked in Boston, Reynolds confessed to Southard that he was "still full of anxiety, to go to the south seas once more . . . if an official enterprise could be got underway."[77]

Once in the United States, Reynolds came to believe he could harness the white supremacy of Democratic political economy to his advantage. Using the *Potomac*'s logbook and records from Downes and the Navy Department, Reynolds authored an account of Downes's cruise as a way to curry favor with the Jackson administration.[78] Aware that Whig politicians like Henry Clay and John Dearborn had tried to portray the Kuala Batu massacre as another example of Jackson's inhumanity, Reynolds released his *Voyage of the United States Frigate Potomac* in 1835 as a full-throated defense of Downes's actions.[79] While naval historians have recently demonstrated how flawed Downes's strategy was—and that a mixture of diplomacy and show of force would have better protected US commerce—Reynolds's *Voyage* took a different approach.[80] It presented Sumatrans as lawless pirates who had no proper government with which Downes could have lodged a formal complaint. Without such governance, Reynolds asked, how could any citizen reasonably expect the Sumatrans to collect and return the stolen property of the *Friendship* and deliver the murderers over to the *Potomac* for justice? In other words, the lack of a capitalistic legal regime, combined with the Sumatran's piratical actions, had made them "outlaws" who deserved the "most summary chastisement."[81] "The smouldering ruins of Quallah-Battoo," Reynolds concluded, "might be gazed upon as a monument of American justice."[82]

Reynolds used his account to argue for increased US naval activity in the East Indies and South Pacific. He centered his appeal on the image of the unlucky, victimized white mariner in the South Seas. Reynolds bemoaned the lack of suitable charts for the Indonesian archipelago, the exposure of the US whaling fleet, and the brutality of Indigenous peoples. He compared the South Seas to Indian Country, noting that when Native North Americans committed crimes against whites, the "nearest local authority immediately makes a demand that the culprits be forthwith given up; and, if refused, the demand is quickly enforced by the arm of military power. . . .

Ought the bloodthirsty inhabitants of Sumatra be treated with any more lenity than the much wronged and oppressed aborigines of our own country?"[83] Reynolds's answer was a resounding negative: "Our flag should be borne to every portion of the globe, to give to civilized and savage man a just impression of the power we possess."[84]

While Reynolds's comparison of Sumatrans to the Indigenous nations of North America was not particularly original, it was a savvy political move.[85] Sadly, his suspicion that he could enlist Jacksonian xenophobia to his advantage in a renewed push for exploration was correct: Jackson hated pirates as much as Indigenous Americans (indeed, he frequently conflated the two), and he savored the navy's ability to strike back at aggressors as far away as Sumatra.[86] As one biographer notes, Jackson was one among the many whites who had "learned to fear and hate Indians from an early age."[87] These early prejudices, formed on the Carolinian frontier during the Revolution, were hardened during his campaigns against British-allied Indians in the Southeast during the War of 1812. At the time of Reynolds's return to Boston, Jackson's antipathies had resulted in the Indian Removal Act of 1830 and in intense pressure on southern Indian nations to give up their lands and move west.

In the political campaign to follow, Reynolds also knew he could rely on the support of his former allies and the old explorationist constituencies of the previous decade. These included upper-class elites, scientists, naval officers, mariners, and the coastal communities of the Northeast. While writing his *Voyage* in Boston, in fact, he forged close friendships with the members of the Boston Society of Natural History, to whom he donated his natural history collection from South America.[88] In Washington, meanwhile, Reynolds was delighted to find that Southard had been elected as a Whig senator from New Jersey and had taken Senator Robert Hayne's former position as chairman of the Committee on Naval Affairs. Ex-president John Quincy Adams, for his part, had taken the unusual step of returning to national politics as a congressman from Massachusetts.

The explorationist effort of the 1830s further benefited from the wide circulation of lurid tales of white male victimization in the Pacific World. Such accounts described how the lack of accurate sailing charts increased the risk of shipwreck on uncharted reefs, islands, or shoals. For those lucky enough to escape a watery death, navigational mishaps still left shipwrecked sailors at the mercy of Oceanian captors. One influential publication in this regard was Horace Holden's *Narrative of the Shipwreck, Captivity and Sufferings of Horace Holden and Benj. H. Nute* (1836). Holden's misfortunes began when, on the night of May 21, 1832, his whaleship suddenly struck an uncharted reef in the Palau Islands.[89] Safely ashore, but with their vessel

DRUMMOND ISLAND WARRIORS.

Figure 2.2 *Drummond Island Warriors*, 1844. This woodcut from Charles Wilkes's *Narrative of the United States Exploring Expedition* (Philadelphia: C. Sherman, 1844, 5:50) reflects US anxieties about Oceanian societies. Such negative representations contributed mightily to the dispatch of the nation's first naval exploring expedition. (Courtesy of Biodiversity Heritage Library, contributed by Smithsonian Libraries)

hopelessly wrecked, Holden and his shipmates agonized over whether to risk an open-sea passage with limited provisions or surrender to the unknown inhabitants of a nearby island.[90] They decided to gamble on the latter. While the first locals they met with were friendly, the second group enslaved them and subjected them to harsh labor and sudden violence. By the time Holden managed to escape to a British China trader, only three out of the ten of the shipwrecked had survived their captivity.[91]

The enslavement and death of white men was not how white male democratic capitalism was supposed to work. For a nation that believed in white supremacy and in the unalienable rights of life, mobility, and the pursuit of wealth for white men, reports from the South Seas had a galvanizing effect. It helped that the United States had already fought several wars for "free trade and sailors' rights," and that the federal government had embraced the sailor as a kind of sacred cow.[92] There were ironies here, of course: Jacksonian elites bewailed the cruel fate of men like Holden while turning a blind eye to Black slavery, Indigenous removal, and the daily, vicious violence inflicted on sailors by heavy-handed captains. Notably, the very act of voyaging under the US flag "whitened" citizens of color, who often felt the same protective gauntlet as those enjoyed by their white shipmates. Thus, in 1855 in Fiji, the USS *John Adams* took drastic measures to protect the property of a US beachcomber and Seminole Indian.[93] While the rallying cry of the Ex Ex was the victimized white mariner, there were plenty of Black men who experienced similar conditions to Holden, and who would now, paradoxically enough, benefit from an assertion of white supremacist state power.

Ignoring contradictions, explorationists leaned hard on the trope of the injured white male. In October 1834, the Rhode Island Assembly approved a memorial that called for an exploring expedition to "open friendly intercources [*sic*] with the natives, which may be the means of preventing the effusion of blood."[94] Dutee J. Pearce, a congressman from Rhode Island, resurrected the subject on Capitol Hill when, on February 7, 1835, he submitted a bill authorizing and funding an exploring expedition to the South Pacific. Pearce admitted that "years ago, it would have been adventurous for a discovery ship," but now, in light of the nation's rising commerce in the South Seas, exploration had become a necessity to protect US labor and capital.[95] Summarizing a memorial from the East India Marine Society of Salem, Massachusetts, he argued that the government had failed to protect mariners "against the natives, who had seen nothing of our power to restrain them from unlawful attacks upon their vessels and their lives."[96] When Pearce's bill went nowhere, Southard reintroduced the measure in the Senate in March 1836 and used similar language. He observed that "many of those islands [in the Pacific] are inhabited by savages, who render access to them dangerous, and whom it is the duty of the government to conciliate."[97]

With Southard's bill in the Senate, Reynolds took center stage for an evening address to Congress on April 3, 1836.[98] Statesmen and their guests packed the House of Representatives, their curious faces illuminated in the light of a hundred candles.[99] Under their flickering gaze, Reynolds took the rostrum and began the speech of his career. He urged legislators and fellow citizens to see how an exploring expedition would safeguard US mariners from Indigenous abuse. "Almost every arrival from the Pacific," Reynolds lamented, "brings some melancholy intelligence of shipwreck, mutiny, or massacre, among the South Sea islands."[100] He asked lawmakers how they could "look supinely on, while our citizens are . . . massacred by savages, for lack of such a judicious exhibition of maritime strength as would command respect."[101] Rather than sit on their hands, lawmakers should empower the navy to negotiate with these "untutored beings" in the South Seas: "Conferences should be held with the natives of the remotest groups, and their confidence gained as far as possible, by a judicious exhibition of our power and policy."[102]

It worked. Reynolds's impassioned speech on behalf of sailors' rights and commercial expansion helped Southard's bill clear the Senate and reach the House. On May 9, explorationist allies in the House rose to defend the measure in similarly militaristic and diplomatic terms. Congressman Thomas Lyon Hamer, a Democrat from Ohio, contended that charts of the South Pacific would rescue the mariner "who suddenly finds himself shipwrecked in an unknown sea, far from the haunts of civilized man, and destined to become a prey to the cruel and remorseless savages who inhabit the islands."[103] To protect such a man, Hamer called for a "demonstration of our power in those seas which would make an impression upon the savages favorable to the future security of our mariners."[104] Congressman John Reed of Massachusetts agreed; holding Horace Holden's captivity narrative aloft, he urged his colleagues to read it. "I wish gentlemen could examine it for a short time," Reed declared, for "many [other sailors] are still in captivity, still suffering the evils from which he has escaped."[105] The congressman ended his speech thunderously: "Our navy," he declared, "should visit those islands, and give the most conclusive evidence of our power, which would make those savages afraid to perpetuate cruelty and murder."[106]

Explorationists made other arguments as well. They did, at times, suggest that a voyage of discovery would have the additional benefit of enforcing law and order in the US whaling fleet. It was not only perceived "savages" who made the South Seas lawless, but also the figure of the "savage" whaler. Melville himself had reveled in this image; in *Moby-Dick*, he proudly chirped that "your true whale-hunter is as much a savage as an Iroquois. I myself am a savage, owning no allegiance but to the King of the Cannibals; and ready at any moment to rebel against him."[107] In 1836, one correspondent with Reynolds asked why there should be a judicial system in the territories but no "superintending influence abroad, where . . . the savage may be awed into respect, and the mutineer's hand be bound down in submission."[108] In *Voyage of the Potomac*, Reynolds worried that "abuses of the most serious nature not only exist, but are of daily occurrence in the whale fleet. The cause of some of these abuses can be corrected by the owners, and others can only be reached by the strong arm of our government."[109] Such classist rhetoric, however, was rarely emphasized—even if it reflected the longstanding views of poor whites on the frontier, the degradation of the common man did not match with Jacksonian rhetoric.[110]

While Jacksonians knew full well that labor had to be bound by capital at sea, they preferred not to dwell on the subject.[111]

In the end, anti-Indigenous rhetoric and the needs of democratic capitalism prevailed; the House approved the bill shortly after Reed sat down from his speech. By May 14, both houses of Congress had agreed on a single bill. Unsurprisingly, the chief Jacksonian himself fully embraced the expedition and became a strong supporter. The secretary of the navy, Mahlon Dickerson, sought to derail Jackson by pointing out the expedition had been the idea of one of his most vehement enemies, Samuel Southard. Jackson's reply was that that "scoundrel" Southard had "had at least one good idea."[112] He signed the bill soon after.[113] In his last annual message on December 6, 1836, Jackson called for an expansion of the navy and pledged that the executive branch would dispatch the expedition as soon as possible.[114] Thanks to the Jacksonian conversion, the explorationist vision appeared closer to reality than ever before.

WAGING INDIAN WARFARE AND DIPLOMACY IN THE SOUTH PACIFIC

By the summer of 1838, the Ex Ex was close to sailing. It was to be a massive undertaking: comprising six ships and manned by two hundred and forty-six officers and men, the expedition dwarfed European voyages of discovery, which rarely included more than two ships. On July 26, 1838, Jackson's friend and presidential successor, Martin Van Buren, visited the exploring squadron in Norfolk, Virginia, and offered his blessing.[115] On the afternoon of August 18, 1838, the US Navy's first voyage of discovery dropped down Hampton Roads, discharged its pilots, and began spreading canvas for the South Seas.[116]

Jeremiah Reynolds was not with them. The period from 1836 to 1838 had featured a bitter battle over whether the Ex Ex would sail at all. The responsibility for organizing the venture fell on Secretary of the Navy Dickerson, who had little stomach for it. In his late sixties, Dickerson was a sickly man who felt enslaved by the Navy Department.[117] Reynolds, despite all his high-placed friends, was one of the casualties of Dickerson's malcontent. In a bold move, Reynolds had decided to sacrifice his own position on the expedition in order to see it sail. Frustrated with the secretary's delay tactics, he pilloried Dickerson in a series of public letters published in the *New York Times* between June 1837 and January 1838.[118] The gambit worked, but it destroyed Reynolds's reputation with the Navy Department. Reynolds sought to console himself. "It was the expedition for which I had laboured," he explained in March 1841, "not a place in it."[119]

Reynolds had labored hard because he believed that the sailing of the Ex Ex would be the clarion call of US national maturity. William Reynolds, a passed midshipman aboard the flagship *Vincennes* (and of no relation to Jeremiah), captured this sentiment perfectly in his journal: "And behold! now [*sic*] a nation, which but a short time ago was a discovery itself and a wilderness, is taking its place among the enlightened of the world, and endeavouring to contribute its mite in the cause of knowledge and research."[120] Though neither Reynolds, Southard, nor Adams were there to witness it, the sailing of the Ex Ex was the moment they had yearned for—and a moment Adams had never expected to see in his lifetime.[121]

The voyage of the Ex Ex gave US citizens ample opportunity to relish their national maturity in comparison to the Indigenous peoples of the Pacific World. Like other US mariners, the crew of the Ex Ex looked to Native North Americans to make sense of the inhabitants of the South Pacific.[122] Upon reaching Australia, Charles Erskine, an ordinary sailor from Boston on the Ex Ex, was surprised to find that Australian Aborigines did not have dogs as pets, as "it is generally believed that all Indians are very fond of dogs."[123] Later, when the commander of the expedition, Lieutenant Charles Wilkes, invited warring chiefs from Christian and pagan factions on Tongatapu to make peace aboard the *Vincennes* in April 1840, Erskine called the conference a "great powwow."[124] While in Fiji in the summer of 1840, Wilkes noted that the Fijians regularly traded their weapons and tools in exchange for valuable Western goods.[125] Accordingly, he acquired three bundles of Fijian war clubs, labeled them as "Indian curiosities," and shipped them back to the United States.[126]

Perception guided behavior. White US citizens believed they had to approach peoples of various races differently, and that some people were in different stages of development; those whom they believed were in the savage stage of development, such as Native Americans and Oceanians, had to be treated like children, who understood only self-interest and self-preservation. This helped to explain their predilection to theft, why they had to be bribed with presents and gifts, which were cornerstones of government dealings with Native nations, and why US officials encouraged Indigenous people to call the president of the United States their "Great Father."[127] White US citizens also deployed Anglo-Saxonism to justify such harsh policies as forced removal, wars of extermination, and excessive retaliatory violence, including the one at Kuala Batu. Wilkes's instructions—drawn up by himself but officially issued by the new secretary of the navy, James K. Paulding—reflected these supercilious views. Paulding's instructions warned Wilkes that "savage nations" had "but vague ideas of the rights of property," and that he should avoid conflict on this front as much as pos-

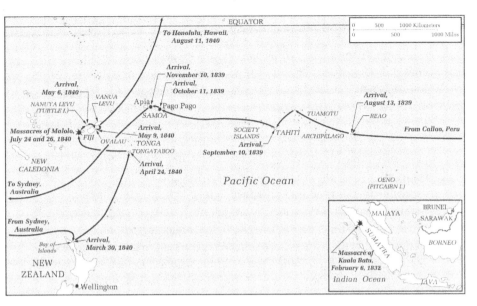

Figure 2.3 Map of the USS *Vincennes* in the South Pacific, August 1839–August 1840. The inset shows the location of the navy's massacre at Kuala Batu in 1832. (Created by Chris Robinson)

sible.[128] He further urged Wilkes to beware of treachery, which he called "one of the invariable characteristics of savages and barbarians." Finally, he exhorted him not to "commit any act of hostility, unless in self-defence."[129]

Wilkes's reliance on Indigenous American analogies when dealing with Oceanians was apparent in the expedition's first interaction with Islanders. It was July 1839, and the Ex Ex had just reached the Tuamotu Group in the eastern edge of Polynesia. While surveying Reao Island, Wilkes sought to engage those Tuamotuan Islanders who had gathered on the beach. He recruited another "Indian" for this purpose—in this case, a sailor and Maori named John Sacs. When Wilkes and his party rowed close to the beach, he directed Sacs to strike up a conversation. Sacs found that he could understand them. In response to his overtures, the Tuamotuans shook their spears and ordered Sacs and his comrades to "go to our own lands; this belongs to us, and we do not want to have any thing to do with you." Ignoring their wishes, Wilkes threw presents ashore. When these failed to dissuade the Tuamotuans from their defensive posturing, Wilkes began to perceive their stance as a challenge; he feared that retreating would only allow the islanders to believe that they had driven him off. He had wished to land his officers and scientists in order to complete the survey and collect specimens, but now he had an additional reason for doing so: to assert US dominance. Disgusted, he ordered his crew to fire volleys of mustard seed (similar to bird shot) on the Tuamotuans and so cleared the beach.[130]

As the Tuamotuans' words and actions suggest, many Oceanian societies did not see the arrival of the Ex Ex as a positive development. This was especially the case in more remote and isolated portions of the Pacific, places far removed from more cosmopolitan locales like Tahiti and Hawaii. In many Oceanian societies, the arrival of other men by sea was a dangerous circumstance, presaging war and usurpation.[131] Western warships in particular brought additional dangers, including disease, firearms, rockets, cannonades, and torches for burning Oceanian villages. Further, the surveying methods of the Ex Ex, which relied on using a cannon or blunderbuss to calculate distances by sound, must have seemed unnerving.[132] Whether at the tip of South America or in Oceania, several Indigenous societies divided themselves between men, who went to investigate the dangers of the Ex Ex, and women and children, who fled to secret locations to wait the passing of the squadron.[133] The Tierra Fuegians in South America, for example, "had secreted the women away" in a cave.[134] On Wytohee, an island in the Tuamotu Group, a band of Tuamotuan men laughed when US sailors asked where all the women were. They believed the Ex Ex had come because the sailors were from an island without women, so the Tuamotuans had wisely hidden theirs.[135] For some Indigenous societies, the dangers might have reached supernatural proportions; Ex Ex members relished reporting that some Oceanians saw them as emissaries from the spirit world, "strange beings who came in huge things that moved through the water without visible help, who covered their whole body, & who had thunder & lightning at their command."[136] However, this may have also been just an echo of a longstanding white fantasy that appears in the accounts of many European explorers.[137] Whether Oceanian societies saw the members of the Ex Ex as invaders, rapists, or spirits, the Ex Ex was clearly an unwelcome intrusion into what Epeli Hau'ofa once famously described as "our sea of islands."[138]

With a few exceptions, the mariners of the Ex Ex generally saw themselves as the forces of law and order in a saltwater wilderness that mirrored the North American West. Nowhere did they feel this contrast more keenly than in Fiji. By the early nineteenth century, Fijians had crafted a fiercely warlike society. Until muskets became more common in Fiji later in the nineteenth century, a "boy became a man only when he had killed an enemy with a war club."[139] In the early 1800s, the war god Bau expressed Fijian sentiments perfectly when he spoke through his priest: "War is that by which I amuse myself. I love it. I wish now to sport in war."[140] Perhaps most important from the US perspective was the fact that Fijians practiced ritual anthropophagy and human sacrifice.[141] The launching of *druas* (massive double-hulled Fijian war canoes), the raising or replacement of building posts, and victories in war were all occasions for sacrificial victims. The hierarchical consumption of human beings was so prevalent in Fiji that the phrase "'Eat me!' was a proper ritual greeting from a commoner to a chief."[142]

Fijian war and sacrificial practices extended to US citizens as well as to other Fijians. These attacks, combined with limited Western knowledge of the region's dense clusters of islands and coral reefs, drew the Ex Ex to Fijian shores. Wilkes arrived on May 6, 1840, believing that a proper survey of the Tuamoto Group was "among the most important objects of the Expedition."[143] William Reynolds agreed, noting in his journal that Fiji "has a hard name with navigators," as the Fijians "are generally believed to be ferocious cannibals, & numerous reefs & shoals & labyrinths of rocky passages among the cluster are so many snares, for the seaman's destruction."[144] In early July, after nearly two months of surveying, Wilkes examined the progress of the squadron's cartographic efforts and decided he needed to postpone the expedition's visit to the Northwest Coast of North America and risk giving up a visit to Japanese waters in order to complete the work. Reducing their rations by a third to conserve resources, Wilkes directed his men to finish the survey as quickly as possible.[145]

In addition to its surveying duties, the Ex Ex had also been charged with establishing diplomatic arrangements favorable to US commercial capitalism in the Pacific World. Across the Pacific, Wilkes and his second-in-command, Lieutenant William Hudson, had demanded that Indigenous polities commit to protecting US capital and labor. This was by no means a novel arrangement, as naval officers had long arranged such treaties, especially in regions where no diplomats were stationed. While the Senate generally did not ratify such agreements, they were frequently effective and US officials perceived them as lawfully binding.[146] The commercial treaties that the Ex Ex composed in the Pacific mirrored those signed with Indigenous North Americans, which frequently discussed trade relations and safe passage through tribal territory.[147]

The concentrated perils that Fiji posed to US capitalism underscored the importance of making diplomatic agreements with local powerbrokers. The eleven articles of the "Feejee Regulations" that Ex Ex officers pushed on Fijian chiefs represented an effort to assert US capitalist governance over Fijian territories. The articles included the protection on the part of Fiji of US foreign consuls, vessels, and shipwrecked crew and property, and US pledges to pay port charges and fair compensation for refreshments, the use of pilots, and the arrest of deserters. Like the Indian Trade and

Intercourse Act of 1834, it also attempted to regulate alcohol, banning the sale of "spirituous liquors." Article IV, meanwhile, stipulated that Fijian chiefs would either punish any subject accused of murdering a foreigner or surrender the accused to US authorities.[148] It was a judicial process that closely paralleled those involving Indigenous murders of US citizens in North America. In 1817, for example, Congress passed a law that required tribes to hand over those who had harmed whites in Indian Country or risk a military intervention.[149]

Article IV of the Fiji Regulations soon came into play with the case of Veidovi.[150] Veidovi was a chief from Rewa on the big island of Viti Levu who was accused of murdering eight crewmen of a Salem brig engaged in the sea cucumber fishery. According to US accounts, Veidovi and his men had reportedly killed the sailors with their war clubs and then ate them.[151] Wilkes assigned the task of seizing Veidovi to Lieutenant William Hudson, in command of the *Peacock*. Hudson planned to capture the accused by inviting him and other Fijian chiefs (including Veidovi's brother, the king of Rewa) to visit the *Peacock* and receive gifts. When Veidovi failed to appear by late afternoon, Hudson ordered his men to quarters, seized the Fijian nobles as hostages, and locked them up in the *Peacock*'s cabin.[152] When Hudson informed them that they would be held until Veidovi was captured, one of the chiefs volunteered to help. He managed to retrieve Veidovi and bring him to the *Peacock*. After the accused confessed his guilt, Hudson put him in irons in the ship's hold.[153] Ex Ex officers would later use the story of Veidovi's capture to intimidate other chiefs within the Fijian Group and to get them to sign the "Feejee Regulations."[154]

Before raising anchor, Hudson assured the king of Rewa that he would not harm his brother. Instead, US officials would return Veidovi after the Ex Ex had brought him to the United States, taught him English, and showed him their country. By then, Hudson promised, Veidovi "would be a great benefit to his own people by being able to tell them . . . how rich & great a people we were, & how, by a peaceful & honest intercourse, every thing that a Fegee man wanted would be brought to their shores."[155] The plan mimicked the visits of Indian chiefs to Washington, DC, which frequently included tours of military and naval facilities and which sought to impress Native delegations with US power and sophistication.[156] It also looked forward to US capitalistic penetration of Fiji, with Hudson envisioning Veidovi as an advertiser for US goods. However, the scheme did not work out as planned; Veidovi was taken sick by tuberculosis, and he died the day after the *Vincennes* returned to New York, in June 1842.[157] Rather than return his body to his relations at Rewa, navy surgeons decapitated him, preserved his skull, and catalogued it as a specimen of natural history.[158] They buried his headless body in an unmarked grave at the Brooklyn Navy Yard.[159] For Veidovi and his relatives, there would be no traditional Fijian burial rites to bring closure or to assist his journey to the underworld.[160]

As Veidovi's case illustrates, the officers and men of the Ex Ex rarely fulfilled their pledges to Oceanian peoples, nor did they ever really trust the Fijians. Accordingly, when Wilkes arrived in the Fiji Group in May 1840, he issued special directives for the squadron's safety. These included prescriptions against going ashore on all but uninhabited islands, that "all trade must be carried on over the stern of the boats, and the arms and how-itzers ready to repel any attack," and "never be off your guard," as "they [Fijians] are in no case to be trusted."[161] Officers like William Reynolds saw the wisdom in Wilkes's caution. "All over Fegee it is necessary to have your weapons with you," he wrote, observing that the "natives themselves never move without their spear or club."[162] Finding them not only treacherous but also ugly, Reynolds actively hoped for their destruction. "May they be smitten from the Earth!" he penned in his journal.[163]

Wilkes's precautions proved unsuccessful; dwindling rations meant that the squadron had to barter with Fijians for yams and hogs. Such ne-gotiations were delicate, with US forces generally taking a prominent Fi-jian hostage for the duration of talks ashore.[164] On July 24, 1840, tensions exploded on the island of Malolo. Nine sailors had rowed to the beach to haggle with the chief and his men for the price of hogs. They left their cutter offshore, with their shipmates holding the chief's son hostage. In the midst of negotiations, the hostage suddenly escaped, launching himself over the gunwales and running for shore. When the cutter's crew fired a warning shot, the chief shouted that the whites had killed his son. He ordered his men to attack. In the ensuing fight, nine Fijians and US two officers died.[165] Ex Ex forces retook the beach, but they were enraged and grief-stricken. When they discovered a wounded Fijian, the commanding officer ordered "him dispatched."[166]

In US eyes, the bloodshed at Malolo was a premeditated massacre. They overlooked its murky and tense origins and the fact that the Fijians had suf-fered nearly five times as many casualties as the Ex Ex.[167] What mattered to them far more was the fact that both slain officers had been beloved mem-bers of the expedition—one of them, in fact, Midshipman Wilkes Henry, had been the only son of Wilkes's widowed sister.[168] More important, they saw Malolo as a direct challenge to the national and racial hierarchy of the Jacksonian-era United States. Wilkes believed that if he did not correct the Fijians' mistake with a "salutary lesson," all the months of surveying and diplomacy would amount to nothing; white democratic capitalism would have been less secure than when he had arrived.[169] Accordingly, after a patriotic burial for the slain officers, the Ex Ex prepared for vengeance. They organized into divisions, divided small arms between them, and sent the squadron's boats around the island to prevent the Fijians from escaping. Wilkes gave orders for Lieutenant Cadwalader Ringgold to march on the town of Sualib. This place he had deemed guiltier than Malolo's other settlement at Arro, which he would torch nonetheless. On the way, Ringgold would destroy "all the plantations they should meet . . . sparing none except women and children."[170] After leveling Sualib, he would reunite with Wilkes at the smoking ruins of Arro.[171]

At nine o'clock on the morning of July 26, the Ex Ex landed in force. The invaders bristled with rockets and weaponry.[172] After destroying yam and taro fields and burning a deserted village, Ringgold's force arrived at Sualib. Here the Fijians had holed up behind the town's palisade and several defensive ditches. When a hail of US rockets began bursting among the town's thatched roofs, the Fijians retreated. "In about half an hour," the sailor Charlie Erskine remembered, the village "was reduced to ashes."[173] Continuing on, the mariners used their rockets to set a second fortified town ablaze. When "it became too hot for the savages," Erskine recalled, they tried fleeing in groups of fives and tens and "were riddled with bullets."[174] As Ringgold's forces burned and slaughtered their away across Malolo, Wilkes's small-boat blockade overturned any canoes that tried to escape—in one seaman's words, "its occupants became food for hungry sharks."[175] By the late afternoon, Ringgold and his force had joined up with Wilkes at the smoldering embers of Arro. In retaliation for their two slain shipmates, the Ex Ex had taken the lives of almost one hundred Fijians.[176] William Reynolds's earlier wish, that the Fijians "be smitten from the Earth," had been partially accomplished on Malolo.[177] The following day, the island's surviving residents groveled before Wilkes and his men in a ceremony of abject surrender.[178]

Members of the Ex Ex justified their response on commercial and racial grounds. Wilkes believed that nonaction would have imperiled future enterprising mariners. "Had [the Fijians'] great crime been suffered to go unpunished," he explained, "[they] would in all probability have become more fearless and daring than ever."[179] Like his commanding officer, William Reynolds also pointed to commerce in order to justify the massacre at Malolo. By describing the Fijians as "a set of Pirates" who were "the terror of all their neighbors,"[180] he fashioned them into the archenemies of capitalism—men who challenged the basic principle of right to property. But Reynolds went even further, wading darkly into religious and racial grounds. In addition to being pirates, Fijians were "Hell Hounds" and "bloody fiends."[181] He compared them to saltwater fish, exclaiming that he felt "the same kind of inward joy in killing them in battle" as when he killed a shark.[182] Malolo "was bloody work," he admitted, "but all the lives in Fegee would not pay for the two we lost."[183] Even if one takes a military man's strong fraternal feelings for his comrades into account, Reynolds's words are extraordinary; only the presence of a racialist ideology that valued Anglo-Saxon lives far above those of other racial or ethnic groups helps to explain them.

What happened on Malolo was the Pacific parallel to settler colonialist violence in continental North America. Just as in North America, white citizens in the Pacific struggled with Indigenous peoples over resources. In North America, the primary resource was land, whereas in the Pacific, resources were largely flora (sandalwood) and fauna (especially marine species). In the West, settlers and the state relied on forced removal and extermination to acquire Indigenous lands. In the Pacific, commercial imperialism required something else: either active Oceanian participation in the production of wealth, or the willingness to allow others to pursue that wealth. When Oceanians declined or resisted the harvesting of their region's natural resources, the US government could respond with brutal, genocidal violence, as it did on Malolo. "Sailor colonialism" had other similarities with settler colonialism, too: both entailed the extension of federal criminal jurisdiction into Indigenous territory, and both relied on missionary labor to teach Indigenous peoples how to participate in the expanding US market.[184] It was for these reasons that Wilkes so frequently praised missionaries; as on the continent, they made the Pacific a friendlier space for US capitalism. For instance, on the island of Raraka, he claimed that the labors of the missionaries meant that "all shipwrecked mariners would be sure of kind treatment."[185]

POLICING SAILORS IN THE SOUTH PACIFIC

In addition to forcing Oceanians into the orbit of US commercial governance, the Ex Ex also sought to protect sea-borne capitalism from its workers. All US ships, whether public or private, were riven into two factions: seamen and officers. According to Melville, these "antagonistic classes" were engaged "in perpetual conflict."[186] While the force of law was firmly on the side of officers, every master knew that he and his mates were outnumbered by those in the forecastle. And they did not like what they saw in the opposing force. The records of Ex Ex officers are rife with condescension, even hints of fear. On the voyage out to Madeira, Wilkes found himself amused to see ordinary sailors clustering around scientists on deck, and "to hear scientific names bandied about between Jack and his shipmates."[187]

Joseph Clark, a corporal of marines on the Ex Ex, freely admitted that some sailors were "degraded and brutalized . . . reveling in the haunts of pollution and drunkenness."[188] "They are sometimes inclined to a spirit of insubordination, and entail upon themselves many evils," he explained.[189] In Tahiti, William Reynolds watched as a group of sailors caught a shark and tortured it to death, noting "the degree of savage satisfaction that sailors enjoy in the capture & destruction of one of these monsters."[190]

To restrain such men, Ex Ex officers deployed many strategies. One was to mediate between capital and labor. Off the Peruvian port town of San Lorenzo, in June 1839 a man on watch spied two whaleships with red shirts "tied in the fore rigging"—"Jack's signal of distress," as Erskine explained. Wilkes paid the vessels a visit, drawing pledges from the captains to "treat the men better and give them better rations."[191] Wilkes repeated the feat while at Pago Pago Bay, on Tutuila, Samoa, where he listened patiently as whalemen unloaded their grievances against their captain.[192] Such activities are similar to the ways Wilkes sought to mollify Oceanians who had also been injured by unfair shipmasters. In his published narrative, Wilkes derided unscrupulous merchants as those whose "sole object" was "to make money" to the detriment of "the welfare of the natives."[193] He criticized merchants and sea officers for violating Indigenous laws, refusing to pay port charges, and sailing off without compensating for provisions. In Apia, on the Samoan island of Upolu, he offered to compensate the Samoans for their back losses in addition to paying for an anchorage.[194]

Perhaps the most notable way the Ex Ex aimed to instill order in the US commercial fleet was by its own example. In Callao, Chile, three men tried to desert the Ex Ex. At the same time, a group of marines snuck whiskey from the "spirit-room" when they were supposed to be guarding it. Wilkes was outraged—and fearful that such insubordination could spread. By law, only the ruling of a court-martial could allow a navy commander to inflict more than twelve lashes on a seaman. Pressed for time, however, and believing that the crimes called for greater chastisement, Wilkes threw navy regulations overboard. He ordered the accused parties punished with at least twenty-four lashes each. He even extended the sentence for one offender to thirty-six and to forty-one for a second. He justified his response in remarkably similar ways to what happened in Malolo: "To let such offenses pass with the ordinary punishment of twelve lashes," he explained, "would have been in the eyes of the crew to have overlooked their crime altogether. I was, therefore, compelled, in order to preserve order and good discipline, to inflict what I deemed a proper punishment."[195] It would not be the last time—over the course of the voyage, Wilkes would go above the legal limit of punishment without a court-martial twenty-five times.[196]

The lieutenant's savagery was on even greater display in Honolulu in October 1840. Three men had earned his ire: two were marines who had imbibed too much and had threatened to kill officers on board the *Peacock*; the other, Peter Sweeney, was a bellicose Briton whose hatred of the United States had resulted in numerous infractions. When the US Consul informed Wilkes that the whaling fleet had experienced several disturbances of late, the commander of the Ex Ex decided a lesson was in order.[197] He would flog the three men through the fleet, thereby ensuring that every vessel in the squadron—let alone the nine whalers clustered in the harbor—would have a good view.[198] On October 31, Wilkes called for the crews of the Ex Ex squadron to assemble and witness the punishment.[199] In the roadstead, whalemen jostled and angled for the best perspective from the rigging and gunwales of their whaleships. Ashore, nearly the whole town of Honolulu seemed to manifest on the town's docks and beaches. One after another, each man was lowered into the ship's launch, tied to the gallows, and rowed to the various vessels of the squadron. At each stop, the condemned received a portion of their lashes in violent, lacerating strokes. The marines received eighty-six in total, and Sweeney, twenty-four.[200] The Ex Ex took back the marines, but they dumped Sweeney on the sands of Honolulu. Sandy, red-faced, his back trailed with bloody ruts, he staggered off into town and disappeared.[201]

How would the common sailor have seen such violence? We can infer their response from the sentiments of other antebellum US Navy sailors. The novelist Herman Melville served as an ordinary seaman on the USS *United States* in 1843–1844 and had plenty to say about the practice of flogging in his autobiographical novel *White Jacket*. He especially railed against flogging through the fleet, which he called a "remnant of the Middle Ages" and thought was even worse than keelhauling.[202] A tar who had been flogged through the fleet, Melville explained, required weeks or even months before being able to return to active duty. And when he did, "he never is the man he was before, but, broken and shattered . . . sinks into death before his time."[203] He believed that the punishment was so rarely applied in home waters because sailors ashore would riot.[204] Enraged, he urged his readers to agitate for the abolition of the lash.[205] Other tars agreed; Navy Steward Edward P. Montague believed that if sailors "were treated more like men, and less like dogs, there would be no occasion for the 'cat o' nine tails.'"[206] The Arctic seaman William Godfrey thought naval service was "grievously oppressive to any seaman . . . who has that nice sense of honor, and that innate feeling of justice, which impel a man to resist tyranny and wrong."[207]

Public opinion eventually swung around. Opposition to the lash was rising at the time of the Ex Ex's return in 1842, such that the navy would officially abolish flogging in September 1850.[208] It is telling, in fact, that of all the charges leveled against Wilkes by his men and officers after the squadron's return, the only one that stuck was his brutality against his sailors. On the charge of cruelty and use of excessive force at Malolo, for example, the jury exonerated Wilkes.[209] It was a verdict that reflected both the white supremacy of Jacksonian maritime expansion as well as the mixed legal place that white sailors occupied in capitalist governance at sea. In the end, the court convicted Wilkes on seventeen counts of punishing his sailors beyond the legal limit.[210] For this, the secretary of the navy delivered a public reprimand: "The country which honored you with a command far above the just claims of your rank in the navy, had a right to expect that you would, at least, pay a scrupulous respect to her laws."[211] Wilkes seethed under the admonishment.[212] But for those whose backs would forever bear the scars of their commander's severity, it must have seemed mild punishment indeed.

AN EMPIRE OF COMMERCE RELIEVED

When the expedition's flagship, the USS *Vincennes,* finally returned to New York in June 1842, Wilkes believed he had achieved many of the Ex Ex's original objectives. In his mind, he had bolstered US capitalism against numerous threats—especially hostile Oceanians and upstart mariners. Historians, however, believe their actors' words at their own peril. How relieved were the captains of the empire of commerce? How effective was the Ex Ex in safeguarding Jacksonian capitalism?

The answer can be found partly in the mission's cartographic achievements. As discussed previously, US shipmasters encountered steep challenges when traversing the Pacific World. They simply did not possess the sophisticated ken of Oceanian mariners, who knew how to navigate with extraordinary precision based on observations of the natural world.[213] In the absence of accurate charts, seamen developed ways to try and guard against the calamities of shipwreck. Whalers, for instance, stationed two men aloft to sing out for navigational hazards as well as whale spouts.[214] Mariners also determined water depth and the composition of the ocean's bottom through lead lines smeared with tallow. These soundings helped them determine the area's marine geography. To gauge the proximity of land and shallow water, sailors paid close attention to aquatic life, including seabirds and seaweed.[215] At noon, they used sextants or octants to fix their latitudinal position.[216] Determining longitude, however, was far more difficult. Before the widespread adoption of chronometers later in the century, captains had to perform complex lunar distance observations and calculations to ascertain their longitudinal position.[217] In 1802, the US navigator and mathematician Nathaniel Bowditch published his *New American Practical Navigator*, which simplified the process of calculating lunar distances at sea.[218] Yet even with the "Bowditch" in hand, venturing into uncharted seas remained a dangerous game.[219]

The result of poor Western cartographic knowledge was predictable. Between 1828 and 1840, five US vessels shipwrecked in Fiji.[220] The dangers were so intense that marine insurance companies refused to underwrite voyages to the island group.[221] Elsewhere, shipwrecks in the Pacific whaling industry were so frequent that a US brig returning to port with one, two, or even three whaling captains who had lost their ships and crews was not an uncommon sight in the early nineteenth century.[222] On Nantucket, nearly a quarter of women of marriageable age and older had lost a husband to the sea.[223]

It was primarily to address this situation of navigation that the Ex Ex had been organized at all. Despite this, some of the previous historians who have written on the Ex Ex were carried away with enthusiasm for the space race and Cold War–era science.[224] In 1955, for instance, John P. Harrison claimed that the Ex Ex had done "nothing . . . to stimulate United States commerce and there is no evidence that the whaling industry benefited from the voyage."[225] D. Graham Burnett and Jason W. Smith have been far closer to the mark: while the exploring squadron carried twelve members of a scientific corps and amassed a wealth of natural history specimens and ethnographic data, its chief function was to promote maritime commerce, not the higher sciences.[226] Had the Ex Ex been organized by the administration of John Quincy Adams, far more might have been made about extending the empire of knowledge. However, this was not the case. Instead, practical, narrow-minded Jacksonians were largely responsible for the enterprise. These were men who, in Secretary Dickerson's words, "would not give one drydock for a mountain of molluscous treasures."[227] In Wilkes's instructions, Secretary Paulding wrote that the mission of the expedition was "to extend the empire of commerce and science."[228] His word order was deliberate—this was a voyage for capitalism first, natural history second.

Accordingly, Wilkes and his subordinates worked tirelessly to survey uncharted geographical features during the cruise. It was hard, backbreaking work; officers and men suffered sunburn, clouds of mosquitoes, and sore feet from wading over coral reefs.[229] Surveying also required the close, hierarchical supervision of the unforgiving Wilkes. Some of the trials that unfolded after the voyage's return, in fact, were squabbles over "hydrographic discipline."[230] Nevertheless, by the voyage's end, Ex Ex personnel had made careful notations of 154 islands and fifty isolated reefs.[231]

When the expedition returned home, one of Wilkes's primary tasks was producing navigable charts of the South Pacific. He and his subordinates poured hours into drafting charts and transferring them onto copper sheets for printing. In total, they prepared 249 charts of islands, island chains, harbors, and submerged reefs.[232] One hundred and eighty of them appeared in a two-volume *Hydrographical Atlas* produced by the expedition between 1850 and 1858.[233] The Treasury Department sold individual Ex Ex charts from US custom houses at the cheapest rate possible, barely covering the cost of engraving and printing.[234] Wilkes's five-volume narrative, published in various editions and formats between 1844 and 1858, provided helpful advice about safe anchorages, whale populations, the availability of fresh provisions, and the friendliness of Islanders.[235] Wilkes expanded on these recommendations in 1861, when he finally published a volume on hydrography and sailing directions.[236]

Shipmasters applauded the cartographic and navigational data of the Ex Ex. In 1846, Senator James Alfred Pearce submitted a report to Congress on the value of the Ex Ex publications, including the charts. He observed that Wilkes had received many letters from grateful sea captains engaged in the Fiji trade. These missives demonstrated that "the labors of the expedition have given security to our vessels trading in those seas."[237] Among those who wrote was a Captain Osborn, a trader in the bêche-de-mer fishery. Osborn reported that the Fijian charts allowed him "to sail night and day . . . without fear of reefs and shoals. I have been enabled to have three and four biche-da-mar [*sic*] houses in operation at one time, by which I soon filled up, and made a much shorter voyage than was ever before made."[238] From New York, another merchant wrote directly to the publisher of Wilkes's narrative volumes, Lea & Blanchard, asking for "a copy of Capt Wilkes Chart of the Columbia River."[239] And in London, the *Times* begrudgingly credited Wilkes with achieving what he had set out to do: they recommended Wilkes's narrative and charts "to the careful perusal of our own South Sea whalers."[240]

Indeed, the overwhelming evidence suggests that the cartographic resources of Ex Ex provided additional security to the US maritime empire in the Pacific World. US and British whalers might still have to face what Melville called the "undeliverable, nameless perils of the whale,"[241] but with the Ex Ex charts they were less likely to strike an unknown reef. Accurate charts also calmed the nerves of investors who had previously refused to underwrite voyages to Fiji. Letters written in the 1840s and early 1850s by David Whippy, a US beachcomber in Fiji, further suggest that a residual fear of the Ex Ex kept Fijians "very friendly and civil" during that time.[242] Indeed, whether due to the massacre at Malolo or not, Fijians did not run afoul of the US Navy again until 1855.[243] US investment capital could now flow more freely into the Pacific. As a result, the US whale fishery ballooned. During the late 1840s, seven hundred of the nine hundred vessels in the world's whaling fleet hailed from the United States.[244] A veritable army of men, twenty thousand strong, scoured the globe for whales.[245] Their presence inspired more US naval activity in the Pacific in the 1850s, culminating with Commodore Matthew Calbraith Perry's mission to Japan in 1852–1854 and the North Pacific Exploring Expedition of 1853–1855. As the name implies, this later mission was a northern version of the original Ex Ex, and was undertaken largely to secure charts of the Japanese coast and North Pacific rim as whalers pursued new species in and around Japan and the Bering Straits.[246]

The cartographic work of the Ex Ex even aided US westward expansion. Despite Secretary Paulding's claims that the Ex Ex was "not for conquest, but discovery," it had very clear territorial ambitions.[247] The West Coast, boosters believed, would soon anchor an expanded US maritime empire in the Pacific World. They hoped that an official government reconnaissance would bolster claims to the region and facilitate its settlement by US citizens. Accordingly, from April to November 1841, the Ex Ex was busily employed in surveying the Pacific Northwest and the coast of California. When Wilkes arrived in San Francisco Bay in August 1841, he marveled at its size and protection from the sea. He predicted that California would soon separate from Mexico and form a political union with Oregon. The resulting nation would "control the destinies of the Pacific."[248] As a good Jacksonian Democrat, Wilkes confidently asserted that California would come to be "possessed . . . by the Anglo-Norman race."[249] He believed that Mexicans, as the "indolent inhabitants of warm climates," would put up little resistance. Once in US hands, the Pacific coast would "fill a large space in the world's future history."[250] In addition to surveying San Francisco Bay, Ex Ex servicemen explored the rivers flowing into it, including the Sacramento and the Feather, and wide swathes of Northern California's interior via an overland expedition from Oregon.

The data that the Ex Ex retrieved from the West Coast cleared the way for more US expansion. The Oregon survey, for example, would be of enormous value to the US settlers who would soon invade Indigenous lands in Oregon Country. In 1843, the army dispatched John Charles Frémont to "connect" his previous western surveys to those of "Commander Wilkes on the coast of the Pacific ocean, so as to give a correct survey of the interior of our continent."[251] In 1849, Wilkes drew on his expedition's discoveries and published a volume titled *Western America*. His stated aim was to provide information and cheap maps to lawmakers and to "those who intend emigrating to California."[252] Lea & Blanchard in Philadelphia published 1,900 copies and hawked it to forty-niners at thirty cents apiece.[253] Missionaries, too, would benefit; as Senator Pearce noted in 1846, the Ex Ex's data on the cultures and languages of Northwest Coast would equip "the public Indian agents, and the missionaries" for their labors on Indian lands.[254]

Diplomatically speaking, the Ex Ex surveys expanded US claims to Oregon. In 1818, the United States and Britain had agreed that persons of both nationalities could settle in Oregon Country for ten years. They renewed this ten-year commitment repeatedly as each angled for a better claim.[255] In Wilkes's secret report to the Navy Department, he pressed the John Tyler administration to disregard British treaties and seize the entirety of Oregon country. He urged such an aggressive step on account of Oregon's rich forests, fisheries, and plentiful stock of fur-bearing mammals. While Tyler initially suppressed Wilkes's recommendations for fear of jeopardizing ongoing negotiations with the British, he came around to backing them: in his December 1843 address to Congress, Tyler called for US occupancy of the Pacific Northwest all the way to the 54° 40' line.[256] In the 1844 presidential campaign, James K. Polk stole Tyler's thunder and trumpeted the idea as his own.[257] When Polk's bombast provoked a belligerent response from the British, the US Senate directed printers to make ten thousand copies of Wilkes's Oregon map in case war actually broke out.[258]

Similarly, Wilkes's accounts of California may have informed Polk's decision to pursue national aggrandizement even if it meant war with Mexico.[259] After all, Polk was intensely interested in seizing the three great harbors of Puget Sound, San Francisco, and San Diego for the benefit of US commerce.[260] Polk's public speeches on the issue support this interpretation. After the Mexican War, for instance, Polk proudly noted that "we have now three great maritime fronts—on the Atlantic, the Gulf of Mexico, and the Pacific."[261] He predicted that San Francisco would become the New Orleans for the Pacific coast, a sheltered port for the expanding whale fishery, and even "our great Western naval depot."[262]

All told, the cartographic resources of the Ex Ex were a perfect expression of Jacksonian political economy. They made the resources of the Pacific and the West much more accessible to white male US citizens. Much of the Democratic program was a war on economic privilege. Democrats fought to equalize economic opportunity for white men, to soften the effects of their failure, and to encourage their competition "without the aid of legislative favour."[263] The so-called Bank War is the most prominent national example of this trend, but they were many more at the state and local level.

The Jacksonian program in the Pacific was similar. Previous to the Ex

Ex, US navigators in the Pacific had to rely mainly on difficult navigational techniques, past experience, and perhaps, if they were lucky, the knowledge of others. In New England, elite merchants established marine societies to share knowledge of lands and seas beyond the Capes.[264] The East India Marine Society in Salem, for instance, provided blank logbooks that its members would fill out and then donate to the society's library for the benefit of future voyagers. Such knowledge, however, was exclusive; membership was restricted only to those who had already braved the Pacific or Indian Ocean. In Jacksonian eyes, the knowledge reservoir of the society could be seen as a form of special privilege.[265] The same might be said for the scattershot of maps, memoirs, and word-of-mouth and letter-by-letter knowledge of the North American West.[266] If one had access to such knowledge, one was privileged and had a special economic advantage over other aspiring white men.

The Ex Ex charts, whether of the Pacific or of the West Coast, was an attempt to equalize opportunity for working white men and the capitalist investors who supplied them. When Peter A. Browne gave opening remarks at the dedication of the Franklin Institute building in Philadelphia in 1825, he claimed that this was an era in which "knowledge cease[d] to be monopolized by few and [was] becoming the property of the many."[267] He might as well have been speaking about the results of Ex Ex. With the publication of its charts in the mid-1840s, the expedition made US capitalism safer than ever before in Oceania. To say that Wilkes succeeded is in no way to imply that he was right; on the contrary, the Ex Ex's responses to Indigenous violence and, to a lesser extent, sailor disobedience was immoral, cruel, and grossly disproportionate. Nor were the extensive diplomatic negotiations and judicial operations that forced Oceanian societies into the jurisdiction of US authorities any more just. What it does mean, however, is that by 1860 the Pacific was much closer to an extension of the domestic US market than it had ever been.

In spite of this achievement, the Ex Ex never received the praise that its leaders had expected. The lackluster reception in the United States surprised Wilkes. Of course, he had himself to blame, at least in part. As we have seen, the stress of managing the expedition turned Wilkes into a nasty martinet. The Navy Department's refusal to promote Wilkes before the expedition compounded his diffidence, which he expressed by beating up on his subordinates, officers as well as ordinary seamen.[268] His viciousness ensured that he returned home with a boatload of enemies. By the end of the cruise, William Reynolds described Wilkes as "either crazy beyond redemption" or "a rascally tyrant & a liar black-hearted enough to be the Devil's brother."[269] In August 1839, the brother of one officer wrote his sibling with advice: "The best revenge is to fight him" and to "assail him and his humbug expedition." When the Ex Ex returns, he wrote, "fasten your teeth into Wilkes' throat. By God, he must be made to suffer."[270]

Since many naval officers had political patrons in Washington, Wilkes's unpopularity in the navy affected his reputation with lawmakers. The House voted down a resolution to commend the expedition, while the Senate failed to pass a measure that would have invited Wilkes and his officers to be publicly recognized in the Senate chamber.[271] The hostility of President John Tyler's secretary of the navy, Abel Upshur, was particularly notable because the man had otherwise been an avid naval reformer and expansionist. In 1842, he convinced Congress to dramatically increase naval spending to $8,397,000, or one-third of the federal budget; to abolish the Board of Navy Commissioners and replace it with the far more efficient bureau system; and to appropriate funds for the construction of the world's first screw-driven warship, the USS *Princeton*.[272] Despite his enthusiasm for a more active, muscular, and efficient navy, Upshur had little affection for Wilkes or for naval exploration. This may have also been because Upshur, as a Whig, saw both as linked too closely to Democratic policies.[273] After five separate court-martials over Wilkes's tenure as commander of the Ex Ex, it was Upshur who gave Wilkes the public admonishment for the treatment of his men and officers.[274]

Wilkes was incensed; where he had expected a parade, he received a censure. When Wilkes visited the White House after his return, President Tyler invited him to join him and his friends by the fire, where they sat, chewing and spitting tobacco. "It was exactly like a Virginia or North Carolina bar room," Wilkes recalled. The president asked the lieutenant no questions, virtually ignoring him.[275] One source even suggests that Tyler had no idea who Wilkes was.[276] With few political friends and fearing that the bitterness of the court martials might overshadow the mission's accomplishments, Wilkes and his allies embarked on a bold public relations strategy. His countrymen needed to hear the expedition's story, and to see firsthand the marvels of the Pacific World. He would have to reconvene the scientists, for they all had work to do. Putting down the lash and the saber, Wilkes picked up the pen. He would write his way to fame.

CHAPTER 3

The United States Exploring Expedition in Popular Culture

Charles Wilkes was in despair. Since his return to New York aboard the *Vincennes* in June 1842, he had labored to publish the results of the United States Exploring Expedition—or the "Ex Ex," as contemporaries called it. It was a task that had weakened him body and soul. Responsible for supervising the expedition's collections and the publication of its accomplishments, he often worked late into the night, scribbling his own contributions to the Ex Ex volumes.[1] By December 1853, the mission was approaching its end: his five-volume narrative of the voyage had been published, as were titles on ethnology, philology, zoophytes, physical anthropology, geology, and meteorology. Other scientific tomes on mollusks, ichthyology, and crustaceans were finally ready for the press. Wilkes's own last volume, on physics, was at Lewis's print shop in Philadelphia. Joseph Drayton, an artist on the Ex Ex and Wilkes's right-hand man in Philadelphia, was away in New York, working with artisans and "up to his eyes in colouring and printing plates."[2]

The fire struck in Drayton's absence. It consumed all his records and his artistic drawings from the expedition. A set of weaving equipment went up, in Drayton's words, "like a pinch of cotton in a lighted candle." More important, the blaze devoured most of the stereotyped plates then in press. While other plates remained safe in a fireproof box, the fire proved "an unexpected blow to us," Wilkes wrote, for he and Drayton had hoped "to give the work the finishing stroke." Sunk in gloom, the weary captain penned one of his few remaining friends and patrons—ex-senator Benjamin Tappan, in Ohio. Wilkes confessed he had often found himself in a mood "difficult to get rid of or conquer." The work of publishing the results of the Ex Ex, he told Tappan, had been "far more than all the duties which devolved upon me during the arduous cruise." "I have great difficulty in keeping the Squadron together," he had earlier explained. Most painful of all was the lack of recognition, "on the part of the Nation for the labours we had gone through." Embittered and lonely, Wilkes felt that his "labours" had been a "curse" for him and his family.[3]

Figure 3.1 Brady's National Photographic Portrait Galleries, *Portrait of Rear Admiral Charles Wilkes, Officer of the Federal Navy*, between 1860 and 1865. Note the intensity of Wilkes's gaze and his careworn, craggy face. (Courtesy of Library of Congress Prints and Photographs Division, Washington, DC. LC-B813-1371 A [P&P], https://www.loc.gov/item/2018666524/.)

Ensnared in his own struggles, Wilkes had failed to see the larger picture. It was true that he had fought many political battles over publishing the results of the Ex Ex, and that he had the scars to prove it. While his cantankerous nature had left him isolated from many of his subordinate officers and former friends, the greater truth was that naval exploration was extremely popular with the white middle-class public by the end of 1853. By then, his own *Narrative of the United States Exploring Expedition* had gone through at least nine domestic and four foreign editions. It would go through two more US editions before the decade was out. Narratives of naval discovery were in such great demand that readers and booksellers wrote directly to publishers, requesting copies for their libraries and shops, while book peddlers clamored for lucrative contracts to sell copies in the hinterlands.[4] The profits anticipated and reaped by publishers were immense; when a fire in New York City destroyed nearly the entire first printing of the navy surgeon Elisha Kent Kane's narrative of an exploring expedition to the Arctic, the publishers decided to absorb the loss and produce a second edition.[5]

Like books, museums also played a role in bringing the fruits of the Ex Ex to the nation's curious middle class. While some specimens went to well-established private museums like the Academy of Natural Sciences or the Peale Museum, most went to Washington. In fact, the first federally funded national museum of natural history was not the Smithsonian Institution, but the National Gallery. Located on the upper floor of the Patent Office, the National Gallery soon became the primary repository for the collections of the Ex Ex. Beginning in the early 1840s, US citizens could not only read about the expedition's adventures, but could also go to Washington and see the imperial trophies firsthand. The exhibits were an instant success. Visitors were thrilled by the gallery's rare birds, mounted mammals, exotic plants, fossils, corals, and most of all the anthropological artifacts from the South Pacific—especially Fiji.

Why were mostly white, antebellum US citizens so fascinated by these publications and specimens? Simply put, the results of the Ex Ex reassured them about themselves, their nation, and their place in the world. The early US republic underwent wrenching change in the 1840s and 1850s; the upheaval of the market, transportation, and communication revolutions increased opportunities for social mobility as well as economic failure. At the same time, abolitionists and first-wave feminists challenged the traditional racial and gendered hierarchy of US society. In this world of transformation, the Ex Ex publications and the "National Cabinet of Curiosities" in Washington reaffirmed white middle-class values.[6] These included commitments to self-improvement, education, US exceptionalism, and white supremacy. Both the Ex Ex volumes and the National Gallery highlighted so-called "savage" and "barbaric" or "semi-civilized" cultures. Both confirmed white US citizens' sense of themselves as denizens of a special, advanced type of nation—one that could categorize global cultures as well as contribute to the scientific knowledge of mankind. In fact, evaluating other

peoples was an essential part of the US diplomatic mission to achieve recognition as a great Western power; after all, only truly "civilized" nations
could pass judgment on peoples who were supposedly in lesser stages of
development. This diplomatic aspect was so salient that the US State Department disseminated the tomes of the Ex Ex to foreign governments as
evidence of national attainment.

The national maturity that the Ex Ex materials represented was mean-
ingful to members of the white middle class. These were folks who were,
like their nation, striving for worldly recognition, success, and status. They
may not have made it yet, but the "national" quality of the productions
of the US Exploring Expedition reassured them that they were members
of a nation of winners—and that there were other peoples, both at home
and abroad, who were beneath them. Thus, the productions of the Ex Ex
affirmed racial and class hierarchies and contributed to the raising of an
imperial society. Moreover, the global dimensions of naval exploration
contributed a sense of universal truth to what might have otherwise been
dismissed as mere provincial knowledge. White readers and museumgoers could now draw comparisons between the perceived savagery of Oceanians, enslaved African Americans, and besieged Native Americans. They
could read about how happy Black slaves were in Rio de Janeiro, study the
skulls of reputed Fijian cannibals, and examine the bone-splitting clubs of
Oceania. The social "truths" they had ingested at home, in school, and on
the street in the early republic were now reinforced by imperial imports
from abroad. Whether white citizens read the publications of the Ex Ex or
visited the National Gallery, they encountered confirmations of their values
and social status in an increasingly diverse, complex, and shifting world.

On a greater political level, the popular culture of naval exploration
raised public and private interest in global adventurism. As imperialists
and scholars have long recognized, the project of empire always requires
buy-in at home.[7] Oftentimes, that cultural support is best seen in the marketplace—a "consumer's imperium," as Kristin Hoganson has termed it.[8]
While the dramatic expansion of US naval exploration in the 1850s can be
attributed to many factors (including those discussed in later chapters),
what cannot be overlooked is how the domestic production and consumption of empire buttressed the explorationist movement in the last decades
of the early US republic. Indeed, the curated results of the Ex Ex—whether
in print or behind glass—created a frightfully powerful alliance between
expansionists in the federal government, publishing houses, and the white
middle class. The impact of this development was predictable: as global imperialism grew more attractive and profitable at home, it became increasingly desirable to reproduce imperial activity abroad. In the "little Ocean

of politics" that was popular culture in the early US republic, the results of the Ex Ex caused "the great wave of democracy" to rise in favor of empire.[9]

EXPLORATORY TEXTS AND FOREIGN RELATIONS

From the start, the publication of naval exploratory texts had a strong foreign policy dimension. As Wilkes and many of his friends and scientists understood, the mission of the Ex Ex did not end with its return in 1842. What awaited them was an even larger and perhaps more daunting task: the publication of the historical and scientific results of the voyage. If the United States was to claim equality with the Great Powers, this documentation was a diplomatic necessity. As one correspondent wrote Senator Benjamin Tappan in June 1842, "The world will expect much for the preparations made & the time spent on making this Voyage of discovery."[10] Jeremiah Reynolds agreed; recently established as a young lawyer in New York City, he wrote Tappan to express his anxiety "that the whole should be carefully prepared and properly published."[11]

Wilkes and his allies on Capitol Hill were determined to produce a work that would rival any European publication. That meant matching France. In the nineteenth century, the French were widely acknowledged as the leading power in publishing fine scientific texts—one British reviewer called French folio atlases of scientific exploration "the most splendid productions of the age."[12] US officials concurred. In August 1842, when Congress directed the Joint Committee on the Library to oversee the publication of the Ex Ex results, they chose a French model for the committee to follow: the Ex Ex volumes should mimic "the voyage of the Astrolabe, lately published by the Government of France."[13] Here Congress was referencing the *Voyage au Pole Sud et dans l'Océanie sur les Corvettes l'Astrolabe et la Zélée*, which recounted the start of a French voyage of discovery led by Captain Jules-Sébastien-César Dumont d'Urville. Published in Paris in 1841, the work was the first of ten that would together narrate the history of the expedition. With the exception of a foldable chart of the Straits of Magellan at its end, the first volume of d'Urville's *Voyage* contained no images and was bound in simple pasteboard.[14] While this first volume was unpretending, the Library Committee knew that the forthcoming French scientific folios would be the envy of the world.

To emulate them, the committee turned to Senator Benjamin Tappan of Ohio. A strong Democrat and an amateur conchologist, Tappan was a promising candidate to serve as primary overseer of the Ex Ex publications. He viewed the assignment as one of the most important of his life.[15] From Wilkes's perspective, however, perhaps Tappan's greatest qualifica-

tion was that he agreed to acquiesce to Wilkes, with the lieutenant directing the project's daily operations and reporting to him. The committee con-
sented to the arrangement, and the pair quickly formed a close working
relationship.[16] Their goal, Wilkes declared, was "to vie with, if not surpass"
any similar European productions.[17]

The national identity of the publications mattered. The Library Committee required that only US artisans and scientists could labor for the
project. For a time, they even insisted that the scientists charged with describing the voyage's specimens live and work in Washington, DC.[18] Because Washington remained a relative cultural backwater in the 1840s and
1850s, the committee's order hampered the specialists' abilities to excel in
their fields; as one frustrated geologist fumed to a colleague in March 1846,
"It is perfectly absurd that I should . . . prepare my reports in a city where
there are no books!"[19] Moreover, because the original law had stipulated
that Congress would pay for only one hundred copies of each of the Ex Ex
volumes, Wilkes and Tappan felt justified in hiring the best talent and using
the finest possible materials the country could produce.[20] For printer, the
committee selected Conger Sherman, a Philadelphia artisan who had some
experience publishing scientific tomes.[21] For binder, they opted for Benjamin Gaskill, another Philadelphian and one of the leading book binders in
the country.[22] Likewise, Drayton ensured that only the best artists would
engrave the work's copper and steel plates and wood blocks. By May 1846,
Tappan could assure the chair of the Joint Library Committee that the
work employed "a great number of the best Engravers in the Country."[23]

Women also played an important role in beautifying the Ex Ex publications. Given the trends of the time, it appears that at least some of the
industrial labor that produced the Ex Ex publications was female. By the
1850s, publishing houses had grown accustomed to hiring more and more
women as skilled typesetters.[24] Young women also found work as atten-
dants for folding machines and in pressrooms, where they fed sheets of paper into the presses.[25] Whether or not they did so for the Ex Ex volumes is
unknown; what is clear, however, is that female artists colored many of the
specimen prints for the scientific volumes. Lavinia Bowen, the co: propri-
etor of a fine-book coloring studio in Philadelphia, received the contract to
color the plates.[26] After Drayton colored the plates of one volume, Lavinia's
"girls" would replicate it for the next ninety-nine.[27] Their labor was frequently elided; in 1846, for example, Senator James Alfred Pearce credited
only Drayton and the geologist, James Dwight Dana, for the "surprising
richness and beauty" of the "colored drawings . . . of many coral animals."[28]
Like the countless men who did the hard, manual, and repetitive labor of

printing and binding the Ex Ex volumes, the contributions of female workers were largely ignored.

The final product was brilliant. When the official copies of Wilkes's five-volume *Narrative of the United States Exploring Expedition* were issued in late 1844, members of the Library Committee laid their hands on a set of books that were as handsome as any book ever produced in the United States. The contrast with the d'Urville volumes was striking: the US tomes were much larger, for one, "of super-royal quarto size" versus the smaller French octavo. While the French government would have doubtless enhanced the binding of the official d'Urville volumes, it would have been hard to outdo the US tomes. Wilkes's *Narrative* and later scientific volumes were bound in fine dark-green morocco with boards "of the best quality, firm and stout."[29] Gilt lettering and tooling on the boards and spine shone with nationalist imagery. On the front cover, a gilt eagle crouched over a shield adorned with the US colors, shrieking at two of the expedition's vessels. Whereas d'Urville's *Voyage* had been printed on inferior paper, the pages of the US *Narrative* were impressed on thick, large, cream-colored cloth. These were tightly sewn together by hand, with the bound strings masked by five raised bands on the spine. Finally, unlike the French volume, the *Narrative* abounded with images: in total, there were sixty-four fine plates, forty-seven steel vignettes (or smaller plates produced by engraved steel), and 247 woodcuts inserted throughout the five volumes.[30] While the French released their own atlas of plates to correspond with d'Urville's *Voyage* in the early 1850s, the integration of the text with images in Wilkes's *Narrative* greatly improved the aesthetics of reading them.[31] Senator Pearce, the chairman of the Joint Library Committee, was well pleased; after having compared the US volumes "with the most celebrated voyages of English and French navigators," he was "satisfied . . . of the superior merit of this first and only similar American work."[32]

The federal government used the Ex Ex tomes as tools for asserting US cultural maturity. In February 1845, Congress stipulated how the hundred official copies of the Ex Ex publications would be divided up. They gave two to every state in the Union and two copies each to France, Great Britain, and Russia.[33] Later bills would add more nations, including the Argentine Confederation, Brazil, and China.[34] Initially, the secretary of state simply forwarded copies to the foreign delegations in Washington, DC, without letters of introduction. However, when the French legation turned around and exchanged them for storage space in New York, the department changed course; as soon as it received shipments of the scientific volumes, it sent them directly to US ministers in foreign capitals to present to their host governments.[35] In April 1855, for example, Secretary of State William Marcy shipped volume 16, a botanical tome, to the US minister at Rio de Janeiro "to present [it] to the Government of Brazil in the name of the Government of the United States."[36] Some US diplomats assigned to lesser (nonministerial) posts believed that the volumes of the Ex Ex were valuable enough to bypass the State Department and ask Wilkes directly for copies. As the new chargé d'affaires for Naples told him when he requested his own copy in July 1853, "the Italians . . . value highly such works."[37]

By giving copies to major foreign nations, the United States was consciously acting like a member of what might be called Europe's "diplomatic republic of science," in which the Great European Powers would aid each other in scientific endeavors and share the results (and sometimes the credit) for their voyages.[38] After Captain James Cook's voyages, for example, the Royal Society gave gold medals to the king of France and the empress of Russia for their assistance during Cook's circumnavigations.[39] (Wilkes himself was later awarded a gold medal by the Royal Geographical Society).[40] The fact that the Library of Congress had a collection of official European accounts of voyages of discovery for members of Congress to scrutinize suggests that the United States was simply following European precedent. Indeed, the Library Committee was familiar with older D'Urville volumes, which he composed after his first voyage in the Pacific between 1826 and 1829, because France had sent them as diplomatic gifts in 1836.[41] Jeremiah Reynolds praised them as "a pretty conception, honourable to the French; and it will be honourable to us when we shall be able to return the compliment."[42] Other nations in the Western Hemisphere acted similarly; in 1857, the Empire of Brazil gifted a copy of *Ornithologia Brazileira* to the United States. Secretary of State Lewis Cass thanked the emperor, calling it "a happy illustration of His Majesty's well known interest in the promotion of . . . arts and sciences," and forwarded the volume to the Library of Congress.[43]

THE EX EX PUBLICATIONS IN POPULAR CULTURE

Neither Wilkes nor the printers were content with the Ex Ex volumes being used solely for diplomacy, however. Wilkes was still fuming about his poor reception at the hands of the Tyler administration, and was determined to redeem his reputation by publicizing the expedition's achievements.[44] A common refrain for Wilkes was that he wanted the publications to be "a great National Monument to our Country."[45] "Time will do me full justice," he wrote, "and my narrative of the Expedition will remain a monument to my exertions."[46] In using the word *monument*, Wilkes revealed just how public he hoped these volumes would be, and how they would be received by the literate middle class. The firms that had produced the original hundred volumes, too, hoped for a broader distribution.[47] Accordingly, Wilkes took out a copyright on the *Narrative* and prepared to raise the profile of the Ex Ex through the popular press. Gaining the copyright over an official government publication was a controversial move, but his determination carried the day.[48]

Wilkes's faith in the marketability of his *Narrative* was well founded. White US citizens in the early republic moved in a disorienting world of transformation. They craved reassurance about the nature of the world and their place in it.[49] For decades now, scholars have sought to comprehend the enormous changes that transformed life in the United States between the War of 1812 and the Civil War. Some have emphasized political metamorphoses, especially the rise of populist politicians like Andrew Jackson and the relative democratization of the franchise that fueled his rise.[50] Others have shied away from defining the era as the "Age of Jackson" (or even the "Age of Clay"), preferring to dwell on the changes attendant to a "market revolution."[51] Likewise, other historians have expounded on technological advances, whether in transportation or communication.[52] Still others have scrutinized the nation's gargantuan territorial growth and its rising aspirations to play an active role in global commerce, international affairs, and Christian missionizing.[53] Closer to home, abolitionists railed against slavery and even implicated white supremacy itself. Feminist pioneers, meanwhile, called for the same legal and political rights as men. Wherever early republicans looked, they perceived a world in flux.

Nowhere was this disorder more prevalent than in issues of class and social status. In the colonial era, the gentry elite had been the social, cultural, and political leaders of their societies. Below them sat preindustrial artisans. These were men whose skills not only earned them comfortable incomes, but who were also largely respected and recognized in the community. The Revolution changed everything; the war for independence and its roiling aftermath swept away the colonial-era gentry—first by disposing of Loyalist elites and their property, and then by sweeping the aristocratically inclined Federalist Party into oblivion.[54] Similarly, the industrial, market, and immigration revolutions threatened to undo the artisanal class in favor of wage laborers.[55] The growing pains of an expanding economy resulted in devasting financial panics in 1819, 1837, and 1857.[56] Stiff economic headwinds encouraged families and ambitious youths to migrate westward, sometimes even outside the borders of the United States.[57]

To compensate for the insecurity of larger forces, US citizens began reinventing the domestic social hierarchy. That began with divorcing wealth from class; instead of having income and property determine one's social status, denizens of the US began emphasizing culture, or what they frequently termed "character." Character in the early republic was signified by self-control and virtue. It also meant self-cultivation and an earnest commitment to self-improvement.[58] Antebellum citizens valued character so deeply that some voyaged far oversees to pursue it; Nancy Shoemaker, for instance, has argued that the primary motive for US nationals to venture to Fiji was not empire or even wealth, but social respectability.[59]

Race was another factor that weighed heavily on the minds of the white middle-class. Indeed, the concept of "character" had racial overtones; as the pseudosciences of craniology and phrenology developed, white US citizens believed that science justified their sense of social superiority.[60] As economic insecurity grew, more and more white laborers found themselves working alongside—and competing with—free Blacks. Suddenly, they faced the possibility of admitting social equality with people who were increasingly viewed as inferior. In this context, racism became an economic means for white social mobility and a psychological strategy for white self-esteem. In *How the Irish Became White*, Noel Ignatiev has argued that Irish immigrants consciously sought social classification as white in order to gain a leg over lower-class Blacks.[61] On a larger scale, both Whigs and Democrats relied on varying levels of race-baiting in order to amass and maintain political power.[62] Finally, in the so-called free North, segregationists excluded Blacks from the very same social venues being used to claim middle-class identity, including schools and lecture halls.[63] In a world of economic upheaval, then, class and race became reassuring tools for middle-class whites. Whatever a white person's economic fortunes were, they could always point to their character and their skin color to differentiate themselves from coarser whites or even wealthier, more talented, and more refined Blacks.

One way that whites could demonstrate their middle-class credentials was through reading. Each night, many well-to-do families clustered in their living rooms to read together or have books or periodicals read to them by a father, mother, or elder sibling. When Elisha Kent Kane's *Arctic Explorations* hit the press in 1857, *Happy Home & Parlor Magazine* declared, "We can conceive of few better employments for these long winter evenings than for a family to read them while circling their centre-table or sitting around their social fireside."[64] The widespread accessibility of kerosene lanterns, not to mention Argand or astral lamps, made such evenings possible.[65] In at least one respect, this led to an imperial circuit whereby readers used the light produced by whale oil to read about whaling in the Pacific. When Melville pleaded with readers of *Moby-Dick* to "be economical with your lamps and candles," for "not a gallon you burn, but at least one drop of man's blood was spilled for it," he was partly addressing the families that gathered each evening to enjoy literary pleasures.[66]

What they read mattered. Because literacy rates in the United States were so high, middle-class citizens had to be discriminating in their literary choices if they wanted to affect gentility. According to the Census of 1850, 77 percent of whites in the United States could read and write. Nearly as many women as men could read, and between 5–10 percent of Blacks (slaves included) were literate. In comparison, only about 60 percent of Her Majesty's subjects in Great Britain could read.[67] Thus, literacy itself was not the best metric for determining a middle-class identity. Instead, it was important to know *what* to read. In 1859, a columnist for *Moore's Rural New Yorker* declared that "perusal of the productions of genius" would improve the mind, but reading "a poorly written book" was "injurious" to one's character.[68]

Wilkes may or may not have understood how his volumes boosted white middle-class egos. What he and his publishers did understand, however, was that there was significant demand for informative travelogues in the early republic. In the words of one travel writer, the late 1840s was an era "when all Anglo-Saxondom [was] on the qui-vive for novelty."[69] Plenty were the Americans, he claimed, who enjoyed voyages "to the ends of the earth in their comfortable arm-chairs."[70] Library statistics bear him out: Of all the books that male patrons of the New York Society Library checked out between 1847 and 1849, 19 percent of them were travel books. For female patrons, that statistic was just slightly less, but still significant—14.65 percent.[71] In 1849, nearly 15 percent of the collections of the Library of Congress were classified under "geography," a category that largely comprised travel narratives.[72]

Travelogues were popular because of a middle-class "culture of curiosity" that combined self-improvement and entertainment.[73] Members of the middle class desired to appear knowledgeable about the world; in this they subscribed to an older, European tradition of education. A central component of the education of any young, eighteenth-century aristocrat was the "Grand Tour" of southern Europe and western Asia. If one could not afford to embark on such an extensive and costly voyage, reading accounts of the Grand Tour was the next best thing.[74] A "defect of personal observation," one writer claimed, could be relieved "by reading the reports and narratives of . . . intelligent individuals."[75] On a larger scale, curious crowds came to view the oddities of Phineas T. Barnum's museum in Philadelphia, watched the spiritualist seances of the Fox sisters, borrow books from public libraries, and attended lectures by professors and explorers.[76]

Many, if not most, travelogues were accounts of sea voyages. Throughout the nineteenth century, merchant captains, naval officers, ordinary
seamen, and female travelers released narratives of "voyages around the
world"—an immensely popular genre of travel writing with strong traditions in European literature and print culture. For landlubbers, sea literature had the double allure of describing two unknown worlds at once: first,
the exposed, circumstantial life of the blue-water sailor, and second, the
lands, peoples, and cultures that lay across the sea. Thus, sales of Herman
Melville's *Typee*, a highly fictionalized account of the author's residence
in the Marquesas, far outstripped those for the ponderous, pelagic *Moby-
Dick*.[77] Similarly, Richard Henry Dana Jr.'s *Two Years before the Mast* had
the advantage of describing forecastle life in exquisite detail as well as the
Pacific coast of North America. Interest in navigational voyages extended
into communities far removed from saltwater; growing up in backwoods
Ohio, Jeremiah Reynolds had been among those who had "imbibed a relish . . . for books of voyages and travels," even when he "had not yet seen
the ocean."[78]

Adventurous narratives inspired readers to replicate similar experiences
and feats. Reynolds's story is a case in point, but there were plenty of others as well. One of the most accomplished US Army explorers of the West,
John C. Frémont, shared with Reynolds an insatiable appetite for travel
narratives.[79] After each of his western expeditions, he worked closely with
his wife, Jessie Frémont, in crafting his own romantic epics of discovery.[80]
These, in turn, bedazzled other would-be conquerors. After reading Frémont's *Report of the Exploring Expedition to the Rocky Mountains* (1845),
one young man so talked up its "glowing pages" that his cautious parents finally relented and permitted him to become a western adventurer.[81] Oceangoing narratives, too, played their part in forging what Martin Green called
"the energizing myth of empire."[82] As Dana famously remarked, "There is
a witchery in the sea . . . which has done more to man navies, and fill mer-
chantmen, than all the pressgangs of Europe."[83]

Gender certainly played a role in determining how readers sought to
reproduce adventure in their own lives, but it does not appear to have been
a major factor in the general popularity of travelogues. Men and women,
boys and girls appear to have been equally enamored with travel narratives.
Jessie Frémont, for instance, cherished her collaboration with her husband.
She relished the opportunity to live vicariously through him and translate
his western experiences into more sentimental, vivid language.[84] Later,
young girls practically worshiped the Arctic explorer Elisha Kent Kane,
whose volumes took the book market by storm in the mid-1850s.[85] And as
will be demonstrated later, loved ones gave exploratory accounts to family

members of both sexes. Thus, while the doctrine of separate spheres often channeled males and females into particular modes of travel (including, for men, attempts at foreign conquest), the broader appeal of adventuresome texts for middle-class readers was not particularly gendered.[86]

Regardless of whether they identified as male or female, nationalism increased the emotional appeal of US travel accounts. As scholars have recognized, nations are "imagined communities" that encourage citizens to identify emotionally with each other. The printing press was critical in forming and then perpetuating this national consciousness in the early modern and contemporary eras.[87] In the United States and other Western countries, a dynamic print culture allowed citizens to hear about their compatriots' experiences at home and abroad. Whether set in the North American West or beyond, travel narratives nationalized non-US territory. They annexed land and waterscapes on a cultural level, stitching disparate regions into an expanding saga of US nationhood.[88] Nationalism further encouraged patriots to ascribe special emotional meaning—pride or shame, for example—to their countrymen's actions. This was especially so for persons operating in a national capacity or otherwise associated with the flag. When the Royal Geographical Society awarded a gold medal to Frémont in 1850, the US minister to Great Britain called it "a national, as well as an individual honor."[89] White citizens were enamored with tales of rugged travel because they affirmed a sense of US spirit and virtue. They were special, they believed, because their books told them so.

Furthermore, Wilkes had specially crafted his *Narrative* to appeal to the white middle class. He drew on the popular genres of the day and portrayed himself as a highly dramatic, sentimental commanding officer. Such passages encouraged readers to identify with the emotions of the narrator. After the expedition left Norfolk, for instance, Wilkes recounted that the crew of the flagship *Vincennes* gathered for a benediction by the ship's chaplain. "I shall never forget the impressions that crowded on me during that day in the hours of service," Wilkes wrote. "It required all the hope I could muster to outweigh the intense feeling of responsibility that hung over me. I may compare it to that of one doomed to destruction."[90] In Wilke's hands, an event as ordinary as a Christian service at sea—a regular event—became a dramatic scene of brooding fatalism.

Aside from sentimentalism, Wilkes gave other reasons for middle-class readers to identify with the *Narrative*. For one, he wrote from the perspective of the expedition's middle-class officers, not its brawnier, working-class members. While the plural first-person *we* normally encompassed the entire expedition, Wilke's use of the term sometimes meant only its officer class.[91] In the first volume, as the Ex Ex drifted past St. Michael's Island in the

Atlantic, Wilkes noted that "we amused ourselves by a view, through our glasses, of its villas, groves, and cultivated fields."[92] Since very few ordinary sailors had spyglasses, Wilkes's circle of "we" here was restricted to himself and his subordinate officers. Similarly, when recognizing the assistance of white missionaries on the Samoan Islands, Wilkes acknowledged they had provided "a great part of the facilities we enjoyed of becoming acquainted with the manner, habits, and customs of the Samoans."[93] Here again was a view of the expedition from a particular strata of naval society—the officers and scientific personnel who would have interacted with missionaries for the purposes of observing Samoan society. It was with these figures—the expedition's "middle class"—that striving, upwardly mobile readers wanted to associate themselves with. Through Wilkes's class-conscious eyes, even Indigenous dress was related to middle-class fashion, with Samoans wearing leaves around their waists almost as "a kind of short petticoat."[94]

Middle-class readers could identify with Wilkes partly because the evolution of the naval officer corps mirrored the construction of the middle class. As the sea duties of naval officers encompassed more and more peacetime operations after the War of 1812, officers began emphasizing other, more refined skills alongside naval science and seamanship. These included diplomacy, foreign languages, and, increasingly, scientific pursuits.[95] In fact, scholars have linked the establishment of the US Naval Academy in Annapolis in 1845 to the rise of a middle class that valued improvement, refinement, and education.[96] In Wilkes's own case, he exhausted himself on the voyage by choosing to head up the departments of meteorology, hydrography, and physics in addition to his regular duties as commander of the Ex Ex. Later naval explorers followed in Wilkes's footsteps, with William Francis Lynch affecting an expertise in classical and biblical studies during his survey of the Holy Land in 1847 and 1848 and the navy surgeon Elisha Kent Kane claiming the mantle of Arctic scientist during his polar voyages in the 1850s.

The classism of Wilkes's *Narrative* was perhaps most discernible when he discussed lower-class sailors. Throughout the expedition's voyage, Wilkes disparaged runaway sailors, whom he dismissed as "the outcasts and refuse of every maritime nation," "the lowest order of vagabonds," and "abandoned white men."[97] Time and again, he blamed such individuals for importing vice into native communities and being a "barrier" to the "their improvement in morals and religion."[98]

In contrast, Wilkes repeatedly portrayed middle- and upper-class missionaries as the torch bearers of civilization in the Pacific World. Like many antebellum US citizens, Wilkes believed in social developmentalism, an anthropological system developed by European thinkers in the eighteenth century. Social developmentalists believed that human societies passed through successive stages, beginning with savagery and then progressing through barbarism, half-civilization, and full civilization.[99] Much of the ethnological work of the Ex Ex, in fact, was to categorize the island communities of the Pacific World in these terms. As the expedition passed through geographies shaded by "the darkness of Paganism," the officers and scientists of the Ex Ex looked for signs that would determine the stage of each Indigenous society.[100] When the *Vincennes* arrived at Raraka (Te Marie) in the Tuamotu Group, Wilkes observed that "the half-civilization of these natives" could be explained by the fact that "the missionary had been at work here"; thanks to Christian evangelists, "the savage had been changed to a reasonable creature."[101] Middle-class readers could find much satisfaction in Wilkes's words—not only was their culture the highest in the world, but their coreligionists (if not their countrymen) were actively extending it across the globe.

The authority of the *Narrative* also increased its appeal. Wilkes's work was no ordinary travelogue composed by a civilian author; it was, instead, an official government account from a national scientific expedition. The ostensible purpose of the Ex Ex was to produce knowledge. Here was, by white, middle-class standards, a definitive account of how the world really was. Wilkes embraced his role as myth buster. In describing the flagship's arrival at Madeira, for example, he noted that the island's "first appearance . . . did not come up to the idea we had formed of its beauties from the glowing description of travellers."[102] Likewise, while those on the expedition (the editorial "we") had imagined coral islands as "a kind of fairyland," Wilkes wrote that "the landing on a coral island effectually does away with all preconceived notions of its beauty."[103] Wilkes also included sections in which the Ex Ex debunked rumors of navigational hazards.[104] The published charts, too, enhanced the expedition's status as a trustworthy, scientific accounting of the physical geography of globe.

Wilkes's sentimentalism, classism, and authority quickly won over middle- and upper-class audiences. An early indication of its popularity came when the first unofficial volumes of Wilkes's *Narrative* came up for sale in 1845. Though printed by Sherman, they were published by Lea & Blanchard, one of the older and more prominent of Philadelphia's publishing houses.[105] This early public edition was both fine and limited—only 150 copies, enough to complete the token begun with the hundred copies ordered by Congress. Wilkes helped finance the new limited edition, buying twenty-five for his social circle and leaving another 125 up for sale.[106] Since they had been printed using the same paper, engraved plates, woodcuts, and stereotype plates as the official Congressional editions, they were both impressive and impressively expensive—$60 for a full set.[107] In 1850, one wealthy New Yorker had the means to write the publishers directly and order a set with "same edition paper, binding and &c as the one presentd [*sic*] by Congress to foreign Governments."[108]

Working-class and even some middling readers would have found the price tag for this early public edition prohibitively expensive; $60 a set was not a price that would, in Wilkes's words, "diffuse a full knowledge of the results of the Expedition."[109] He and Lea & Blanchard therefore set out to release new editions that would be accessible to middle-class readers. First, they contracted with Sherman to print a thousand copies of an imperial octavo version, complete with gold tooling, colored maps, and all the same plates and illustrations as the one printed by Congress.[110] They advertised them heavily, delivering twelve copies to newspapers and placing 35,000 ads in the mail and another 29,500 ads in leading periodicals, for a total advertising cost of $235.69.[111]

At $25 per set, the imperial octavos were much more affordable than the special Congressional edition, but still beyond the means of the laboring classes. For these, Wilkes promised the Speaker of the US House of Representatives that he would "publish a complete edition of the work at such a reduced price that all who desire it may possess themselves of a copy."[112] To fulfill this promise, Lea & Blanchard released a "medium" duodecimo edition in the late spring and early summer of 1845.[113] By using cheaper binding and "commoner paper," and by eliminating the more expensive engravings and charts, the publishers were able to charge just $2 per volume or $10 for the medium edition.[114] They published at least five thousand copies of this edition, and possibly more; Wilkes, in his autobiography, says Lea & Blanchard were prepared to publish ten thousand.[115] As with the imperial octavo, the advertising campaign for the duodecimo was aggressive: the publishers had special woodcuts made for newspaper ads, and inserted 12,500 ads in magazines and sixty thousand more in *Literary News*, among others. Overall, a clerk calculated that about two hundred thousand ads were circulating nationally.[116]

Nor did Lea & Blanchard neglect markets in Great Britain; they sent specimens of both the imperial octavo and the medium duodecimo to British editors in London.[117] They further asked Sherman to print the leaves of an edition that would be published and sold by the British firm Wiley and Putnam.[118] They even used a business partner, the China Trade firm Rarule, Drinker, and Co., to sell finer copies—probably the imperial octavo—among the English-speaking merchants of Canton, China.[119]

Lea & Blanchard's attention to the British market was good business, but it also served as a popular version of Congress's diplomatic impulse to share the results of the Ex Ex with the Great Powers of Europe. There was no country where maritime exploration was more celebrated, nor where exploratory accounts proved more popular, than Great Britain. In the 1770s, the British government was so confident about the popularity of Cook's published journals that it paid John Hawkesworth the handsome sum of £6,000 for editing them.[120] They were not disappointed; Cook's journals were among the most popular volumes of the eighteenth and early nineteenth centuries. When, in 1843, Captain Edward Belcher of the Royal Navy published his own recollection of a circumnavigation in command of HMS *Sulphur*, he noted that "voyages undertaken for the express purpose of Maritime Discovery have always been received with so much favour by the British public." He hoped that he, too, would "not be denied that indulgence which has been uniformly accorded to those who have preceded him."[121]

Wilkes and Lea & Blanchard shared the same aspiration. They need not have worried—the Ex Ex *Narrative* was popular enough in Great Britain to be plagiarized. In 1845, an English publisher took advantage of the lack of copyright laws between the United States and Great Britain and released a condensed and abridged, two-volume version of Wilkes's *Narrative* in 1845.[122] This edition appears to have later been translated into German and spread to the Continent between 1848 and 1850.[123] In 1852, the British firm Ingram, Cooke, & Co. printed their own copies of an abridged, one-volume US edition of Wilkes's *Narrative*.[124] Because there were no reciprocal copyright treaties between the United States and Great Britain at the time, such unauthorized reproduction was entirely legal.[125]

British reviewers were generally courteous, if sometimes condescending, when reviewing the *Narrative*. On the positive side, the *Times* of London thought "that in paper and typography," the imperial octavo edition of the Ex Ex volumes could "take rank with the best productions of the British press."[126] (He might have added the French as well). Other reviewers criticized the logistical shortcomings of the expedition itself, portraying the voyage as the venture of an inexperienced, younger nation: "This is but the history of all our own early exploring expeditions," *Westminster Review* opined, "including those of Cook; but experience has taught us some useful lessons, and America in due time will profit by the same teacher." For this reviewer, "the numerous and highly finished steel engravings and vignettes" were, at least, "a great improvement upon the undecorated page of our early voyagers."[127]

US citizens viewed such reviews through a hypersensitive lens. They knew of such reviews because many British literary journals (the *Edinburgh Review* among them) had been popular among middle-class US citizens since at least the 1810s.[128] Thus, when the *London Athenaeum* gave Wilkes's *Narrative* a negative report, the *Banner of the Cross* sniffed that it was the result of "John Bull's national jealousy" for the United States' discovery of Antarctica.[129] Likewise, the *Southern & Western Literary Messenger* was gratified that the *Westminster Review* "treats the work and our Government with liberal justice," especially in terms of the book's quality.[130] Wilkes himself believed that his work met "the approval of those who are able to judge of its contents, both abroad and at home, and has & is doing much to elevate the character of our country."[131]

Like British reviewers, US actors perceived the *Narrative* in national terms. An ad for the imperial octavo edition hawked it as "this great and truly national work."[132] "Nothing has been used in its preparation," another advertiser continued, "that is not STRICTLY AMERICAN."[133] In May 1845, the *Banner of the Cross* posited that, as the Ex Ex was the "first scientific expedition fitted out by our government, every American must feel interested in its results."[134] The *Columbian* agreed, claiming that the work "should be possessed by every American citizen." It was, mused the *Columbian*, the first exploring expedition "that ever left our shores fitted out by national munificence, and will be an imperishable monument of American enterprise, intelligence, and liberality."[135] *Pride* was a keyword for many reviewers; when the *North American Review* received their copy, they observed that the "first feeling excited by the appearance of these volumes is that of national pride,—that our country, prosperous in her resources, and liberal and enlightened in the use of them, has made a contribution to general knowledge and the security of navigation worthy of her extended commerce, and her undoubted position among the cultivated nations of the world."[136]

This does not mean that domestic reviewers gave only positive accounts of the *Narrative*. The *North American Review* called it a "work of oppressive dimensions," one that displayed "more eagerness for accumulation, than skill in arrangement."[137] Other readers were scandalized to find Wilkes so critical of his junior officers in a work officially endorsed and gifted around the world by the State Department.[138] A few even questioned the wisdom of giving copies to nations like Brazil, which Wilkes had criticized in his summary of the expedition's visit there.[139] The *Southern Literary Messenger* was Wilkes's harshest critic. While it claimed to have been broadly supportive of the expedition, it found his leadership flawed and his writing "bad." It even accused him of plagiarizing from his officers' journals, which he had collected at the end of the cruise.[140] Wilkes denied the charge in his autobiography.[141] He might have also pointed out that the collection of officers' journals after a voyage of discovery was an old practice, dating back at least to the days of Captain Cook, and was an important means of controlling information deemed critical to state interests.[142]

Despite these points, the overall domestic reception appears to have been mostly positive. Reviewers admired the publication's many illustrations, describing even the duodecimo edition as being "plenteously interspersed with wood cuts."[143] They also praised the *Narrative* for its thoroughness and veracious character. The *American Journal of Science & Arts* called the Ex Ex tomes "by far the most important contributions to geographical science ever made from this country."[144] They believed that "the historical and commercial information they contain, combined with the varied incidents" of a four-year circumnavigation, "will render it an attractive book to the general reader."[145] Another admirer and correspondent with Wilkes agreed, writing that the volumes would be "interesting to readers of every class, whether scientific or not."[146]

The later publication history of the Ex Ex appears to prove him right. In 1849, Lea & Blanchard released another imperial octavo edition. Public demand prompted them to issue a ninth edition the following year.[147] Meanwhile, in Philadelphia, George Gorton had condensed Wilkes's hefty tomes into a single volume in 1849. Gorton then appears to have sold the stereotype plates to George P. Putnam of New York, who printed new copies of the abridged edition in 1851.[148] Lured by profitability, Putnam went whole hog in 1856, publishing a five-volume edition in New York. By 1858, though, he must have felt that the market for Wilkes's volumes had dried up; his firm published only the first volume of the *Narrative*.[149]

Wilkes was to some extent a victim of his own success—by the late 1850s, other accounts of the Ex Ex and other naval exploring expeditions were in broad circulation. Some of these were the edited journals of Ex Ex officers, who had somehow managed to regain access to their expeditionary entries or lean on secret (and illicit) journals from the cruise, or were able to rehash them from memory.[150] Other publications, often by non-expedition members, were paraphrased summaries of Wilkes's own writing. These included John S. Jenkins's *United States Exploring Expeditions*, which went through at least five printings or impressions between 1850 and 1855. Jenkins's appealed to national pride by contextualizing the Ex Ex within a larger framework of European voyages, including those by Dumont d'Urville, Wilkes's rival at sea and at the press. The message was clear: Wilkes was the latest in a string of "civilized" European explorers who braved strange seas for the sake of knowledge and glory. It was a theme that appeared to resonate in the marketplace, with publishers in New York, Illinois, and Michigan arranging for the shipment or reproductions of the stereotype plates of Jenkins's book.[151]

Perhaps the best evidence for the popularity of explorationist volumes, however, comes from the fact that they were given as gifts. A commonly gifted book was George M. Colvocoresses's *Four Years in a Government's Exploring Expedition*, published in 1855. Colvocoresses, who served as a passed midshipman on the expedition, aimed "to furnish a work which should have the merit of being instructive and entertaining, concise and cheap."[152] He appears to have been highly successful. According to one inscription, for example, a woman named Eliza gave her cousin, Charles Perry, a copy of Colvocoresses's work on June 18, 1859.[153] Similarly, in 1855, an elder relative or mentor gave a boy named Charley a copy of Colvocoresses's work as "a New Year's Present."[154] Matthew Irwin Scott was sufficiently enamored with Jenkins's *U.S. Exploring Expeditions* that he gave a copy to his "beloved sister, Mary Jane Scott Irwin."[155]

Thoughtful, middle-class citizens in the United States felt that books on the Ex Ex had value—most likely in terms of education as well as entertainment. The present to Charley is especially revealing; the anonymous presenter believed that such a work would be valuable to a young, aspiring boy. Perhaps they were persuaded by a review similar to the one that appeared in the *Christian Parlor Book* in March 1855, which chirped that it was "worth more than a ship-load of the light reading of the day. The reader travels round the world with the author, and instead of seeing fictions and castles in the air, sees the grandeur of the ocean, and views all those places visited by the Expedition." In other words, here was a title that was "useful," "highly instructive," and "a treasure to any family"—or to any reader who wanted to affect an informed, middle-class, and patriotic attitude.[156]

THE EX EX PUBLICATIONS AND EMPIRE

If he read his present, young Charley would have also walked away with reinforced notions of his own racial superiority. Indeed, a major attraction for US and British readers was how Ex Ex authors like Colvocoresses described nonwestern peoples in the Atlantic and Pacific Worlds. Throughout the cruise, Ex Ex authors scrutinized other peoples and frequently found them wanting. The visages and physiques of many ethnicities came under special attack; on St. Jago, Colvocoresses perceived the women as particularly ugly, apparently because two-thirds of them were of mixed race.[157] Of the Natives in Tierra del Fuego, Colvocoresses wrote that it was "impossible to imagine anything in human nature more filthy and disgusting."[158] Wilkes concurred; "they are an ill-shapen and ugly race," he wrote.[159] Similarly, Wilkes found the Maori of New Zealand displeasing to look at. When a party of Maori chiefs visited the *Vincennes* in Cloudy Bay, Wilkes described them as "fierce-looking savages, with coarse matted hair, tattooed visages, and bodies besmeared with red earth and oil . . . and all exceedingly filthy." One "truly fiendish" chief had "small deep-sunk eyes" that shone "with the ferocity of a tiger."[160]

It should be noted that not all nonwhite peoples met with disapprobation. Wilkes thought that the Samoans were a "fine athletic race," and called the males of Tutuila "a remarkably tall fine-looking set, with intelligent and pleasing countenances."[161] He also expressed admiration for Oceanian watercraft and navigational skills, raged against the segregation of Hawaiian and white schoolchildren, and thought a charismatic Samoan chief looked for all the world like "General Jackson."[162] Other officers, meanwhile, experienced their own touching moments when the veil of racial prejudice lifted and they saw the unity of humanity. While visiting a Samoan village, for example, William Reynolds found that his "pride as a white man melted away, & I thought in my heart, *these people have more claim to be called good, than we.*"[163] Such compliments notwithstanding, the mere act of evaluating foreign peoples reveals the superciliousness of Wilkes and his brother officers; after all, the height of their yardstick was the white, Christian, US middle class that they represented.

No Oceanian society was of greater interest to Western readers than the Fijian. Their reputation as fierce warriors and reputed cannibals had already preceded them in US and British imaginations long before the release of Wilkes's *Narrative.* His work was no myth buster in this regard. While in Fiji, he painstakingly recorded every instance of cannibalism observed by the Ex Ex. In his third volume, he recounted a scene in which a US purser had attempted to barter with some Fijians for the remains of a cannibalized skull. They were on the verge of reaching an understanding when the Ex Ex sailors grew distracted by another Fijian watching the proceedings. According to Wilkes's account, he was nonchalantly chewing on an eyeball.[164] Nor was this an isolated account; instead, the lieutenant claimed that Fijian cannibalism persisted for "the mere pleasure of eating human flesh as a food." "The greatest praise they can bestow on a delicacy," he added, "is to say that it is as tender as a dead man."[165]

Such sensationalized depictions of Fijian customs thrilled readers and reviewers in the US and the UK alike. The *Times* of London was morbidly delighted: "In the Feejee group, we find savage life in all its unmitigated ferocity. Cannibalism,—not as a demonstration of triumph, or in pursuance or revenge, but avowedly under the influence of an appetite for human flesh, was exhibited before the eyes of the horror-struck Americans."[166] Likewise, the *North American Review* sought "to excite the curiosity of the reader, by giving an outline of this novel form of savage life."[167] Unsurprisingly, when Wilkes issued a condensed, one-volume edition of his *Narrative* in New York in 1849, he made sure to keep "full descriptions of the places we visited, and of the habits, manners, and customs of the natives"—especially Fiji.[168]

Wilkes's reports of cannibalism and savagery, amplified by enthusiastic reviews in the popular press, help justify his actions at Malolo. His writings represented what Gananath Obeyesekere has called "savagism"—the conscious portrayal of Indigenous peoples as primitive and barbaric Others who could be missionized, colonized, and even exterminated.[169] While a handful of reviewers criticized Wilkes's brutal response to the killing of his two officers at Malolo, most rallied to his defense. The *North American Review* expressed "unqualified approbation" for "the punishment [Wilkes] inflicted upon the natives."[170] After recounting the incident and Wilkes's retaliation, the *Southern Literary Messenger* beamed with pride. Summoning a parade of US naval heroes from the War of 1812, it proclaimed that "the spirit of our Hull, Lawrence, Decatur and their contemporaries still lives in the officers of the Navy of the present day."[171] In Scotland, the *Edinburgh Review* concurred, arguing that the islanders' conduct had "clearly left Captain Wilkes no alternative." "Further hesitation in commencing hostilities," they added, "would have been nothing short of unpardonable weakness."[172]

Across the Atlantic, Wilkes's volumes and their British reviews likely reinforced Victorian Britain's commitment to empire. After all, such major publications as the *Times* of London and the *Edinburgh Review* reproduced Wilkes's characterization of Fijians as "the most savage and treacherous race in the Pacific" and "cannibals of the most inveterate kind" extensively in the British press.[173] While the foreign impact of any of these writings is hard to judge, such portrayals may have contributed to cultural justifications for Great Britain's annexation of the Fiji Group in 1874.[174]

The writings of the Ex Ex helped strengthen white supremacy at home as well. The trope of the Fijian cannibal was so deeply ingrained that when George Fitzhugh sat down in Port Caroline, Virginia, to compose another treatise in defense of Southern slavery, he decided to compare Northern, Free Labor ideology to Fijian cannibalism. In *Cannibals All! Or, Slaves without Masters* (1857), he accused Northerners of being cannibals who took "pride . . . on the number of [their] victims, quite as much as any Feejee chieftain, who breakfasts, dines and sups on human flesh."[175] Similarly, another slavery apologist, Matthew Estes, cited Wilkes's writings on Pacific peoples when arguing that so-called lesser races were incompatible with civilization—and that slavery was therefore the natural place for people of African descent.[176] Both Fitzhugh and Estes might have

MASSACRE OF LIEUT. UNDERWOOD AND MIDSHIPMAN HENRY.

Figure 3.2 *Massacre of Lieut. Underwood and Midshipman Henry*,
frontispiece to George M. Colvocoresses's *Four Years in a Government's
Exploring Expedition* (New York: Cornish, Lamport, 1852). (Courtesy of
Biodiversity Heritage Library, contributed by Smithsonian Libraries)

also marshaled other proslavery evidence from Ex Ex authors; both Wilkes
and Colvocoresses depicted Black slaves in Rio de Janeiro as cheerful and
happy with their condition.[177] "In general they are kindly treated," Wilkes
concluded, "and become firmly attached to their masters."[178] Wilkes recognized the inhumanity of the transatlantic slave trade, but he seems to
have doubted whether or not Blacks could ever attain full civilization.[179]
While African slaves were often baptized at purchase and went to church
and confession, "they [were] never thought to become entirely civilized,"
he wrote.[180] Those who read his first volume would be hard pressed to avoid
the conclusion that benevolent slavery, Brazilian-style, was the most ap-
propriate social position for people of African descent.

Images, too, could convey powerful racial judgments. When little Charley opened his New Year's present in 1855, he surely noticed the frontispiece. A wood engraving titled "Massacre of Lieut. Underwood and Midshipman Henry," it depicted the bloodshed that had unfolded so suddenly
at Malolo in July 1840.[181] If he had looked closely enough, Charley might

have noticed how similar the club-wielding natives appeared to images of Black slaves striking for their freedom.

With the printing of the popular editions of the *Narrative*, US citizens could learn about the Ex Ex fairly easily. In the 1840s and 1850s, though, they could also visit Washington, DC, and see the missions' specimens firsthand. In 1841, the federal government rearranged the cavernous second floor of the US Patent Office for precisely this purpose.[182] The formation of this "National Gallery," as it came to be known, was not predetermined. The first boxes from the Ex Ex were actually shipped to the Peale Museum in Philadelphia. This was in line with the precedent established by the Lewis and Clark Expedition, whose collections had ended up in private institutions.[183] In an uncharacteristic move, however, the outgoing secretary of the navy intervened. While Abel Upshur had been generally hostile to Wilkes and the Ex Ex, he seemed to recognize the value of the squadron's scientific collections. Declaring them the official property of the US government, he redirected their flow to Washington, DC.[184]

The collection's first official caretakers were the members of the newly established National Institution for the Promotion of Science. Its founder, Secretary of War Joel R. Poinsett, believed that the institution would serve an important diplomatic and imperial purpose. In an address to his colleagues in June 1842, Poinsett argued that scientific progress was "important to the character and to the independence of the country. . . . If we look abroad, we shall see that the people the most advanced in science and the arts possess the greatest share of wealth and power."[185] Leading statesmen, including John Quincy Adams and President John Tyler, rallied around Poinsett's vision for an empire of science; after all, the Great Powers of Europe had their own scientific societies in their capital cities, so why not the United States?

Wilkes was initially a supporter of the National Institution. He was docked with the Ex Ex in Honolulu when he first learned about it. He lost no time, firing off a letter to Poinsett and requesting admission as a member.[186] The move made perfect sense—like Reynolds, Wilkes intended to become a mover and shaker in the empire of knowledge as well as of commerce. He also had a relationship with Poinsett, who had officially appointed him commander of the Ex Ex in April 1838.[187] Poinsett assented. After Wilkes's return in June 1842, he invited the lieutenant to present the expedition's findings before the other members of the institution. The membership, which included many of Washington's political elites, turned out in droves to hear him speak.

From that high mesa, however, Wilkes's relationship with the institution soured. The Ex Ex scientists complained bitterly about the institution's mismanagement of their specimens, which reduced some to uselessness as scientific samples. The geologist James Dwight Dana fumed that some crustaceans "were rendered wholly unfit for description," while others, pierced with pins, suffered "the obliteration of many of their characters."[188] Accordingly, when the institution's curator, Charles Pickering, resigned to work on his expedition report, the Joint Committee on the Library handed oversight to the commissioner of patents, Charles Ellsworth, and made Wilkes the new curator of the Ex Ex materials.[189]

Wilkes's new base of operations was a massive room named the Great Hall, on the second floor of the US Patent Office. Technically, it was in the second office, too—a fire had consumed the first one in 1836.[190] This second incarnation was far grander than the first: hewed from solid stone and supposedly fireproof, it had a portico composed of sixteen Doric columns, "the same extent as that of the Parthenon at Athens," as one patriotic guidebook explained.[191] Visitors would have sauntered up the building's front steps, strolled past these neoclassical behemoths, ambled under a vaulted hallway, and then finally climbed their way up an elegantly curved staircase to the second floor. At the entrance to the Great Hall, another neoclassical design greeted them in the shape of pilasters under a curling archway. Above it, in "large Golden letters," was a massive sign with the words "Collection of the Exploring Expedition."[192] Here one stood at the threshold of the first publicly funded museum of natural history in the United States.

On entering, visitors would have been immediately struck by the grandeur of the space before them. The Great Hall dominated the upper floor; at 273 feet long, sixty-three feet wide, and more than thirty feet from floor to ceiling, it was one of the largest rooms in Washington.[193] A series of red rectangular pillars punctuated the gigantic space, which stretched far out of sight through two wings on either side. Above, a central stained-glass atrium arose like a daffodil pyramid surrounded by blue posies. Visitors had only a moment to take in the space before being greeted by a friendly and "courteous" doorman. He may have taken their coats and umbrellas if it was raining, asked them to sign the register of visitors (though few ever did), and perhaps good-humoredly pointed out a few architectural flaws.[194] The distractions during this conversation would have been many— murmuring echoes, the tap and scuff of shoes on marble, and most of all, the main attraction itself: a maze of tall wood-and-glass cases, full of specimens and expanding in all directions.

Wilkes had worked hard to refashion the Great Hall into a pleasing, organized, middle-class space. Soon after becoming curator, he shunted the

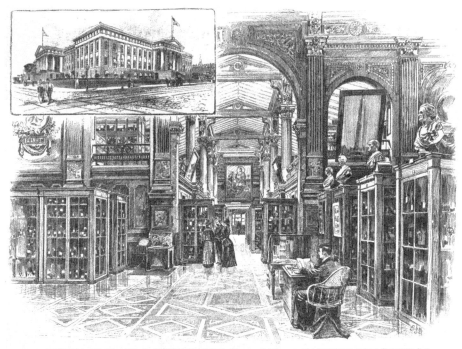

THE EXTERIOR AND INTERIOR OF THE PATENT OFFICE.—DRAWN BY E. J. MEEKER, AFTER PHOTOGRAPHS BY BELL, WASHINGTON, D. C.

Figure 3.3 E. J. Meeker, engraving of the exterior and interior of the US Patent Office building, 1891. While this image was engraved from a photograph in the late nineteenth century, it still provides a sense of what the Great Hall of the Patent Office would have looked like in the 1840s and 1850s, when these wood-and-glass cases would have been stocked with the collections of the Ex Ex. (Courtesy of Smithsonian Institution Archives. Image SIA2007-0134.)

National Institute (recently renamed) out of the hallway.[195] Underfunded and restricted to a "a handful of exhibit cases and one or two rooms in the basement of the building," the National Institute limped on until the expiration of its charter in 1862.[196] In the meantime, Wilkes professionalized the vacated hall, filling cases according to science rather than visual effect, posting signs, placing spittoons around the green bases of the red pillars, and directing an employee to follow anyone seen chewing tobacco.[197] Their mission: to quickly and grumpily sponge up any tobacco spit that did not make it into the spittoons.[198] The result of these efforts, according to Wilkes, was that "the Hall no longer became the resort of idlers and a place for exercise and smoking."[199] It was also soon rid of errant tobacco juice, a "filthy custom" that had appalled Charles Dickens during his visit to Washington in 1842.[200]

The revised National Gallery was hugely popular. Edgar Allen Poe praised its collections, and Ralph Waldo Emerson called it "the best sight in Washington."[201] Other prominent intellectuals, including Harvard's naturalist Louis Aggasiz, rushed to the capital to see what the Ex Ex had brought home.[202] Once in the hall, such men of prominence found themselves part of a throng of curious humanity. Contemporaries estimated that visitation rates exceeded more than one hundred thousand annually.[203] While this figure is probably exaggerated, the surviving visitor registers at the Smithsonian Institution Archives clearly demonstrate the immense popularity of the National Gallery. In March 1845 alone, for example, a clerk scribbled that 10,323 patrons had entered the museum. While those numbers decreased considerably during the hot summer months, they were still striking; in July, 1845, for instance, the museum had 3,209 visitors.[204] What was more, museum patrons came from all over—while many listed a DC-area place of residence, others came from as far away as Pittsfield, New Hampshire; Hanging Rock, Ohio; Mobile, Alabama; St. Louis, Missouri; and Natchez, Louisiana.[205] They came as couples, families, and coworkers; as gangs of navy sailors on liberty; and as foreign dignitaries from Constantinople, Venezuela, Egypt, and Scotland.[206]

Why was the National Gallery so popular? The charm of admiring nature certainly played a role—after all, the museum sported a huge variety of items of natural history. Patrons could encounter everything from vivid, branching corals and fossilized fish to stuffed toucans, Hawaiian honey birds, and spiny-backed echidnas. Leathery fruit bats could be seen as well, along with oily whale skulls, rocks retrieved from icebergs, and the lumbering bones of elephant seals. In 1844, the *Guardian* claimed that visitors to the National Gallery could count 2,000 birds, 829 fishes, 140 reptiles, 900 crustaceans, 1,500 insects, 450 corals, and 3,000 shells on exhibit.[207] Gawking at the variety of the earth's riches, one patron remarked that "everything almost in the wide world is here by sample. . . . I could spend a week in the Patent Office with great interest."[208] Especially popular was the greenhouse, located in the rear of the complex. Initially it was just fifty feet in length, but the addition of new specimens and rising foot traffic necessitated continual expansion. By 1845, it was seventy-eight feet long and desperately in need of heat. That year, museum staff installed a small stove to help hold off the cold Washington winters.[209]

This middle-class delight in nature stemmed at least in part from a passion for order. As Mary Louise Pratt argues, the publication of Linnaeus's *Systema Naturae* in 1735 represented a turning point in the history of Western empires.[210] Linnaeus sought a totalizing, classificatory scheme for organizing all the plants in the world. In the 1750s, he began to classify plants by genus and species, which he determined from the morphology of their reproductive parts. The Linnean system soon expanded to other fields of natural history.[211] In doing so, Linnaeus helped construct a European "planetary consciousness" that encouraged Westerners to explore the world in search of greater systemic knowledge.[212] Antebellum US citizens, too, seemed warm to this project; knowing that the natural world could be easily catalogued, organized, and intellectually understood may have helped them situate themselves in a rapidly changing world. The author of one guidebook claimed that "nothing can be more interesting to man, or more gratify his thirst for knowledge, than a survey of the materials which compose the earth which he inhabits."[213] For him, this experience was even religious, with "the varieties of creation, and infinitude of the forms inhabiting it" increasing "our admiration of the power of the Creator."[214] The achievements of discovery and science, he assured his readers, "have rendered many modern collections accurate, minute, comprehensive, and complete."[215]

Nationalism was another major attraction. Antebellum citizens interpreted the rich scientific harvest of the Ex Ex as proof of national maturity. In 1851, the first secretary of the Smithsonian Institution, Dr. Joseph Henry, expressed this line of thought when he observed that "a general museum appears to be a necessary establishment at the seat of government of every civilized nation."[216] For many US citizens, the Ex Ex collections matched those of any European museum. "On the receipt of the objects brought home by the exploring expedition," Joel Poinsett declared, "we shall possess a museum . . . unsurpassed in any country."[217] In 1844, the expedition's conchologist, Augustus Gould, beamed with pride in a letter to Senator Tappan about the visit of "our most accomplished zoologist," a "Dr. Wyman of Boston." Wyman "spent a day in examining the collection," Gould reported; afterward, Wyman remarked that it required "only a thorough arrangement . . . to vie with any of the London or Paris museums."[218]

If scientific attainment was not enough to stir the hearts of patriots, visitors could also see important US political and military relics exhibited at the National Gallery. While these items had not originated with the Ex Ex, the gallery exhibited them alongside its ethnographic and natural history collections. A museumgoer might, for example, encounter Benjamin Franklin's cane, the "Sword of Washington," the coat that Washington wore "when he resigned his commission at Annapolis," "General Andrew Jackson's Military Coat," "and an original copy of the Declaration of Independence."[219] Elsewhere, patrons could feast their eyes on trophies of US diplomatic and imperial triumphs. Among these were mementos from the Barbary coast of North Africa, including "Moorish swords, presented to

the officers of an American squadron by a Barbary power," and "two elegantly embossed muskets, inlaid with gold . . . presented to Thomas Jefferson by the Bey of Tunis."[220] Well represented, too, were artifacts from
Native American wars and the conflict with Mexico, including a "Seminole
war-plume," various "Indian pipes from the War Department," and "a shell
thrown by the Mexican forces . . . during the siege of the Alamo."[221]

Of all the exhibits, however, it was the Fijian display that transfixed visitors the most. At four thousand items, the Ex Ex's anthropological collection was larger than that of any other European exploring expedition—for
example, it was one and a third times larger than all of Captain Cook's
Pacific ventures combined.[222] A significant portion of that collection (any-
where from a fourth to nearly half) had come from Fiji. Public anticipa-
tion to see the ethnographical collections was so great, in fact, that the
museum staff at the National Gallery had made cataloguing and exhibiting
them their first priority.[223] It was perhaps for this reason that the very first
case a visitor would come to displayed "a large collection of spears and war
clubs from the Fegee Islands."[224] Among them was a dark, stout wooden
club with a squiggly wave pattern at one end. According to a visitor's guide,
it was the weapon that had killed Lieutenant Underwood in the skirmish
on Malolo.[225]

As its first case reveals, the National Gallery presented Fijians as a particularly dangerous, warlike people. While the club that had felled Underwood was relatively humble in appearance, the wooden maces that
surrounded it were heavy, curved, ornate things. Some were shaped for
splitting flesh and smashing bone, while others were designed to crush and
puncture skulls. There were throwing clubs, too, used to stun the enemy
before the combatants closed in, as well as paddle-shaped clubs that might
deflect an opponent's blow. Regardless of their precise function, all were
expertly designed for effectiveness in hand-to-hand combat. They were
also all incredibly dense and heavy, having been "carved from the hard
roots of mangrove trees."[226] The irony in this display, of course, was that
many of the expedition's collection of Fijian war clubs had actually derived
from a *meke wau*, or club dance, which the Fijians of Ovalau had performed
for Wilkes as a traditional ceremony of "friendship from one sovereign nation to another."[227] Taken out of this cultural context, the museum's dis-
plays encouraged patrons to meditate on the Fijians as addicts to human
strife, not as cross-cultural diplomats. One guidebook described the Fijian
clubs as the "most curious and frightful bludgeons." "No weapon of civilized nations," it declared, "possesses more convenient or elegant forms for
belligerent purposes."[228]

Far more sensational, however, were the items that appeared to offer proof of Fijian cannibalism. Case 4, for instance, contained a necklace of human teeth. Had US citizens purchased one particular guidebook, they would have been informed that the dangling molars had been "received from one of the great Chiefs, taken from the heads of prisoners that he had killed and eaten three days before."[229] In the opposite wing of the museum, meanwhile, visitors could study the pickled and embalmed head of Vei-dovi, the Fijian noble accused of murdering and eating eight US sailors in 1834.[230] Following Veidovi's death and decapitation in New York, naturalists sent his head to the National Gallery at Washington. There it sat behind glass, an object of fascination for museumgoers who thronged to see it. One guidebook studiously pointed out Veidovi's facial tattoos, his preserved hair, and his pointed teeth — "filed," as he claimed, "with the shark skin, so as to keep them ready for use."[231] Other Oceanian skulls surrounded Veidovi's, including another one from Fiji that came from a reputed victim of cannibalism.[232]

For white, middle-class nineteenth-century visitors, the necklace of human teeth, Veidovi's preserved head, and the cannibalized cranium offered solid proof of cultural and racial hierarchies. At the time, craniology was an esteemed science that was widely thought to prove white racial superiority. The ideas of Samuel George Morton, the country's leading craniologist, were regularly cited as justifications for slavery and the exclusion of Blacks from political life. After studying the cracked crania of ancient Egypt, Morton proclaimed that the ancient Egyptians were a white race who had enslaved Black Africans. In other words, since the dawn of recorded history, Black people had been consigned to slavery.[233] In 1857, one of Morton's disciples, James Aitken Meigs, argued that craniology was especially relevant for debates on racial policy: "The civil history of a nation in great measure arises from, and is dependent upon, the natural or physical characteristics of its citizens."[234] For Meigs and many of his white countrymen, "the problem of human destiny on the one hand, and the stability of our boasted republic on the other" rested on the insights of physical anthropology.[235]

What all this means is that when white, middle-class visitors feasted their eyes on Veidovi and other human crania at the National Gallery, they were not merely indulging in the macabre—they were also affirming contemporary theories of white supremacy. No matter their economic standing in a dynamic, pulsating economy, white visitors could pride themselves on having educated, middle-class values; regardless of how prosperous people of color might get at home, white visitors could reassure themselves that they belonged to a superior race. And finally, irrespective of how much "progress" an Oceanian or Native American society might make toward "civilization," white US citizens and Europeans were still the teachers who tutored, evaluated, and studied them. By the time they left the National Gallery, these visitors had seen physical evidence of the supposed inferiority of Black and brown peoples. In contrast, the museum's patriotic relics and the models of inventions on display on the first floor of the Patent Office offered proof of what one guidebook called the "universal genius of the Teutonic blood and brain."[236] Little wonder, then, that the National Gallery was such a popular sight for members of the white middle class: not only was it intellectually stimulating, but it was also psychologically soothing.

Gradually, the publications and collections of the Ex Ex shifted US public opinion in favor of federally directed global imperialism. When the expedition had returned in 1842, there had been very little pomp and circumstance to greet it. Instead, as we have seen, five court-martials litigated the many conflicts of the cruise. After the court found Wilkes guilty for his cruel conduct as a commanding officer, the secretary of the navy issued him a public reprimand.[237] The humiliation of these trials lodged deep in Wilkes's soul. He grew determined to revive his reputation through publishing the history of the Ex Ex and displaying its specimens. Only a few years later, his strategy appeared to be working; when Wilkes visited Boston in May 1845, he wrote triumphantly to Tappan that "the feeling about the Expedition is very different from what it was before the Narrative made its appearance."[238] He may have said the same thing about the effects of the National Gallery in Washington, DC. Indeed, the numerous US Navy expeditions around the world in the late 1840s and 1850s strongly suggest that Wilkes was right: by the late 1840s, naval exploration had become a popular item of consumption for the white middle class.

This seismic shift toward federally directed global imperialism was the result of a crucial but forgotten symbiosis. Naval imperialists, businessmen, and the curious middle class all found common cause in the 1840s and 1850s. For explorationists like Wilkes, the public's fascination with the findings of the Ex Ex affirmed the cultural and social value of global, state-sponsored, imperial endeavors. More personally, publicizing the Ex Ex results finally won Wilkes the laurels he had failed to receive after the squadron's arrival home. Commercially, artisans and businessmen (and some businesswomen) profited from government contracts and the quick sales of expeditionary volumes. Finally, and most important, the literature and museum exhibits of the Ex Ex offered upwardly mobile white citizens a chance to stroke their egos and prove their gentility in a world of wrenching change. In the years that followed, their continued curiosity about the world and its peoples generated popular enthusiasm for new voyages across the globe. With the return of the Ex Ex, the empire fed itself; in so doing, it found an even greater hunger.

CHAPTER 4

The Dead Sea Expedition and the Empire of Faith

Bearing torches and prayers, the pilgrims came down toward the US encampment, on the banks of the river Jordan, in the last few hours of the night, April 18, 1848. A sentry sounded the alarm. Stirred from their beds, navy officers and seamen rushed out of their tents to see "thousands of torchlights, with a dark mass beneath, moving rapidly over the hills."[1] The approaching throng numbered many thousands.[2] Its members had come from all portions of the world to mark the anniversary of the baptism of Christ.[3] They came by mule, camel, horse, and foot, alone and with their families, a dozen languages on their tongues, and in all varieties of dress, equipage, and comfort.[4] Now, in a state of religious frenzy, they were headed straight for the explorers' bivouac and the sacred river beyond. Lieutenant William Francis Lynch, the commanding officer of the United States' Expedition to the River Jordan and the Dead Sea, barked orders for his men to strike their tents and drag their supplies to one side, away from the pilgrims' path. "We had scarce finished, when they were upon us," Lynch recalled, "men, women, and children . . . talking, screaming, shouting." With "the wild haste of a disorderly rout," they threatened to overrun the Yankees' hastily dismantled camp.[5] Fortunately, Lynch's allies, a bevy of Bedouin tribesmen, drew up around them, "sticking their tufted spears before our tents," and mounting their steeds.[6] With their flowing black *abas* or cloaks, black beards, yellow keffiyehs, and eighteen-foot spears, they held off the pious torrent of humanity.[7] "But for them we should have been run down," Lynch admitted: "nothing but the spears and swarthy faces of the Arabs saved us."[8]

The last of the pilgrims departed a few hours after dawn. A storm sprung up in their wake, drenching the scene with lightning, thunder, and rain. By the early afternoon, Lieutenant Lynch and his men and allies were wet, exhausted, and low on fresh provisions. Nonetheless, they gathered themselves and set out for the objective that had drawn them from the distant shores of the United States to the interior of Ottoman Palestine: the Dead Sea. By then, it was "only a few hours distant."[9]

The United States Expedition to the River Jordan and the Dead Sea has alternately fascinated, confused, and vexed scholars for generations.[10] While its ostensible purpose was to study the descent of the Jordan River and make a careful, scientific survey of the Dead Sea, the mission's deeper agenda and raison d'être has long been a subject of debate. Some historians have tried to pin down commerce as the expedition's underlying impulse.[11] On the surface, this would fit the pattern of what we think we know about early US governance: surely a parsimonious, practical, and secular government would send a state expedition to the Holy Land only for pragmatic purposes. In making the case for trade, however, these scholars have ignored the fact that the United States had minuscule economic interests in the Holy Land, and that Lynch himself made very limited commercial investigations during his expedition.[12] Another group of historians have argued that culture served as the primary impetus for the Dead Sea mission.[13] One has argued that the single defining characteristic of the Dead Sea expedition was its marketability in the expanding world of mid-nineteenth-century print. According to this interpretation, the expedition failed to accomplish its central scientific or theological goals. Instead, the mission's real treasure was the "thrilling uselessness" of producing an "interesting story."[14]

Approaching the expedition in terms of empire and evangelical culture suggests a different narrative. As an evangelical Christian, Lynch perceived history as a morality play. God had gifted human societies with free will; like individual human beings, they could determine their own course — whether to uplift themselves to higher spiritual planes or debase the purposes of their existence through sensual excesses. The former path exalted nations and individuals alike, blessed their lands, and bequeathed them power; the latter path resulted in unutterable ruin. According to Abrahamic traditions, this latter path was precisely what had happened to Sodom and Gomorrah. Nestled on the banks of the Jordan in the midst of a luxurious plain, both had been prosperous, thriving cities. Despite their many blessings, the denizens of Sodom and Gomorrah had chosen sin over virtue. God unleashed His righteous rage. In a storm of fire and brimstone, He annihilated the cities. The fertile plain collapsed. The Dead Sea arose to swallow their smoking ruins.[15] The US Holy Land expedition was designed to prove the veracity of this biblical tradition. Like most devout Protestants in the middle of the nineteenth century, Lynch believed that Christianity and science were perfectly compatible. He was convinced that a scientific survey of the Dead Sea could uncover what he termed "the record of God's wrath."[16]

Seen from this evangelical Christian perspective, the Dead Sea expedition was anything but useless; it was, instead, an effort to nourish the roots of an empire of faith. And since evangelicals believed that possessing the right faith would be the primary source of national strength, the expedition was, fundamentally speaking, a voyage of power.[17] As Lynch and his coreligionists understood, spiritual empires are vertical as well as horizontal. The vertical aspect represents depth of faith and religious commitment, while the horizontal comprises all the institutions, activities, and persons who spread that faith. In the US context, the horizontal aspects of religious empire were composed primarily of missionaries, their sponsoring institutions, and the government forces that protected them. While the missionary's primary goal was always the conversion of non-Christians, evangelicals had long believed that missionary activity also strengthened faith at home. Ideally, then, both aspects of spiritual empire were mutually reinforcing, with faith dispatching missionaries and missionaries building faith. Lynch's Dead Sea expedition shared this objective. A key difference, of course, was that the expedition was an official state enterprise. In 1847, Christian faith became a national asset; it required government intervention overseas.

Religious expansionism and its relationship to political and commercial empires has been a subject of much discussion in the scholarly literature. Some, especially those who study the British Empire, have argued that missionaries aided and abetted territorial expansion.[18] Others have not been quite so certain, contending that missionaries, merchants, and colonial officials were very different imperial agents.[19] As Jeffrey Cox writes, British evangelicals "had very little concern for issues of state power except insofar as they were an impediment, or a providential help, to the spread of the Gospel."[20] Andrew Porter agrees: "Missionaries viewed their world first of all with the eye of faith."[21] "For the missionary, faith placed the empire in perspective. . . . At best," empire was "something to be turned to missionary advantage, a means to an end but equally something to be ignored or rejected out of hand if it failed to serve the missionary's main purpose."[22]

This chapter takes up Cox and Porter's challenge of taking faith seriously.[23] It contends that the Dead Sea expedition was in fact an imperial venture that emerged out of a moment of Christian spiritual crisis for the United States. At home, evangelicals felt that the Christian soul of the nation was stretched thin by Catholic immigrants, intemperance, westward expansion, and, most important, the biblical criticism of liberal Unitarian Christians. Abroad, meanwhile, it was unclear whether US commercial expansion—including that fostered by the United States Exploring Expedition—would help or hinder missionary efforts to convert the world. Sin, in its many guises, appeared to threaten the heart of the United States' power by diminishing national faith.

Lynch organized his expedition to address that threat: by proving the Bible, he could put unbelievers and sinners to flight at home while simultaneously persuading his fellow evangelicals that naval exploration and religion could coexist harmoniously. The publications that heralded the expedition's return continued this trajectory, shoving aside concerns over religious liberty and embracing romantic Christian nationalism as a national ethos. The result, Lynch and other evangelicals believed, strengthened the United States as God's chosen empire.

Whether it succeeded in this or not is beyond the ken of any historian; what is clear, however, is that the Dead Sea expedition carried evangelicals into the explorationist camp. The United States was already hierarchical in terms of race, gender, class, and even religion, with Christian evangelism enjoying the protection of the law while outspoken atheists risked jail time.[24] Now, however, evangelicals came to believe that naval exploration could raise their brand of Christianity even higher in the nation's imperial pecking order. Like mariners, scientists, Jacksonian Democrats, and the members of the curious middle class, evangelical Christians discovered that naval surveys could serve their most cherished imperial ends.

There is an irony to this story of Christian awakening. As this chapter's opening anecdote suggests, the achievements of the expedition were not Lynch's alone; nor did they belong solely to his subordinate officers, seamen, countrymen, or even to the Navy Department. From start to finish, the Dead Sea mission relied on Islamic actors. Lynch understood this paradox. Reflecting on how closely his party had come to being trampled by Christians, he observed how "strange that we should have been shielded from a Christian throng by wild children of the desert—Muslims in name, but pagans in reality."[25] Through the Dead Sea expedition, Ottoman officials, Arab holy men, and Bedouin tribesmen became active partners in a US empire of faith.[26]

A CHRISTIAN NATION?

William Francis Lynch was the product of an increasingly Christian nation. At the time of his birth on April 1, 1801, in Norfolk, Virginia, the United States was entering a new phase of Christianization known to scholars as the "Second Great Awakening."[27] Popular memory recounts a declensionist model of Protestant Christianity in North America, with Puritan pilgrims forming the apogee of Protestant faith and the rest of colonial and national history experiencing a decline. Historians, however, tell a different tale: the pilgrims of New England were minorities in the English North American colonies, religious extremists whose legendary status as honorary founding fathers was established only with the Union's victory in the Civil War.[28] The real narrative is one of increasing Christianization over the course of US history.[29] In 1776, for example, only about 17 percent of the population of the thirteen colonies claimed membership in a church; by 1850, 35 percent of the US population did.[30] To meet this burgeoning demand, the number of churches, ministers, and religious organizations exploded in the first half of the nineteenth century.[31]

Emboldened evangelicals pressed on the Revolutionary generation's separation of church and state. The founding fathers and others of their generation adhered to an older European tradition of religious liberty. They wrote a federal Constitution that forbid religious litmus tests and that guaranteed freedom of religion. They took pains to reassure Jews and Catholics that they were welcome in the United States. Their commitment to religious toleration even led them to consider, and endorse, the possibility of Muslim citizens, representatives—even presidents.[32] When the US diplomat Joel Barlow drafted a treaty with Tripoli in 1796, he made sure to include a statement that the United States was not a Christian nation.[33]

Some religious and political leaders took issue with such liberalism. Ministers and clergymen had served as bastions of independence during the Revolutionary era.[34] After the Treaty of Paris, evangelicals among them sought to bind government, Christianity, and nation together. In the words of David Sehat, they created a "moral establishment" at the state level that promoted Protestant Christianity in public life and discouraged the civic participation of atheists and nonbelievers.[35]

Nowhere was this trend more visible than in New England, where Puritanism had morphed in the eighteenth century into Congregationalism. Still Calvinist and almost as stern as their predecessors, Congregationalists had enough clout to make their church the official state religion for several New England states—Massachusetts, for example, required residents to pay state church tithes until 1832.[36] Like many other states, it protected Christian messaging in public but made promotion of blasphemy a crime. State courts routinely upheld such laws, and the federal government backed them.[37] In 1833 and again in 1855, the Supreme Court decided that the religious liberty clause of the First Amendment was guaranteed only at the federal level, not within the states.[38] The result was a religious hierarchy within the United States, or what Alexis de Tocqueville called America's "moral empire."[39]

Figure 4.1 *Commander William Francis Lynch of Confederate States Navy in Uniform*, photographer unknown, between 1861 and 1865. (Courtesy of Library of Congress Prints and Photographs Division, Washington, DC. LOT 14043-2, no. 192 [P&P], https://www.loc.gov/pictures/item/2016647910/.)

Lynch's early life reflected these transformations. While his father was more preoccupied with business than faith, his mother was a born-again Christian who left a powerful impression on her son.[40] She died young, but Lynch had known her well enough to praise her piety and to remember listening to her "beautiful but neglected precepts."[41] When he became a midshipman in 1819, his faith followed him to the navy.[42] At sea, he saw the ocean as the perfect mirror of God, a reminder "of the majesty, the beneficence, and the terrific wrath of the Great Maker."[43] Furthermore, as a man of faith, he saw God's hand in everything: when, during a stay in the Philippines, a boatswain's mate died of cholera, Lynch noted the man's "obscene profanity" and attributed his death to "a peculiar visitation of Providence."[44] "We are in the hands of God," he wrote, "and, fall early, or fall late, we fall only with his consent."[45]

This kind of Calvinist fatalism did not prevent Lynch from promoting righteous action, however. On the contrary, he was a devout reformer who believed that good works would allow the United States to realize its providential destiny. Like other Christians, his sense of history revolved around the twin concepts of God's covenant and free will. He saw Western history as a succession of broken covenants with God. While the Lord had told the ancient Israelites, "Ye shall be unto me a kingdom of priests, and a holy nation" (Exodus 19:16, New King James Version), the Jews had repudiated their holy status by turning the Messiah over to the Romans. The early Christians had taken on the mantle as God's chosen people, but the corruption of the Catholic church had abrogated that commitment. With the Protestant Reformation, the divine covenant passed into the hands of Northern European Protestants, who in turn brought the Good News with them to the New World. Like his coreligionists, Lynch saw God's hand in shielding the Western Hemisphere from Catholic eyes until the Reformation.[46] For US evangelicals, the Revolution was a kind of second era of revelation, with the Declaration of Independence and the Constitution approaching the status of sacred covenants.[47] Lynch would have fully agreed with Melville's famous description of the United States as the "political Messiah" of the world, and of white US citizens as "the peculiar, chosen people—the Israel of our time." "We bear the ark of the liberty of the world," Melville declared.[48]

When Lynch and other evangelicals looked around the United States, however, they feared that the nation was on the verge of breaking their covenant with God. One such threat came through immigration. It is no mistake that the Dead Sea expedition coincided with the high-water mark of Catholic immigration in the antebellum era. Irish and German peasants, their homelands stricken with blight and political repression, fled to the United States in record numbers in the 1840s and 1850s.[49] By 1855, nearly three million Irish and Germans had reached US soil.[50] In nativist eyes, they brought with them two great evils: intemperance and false religion. Temperance activists were distressed by Irish and German traditions of alcohol consumption, whether it was the binge-drinking of young Irishmen or the cherished Sunday lager of the German farmer.[51] Evangelical Protestants were even more unnerved by the increasing number of Catholics in the country. Extreme nativists saw Catholic immigration as part of a popish—even devilish—plot to overrun God's chosen people and sink the "ark of liberty" back into the ocean of error. To counter this grand conspiracy, native-born white Protestants established the "Native American Party" in the 1840s and flooded society with anti-Catholic propaganda. They even turned to violence, burning down a Catholic convent outside Boston in 1834 and instigating nativist riots in Philadelphia in 1844.[52]

A second danger to national holiness came from the West. Ideally, the West should have been a cradle of piety for the new nation. Indeed, many white US citizens seemed to think it already was. When white settlers arrived in southwestern Missouri in the 1830s and 1840s, they changed the name of the local stream from "Wilson's Creek" to "Jordan Creek."[53] Similarly, when, in 1850, William S. Jewett sat down to paint his masterpiece *The Promised Land—the Grayson Family*, he chose as his setting not the Holy Land but California's Sierra Nevada. For Jewett and other white US citizens, pioneering families like the Graysons were God's new chosen people, and the West was their Canaan.[54] It this kind of providential thinking that led the army explorer John C. Frémont to espouse California as "the modern Canaan, a land 'flowing with milk and honey,' its mountains studded and its rivers lined and choked with gold!"[55]

In reality, however, the West posed significant challenges to Protestant expansionism. First, true Native Americans (the modern Canaanites in Protestant thought) held steadfastly to their own spiritual traditions. For a brief period in the early nineteenth century, white missionary societies had grown so discouraged at the spiritual resilience of North American Indigenous peoples that they began diverting missionaries to Asia instead.[56] Secondly, much of the West was claimed by the Catholic power of Mexico. Even after the US–Mexican War, Protestant fears of having to incorporate a vast population of racially mixed Catholics threw a dampener on exuberant expectations of expansionism.[57] As much as Democratic boosters like the Irish American John O'Sullivan might crow about a "manifest destiny to overspread the continent allotted by Providence," the race and religious diversity restricted expansion.[58] Thirdly, Protestants fretted over the true Christian character of white western pioneers. The Catholic German immigrants who preferred to settle in the Midwest were bad enough, but Mormons were worse; nativist mobs chased them from state to state throughout the antebellum era. Even poor white settlers were suspect: they drank, dueled, married Indigenous people, and put more faith in the hoe than in the Bible. As one Illinois pioneer put it, "When I look upon the vast and beautiful prairie surrounding our town . . . I feel a most intense desire that the right kind of moral institutions should grow up with the increasing population."[59]

The fourth challenge to US holiness was the most serious of them all: the highly educated, liberal white US Protestants who adhered to biblical

criticism. This was the crowd of Ralph Waldo Emerson—ministers and intellectuals who found inspiration in the works of German and French biblical scholars. The Bible was not infallible, they argued, but was a product of
both divine revelation and errant human hands. Biblical symbolism, not lit-
eral interpretations, revealed God's true message and plans.[60] Evangelicals,
by contrast, held fast to the Puritan faith in the Bible's infallibility. In their
minds, the Word was the Word; questioning its accuracy or approaching it
as a human literary document threatened the very fundamentals of Christian faith. And yet, that was precisely what increasing numbers of Unitarian Universalists in eastern Massachusetts were doing. Ensconced in such
educational bastions as Harvard University and Concord, Massachusetts,
Unitarians seemed dangerous indeed.[61]

To parry the "intellectual pride" of the Unitarians, evangelicals embraced
intellectual piety.[62] Evangelical Christians established Andover Theological
Seminary, in Andover, Massachusetts, in 1807, to counter Harvard's yearly
crop of liberal graduates.[63] The ministers that they trained there would
joust with Unitarians from the pulpit and in the press; they would serve as
the front line in their crusade to preserve the country's covenant with God.
While many ended up in evangelical strongholds in western and northern
New England, some of them would also go abroad as missionaries.[64] Indeed, evangelicals deployed the letters and reports of missionaries to, in
Christine Heyrman's words, "show that the wrong kind of religion fostered
gross inequalities, despotic regimes, and despicable customs."[65] As one
evangelical put it in 1855, "We purify California in the streets of Canton."[66]

Evangelicals also wielded biblical archaeology in their combat with
Christian liberalism. Unitarians might have Emerson, but born-again
Christians had Edward Robinson. Robinson was a brilliant scholar and
devout Christian who almost single-handedly invented the field of biblical archaeology. The son of a Congregationalist minister from Connecticut, Robinson's talents were so impressive that he quickly became one of
the leading scholars of ancient languages in the United States. When he
graduated from Hamilton College in upstate New York, his faculty mentors
immediately hired him as a colleague. His evangelical fervor led him to Andover, the nexus of US evangelical Christianity. Taken with his talents, his
Andover colleagues dispatched him to Europe in 1826 to learn how to use
the methodologies of biblical criticism against their liberal competitors.

On returning to the United States in 1830, Robinson decided that lin-
guistic analysis was not enough; to really counter the Unitarians, he had to
go to the Holy Land and prove, scientifically, that the Bible was an infallible
historical text. He arrived in the Holy Land in 1838 with a missionary colleague from Andover.[67] In a preview of Lynch's own reliance on Muslims,

Robinson's excursion was dependent on the liberality of Mehmet Ali, the former Ottoman governor of Egypt who had rebelled against the sultan and established his own empire in Egypt and the Holy Land in the 1830s. Robinson dismissed centuries of Catholic and Orthodox traditions about religious sites, relying instead on the similarities between Arabic and ancient Hebrew names to locate Old Testament sites. His erudition and careful analysis paid off; in 1841, he published a highly acclaimed two-volume study of the Holy Land. *Biblical Researches in Palestine* argued that the Bible was an authoritative, truthful historical document—and not merely symbology. The work represented a significant setback to liberal interpretations of the Bible, even in Europe. The *Times* of London called it "by far the best work on Palestine that has hitherto appeared."[68] In 1842, the Royal Geographical Society in London honored Robinson with a gold medal. He was the first US citizen to be so awarded (Charles Wilkes was the second, receiving his in 1848).[69]

Lynch's Dead Sea expedition was deeply indebted to Robinson. Indeed, the entire operation was based on Robinson's premise that a scientific analysis of the Holy Land would prove the veracity of the Bible and put Unitarians and skeptics to flight. Lynch praised Robinson's "elaborate work," confirmed many of his findings, and may have even consulted the scholar in person before his departure.[70] Robinson, for his part, took an active interest in the mission, corresponding on the subject with the Navy Department.[71] As Robinson knew, the Dead Sea expedition was not simply a generic Christian operation; it was, instead, an effort to arm the faithful in their fight with the Unitarians.

THE PROPOSAL

Lynch formally proposed his venture to the Navy Department on May 8, 1847. His pitch was that a survey of the salt lake would be easy, cheap, and a coup for the navy, for the United States, and for biblical and scientific knowledge. Resolving the "mystery" of the Dead Sea, Lynch told Secretary of the Navy John Young Mason, "will advance the Cause of science and gratify the whole Christian world." Noting that naval supply ships had to stop regularly at Mediterranean ports in order to provision the squadron there, Lynch suggested that the expedition could be executed according to their schedules. As for men, there was need for only a handful, while "the frame of a boat could be transported on camels from Acre to Tiberias," on the shores of the Sea of Galilee. There, the party could launch their boats and let the Jordan carry them down into the Dead Sea. The canvas for the tents, as well as camp provisions and weapons, could be taken from the

supply ship itself. Overall, Lynch assured Mason, "the expense will be tri-
fling, and the object easy of attainment."[72]

There can be little doubt that Lynch was, in some sense, an opportun-
ist. David H. Finnie's assertion that the Dead Sea expedition was simply
Lynch's touristic fantasy is, in part, correct.[73] Lynch was an inveterate traveler and one of the most exploration-minded officers in the navy. As a devout Christian, he confessed to "an insatiate yearning to look upon . . . the
soil hallowed by the footsteps, fertilized by the blood, and consecrated by
the tomb, of the Saviour."[74] If he was unable to embark on his expedition or
see service in the US–Mexican War, he had made arrangements to take a
year's leave and traverse the Holy Land on his own.[75] Even after his survey
of Palestine, Lynch would thirst for more; he described Africa as "a vast
and glorious field for exploration," and in 1852 led a brief mission to explore
the interior Liberia.[76] During the same decade, he offered to explore the La
Plata River in South America, reconnoiter Manchuria for the benefit of US
commerce, and pilot a warship around the world, collecting useful plants,
animals, and seeds to improve the nation's farms.[77] To his great disappointment, none of these missions came to fruition. Like Jeremiah Reynolds,
Lynch worked tirelessly to become the New World's Humboldt—a man
whom, like Reynolds, he deeply admired.[78]

However, it is also equally apparent that Lynch's proposal emerged
from a grander imperial design. Like Robinson, he wanted to buttress the
US spiritual empire through faith. Lynch's explicit goal was, in his words,
"to refute the position of infidel philosophers" who disregarded the divine
origins of the salt sea.[79] Like many evangelicals, Lynch fretted over alcohol, Catholics, and immigrants. But he reserved his greatest ire for liberal
Christians. He described "hard-hearted scepticism" as being "nearly allied
to infidelity."[80] "There is nothing which so perverts the heart as intellectual
pride," he wrote, describing it as "a crime which the dread Creator has reserved for special retribution."[81] If Lynch could convince biblical skeptics
of the errors of their ways, he might preserve the United States from "the
terrific wrath of the Great Maker."[82]

The Dead Sea appeared the perfect venue for a lesson on national morality, power, and ruin. Jews, Christians, and even Muslims had long believed that the inland sea was the result of God's punishment of Sodom
and Gomorrah.[83] The celebrated travel writer John Lloyd Stephens is a
case in point. In 1837, he published what proved to be an immensely popular two-volume travelogue on his wanderings through the Dead Sea region and its environs. Stephens was no scientist and was, in fact, a former
atheist, but he claimed to have seen "abundant tokens that the shower of
fire and brimstone which descended upon the guilty cities of Sodom and

Gomorrah, stopped the course of the Jordan, and formed it into a pestilential lake."[84] His experiences abroad made him a believer.[85] He hoped that future investigations would reveal even more evidence of the veracity of the Bible—especially the actual ruins of the guilty cities.[86] Similarly, in his *Biblical Researches*, Robinson had concluded that the Old Testament account was correct, and that God had used volcanoes to incinerate Sodom and Gomorrah.[87]

Lynch aspired to perfect this work. In a published letter from December 1847, he pledged that his expedition would "reveal those ruins, upon the non-existence of which the unbeliever states his incredulity." He reminded readers that the Dead Sea had been a mystery "for upwards of four thousand years," and cited some of the major questions that still remained unanswered. In addition to resolving ancient biological and ecological questions about how "dead" the Dead Sea really was, Lynch hoped to determine whether or not a subaqueous volcano lurked within its depths or a "subterranean aqueduct" linked it with the Mediterranean. Like Reynolds and John Quincy Adams before him, he appealed to white US citizens' insecurities about their cultural status vis-á-vis European powers. He further linked his mission with the US–Mexican War: "We owe something to the scientific and the Christian world," Lynch contended, "and while extending the blessings of civil liberty in the south and west, may well afford to foster science and strengthen the bulwarks of Christianity in the east."[88]

Secretary Mason may have well scratched his head after reading Lynch's letter. The bland but affable gentleman from Virginia would have known that, outside of a handful of US citizens who profited from commerce with Smyrna and Turkey, US economic interests in the Holy Land in 1847 were essentially nonexistent.[89] As one of Lynch's own sailors put it in 1849, the Holy Land was "distant from the great marts of commerce, and of but little interest except for their historical associations."[90] That perception would change in the 1850s and 1860s, when some US citizens (including Lynch) followed Britain's lead and began emphasizing Syria as the new route to Asia.[91] In 1847, however, that development was still in the future. Mason knew that the proposal on his desk was an effort to address scientific and religious concerns, not commerce. Later, in fact, when Lynch attempted to extend his expedition to the Euphrates River, Mason rejected the idea on the grounds that the extension "would be political and commercial; while the observations at the Dead Sea are scientific."[92]

In the end, Mason decided in favor. He wrote to Lynch on July 31, 1847, and ordered him to New York to procure supplies, vessels, and men for the expedition.[93] He explained his reasons for doing so a few months later: "The object, with which I have yielded to your request, is to promote the cause of Sciences, and advance the character of the Naval service."[94] The second of these is easier to understand than the first. The Dead Sea expedition promised to cast a positive light on the navy at a time when it had been eclipsed by the exploits of the army. By the summer of 1847, the navy had had its brief moment of glory with the amphibious landing of General Winfield Scott's troops at Veracruz.[95] Afterward, as Lynch explained, there remained "nothing left for the Navy to perform."[96] Navy cruisers searched for prizes that rarely materialized. Now and then, smaller naval vessels darted up Mexican rivers to strike riparian towns of little strategic significance. The army, in contrast, bested Mexican forces in contest after contest. Victories by Zachary Taylor and Winfield Scott captured the public's imagination and even drew praise from the Duke of Wellington.[97] As Robert Rook writes, "The army's campaign in Mexico left it well-positioned to fight budgetary battles in Washington." Thus, the "fame not won on the way to halls of the Montezumas could be attained on the shores of the Galilee and the Dead Sea."[98]

In terms of science, Mason may have known that Lynch's mission could resolve two of the leading geographical questions of the day: the altitude of the Dead Sea and the course of the Jordan River. In 1841, British Lieutenant J. F. A. Symonds of the Royal Engineers claimed to have determined the relative levels of the Sea of Galilee and the Dead Sea. While the Royal Geographical Society (RGS) awarded him a gold medal in 1845, some doubts lingered. Among the most prominent skeptics was Robinson. In November 1847, he presented a paper before the RGS in which he argued that, for Symonds's calculations to be correct, the Jordan River had to descend from the Sea of Galilee to the Dead Sea in a series of grand, Niagara-like cataracts.[99] One of Lynch's primary scientific goals was to explain this mystery and check Symonds's calculations. Unbeknown to him, the Royal Navy was already organizing its own expedition, under Lieutenant Thomas Molyneux, to answer Robinson's questions. Molyneux's plan was nearly identical to Lynch's: by floating down the Jordan in small boats, Molyneux's party would demonstrate that the river shaped a rapid and twisting course. Its tortuous path explained how it could avoid being the perpetual waterfall that Symonds's observations had suggested.[100] However, Mason and Lynch did not know of Molyneux's expedition at the time of their correspondence.[101] His venture, then, was partly designed to answer two geographical questions that appeared up for debate in the spring and summer of 1847.

Mason's primary justification, "the cause of Sciences," also had religious implications. Science and religion had not yet parted ways in the mid-nineteenth century. This explains why Lynch's close friend and brother officer, Matthew Fontaine Maury, frequently employed the Bible in his scientific publications.[102] Mason was similar; like many other white US citizens of his generation, Mason's upbringing and educational background had been deeply influenced by faith. This meant that his sense of knowledge and truth was intimately intertwined with Christianity. His father, Edmund, was an Episcopalian who brought his young family to Methodist services to hear his brother preach. Every night, Edmund would read the Bible to young John and his siblings by candlelight.[103] In preparatory school, Mason studied classical languages and translated portions of the New Testament from ancient Greek.[104] His time as a student at the University of North Carolina was punctuated by morning and evening prayer sessions, Sunday services, and morality examinations on Sunday afternoons.[105] Unsurprisingly, therefore, Mason prized piety; after his marriage in 1821, he praised his evangelical mother-in-law as "religious and saintly."[106] Before she died, she entrusted him with her spiritual diary.[107] In sum, Mason's background would have left him favorably inclined to Lynch's plan.

Nonetheless, the navy secretary's approval represented an enormous breach of the separation of church and state. In acquiescing to Lynch, Mason had firmly arrayed the federal government on the side of evangelical Christianity. Confusingly, this meant that the Democratic administration of James K. Polk had assumed what was normally the Whig position in US politics. The whole plan, in fact, had been conceived by a Southern Whig: Lynch himself. Like other Whigs, Lynch was far more open to using the state to advance public morality than Democrats. His party supplied more temperance activists and nativists than Democrats, and during the US–Mexican War, they were more likely to see the conflict as a religious clash between Protestants and Catholics.[108] Mason's permission caught Whig politicians and newspaper editors off guard; while they bludgeoned the administration on the hypocrisy of rejecting federal power to improve western rivers while exploring Ottoman Palestine, they generally did not challenge its religious or scientific value. "It is lucky," one Whig writer remarked, "that the Dead Sea is not situated in any of the states; for if it [were], the expedition would certainly be unconstitutional."[109]

Whigs likely chose not to make an issue of the religious nature of the expedition because the Christian press rallied to Lynch's side. Few periodicals echoed the criticism of the *Monthly Beacon*, which hoped that the venture had not "been undertaken with any such foolish intent" as "to confute the scoffs of infidels, and prove the scripture account."[110] But of course, that was precisely what Lynch was after—and evangelicals knew it. Their enthusiasm knew no bounds. "I have often wondered that this has not been accomplished before," one writer mused in the *Christian Palladium*, "and it is now very gratifying to me that our Navy is likely to have the honor of accomplishing what the civilized world has hitherto failed to do."[111] The *Presbyterian* of Philadelphia took pride in the fact that "a government of the new world should be the first to explore . . . a region so intimately connected with the common faith of Christendom."[112] It hoped Lynch would confirm "the original record of the Bible."[113] *The Gospel Teacher & Sabbath School Contributor* concurred: "The great point of interest will be to ascertain if any trace can be found of the reprobate cities."[114]

Lynch's expeditionary plans were marked by a nativist, masculine, and martial brand of evangelicalism. When recruiting seamen in New York, Lynch shipped only "young, muscular, native-born Americans, of sober habits, from each of whom [he] exacted a pledge to abstain from all intoxicating drinks."[115] When one of his sailors snuck ashore for "another drop of rum," Lynch sentenced him to three months without grog (the sailor said he would have preferred to have been flogged).[116] In October, Lynch asked Mason to discharge a sailor whom he thought "wanting in physical stamina."[117] He also scrapped his original plan of hauling pieces of a wooden boat across Palestine in favor of something safer but also more novel: two smaller, metal boats, one copper and the other iron.[118] He named them after Mason's children, and felt assured that "their prayers, like guardian spirits, would shield us in the hour of peril."[119] And in case the Mason children skipped their payers, Lynch assembled an impressive arsenal—his team's weapons included a blunderbuss, fourteen rifles with bayonets, four revolving pistols, ten bowie-knife pistols, and swords for the officers.[120] He would suffer no fools in God's country, but neither would he rely on Providence alone.

Unsurprisingly, his handpicked sailors reflected Lynch's nativist and brawny values. They described themselves as "thorough-bred Yankee boys" who were "up to the mark."[121] "We have determined souls, enduring constitutions, plenty of provisions," and "lots of ammunition," espoused one sailor.[122] They practically worshiped Lynch, whom they called "one of the best, most humane, thoughtful, and generous men in the world, who lack[ed] nothing on the score of 'bravery,' and the resolute 'go-ahead' spirit of a real, true-born American."[123] And like their commander, they evinced great interest in their mission. According to the diary of a mariner aboard Lynch's vessel, the store ship *Supply*, "there [was] constant conversation amongst the men about the Expedition." As the store ship neared the coast of Palestine, the crew of the *Supply* began begging members of the expedition to exchange places—to no avail.[124] Later, while setting up tents after landing at Acre on March 31, 1848, one sailor began belting, "O carry me back to Old Virginia shore."[125] His comrades cut him off, admonishing him for singing such a tune before the expedition had even begun. "They [didn't] want to go back till they've been t' bottom o' the Dead Sea," the tars exclaimed, "and seen the spires and churches, and wine stores of old Sodom and Gomorrah."[126]

THE SUBLIME PORTE

By all accounts, the Dead Sea expedition was a mission for US Protestants by US Protestants. Yet almost from the start, Lynch and Mason's evangelical survey would rely on Muslim actors. Lynch's first debt would be to the Ottoman sultan, Abdülmecid I. James Buchanan was to account for this; as Polk's secretary of state, the expedition was partly in his court. He assented to the voyage but required that Lynch win the sultan's blessing in order to proceed.[127] Accordingly, Buchanan ordered the US minister to Constantinople, Dabney S. Carr, to make preparations for Lynch's arrival and to see about acquiring a firman, or imperial passport. It was common practice for Western explorers in the region to seek firmans from the Sublime Porte and even from provincial governors.[128] The firman would allow Lynch to pass through Ottoman territory and, ideally, would secure the assistance of Ottoman officials.[129] It would also make matters far less complicated should the expedition encounter trouble. If a fracas ensued between Lynch's team and Ottoman subjects, the firman would partly shield the Polk administration from public criticism and serve as a basis for negotiation with the Sublime Porte.[130]

The *Supply* left New York on November 26, 1847.[131] The long transit to the eastern Mediterranean gave Lynch plenty of opportunity to meditate on his evangelical theory of history. The key to ruin, in his mind, was lack of proper faith. This led to indulgence in sensuality, especially sexual sensuality, which sapped women of their virtue and men of their virility.[132] Off Cape Trafalgar, he reflected on how the British naval hero Lord Horatio Nelson had suffered "from the thaldrom of a syren."[133] Similarly, the vices of "the licentious cavalier" Charles I and the sexual excesses of the French nation had culminated in ruinous, bloody revolutions.[134] Approaching the Aegean, Lynch praised "the chaste philosophy of Greece," which revealed "the early rays of revelation" and permitted Socrates and others to transcend polytheism.[135] He fixed the fall of Rome on the materialist philosophy of Epicureanism, which, "by denying the superintendence of a Supreme Being, struck at the root of all social and political morality."[136] For Lynch, the primary lesson of the past was that "licentiousness of morals has always preceded and precipitated . . . national calamities."[137] The implications of this interpretation was clear: Christians had a duty "to oppose everything which tends to corrupt morals and promote licentiousness."[138] Nothing less than the US empire was at stake.

It bears mentioning that Lynch never explicitly listed male-on-male intimacy as a major concern. Considering that the Bible attributes God's destruction of Sodom to male homosexual lust, this may seem surprising. Indeed, the city's name lived on as a description for all kinds of illicit sexual activities, including anal sex, with which it later became synonymous.[139] While many historians trace the rise of the modern "homophobic state" to the mid-fourteenth century, its origins date back even earlier, when Constantine's conversion to Christianity in the fourth century began mixing Church sexual codes with civil law.[140] Colonial North America and the early republic inherited this tradition, with colonies and states mandating the death penalty for sodomy.[141] Lynch's omission might also seem surprising in light of his chosen profession: sailor slang, navy codes, and court-martial records reveal that homosexual relations at sea were not uncommon.[142] However, given the repressive values of the age, sodomy was likely too taboo a subject for a gentleman-officer to raise; indeed, Lynch's brother officers worked hard to sweep such matters under the rug as much as possible.[143] Lynch may also have believed that the mission's position on male-to-male intimacy was obvious, and that the expedition would demonstrate that sexual relations between men were a sin without having to say so publicly. Whether the omission was intentional or not, there can be little doubt that the expedition implicitly promoted heteronormativity. If Lynch could convince his countrymen that the biblical account of Sodom's destruction was true, religious justifications for criminalizing gay intimacy would only grow stronger.

When Lynch finally arrived in Constantinople on February 20, 1848, he alighted in an ancient capital city in the midst of profound transformation.[144] The Ottoman world was in the throes of a sweeping era of reform known as the *tanzimat,* or "reordering."[145] The origins of the *tanzimat* lay in the eighteenth century, when the Age of Revolutions and wartime losses against Russia in the 1760s and 1770s reshaped the Ottoman Empire and impelled new modes of organization and governance.[146] Further defeats at the hands of Greek and Egyptian rebels in the 1820s, 1830s, and early 1840s further underscored the necessity for reform. In consequence, a succession of sultans and allied bureaucrats sought to reorganize the Ottoman military-fiscal state.[147] The empire's elite troops, known as janissaries, and their fundamentalist allies, the ulema, or lower-class Islamic scholars, opposed these moves. They countered reformers with an argument that Lynch and other US evangelicals would have recognized: the empire's setbacks were

Figure 4.2 Map of Lieutenant William Francis Lynch's movements in the Eastern Mediterranean, February–May 1848. (Created by Chris Robinson.)

due to a loss of faith, not to an antiquated system of organization.[148] Their appeals fell on hostile ears; in 1826, Sultan Mahmud II launched a surprise attack against the janissaries and wiped them out.[149] For Ottoman conservatives, it was a monumental setback. When Mahmud's son Abdülmecid I came to the throne in 1839, he continued his predecessors' reforms in such areas as tax administration, army conscription, European-style military and diplomatic training, and religious liberty.[150]

Lynch encountered several of these transformations while in Constan-

tinople. On a tour of the Ottoman barracks, for instance, he noted the soldiers' European dress and the prohibition of the bastinado, an ancient form
of Mediterranean punishment.[151] At San Stefano (modern-day Yeşilköy,
Turkey), outside the capital, he met two US citizens who served the sultan as top geological and agricultural counselors.[152] Moreover, US actors
had played an important role in Ottoman naval affairs since the 1830s, and
Lynch soon found himself continuing that tradition.[153] For example, during
his time in Constantinople, he advised the government (negatively) on the
purchase of a British steamer.[154]

    While Carr, the US minister to Constantinople, was enthusiastic about
the sultan's plans "to regenerate his people" through US agricultural and
naval expertise, Lynch was more pessimistic.[155] He generally subscribed to
the more common European perspective that the Empire was on a steep
decline. In the words of one roving US diplomat, only "the protecting
jealousies of the great powers of Europe" kept the invalid standing.[156] As
an evangelical, Lynch attributed Ottoman declension to religion. He described "Muhammedan rule" as "that political sirocco, which withers all
before it."[157] A primary mechanism of decay was women's rights. While he
believed that Christianity empowered women to refuse male sexual appe-
tites, he thought that Islam offered no such protection. The consequence
was a cycle of sensuality and degradation between men and women that
drained the spirit of the nation.[158] On a tour of the Seraglio, or the sultan's
harem, Lynch's Protestant soul revolted. "What scenes have been enacted
in these apartments! What intrigues, murders and sewing up in sacks! Alas,
poor woman!"[159] "Could Christianity but shed its benign influence over
this misguided people," he averred, "their national existence might be prolonged, and the sad catastrophe averted."[160]

    The theme of Ottoman sickness hangs heavily over Lynch's account of
his meeting with the sultan on February 24, 1848. The royal conference
took place at the Ciragan Palace, a gray wooden edifice on the banks of
the Bosphorus. The naval lieutenant described it as "oriental," "light," and
"graceful."[161] He enjoyed its courtyard, fishponds, and staircases, all of
which he praised as being in "exquisite taste."[162] But when Lynch finally
laid eyes on Abdülmecid, his old prejudices resurfaced. He perceived the
sultan as a kind, sickly, and melancholic youth. "There is that indescribably
sad expression in his countenance, which is thought to indicate an early
death," he mused. Lynch attributed his depression to "a boding fear of the
overthrow of his country." He imagined the "souls of the mighty [Otto-
man] monarchs who have gone before" hovering over him, genie-like, and
mourning "the impending fate of an empire which once extended from the
Atlantic to the Ganges, from the Caucasus to the Indian Ocean."[163]

Lynch juxtaposed the sultan's weakness with his own republican vigor. His nerves quaked only briefly when, while waiting for his appointment, he was served a delicate cup of coffee and a chibouk, or Turkish tobacco pipe, made of the most stunning and costly materials.[164] He recovered quickly, finding the nerve to argue with the chamberlain over whether or not he could bring his sword to the royal meeting.[165] Once through the doorway (sword at his side), Lynch scoffed at the quiet shuffling of the Ottoman secretary as they approached the sultan's chamber. In contrast, Lynch took pride in his own heavy footsteps, "which, unaccustomed to palace regulations, fell with untutored republican firmness upon the royal floor."[166] During his audience, Lynch compared his position as one of the "humblest servants of a far-distant republic" with the sultan's status as "the ruler of mighty kingdoms and the arbiter of the fate of millions of his fellow-creatures."[167] Even so, he decided that he "would not change positions with him."[168] He wrote, "My feelings saddened as I looked upon the monarch, and I thought of Montezuma."[169]

As Lynch's comparison of Abdülmecid and Montezuma implies, the naval lieutenant saw much of his mission through the prism of westward expansion. Indeed, the conquistadores were never more popular among white US citizens than during the US–Mexican War. As evidenced by the hymn of the US Marine Corps, white Christian soldiers imagined their invasion of Mexico in 1846–1848 as a restaging of Hernán Cortés's overthrow of the Mexica. Secretary Mason was so enamored with William H. Prescott's *History of the Conquest of Mexico* (1843) that he ordered a copy of "for every vessel in the United States Navy."[170] Perhaps Lynch and his band thumbed through it during their long Atlantic and Mediterranean crossings. Throughout his time in the Near East, Lynch turned again and again to US western analogies. He thought that Turks walked "like our Indians," that Bedouin Arabs reminded him of the same, and that Ottoman Palestine was as lawless as the North American West.[171]

The products of westward expansion even helped Carr arrange Lynch's summit with the sultan. Carr understood that frugality was ill suited to Ottoman court culture, which prized generosity. Just as Wilkes had during the voyage of the Ex Ex, Carr looked to Indigenous American diplomacy as a guide. In June 1847, he advised the State Department "to conciliate the friendship" of the Turks just as it did for "our Indian Chiefs and tribes, by presents."[172] Buchanan approved of this strategy. Acting on Carr's observation that the sultan had "the greatest curiosity about the North American Indians," he ordered three beautiful portfolio volumes of Native North Americans (including one by George Catlin) for the lieutenant to give the sultan in person.[173] "These enabled me to procure for Lt. Lynch an Audience of the Sultan," Carr wrote Buchanan. "I made him the bearer of these presents to His Majesty, who was greatly delighted with them."[174] After looking over the magnificent tomes, Abdülmecid declared them "evidence of the advancement of the United States in civilization." The remark shocked Lynch; it was, after all, a surprising thing for a Montezuma to tell a Cortés.[175]

On the evening of March 7, Lynch received the much anticipated firman. "The objection of the Secry of State are [sic] now consequently removed," Lynch crowed to Mason in triumph.[176] While Lynch credited Carr with engineering the firman, diplomatic skill alone cannot account for his warm reception or for the Ottomans' decision to permit the expedition to proceed.[177] Instead, there were three factors that are most likely responsible for Lynch's favorable treatment in the Sublime Porte. One was defensive: Constantinople struggled throughout the 1830s and early 1840s to eject the Egyptians from Palestine and Syria. Twice, in 1832–1833 and again in 1840, European powers had rescued them from Egyptian arms and restored Ottoman rule over the Holy Land.[178] Abdülmecid and his counselors probably thought that having more-detailed surveys of the region would prove helpful if the Egyptians ever rose again. Secondly, the Ottomans recognized that providing access to holy sites was instrumental in maintaining good diplomatic relations with Western powers.[179] It was for this reason that they provided a strong military escort for the annual Christian pilgrimage from Jerusalem to the Jordan.[180] Lastly, the Ottomans genuinely seemed to have valued their relations with the United States. This can be seen in their hiring of US shipwrights and scientists and in their exceptional treatment of Lynch.[181] The observant Carr thought that the Ottomans "look more to our Country than any other, for aid and sympathy in their great effort at Reform."[182] The Ottoman foreign minister agreed. "However you may act toward us," he told a British businessman, "the Americans will be our good friends."[183]

THE RIVER JORDAN AND DEAD SEA EXPEDITION

Ottoman friendship may have allowed the expedition to proceed, but Bedouin Arabs would help make it a success. When the *Supply* at last disgorged the mission's officers and men on the Syrian beach of Acre on March 31, 1848, Lynch was distressed to receive word that the Dead Sea region was in an uproar.[184] By then, he had also learned that Bedouins had ambushed Lieutenant Molyneux's party on the Jordan, and believed (wrongly) that Molyneux had been "mortally wounded" in the attack.[185] He conferred with the local Ottoman governor, Sa'id Bey, but suspected that the latter sought

to take advantage of the situation and scare the expedition into buying protection from him.[186] In his next moves, Lynch proved himself surprisingly
conscious of the geopolitical complexities of the region. He knew, for example, that while the Ottomans held fast to their authority in the region's
major cities, Arab Bedouins in the countryside detested their governance.
He decided that leaving Acre with a strong complement of Turkish troops
would only invite hostility and attack.[187] Refusing to deal with Sa'id Bey, he
cast about for other, more culturally attuned options.

He was not long in finding them. During his opening interview at the
governor's palace, Lynch had encountered 'Akil Aga el Hasseé. 'Akil was
a sheikh, a Bedouin leader responsible for managing his tribe's diplomatic
affairs.[188] Sitting at the Ottoman divan with the governor and other Turkish notables, Lynch found himself awestruck at 'Akil's appearance: "En-
veloped in a scarlet cloth pelissee, richly embroidered with gold," the lieutenant thought him "a magnificent savage," and the "handsomest," "most
graceful being [he] had ever seen." As Sa'id Bey described the unsettled
state of the interior, he gestured to 'Akil as a witness. "It immediately occurred to me," Lynch reflected, "that the Bedawin sheikh had been brought
in as a bugbear to intimidate me." When Lynch declined the governor's
protection, 'Akil interjected, warning Lynch that "the Bedawin of the Ghor
would eat us up." Lynch coolly replied that "they would find us difficult of
digestion."[189] Afterward, he caught up to the sheikh and showed him his
"sword and revolver—the former with pistol barrels attached near the hilt."
Lynch described his party's strength in terms of men and arms and then
"asked him if he did not think we could descend the Jordan." "You will, if
anybody can," 'Akil replied.[190] Perhaps the sheikh was as impressed with
the lieutenant as Lynch was him; through messengers, he agreed to accompany the expedition, so long as Lynch could keep the arrangement away
from Ottoman ears.[191]

Lynch met his second Arab ally at the US consul's house, where a stream
of locals came to visit and mingle with the exotic US officers. Among them
was Sherif Hazza, "a fine old man . . . about 50 years of age, of a dark Egyptian complexion, small stature, and intelligent features."[192] Lynch was impressed to see that "every Muslim who came in, first approached him and
kissed his hand with an air of profound respect."[193] He soon learned that
Sherif was a descendant of the Prophet Muhammad, and that his family
had served as the governors of Mecca for generations.[194] The Egyptian oc-
cupation had put an end to that tradition, with much suffering and trials
for Sherif and his family. At the time, Sherif was awaiting the result of his
application for redress from Constantinople.[195] Lynch saw an opportunity
and sprung, asking Sherif to join them. "At first he smiled," Lynch recalled,

"as if the proposition were an absurd one; but when I explained to him that, instead of a party of private individuals, we were commissioned officers and seamen, sent from a far distant but powerful country to solve a scientific question, he became interested." Lynch even appealed to Sherif on the basis of faith, pledging that "we hoped to convince the incredulous that Moses was a true prophet."[196] Sherif assented.[197]

Why did 'Akil and Sherif agree to join a US exploring expedition to the Dead Sea? Money does not seem to have been a major factor. There is no mention, in any of the archival or published documents of the expedition, about a specific financial arrangement with 'Akil. In fact, Sherif shocked Lynch by letting him determine how much he ought to be compensated.[198] And even the naval lieutenant did not ascribe their assistance to this factor. Considering that Lynch characterized Arabs as having "an insatiate love of gold," and that he had the impression that 'Akil's people thought that the US party was surveying for precious metals, this is surprising indeed.[199]

Instead, the surviving evidence suggests that the Muslim leaders' decision was a diplomatic one. The year before, 'Akil had led a desert rebellion against the sultan. "Unable to subdue him," Lynch narrated, Constantinople did a very Ottoman thing: they restored 'Akil's loyalty (or so they thought) by giving him rank and title and a share of local governance.[200] Nevertheless, it appears that 'Akil was still casting about for greater opportunities. In a long evening conversation with Lynch, the sheikh ventured the possibility of a US–Bedouin alliance against Constantinople.[201] Both 'Akil and Sherif knew that the distant republic had fought two wars with Great Britain. And since the British were close allies of the Ottoman Empire, the Bedouins "look[ed] around with eagerness for some power able to [contend] with the Great ally of the Porte."[202] Sherif may have had a different objective in mind. The Ottoman Empire's identity as an Islamic power had long granted Ottoman rule a special legitimacy in the eyes of urban Arabs.[203] As an elite Arab whose family had long profited from Muslim empires, Sherif may have therefore sought to curry favor with the Ottomans in advance of their decision on his case. After all, Lynch carried several Ottoman firmans with him—one from the sultan, and another from the pasha of Jerusalem.[204] This was clearly a man who possessed Ottoman goodwill.

Regardless of why they joined, 'Akil and Sherif proved invaluable. Lynch's "dearest wish" was to avoid the kind of ambush that had befallen Molyneux's men on their trip down the Jordan.[205] Accordingly, he divided the party in two, sending a caravan down the river's Palestinian side while he navigated the boats down the sacred stream. Whether guarding the caravan or assisting the tars with the metal craft, Arab manpower was essential. 'Akil brought fourteen fighting men to the party, nearly doubling its physical strength.[206] Those Arabs assigned to the water route helped carry the boats out of the Jordan and around the river's frequent rapids.[207] At other times, Lynch "employed" the "most vigorous Arabs" in swimming and guiding the boats through white water so as "not to risk the men."[208] Most critical of all was the simple prestige that 'Akil and Sherif carried with them. Both of these headmen traveled with the caravan and served as the mission's emissaries and diplomats.[209] With them by his side, Lynch and his sailors were still "Franks," as the Arabs termed all Europeans, but they were also the allies of respected local leaders.

While race figured prominently in Lynch's writings about his "Bedawin friends," class may have been more important.[210] For both professional and racial reasons, Lynch was more comfortable risking the lives of lower-class Arabs than those of US sailors in the rapids of the Jordan. When meeting Arabs, he relied on comparisons with Native North Americans, African Americans, and even Oceanic Islanders to make sense of his encounters.[211] Nonetheless, he seems to have formed a close partnership with 'Akil and Sherif based on their shared leadership status. This comports with what scholars have perceived in English (and later British) colonial and imperial relations. As Karen Ordahl Kupperman writes, "Neither savagery nor race was the important category" in early English encounters with native North Americans; instead, "the really important category," she writes, "was status."[212] Thus, 'Akil might be a "barbarian," but "he had much of the manners and feelings of a gentleman."[213] Similarly, Sherif was "our counselor, sagacious, and prudent."[214] Lynch relied on both men's advice, noting that they "frequently visited us in our tent."[215] In reading his account, one gets the impression that Lynch saw them as sharing the same rank as his valued second-in-command, Lieutenant John B. Dale. Furthermore, the respect appears to have been mutual; in a letter to Lynch, for instance, 'Akil addressed him as his "dear friend."[216]

The rapport that developed between Lynch and his Arab allies was not shared by the tars under his command. Whereas Lynch could wax poetic about how "Sherif was the Nestor, and 'Akil the Achilles, of our camp," the white, working-class seamen of the expedition never voyaged past their prejudices.[217] The published account of the anonymous sailor who accompanied the mission is rife with stereotypical perceptions of bloodthirsty, violent Arabs. "Day and night," the salt claimed, the Arab "is abroad pursuing his purposes of cruelty, rapine, and murder."[218] Such comments may speak as much to the physical organization of the expedition as to US working-class prejudice. As in other European archaeological expeditions to the Islamic world, Yankees and Bedouins had their own tents, and there appears to have been little crossover.[219] The officers, in contrast, visited, consulted, and socialized regularly with their Arab peers. They also had an Arab cook, Mustafa, whereas the sailors had to hash out among themselves who would fix supper, and when.[220] While the seaman who published his narrative seems either especially ignorant or overly reliant on old tropes of Muslims as violent fanatics, his station may have also given him less opportunities to shatter deeply ingrained stereotypes.[221]

In spite of this intercultural suspicion, the alliance held together. On April 18, 1848, the expedition finally spilled into the Dead Sea.[222] A sloshing storm greeted the boats. It threw the salt lake into a "sheet of foaming brine," doused the party in salt spray, and burned their eyes.[223] The boats slowed, and "it seemed as if their bows were encountering the sledge-hammers of the Titans, instead of the opposing waves of an angry sea."[224] Fearing for their survival, Lynch began weighing whether or not they could beach the boats in safety. Suddenly, however, the wind died, and the sea settled into a deep calm.[225] Lynch later wondered whether "the Dread Almighty frowned upon our effects to navigate a sea, the creation of his wrath."[226] The Arabs shared his concerns. They knew it as the "Sea of Lot" and, like their US allies, believed it possessed a frightful power.[227] Ever helpful, they declared again and again to Lynch and his party that "no one can venture upon this sea and live," reminding him "repeatedly" of the fate of Molyneux, who survived the attack on his boats but later perished of typhus aboard his ship.[228]

Nonetheless, the Arabs continued to provide the same critical support on the Dead Sea as they had on the Jordan. Sherif and especially 'Akil carried on with their diplomatic roles, with Lynch dispatching the latter to conciliate the tribes on the east coast of the Dead Sea.[229] Arabs also provided sustenance, fresh water, and natural knowledge. Sherif went to Jerusalem to oversee the shipment of new supplies, for instance.[230] Local Rashâyideh tribespeople assisted as guides and agents for acquiring provisions.[231] After one full day of surveying, the Yankees collapsed back at camp and wondered what remained of their dwindling provisions. Fortunately, Lynch wrote, "our supper was helped out by some dhom-apples, brought by our Arab guide."[232] "I scarce know what we could have done without the Arabs," he wrote Mason. "They bring us food when nearly famished, water when parched with thirst: They act as guides & messengers, and in our absence faithfully guard our tents, bedding & clothes."[233]

Bedouin assistance allowed the Protestants to focus on their surveying work. Over the next twenty-two days, officers and jack tars would endure desiccating heat, biting brine, and exhaustive labor as they charted and sounded the Dead Sea. Their investigations added immensely to the scientific and geographical knowledge of the salt basin. "We have carefully sounded this sea," Lynch would later inform the readers of his narrative,

MUSTAFA THE COOK.

Figure 4.3 This image, *Mustafa the Cook*, from William F. Lynch's *Narrative of the United States' Expedition to the River Jordan and the Dead Sea* (Philadelphia: Lea & Blanchard, 1849, 318), reflects the critical supporting role that Arab Bedouins played in guarding and supplying the Dead Sea expedition. (Courtesy of Library Company of Philadelphia)

"determined its geographical position, taken the exact topography of its shores, ascertained the temperature, width, depth, and velocity of its tributaries, collected specimens of every kind, and noted the winds, currents, changes of the weather, and all atmospheric phenomena."[234] The expeditionary party also took careful measurements of the elevation of the Sea of Galilee, the Dead Sea, Jerusalem, and the Mediterranean. They confirmed Symonds's old calculations, finding that the inland sea lay just over 1,300 feet below the Mediterranean. They further determined that the answer to Edward Robinson's question about the rate of descent of the Jordan River was its ox-bowed course.[235] Though the Jordan originates only sixty miles above the Dead Sea, the expedition found that its actual length was more than two hundred miles.[236] Their findings therefore seconded those of the ill-fated Molyneux, whose party were the first known navigators of the Jordan.[237]

As to biblical archaeology, the expedition discovered no ruins that they explicitly linked to Sodom or Gomorrah. This was one of the rare ways in which Lynch comes across as scientifically cautious. While previous explorers, including Robinson, had interpreted small, beachside ruins as the remnants of the guilty cities, Lynch was more circumspect.[238] This is surprising; in light of his mission, his previous statements about the expedition's goal of locating the remnants of the Old Testament cities, and the extent of his faith, one would expect Lynch to see a pyramid in every molehill. Furthermore, his writings make it clear that he and most other members of his party entered the Dead Sea already convinced of the Bible's veracity. By Lynch's own count, only two of the entire party were skeptical.[239] Their collective faith even caused members of the party to hallucinate ruins in and around the Dead Sea; when a small party left camp to investigate the ruins of Masada, for instance, they actually saw "a plain covered with towns and villages, marble cities, with columns, temples, domes, and palaces, which, as they advanced, faded away, and finally resolved themselves into curiously-configurated hills."[240] Later, in a moment of reflection, Lynch paused to gaze out over "the calm and motionless sea," knowing that "beneath it lay embedded the ruins of the ill-fated cities of Sodom and Gomorrah."[241]

Perhaps Lynch felt daunted by the prospect of dating ruins or the likelihood of retrieving artifacts from the depths of brine and muck. He might have also agreed with the logic of one of his sailors, who thought that, because "all the unbelieving cities of Galilee [had] been brought to naught . . . it is difficult to determine the site on which they once stood."[242]

What seems most probable, though, is that Lynch believed there were superior ways of proving the Bible. As a naval officer, he pointed to the expedition's soundings as the surest evidence. These had revealed a deeper northern basin and a shallower southern one. It also showed that a central depression ran the length of the sea, which Lynch assumed to be the ancient bed of the Jordan River. These findings, Lynch believed, proved definitively that "this entire chasm was a plain sunk and '*overwhelmed*' by the wrath of God." To him, they backed up the geography of the Bible, which stated that Abraham had seen a huge plain where the Dead Sea presently lies. Toward the end of his survey, he scribbled an enthusiastic letter to Mason: "My hopes have been strengthened into conviction," he wrote, "& I feel sure that the results of this survey will fully sustain the scriptural account of the destruction of the Cities of the plain."[243]

There was other geological evidence as well. On the eastern shore of the Dead Sea, the expedition encountered a massive column of salt. This led to speculation that it was the transfigured body of Lot's wife, whom the Bible narrates as having been turned into a pillar of salt for having looked back at the red majesty of God's wrath during the destruction of Sodom and Gomorrah.[244] The party took samples of Lot's wife for further analysis.[245] Secondly, the Protestants could also point to the basin's rocks, which they believed to bear the scars of volcanic activity. Both Edward Robinson and Lynch's friend Matthew Fontaine Maury were among those pious men of science who saw volcanic activity as an instrument of divine will.[246] As Lynch had informed the public in an open letter before his departure, the mere presence of volcanism would serve "to refute the position of infidel philosophers with regard to [the Dead Sea's] formation."[247]

Lynch and his Protestant sailors invested this conclusion with deep national meaning. Nations rose and fell in accordance with their faith and virtue. The United States had to remain pious if it was to preserve God's covenant; if it did not, it would also find itself "scathed by the wrath of an offended Deity."[248]

Having found the results they were looking for, the small band of Christians and Arabs broke camp on May 10.[249] The expedition's Holy Land tour would continue with a visit to Jerusalem, Bethlehem, and the source of the Jordan River, but their scientific work was done. Lynch brimmed with pleasure. The expedition's findings had, in his words, "confirm[ed] to the very letter the history of the Holy Land, as regards the sunken cities."[250] Packed safely in crates and luggage, they would, he was sure, persuade many Unitarians, liberal skeptics, and atheists to return to the evangelical fold.

THE DEAD SEA EXPEDITION AND THE PRESS

By the time that Lynch and his men disembarked in Norfolk, Virginia, in late 1848, they had become the subject of enormous interest.[251] Throughout their absence, many papers had sustained the public's curiosity in the navy's exotic adventure in the Holy Land through periodic updates.[252] Now that the mission had returned, the press eagerly anticipated an official narrative. A statement in the *New York Herald* was typical: "We may expect from them a highly interesting account of their explorations of the Dead Sea, and their adventures in the Holy Land."[253]

No group was hungrier for intelligence than the evangelical community in the United States. The *Christian Ambassador* posited that "the account of their exploration and adventures cannot fail to be highly interesting."[254] Likewise, a writer for the *Christian Palladium* struggled to contain his excitement over reports of the pillar of salt. "Can this pillar be an abiding confirmation of Genesis 19:26?" he asked. "We shall hope to hear more concerning it."[255] No one was prouder than Maury, Lynch's close friend and brother officer. He had been among Lynch's correspondents over the course of the cruise, and in September 1848, he had published a long article in the *Southern Literary Messenger* defending the mission and championing its accomplishments. His words reveal the ways in which the expedition had breached the separation of church and state and sought to Christianize the people of the United States: "By this expedition, problems, great and important in the eyes of Christendom, have been solved by the American government."[256] He believed that Lynch and his team fully deserved "the approving 'well-done' of a Christian people," and that "the whole Christian world with eager interest await his return and the forthcoming of his final Report."[257]

The federal government's support for the narrative was more mixed. In terms of publishing, Lynch received more backing from the Navy Department than from Congress. On the surface, this makes sense. After all, Secretary Mason had approved the project as a useful publicity stunt for an institution that had been outshined by the army during the US–Mexican War. He had assigned two "excellent draughtsmen," to accompany Lynch and produce images and charts for publication.[258] Mason informed Lynch that he hoped his report "will reflect honor on the Naval service," and "gratify the enlightened curiosity of the Christian, and Scientific worlds."[259] No wonder, then, that after Lynch submitted his report to the Navy Department in February 1849, Mason was happy to grant him permission to publish a personal narrative.[260]

Congress, however, was less interested. Though the government printed Lynch's official report in 1849, it was not a pretty publication; Lynch himself felt "ashamed" at its typographical errors and "unseemly appearance."[261] Lawmakers sought to correct this in 1852 with the release of a "very neat quarto volume, handsomely bound and gilt."[262] While precious, the 1852 report included lengthy scientific papers and the engravings of fossil specimens. It was not designed for mass public consumption.[263] Nor did Congress ever support the publication of Lynch's longer narrative, as they had done with Wilkes's account of the Ex Ex. It seems likely that they did not see great practical value in publishing Lynch's *Narrative*. As will be seen in the following chapter, congressmen took a very different approach when it came to publishing the accounts of naval surveys of South America, a region of great expansionist interest to proslavery leaders.[264] In the aftermath of the Navy Department's invasion of the separation of religion and government, Congress, at least, pulled back.

Lynch, however, did not. In turning to the pen, he embarked on a central evangelical strategy for spreading the faith. Indeed, many evangelical Christian organizations saw publishing as a tool for conversion. Edward Robinson, as an author and as the editor of the evangelical *American Biblical Repository*, certainly did so, as did the American Bible Society, whose central goal was to place a Bible in the hands of every free patriarch and householder.[265] Missionary societies, too, used the letters of their field agents to fundraise and spread the faith at home. One Massachusetts law-maker explained his backing for a missionary society in precisely those terms: "Religion," he told his colleagues, "was a commodity of which the more we exported the more we had remaining."[266] Narcissa Whitman was a case in point: she decided to become a missionary to the Cayuse Nation in Oregon because she had grown up reading hagiographies of US missionar-ies and Hawaiian converts.[267]

Lynch had barely put pen to paper, however, when he learned that an-other of his party was planning to beat his commander's account to press.[268] This sailor, conscious of the venture's cultural and national significance, had kept a diary through the entirety of it—on ship, ashore, and even "whilst mounted on the back of a camel."[269] When the expedition rendezvoused with the *Supply* off Syria, the anonymous sailor shared it with the steward for the ship's surgeon, Edward P. Montague, who began writing it up as a book during the voyage home.[270] Soon after his arrival, Montague raced to a publisher.[271]

Montague's text was a rougher, more democratic version of the genteel volume that Lynch would publish later that year. While the aristocratic commander would inscribe his book to his patron Mason, Montague dedi-cated his *Narrative* to the "People of the United States." He even justified the publication on democratic grounds, claiming that he had concluded to publish his "unpretending volume" in order to satisfy the curiosity of "many readers [who] would be unable to pay a large sum" for Lynch's forth-coming book.[272]

Unsurprisingly, Montague's account overflows with working-class na-tionalism and muscular Christianity. A point of emphasis was the unfurling of the flag, or "the stars and stripes of America given to the breeze" at sea, ashore, and even on the surface of the Dead Sea itself.[273] Moreover, the sail-ors themselves take center stage, with Lynch and the officers retreating to the background. Montague unerringly portrays the party's tars as strong, brave, and determined—the ideal citizens of "this great Republican coun-try."[274] "We Yankee boys flinch not," the author averred; "we fear neither the wandering Arab nor the withering influence of disease; we fear neither the heat of the sun nor the suffocating sirocco."[275] In Montague's telling, the "jolly tars" became the heroes; they assumed the mantle of the "bold navi-gators" that Lynch and countless other middle- and upper-class explorers had always claimed for themselves.[276]

As in the domestic United States, the darker underbelly of this paean to democracy was nativist intolerance. Rather than Lynch's story of alliances and cross-cultural friendships, Montague's was the tale of how a band "of healthy, robust, brave and daring fellows" survived a harrowing journey through the land of "the prowling Bedouin Arab."[277] It is a miracle, it seems, that any of them survived their passage "among professional thieves and murderers."[278] Furthermore, Montague's book is speckled with nativist sentiment. The sailors were "thorough-bred Yankee boys" and "true-born" or "true" Americans.[279] This was in contrast to false US citizens, or those of the Catholic faith, whom Montague tellingly italicized as "*Americans.*" At the scene of the pilgrim's bathing, for instance, Montague noted that "there are a few *Americans* here," though "they have been taught to believe in another mode of being cleansed from their sins—by the blood of Christ."[280]

In contrast, Montague and his band emphasized the necessity of faith over sacrament. His book fulfilled the evangelistic purpose of the mission, but for the common man. In Jerusalem, for instance, the seamen brawled with Ottoman soldiers and compared their subsequent arrest and trial to Christ's audience with Pontius Pilate.[281] In another section of his published diary, he imagined what a conversation with a ghost of the sunken cities would look like. Rising from "the immense sepulchre" at the bottom of the Dead Sea, "might he not contrast the privileges of American people at the present day, with the state of things in Sodom and Gomorrah previous to the fatal overthrow? And before he left us, would he not, on the strength of his experience, with warmth and eloquence . . . conjure *us* to listen with believing attention to the precepts and truths of the Bible?"[282]

It is hard to gauge how working-class readers responded to Montague's book. What is clearer is the middle- and upper-class reaction: almost without exception, reviewers trashed Montague's volume as opportunistic garbage. "We are reluctantly compelled to speak of this book," read an article in *Church Review* in July 1849, characterizing Montague's *Narrative* "as barren almost alike of good taste, interest, and information." Across the sea, the *North British Review* pronounced Montague's language "schoolboy balderdash," and "wretched forecastle slang."[283] The *Southern Literary Messenger* thought the publication was a scheme "to take advantage of public curiosity which is now rife with regard to the late remarkable voyage of Lieut. Lynch." "Mr. Montague's book," it judged, "is certainly not the book which public expectation demands."[284] *Godey's Lady's Book* agreed: the "unpretending narrative," it wrote, "create[d] fresh anxiety to see the forthcoming work of Lieut. Lynch."[285]

Part of their criticism derived from a sense that by publishing in advance of his superior officer, Montague had violated social hierarchies. As commander, so it was believed, Lynch had first right to share the results of the expedition.[286] Montague's publication had usurped that right. As other historians have noted, the directors of scientific and archaeological expeditions often had a possessive sense of their missions, frequently conflating their workers' sweat and labor with their own.[287] Lynch was no different; when he learned that Montague's account was in the press, he was furious. He wanted the Navy Department to intervene and halt the publication.[288] Mason demurred, but he sympathized with Lynch's rage: "I do not think that you should be anticipated by any other, who had not the responsibility of the enterprise," he wrote him.[289]

When Lea & Blanchard finally published Lynch's *Narrative of the United States' Expedition to the River Jordan and the Dead Sea* later that year, they unleashed a publishing sensation. The book itself was gorgeous, "a handsome octavo" and a "magnificent library volume," in the words of two reviewers.[290] The publisher spent a good sum—$933—to hire some of best artists in the country.[291] They worked their craft well: through two foldout maps, the Jordan River and the salt cavity of the Dead Sea practically pooled into viewer's laps. Twenty-eight other wood engravings brought the rest of the Holy Land and its denizens to life. Readers could view the "sagacious" Sherif resting at ease, the honorable and "graceful" 'Akil, the balmy source of the Jordan River, and the crusty, desiccated shore of the Dead Sea.[292] Unsurprisingly, consumers quickly gobbled up the first printing, then a second, third, fourth, fifth, and sixth.[293] Bookstores struggled to keep up with demand.[294]

Sales were so quick that Lea & Blanchard decided to issue a cheaper, abridged edition in 1850. Soon, the publisher's Philadelphia offices swarmed with letters from booksellers and individual readers ordering copies.[295] Backcountry book peddlers, meanwhile, were intrigued with the promise of a brisk sale. "I notice that you are about to publish a 'Condensed Edition of Lynch's Expedition to the Dead Sea,'" George Reynolds wrote from Syracuse, New York. "Being a travelling agent, & having seen the large Edition in some Libraries, I think the smaller work will take well." He requested a copy to examine and a list of prices.[296] J. M. Holland, another roving bookseller, concurred. Writing from North Carolina, he believed that he "could dispose of from 2 to five hundred Copies in a County," if the price could be reduced.[297] By releasing a more affordable copy, "the publishers have done a wise and good thing," wrote one reviewer. "They will have the thanks of many hundreds who will now possess themselves of the long coveted book."[298]

HARVEST

Whether popularity actually translated into evangelical converts is hard to determine. What is clear, however, is that evangelical Christians saw Lynch's *Narrative* as a powerful new weapon in the war on biblical skepticism and atheism. As a writer for the *Church Review* put it, "We are glad, for once, to see the pertness of Infidelity put to the blush, by the deep tone of reverence in which the author has written."[299] The Christian reformist *New-York Organ* put it less diplomatically: "Those who incline to sneer at the Scripture account of the fate of the Cities of the Plain, will do well to read Lieut. Lynch's account of his exploration of the Dead Sea."[300] A reviewer for the *Christian Observatory* called the *Narrative* "a sacred charity" that "disarms criticism." "All the geological features of the region," he concluded, "go to confirm the accuracy of the Mosaic narrative of the destruction of the guilty cities of the plain."[301]

As Candy Gunther Brown has noted, nineteenth-century US evangelicals especially valued publications that promoted the Protestant faith.[302] If we approach the evangelical reception to Lynch's work in those terms, his *Narrative* was as Christian as the crucifix. The *Christian Examiner and Religious Miscellany* observed that the expedition's findings were "already flowing amidst the Christian public in various popular publications."[303] In January 1851, for instance, the *Sunday School Advocate* printed a synopsis and extractions from Lynch's account of his sailors' descent of the Jordan.[304] Likewise, the Baptist Edward Thurston Hiscox took Lynch's description of the Jordan River into theological battle with him. He wielded it against those who thought the Jordan was never deep enough for complete immersion.[305] In 1859, the American Tract Society drew on Lynch's writings for *A Dictionary of the Holy Bible, for General Use in the Study of the Scriptures*.[306] In similar fashion, the evangelical enthusiast Fisher Howe cited Lynch early and often in his own account of travels in the Holy Land. Like the naval officer, he hoped his work would bolster "that noble phalanx" of faith, "the teachers of the Sabbath-school and the Bible-class."[307] Little wonder, then, that Lynch was "mentioned everywhere with gratitude" in Christian circles.[308]

While the Dead Sea expedition may or may not have increased the net faith of the United States, it did help usher evangelicals into the explorationist camp. Prior to Lynch's mission, the precise relationship between exploration and religious expansion was mixed. On the one hand, the Bible frequently followed the flag, with explorers opening new areas for proselytizing worldwide.[309] Western navies also offered protection to religious workers, forcing local leaders to respect missionaries and punishing those who did them harm. After the arrival of new evangelists in Samoa in October 1839, for example, Charles Wilkes ordered the crew of the Ex Ex to hold a drill at the mission house. A crowd of Samoans watched as US Navy bluejackets paraded and flashed their bowie knives, cutlasses, and pistols in the hot tropical sun.[310]

In other cases, however, missionaries and naval officers did not see eye to eye. Some evangelists were opposed to the military character of exploring expeditions; when Wilkes tried to convince a missionary on Samoa to carry arms with him for self-protection, the reverend "declared himself averse to the use of fire-arms or any other weapon in the propagation of the gospel."[311] The commercial impetuses for exploration also drew suspicion from some missionaries, who blamed mariners for importing vice into Indigenous societies and treating them inhumanely. Samuel Wells Williams, a missionary who served as an interpreter on Matthew Perry's expedition to Japan, fretted that he was helping connect the Japanese people with opium and other sinful products.[312] Finally, nineteenth-century maritime explorers generally tended to see themselves more as the sons of the Enlightenment than the agents of the Christian world.[313] In 1830, the Russian explorer Otto von Kotzebue published a highly critical account of British and US missionary activity in the Hawaiian Islands. The evangelical press fumed for years.[314]

The Dead Sea expedition helped tilt the scales in exploration's favor. With the publication of Lynch's and, to a lesser extent, Montague's texts, evangelicals saw that naval exploration could be a potent tool for deepening the empire of faith at home and abroad. They could use the power of the federal government and enlist the navy to wage their battles against Catholic immigrants, coarse western pioneers, and especially liberal Unitarians. Lynch's research allowed them to summon the terrible fate of Sodom and Gomorrah and scare sinners and society into embracing their reforms, whether they be temperance laws, immigration restrictions, or the regulation of sexuality and blasphemy. Already stratified by skin color, wealth, and gender, US society was becoming increasingly hierarchical in terms of religious conviction. In evangelical minds, this was well and fine; if the United States was to be a great imperial nation, it needed the proper foundations. What Lynch sought to do was to sink those foundations deep into the bedrock of evangelical Christian faith. That he relied deeply on Muslim agency to do so is one of the more intriguing elements of this unusual tale.

This Christian conversion left other interest groups in the United States wondering: if naval reconnaissance could serve evangelicals, then perhaps the navy could explore the world in pursuit of other, equally specialized imperial aims. Among those who wondered were slaveholders.

CHAPTER 5

Proslavery Explorations
of South America

Passed Midshipman Lardner Gibbon had just sat down to dinner when he found himself subject to an interrogation. As one of two US naval officers conducting an exploring expedition of the Amazon River Valley, Gibbon had split off from his commander in Peru in July 1851 in order to survey the Bolivian tributaries of the great river.[1] Now, during a lively supper at a private home in La Paz, Gibbon had planted himself right next to the "lady of the house."[2] He may have wished that he had sat elsewhere; his hostess expressed great interest in US expansionism, peppering Gibbon with questions about the annexation of northern Mexico and his nation's designs on Cuba. "Turning suddenly," Gibbon remembered, "she looked up and said: 'What are you doing here, Señor Gibbon; do you want Bolivia, also?'"[3] Gibbon explained that the goal of his mission was to help the Bolivians find an easier route to foreign markets. Though his Bolivian companion "approved of the enterprise," she ended the conversation by exclaiming that the "North Americans will some day govern the whole of South America!"[4]

Gibbon had been less than honest with his hostess. As a Southerner and future Confederate army officer, he had a vested interest in exploring South America.[5] Indeed, international actors and US domestic opposition to the extension of slavery in the North American West triggered aggressive schemes for proslavery expansion beyond the United States in the late antebellum era. Such expansionists led the nation into a war that seized the northern half of Mexico, tried to purchase Cuba from Spain, and sought to conquer other Latin American countries through private armies, or filibusters. Most crucial for this chapter, they also ordered the US Navy to investigate possible new slave territories in South America. Following the Amazon expedition's return in 1853, the navy dispatched a second and larger mission to the Río de la Plata watershed. Between 1853 and 1856 and again from 1859 to 1860, the officers and crew of the USS *Water Witch* searched for future slave states along the lush riverbanks of Argentina, Brazil, and Paraguay. Taken together, the missions to the Amazon and the Río de la

Plata demonstrate that naval reconnaissance was more than just a passing fancy for slaveholding elites and their allies. It was, instead, one of the federal government's persistent strategies for resolving sectional tensions and placating Southern white anxieties in the final decade of the early republic.[6]

The navy's proslavery exploring expeditions represent a remarkable transformation in white Southern attitudes toward overseas imperialism. Back in 1829, the South Carolinian slaveholder and politician Robert Young Hayne had crippled the first push for federal global reconnaissance. He had founded his opposition on republican grounds: the best way to preserve a slaveholding republic, in his view, was to limit federal power and focus more on westward expansion than on scientific exploits on the high seas. Oceanic voyages of discovery would result in oppressive taxation, government overreach, and overseas colonies. They would, in his mind, undermine liberty for white men and perhaps even imperil the institution of slavery. By 1850, circumstances had changed; Hayne was long dead, slavery was more entrenched in the United States than ever before, and even John C. Calhoun's thinking had evolved. When projected outward, federal power could be made to serve the cause of human bondage. Instead of a threat, naval exploration could prove beneficial to slaveholders and their interests by expanding the empire of slavery. Supporters even hoped that the navy's surveys of South America would result in precisely what Hayne had once feared: the establishment of US colonies in faraway lands. Once a danger, overseas colonization had become the means to US slavery's salvation.[7]

The slaveholder's conversion to explorationism significantly expanded the coalition's base of support. This was especially so in the halls of power, where proslavery elites predominated in the antebellum period.[8] It was another example of the many ways in which Southern leaders increasingly leaned on federal state power in order to protect slavery in the run-up to the Civil War. As Matthew J. Karp has demonstrated, slaveholders and their allies arranged their political ideologies according to the dictates of slavery. Southern politicians could field the rhetoric of federalism and states' rights when it served this purpose, but they could also back a robust foreign policy establishment for the same end. It was for this reason that such prominent future Confederates as Jefferson Davis and Stephen Mallory could work so diligently to expand the US Army and Navy in the 1850s and then champion secession in 1860–1861; they expected that the military would continue to serve slaveholding interests. In the 1840s and 1850s, therefore, Southern politicians saw the military and diplomatic branches of the federal government not as threats, but as weapons to be wielded on behalf of the South's peculiar institution.[9]

The rise of antislavery forces at home and abroad played an integral role in this gradual proslavery embrace of federal state power overseas. Within the United States, the stinging publications and passionate activism of Black and white abolitionists worried enslavers. They fretted all the more as the US antislavery movement moved mainstream in the 1840s and 1850s. Abroad, a similar change was underway in the British and French Empires. In 1833, Parliament passed a gradual emancipation law that would eventually free all enslaved persons in the British West Indies. While the terms of that emancipation were highly restrictive, the move nonetheless shocked US slaveholders.[10] When France re-abolished slavery in its colonies in 1848, US slaveholders felt even more isolated from the imperial politics of Europe.[11] Far and away, however, it was violent Black freedom fighters themselves who did the most to cause proslavery elites to do an about-face on naval exploration. These were men like François Dominique Toussaint L'Ouverture and Jean-Jacques Dessalines in Haiti, and, in the United States, Gabriel, Denmark Vesey, and Nat Turner. Their willingness to fight for their freedom—to turn "ploughshares into swords"—kept many white masters and mistresses up at night.[12]

Lastly, there were South American factors that convinced Southern leaders and their allies to embrace naval exploration. The navy's proslavery explorations were formulated along lines that paralleled South American creoles' own plans for national development. US naval imperialists knew that many South American elites aspired to modernize their countries by imitating European and US trajectories. Indeed, whether in Rio de Janeiro, Asunción, or Buenos Aires, South American creoles hoped to clear rainforests, remove Indigenous peoples, build railroads, encourage steam navigation, and increase their nation's agricultural output. Often, these plans had powerful racial components; many South American creoles reasoned that the best way to modernize according to Western standards was to convince European and North American whites to settle and establish colonies in their territories. Furthermore, in the early nineteenth century, the United States, Brazil, and Cuba experienced a renewed commitment to slave-based agriculture in what Dale Tomich has termed "the second slavery."[13] For some South American elites, importing white colonists (and, in the case of Brazil, Black slaves) appeared a sure recipe for growth and power. Proslavery officers in the navy tried to take advantage of these economic aspirations; like Gibbon, they masked their imperial missions under the false flag of friendship and commerce.

In spite of the navy's best efforts, its strong backing by various presidential administrations, and significant public interest, no US colonies emerged in South America before the Civil War. Brazilians, alarmed by the US–Mexican War, were highly suspicious of the United States' goals during the navy's survey of the Amazon. After the expedition's return, the mission's progenitor let his enthusiasm get the best of him. In doing so, he confirmed Brazilians' worst fears about the US intentions. In Paraguay, too, the arrogance of US naval officers led to bloodshed in 1855 and a major showdown between Asunción and Washington in 1858. Officials in Argentina and Bolivia, however, were less suspicious, often encouraging naval explorers with hospitality and praise. The question of whether US colonies would have developed in these countries without the US Civil War is an intriguing but ultimately unanswerable one. It seems likely that the postwar exodus of Confederates to Brazil would not have happened, but that is about as far as any historian can venture. What is clearer and more striking, however, is the fact that proslavery imperialists warmed to naval exploration when they discovered its utility. Rather than a passing fancy or a harebrained odyssey, the Amazon and La Plata expeditions represented a concerted effort, on the part of the federal government, to extend the "Slave South" into the Southern Hemisphere.

THE ORIGINS OF PROSLAVERY EXPLORATION

The central figure behind the US Navy's exploration of the Amazon was a brilliant, petite naval officer named Matthew Fontaine Maury. Maury was born in 1806 to a family of white slaveholders near Fredericksburg, Virginia.[14] When he was five years old, the clan resettled in Middle Tennessee.[15] Yet agrarian life suited neither Maury nor his older brother, John, who left to join the navy in 1809. John's letters home ignited Maury's imagination and inspired a lifelong passion for the sea.[16] He followed his brother into the service in 1825, where he quickly won recognition as a competent officer with a gift for science and oceanography. His skills were such that, in 1837, he was offered a chance to serve on the Ex Ex as an astronomer. He declined the appointment, suffering instead a debilitating stagecoach accident two years later.[17] Unable to serve his country on deck, Maury channeled his genius into oceanographic science ashore. Between 1842 and 1861, he served as superintendent of the Naval Observatory and the service's Depot of Charts and Instruments, both in Washington, DC. He became best known for his sailing directions and wind and current charts, which drew heavily on the countless observations submitted to Maury by mariners and naval officers in customized logbooks. Published between 1847 and 1855, they quickened the pace of Atlantic commerce by revealing faster routes than the ones that were being followed at the time. He was showered with praise from presidents, European scientific associations, and writers— including Melville, who described him in *Moby-Dick* as among those who

Figure 5.1 Jesse Whitehurst, *Matthew Fontaine Maury*, circa 1857. Maury tried to use naval exploration to facilitate the settlement of Brazil with US slaveholders and their enslaved persons. He envisioned that proslavery settlers from the United States would eventually revolt and establish a new Anglo-Saxon slaveholding republic. (Courtesy of National Portrait Gallery, Smithsonian Institution, Washington, DC. Object no. NPG.80.164.)

were revealing "the secrets of the currents in the seas."[18] As numerous studies have made clear, Maury was both a giant of nineteenth-century science and an oceanic (especially cartographic) trailblazer.[19]

Yet there was another side to Maury that has received substantially less attention. While he is better known today as the father of modern oceanography, Maury was also an avid proslavery expansionist. He could be critical of slavery and the transatlantic slave trade, but he nevertheless saw the institution as an essential part of the Southern political, economic, and social order.[20] Thus, while he never appears to have owned slaves himself, he identified closely with those who did.[21] In 1861, in fact, he resigned his post as superintendent of the Naval Observatory to serve the Confederacy. In Britain, he bent his talents to buttressing the South's shore defenses and negotiating for Confederate warships. Having devoted his entire professional life to building a US empire of commerce through science, he spent the war years trying to destroy it.[22] For Maury as for other Confederates, there were higher imperial loyalties that could not be denied—to his home state, for one, but also to the empire of slavery.

Before the Civil War, Maury's great apparition was the Haitian Revolution. A complex slave uprising that emerged from the tumult of the French Revolution, the Haitian Revolution resulted in the self-emancipation of Haiti's slaves and tens of thousands of Black and white deaths in the violence that ensued. Skillful Black leaders like L'Ouverture and Dessalines repelled several European attempts to snuff out their revolution. In 1804, they installed a free Black republican government, the first in the Western Hemisphere. US newspapers followed the twists and turns of the Haitian Revolution closely. Many white readers North and South were horrified by the news. Ignoring the crime of slavery and wartime violence against Blacks, they were particularly troubled by reports (sometimes eyewitness ones) of mass executions of whites.[23] Though no slave rebellions in the United States ever approached the scale or success of the Haitian Revolution, white US citizens often correlated domestic uprisings with what had transpired on Hispaniola. Following Turner's slave revolt in Virginia in 1831, for example, Samuel Warner penned a sensational, blood-soaked account of the rebellion. Nearly half of his pages, however, recounted events in Haiti, not the Old Dominion. Due to the "alarming increase of the Black population at the South," Warner warned, white Southerners might witness "similar scenes of bloodshed and murder."[24]

Samuel Warner was not the only proslavery white who feared the growing population of enslaved African Americans in the United States. To Maury and other masters, slaves were reproducing at a "tremendous rate," resulting in a "frightful ratio" of Blacks to whites in the Southern states.[25] Indeed, between the middle of the 1820s and 1860, the number of bondspeople in the United States grew from less than two million to almost four million.[26] The white population, in contrast, seemed to be decreasing as white families sold their slaves and emigrated to the Deep South or West to free territory.[27] Examining such data, Maury foresaw a racial crisis in the offing: "Is the time yet to come when the United States are to be over-peopled with the black race?" he rhetorically asked the secretary of the navy.[28] He felt sure that, if the demographic pattern continued, racial war would be the result. Unless slaveholders could find a way to "be rid of their surplus black population," he wrote, "the time will come . . . when the two races will join in the death struggle for the master."[29] Blacks in the United States were equally certain that more slave revolts were in the offing; shortly after a foiled uprising in Charleston in 1850, one anonymous Black freedom fighter swore that "the colored American people" would again "arise in the majesty of their nature to become free men."[30]

Violent Black resistance caused masters to reflect deeply on their situation. Their concerns took on Malthusian dimensions. Educated thinkers in the United States were well schooled in the population theories of the English economist Thomas Malthus, who postulated that human populations would naturally increase beyond their food supply and therefore inevitably foster crisis. Unlike Malthus, however, slaveholders tended to think in terms of land, not food, as the determining factor in assessing whether the enslaved population was too high or low. Citing history, the slavery apologist Matthew Estes believed that "no improving nation has ever declined so long as it had territory to settle."[31] John Quitman, the former governor of Mississippi and an ever-eager filibuster, argued that acquiring more land was critical to slavery's safety.[32] Southern masters, he wrote, had to "guard against the possibility that a system of labor now so beneficent and productive might, from a redundant slave population confined to narrow limits, become an ultimate evil."[33]

Like Quitman, Maury believed slavery was stable only as long as it was profitable—and that meant having access to virgin land. According to this line of thinking, enslavers and their sons needed a constant resupply of new land either to move to, with their enslaved workers, or to create new markets to sell their unwanted bondspeople. No new territories meant no place to resettle the increasing enslaved population, whether through involuntary migration or the establishment of new markets for human beings. The only conclusion of such a scenario was a Black uprising, another Haiti.[34] It was for this reason that, after Lincoln's election in 1860, Maury would see disaster. "The South is blocked to expansion," he would write a cousin, "and that in itself is death."[35]

The North American West was the most obvious solution, but the state of national politics in the late 1840s and early 1850s worried Maury. He believed, in typical racist fashion, that white masters and mistresses had as much right to move west with their slaves as Northern farmers with their oxen.[36] From his desk at the Naval Observatory, however, he saw the chances for proslavery expansion shrinking. While tension between Northern and Southern states over slavery dates back to the Constitutional Convention, the passage of the Wilmot Proviso in the House of Representatives in 1846 raised the stakes as never before.[37] David Wilmot, a Northern Democrat, introduced an amendment into a wartime appropriations bill that would have banned slavery in any territory that the United States would acquire from the US–Mexican War.[38] Though the measure was rejected by the Senate, it stoked antislavery sentiment in the North, galvanized a "Free Soil" movement among Northerners of both political parties, and alarmed slaveholders.

After the US–Mexican War, white Southerners fretted all the more when they discovered that President Zachary Taylor, a fellow slaveholder, leaned free soil. In 1850, Taylor encouraged California and New Mexico territories to apply for statehood as free states.[39] When Southern politicians protested, he threatened to lead the army into the South and hang any traitors he found.[40] Taylor rejected the compromise measures of his fellow Whig, Henry Clay, and seemed determined to force a showdown with Southern nationalists. His sudden death on July 9 allowed his milder successor, Millard Fillmore of New York, to sign a succession of bills now lumped together as the "Compromise of 1850." This negotiated assemblage accepted California into the Union as a free state, prescribed that settlers of New Mexico and Utah territories would determine the slave or free status of their states, and forged a tougher federal fugitive slave law.[41] The compromise may have extended the life of the Union, but it did not resolve the fundamental tensions among the white body politic. Many proslavery Southerners despised the compromise, viewing it as an attempt to limit the bounds of slavery. In the North, meanwhile, the new fugitive slave law infuriated Northern antislavery leaders of all races.

In this context, Maury hoped naval exploration would offer another option to slaveholders by locating fresh lands for human bondage. As he later explained to a friend, acquiring US rights to settle in the Amazon River Valley would "reliev[e] our own country of the slaves . . . [and put] off indefinitely the horrors of that war of races, which without an escape is surely to come upon us."[42] On April 20, 1850, Maury elaborated on his vision in a letter to his brother-in-law, William Lewis Herndon, a fellow naval lieutenant whom Maury hoped would carry his plans into effect. In it, he claimed to have foreseen a time when the United States had subdued the entire Caribbean basin, including its shores and major tributaries. This "universal Yankee Nation" would be a slave country, growing Southern crops and exporting them east through the Gulf of Mexico and west through a bustling canal across Central America to markets in the Pacific World.[43] No portion of his imagined nation would be more important than the Amazon River Valley, which Maury described as "the only remaining cotton country on this continent" and possibly the "greatest rice region in the world."[44] Herndon's survey would stimulate US and Brazilian interests in opening the Amazon to US commerce and settlement. In doing so, he would initiate a "chain of events" that would "end in the establishment of the Amazonian Republic."[45] Once Brazil granted foreign vessels the right to navigate its inland waters, nothing could "prevent American citizens from the free as well as from the Slave States [*sic*] from going there with their goods and chattels to settle and to revolutionize and republicanize and Anglo Saxonize that valley."[46] Over time, the settlement of the Amazon would gradually decrease the number of Blacks in the Deep South. By forestalling a mass uprising of enslaved persons, Brazil would therefore serve as the "safety valve for our Southern States."[47]

Why did Maury choose Brazil? Simply put, his job led him to it. Indeed, it was Maury's duty, as superintendent of the US Naval Observatory and the navy's Depot of Charts and Instruments, to harness astronomical, tidal, oceanographic, and meteorological data for the benefit of US commerce. Maury was very much like those who headed equivalent astronomical, hydrographic, and cartographic institutions in Britain and France—they all served practical purposes for the benefit of empire.[48] While studying this data, Maury saw evidence that ocean currents brought Amazonian waters north to the Caribbean, where they mingled with the discharged waters of the Mississippi. This made US Atlantic ports, in his words, "the halfway stations between the mouth of the Amazon and all the markets of the earth."[49] In Maury's eyes, the Amazon was simply part of the same waterscape as the Mississippi. His vision was a kind of oceanographic "manifest destiny," with ocean currents providing the same justifications that contiguous territories in North America offered for the conquest of the North American West.

Secondly, Maury chose Brazil because he knew that its planters wanted more slaves. In the late 1840s, Maury could have read popular travelogues of US citizens sojourning in Brazil. These included Daniel P. Kidder's *Sketches of Residence and Travels in Brazil*, a "best-selling" book published in 1845 that "found a place in many southern libraries."[50] He almost certainly studied Wilkes's five-volume narrative of the United States Exploring Expedition. Volume 1 described Rio de Janeiro, its government, and its enslaved population in depth.[51] From such sources, Maury would have known about the Empire's rising demand for slaves. For centuries, Black slaves had powered Brazil's economy. In the era of the "second slavery," however, bonded labor became more important than ever as Brazilian planters discovered just how lucrative slave-grown coffee could be.[52] By the 1830s, Brazil was the leading coffee-growing nation in the world, and the US was its largest market.[53] Brazilian demand for slaves fueled an ongoing and illicit transatlantic slave trade in which US citizens played a prominent part.[54] Between 1845 and 1850, slavers dodged British (and some US) warships and carried a third of a million African bondsmen to the Brazilian Empire.[55]

Finally, Maury may have known that many other white Brazilian elites (including the emperor, Dom Pedro II) feared that the slave trade would "Africanize" the Brazilian population.[56] In this sense, they shared with Maury a common horror of Black fertility. Dom Pedro II and his allies therefore sought to replace African slaves with white immigrants, particularly from northern Europe. Like many other South American creoles in the nineteenth century, liberal Brazilians believed they could improve the nation's character through a process called "whitening." In Jeffery Lesser's words, "whitening" meant that the "population could be physically transformed from black to white through a combination of intermarriage and immigration policies."[57] In 1824, Brazil began offering subsidies to encourage Central Europeans to immigrate. Brazilian agents in German-speaking countries enriched themselves by piling emigrants onto boats and publishing works that espoused Brazil as a promised land.[58] In 1848, Brazil set aside about 275 square miles in every province for white colonies.[59]

Part of Brazil's calculation was defense. Its empire had vast, unsettled frontiers that were exposed to neighboring powers, especially Argentina and Paraguay.[60] Thus, defining national borders through settlement was of particular concern to political elites. When the Platine War erupted between Brazil and the Argentine Confederation in 1851, Dom Pedro II hired some 1,800 German mercenaries. After the war, he hoped they would settle near the Argentine border.[61] Lastly, the government also worried about Indigenous revolutions and slave uprisings, of which there were several real and anticipated ones in the mid-nineteenth century. As in the United States, Black and Indigenous agency was a thing to be feared. Such resistance convinced officials in Rio that having more white subjects would decrease Brazil's vulnerability to foreign and domestic threats.

For all these reasons, Maury's plans for settling the Amazon with slaveholding white families from the United States was congruent with the aims of many governing Brazilians. In fact, it appears likely that Maury concocted his Amazon scheme partly because he expected Brazilian support. He often emphasized, for instance, how US–Brazilian immigration and commerce would develop Brazil's rainforests and freshwater rivers and generally promote fraternal peace and harmony between the two slaveholding nations. As he wrote in 1852, "Let the South . . . cultivate with Brazil the relations of friends and neighbors."[62] Mimicking Maury, Herndon would later promise that US immigration would "prodigiously augment the power and wealth of Brazil."[63] Maury and Herndon's intermediate goal—of acquiring the right for US citizens to settle the Amazon with their slaves—was also well-positioned to interest both sides of the slavery debate in Brazil. Reformers like Dom Pedro II could welcome white Southerners as non-Black immigrants, whereas Brazilian planters could find a novel source for slaves as well as new political allies. The crucial departing point, of course, was Maury's secret vision of revolution and future conquest, but this he squirreled away in private conversations and correspondence.

Maury had little difficulty securing the support of the Navy Department. This is unsurprising, considering that both Taylor's and Fillmore's secretaries of the navy, William Preston and William Graham, respectively, were Southern Whigs who shared Maury's concerns about the future of Southern slavery. Indeed, Maury was quite candid about the expedition's objectives when he wrote Preston to propose it in March 1850: "Would it be wise to transfer the slaves of [the] Mississippi Valley to the Valley of the Amazon?" he asked him rhetorically.[64] When Taylor's passing reset the approval process, Maury was similarly open with Graham; he even sent him a copy of his letter to Herndon.[65] Like many in Washington, Graham was impressed by Maury's intelligence and scientific accomplishments. He respected his opinions and frequently sought his counsel.[66] He therefore showed little hesitation in approving Maury's proposed reconnaissance of the Amazon River Valley, providing $5,000 for the expedition's completion.[67] Crucially, Graham's approval made the Amazon Expedition an official project of the federal government.

Whigs in the executive branch probably thought that exploration would be an uncontroversial way to expand slavery. They knew how desperate slaveholders were to expand their institution; but as constitutional and foreign policy conservatives, they frowned on outright conquest. In the late 1840s, most Whigs, including Taylor, Henry Clay, and Abraham Lincoln, had scorned President James K. Polk's invasion of Mexico.[68] At the same time, they disapproved of plots by private adventurers and filibusters to conquer parts of Mexico, Central America, and the island of Cuba. When a former Spanish army officer named Narciso López amassed a private army to invade Cuba, Taylor sent the navy to blockade him.[69] Maury, himself a Southern Whig, offered another way: Brazil's opening to commerce and colonies, he believed, should not be accomplished by the "hand of violence" or the "strong arm of power," but rather by "science," "diplomacy," and "peace."[70]

Brazil's reasons for providing passports for Herndon and Gibbon are less clear.[71] Following the US–Mexican War, Brazilian elites harbored grave suspicions about US aspirations in Latin America. As Herndon admitted, the Mexican War and filibustering resulted in a "broadly and openly expressed fear of us."[72] It is unclear whether Maury's proposals struck a chord with either those promoting white immigration or those doubling down on a slave-based economy. What appears most likely, however, is that Brazil saw no diplomatic way to refuse. Like US citizens, Brazilian subjects also wanted to appear advanced and developed according to European standards.[73] In international affairs, promoting science was one of the primary means of demonstrating a nation's cultural sophistication and modernity. Since Brazil was in no position to dispatch its own scientific expeditions abroad, the best way for the empire to acquire a liberal reputation was by allowing outsiders in. On the practical side, too, reformists like Dom Pedro II could use the US Navy's reports to further encourage white immigration from the US or Europe, as they saw fit. Cultural and practical imperatives, then, most likely persuaded Dom Pedro II's government to acquiesce to Maury's expedition.

Back in Washington, the naval lieutenant was ecstatic when he heard the news. "Lewis Herndon is off upon his Amazonian Expedition," he wrote to a relative in March 1851. "Ask M. & E. how they would like to have a plantation there. I suppose Lewis will come back with extraordinary yarns & as extraordinary grants, & that he will give us all a country or two apiece at the very least."[74]

THE EXPLORATION OF THE VALLEY
OF THE AMAZON, 1850–1854

Herndon arrived in the high city of Lima in the winter of 1851. By early April, he had received his orders and diplomatic papers and had been joined by his subordinate officer, Passed Midshipman Lardner Gibbon.[75] Secretary Graham's directions charged Herndon and his party to examine the mineralogical, navigational, agricultural, and commercial opportunities of Amazonia. Describing the free navigation of the Amazon River as a national issue of "future importance," Graham explained that Herndon's mission would "enable the government to form a proper estimate as to the degree of that importance."[76] To achieve these objectives, Herndon eventually decided on splitting the surveying party, sending Gibbon and several others to traverse the Bolivian tributaries of the Amazon while he proceeded down the mighty river itself.[77]

After crossing the Andes, the explorers found themselves overwhelmed by the fertility of the lush South American interior. Herndon confirmed Maury's suspicions of the rice-growing potential of the Amazonian floodplains and compared its cornfields to the richest "bottom-lands in Virginia."[78] As he approached the end of the Amazon in January 1852, he

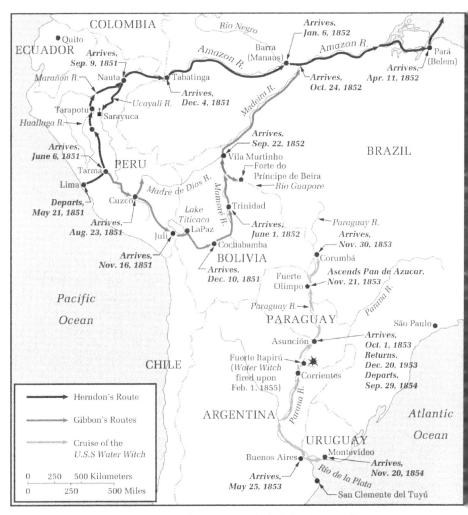

Figure 5.2 Routes of the Amazon and Río de la Plata expeditions,
May 1851–February 1855. (Created by Chris Robinson)

marveled at the network of arable islands that surrounded him. The banks
of these, he believed, could "produce, [*sic*] all that the earth gives for the
maintenance of more people than the earth now holds."[79] Closer to Pará,
on the Amazon's Atlantic estuary, Herndon felt "his heart [swell] with
emotion" as he gazed upon the "rank luxuriance" of fields of sugarcane and
cotton—classic Southern crops.[80]

   What made Amazonia's fecundity especially valuable was its nexus of
navigable rivers. Throughout their journeys, Herndon and Gibbon re-

ported fastidiously on the watershed's capacity for transportation. They made river soundings, judged which rapids were passable, measured the distance between foaming waterfalls, and advised future voyagers whether they should use canoes or steamboats for particular segments.[81] Herndon's writings on the navigability of the Amazon were at times contradictory, but he eventually concluded that the river was perfect for steamboats.[82] Lifting a line from Maury, Herndon wrote that US citizens would soon come to view "the free navigation of the Amazon and other South American rivers . . . as second only in importance to the acquisition of Louisiana."[83]

In their letters and official reports, Herndon and Gibbon portrayed the agrarian and commercial potential of Amazonia as being completely untapped. Like other white US citizens, they believed that South Americans possessed neither the will nor the energy to transform their rich holdings into pastoral paradises. In the words of one US national living in Lima, the result of South American stupor was a vast region "where Nature annually wastes more than would support the population of China."[84] Maury agreed. "In the valley of the Amazon," he wrote, "the plough is unknown; and the American rifle and axe, the great implements of settlement and civilization, are curiosities"; steamboat navigation was "a problem almost untried."[85] The explorers' firsthand accounts appeared to support these claims: "There is scarcely any attempt at the regular cultivation of the earth in all provinces of Amazonas," Herndon wrote.[86]

White US citizens were certain that race and climate explained the lethargy. In Anglo-Saxonist racial theory, the world's productive tropical climates had long spoiled its original inhabitants.[87] Their solution was to import people from the Northern Hemisphere, where the harsher environment had supposedly given rise to a more intelligent and industrious race. Maury expressed this thought clearly when he asked Herndon whether "the great valley of this mighty Amazon" would "be peopled with an imbecile and an indolent people or by a go ahead race that has energy and enterprise equal to subdue the forest and to develope [sic] and bring forth the vast rescources [sic] that lie hidden there?"[88] Even before leaving Lima, Herndon had jumped to the same conclusion, promising Graham that "if Colonies of enterprising & industrious people were planted in these parts, and a free right of Navigation obtained by the Government of the U. States, that an immense impetus would be given . . . to the wealth and power of our Citizens."[89] "Nothing is to be had here but with immigration & settlement," he told the navy secretary in September 1851. The mere "presence of the White Man," would cause Amazonia "to spring into luxuriant life."[90]

Slaves, however, were also necessary. Because the hot and humid climate would enervate white colonizers, planters would need Black slaves to do the hard work of leveling forests, pulling stumps, raising houses and barns, tilling the soil, and planting and harvesting crops. "The constitution of the white man," the proslavery thinker Matthew Estes contended, "is not adapted to long continued exposure in a hot climate."[91] If white Southerners lost their slaves, Estes warned, the "primitive forests" of the Deep South "would again cover our fields."[92] Therefore, white-overseen slavery was the only successful formula for exploiting the fecundity of the tropics. Naval explorers agreed; after leaving Cochabamba, Bolivia, Passed Midshipman Gibbon noted that he was "among fruits and flowers now—a congenial climate for the black man."[93] Herndon arrived at a similar verdict, observing that the "negro slave seems very happy in Brazil."[94] He further noted that the Amazonian manatee "makes capital jerked beef for the Negroes of Brazil," and that the vast schools of freshwater fish could feed slaves, too.[95] As usual, Maury summed it up in one of his articles: "If ever the vegetation there be subdued and brought under," he wrote, "it must be done by the African, with the American axe in his hand."[96]

In the end, Herndon and Gibbon concluded that the Amazon River Valley was a perfect destination for US slaveholders and their human bondspeople. "No territory on the face of the globe is so favorably situated," Herndon wrote of Brazil's capacity for supporting this scheme.[97] If only Brazil would permit foreign immigration, he was certain that "Southern planters," already nervous about "the state of affairs as regards slavery at home, would . . . remove their slaves to that country, cultivate its lands," and "draw out its resources."[98] To slaveholders, Brazil's status as one of the largest slaveholding nations in the Western Hemisphere was an added advantage: in Brazil, at least, Southern settlers would not have to fight for their "liberties" against antislavery activists. As Maury assured a friend in 1851, his Amazon plan was "not seeking to make slave territory out of free, or to introduce slavery where there is none. Brazil is as much of a slave country as Virginia."[99]

The expedition's conclusions were welcome news for Millard Fillmore's pro-Southern administration. The venture had begun, after all, as a federal proslavery project originating out of the executive branch. Their supporting efforts had begun early; while Herndon and Gibbon were preparing to depart Lima in May 1851, Secretary of State Daniel Webster prepared a diplomatic offensive. At the time, Webster was maneuvering to become the Whig nominee in 1852 and needed Southern support.[100] Accordingly, he instructed the US minister to Brazil to begin negotiating with Rio for navigation rights on the Amazon.[101] Other US diplomats in South America joined the effort, including the US minister to Peru, who signed a treaty with Lima in July 1851 that allowed the United States free navigation of the Peruvian

Amazon.[102] In Bolivia, Gibbon persuaded that country's president to de-
clare its rivers open to international commerce.[103] The goal was to pressure
Brazil into embracing a similar course. After Herndon's safe return to the
United States in July 1852, the new secretary of the navy, John Pendleton
Kennedy, put Herndon, and later Gibbon, on special assignment to draft
an official report of their surveys in order to drum up public support.[104]
The navy also sent Herndon's specimens to the US Patent Office in Washington, where visitors could inspect the quality of Amazonian cotton and
manufactures for themselves.[105] In his third annual message in December
1852, Fillmore thanked Herndon for his "interesting and valuable account"
of the Amazon, "which if opened to the industry of the world will prove an
inexhaustible fund of wealth."[106]

Proslavery Democrats in Congress, too, proved to be ardent allies.
When Fillmore handed over Herndon's report, legislators voted to publish ten thousand extra copies in January 1854 and twenty thousand more
copies in April.[107] As Maury worked feverishly to raise popular enthusiasm
with letters and articles in the press, Southern Democrats in Congress became his agents on Capitol Hill. In addition to convincing Brazil to open
the Amazon to foreign navigation, another of Maury's goals was the establishment of a steamship line between a southern port and Brazil's Pará,
at the mouth of the Amazon River. If enacted, the line would provide the
means of transporting Southern settlers and their slaves to Brazil.[108] Southern representatives were eager to help; they shared memorials from Maury
and his allies pleading for a mail line, and, in June 1852, introduced a bill to
put the measure into effect.[109]

All these efforts created significant public interest in the Amazon. *Scientific American* called Maury's plans "a great project."[110] In Iowa, a wandering printer named Samuel Clemens read Herndon's report and found
himself "fired with a longing to ascend the Amazon."[111] Inspired, the future
Mark Twain made short-lived plans for an Amazonian venture, traveling
from Iowa to New Orleans to look for a steamer to Pará.[112] In New York,
meanwhile, the *Times* thought that the Amazon would prove "even more
precious than . . . the mountains of California and the Islands of Japan."[113] In
Cleveland, *New American Magazine* recirculated Herndon's and Maury's
boosterish statements about the commercial capabilities of the Amazon.
It was "indeed the garden of the earth," the magazine asserted, adding that
"to the United States . . . rather than to any other people, does the wealth
of the Amazon belong."[114] Reviewers of Herndon's narrative, meanwhile,
applauded his exploits and his expansionist vision. Herndon "has done his
part, and has done it well," DC's *Daily Globe* declared; "the rest he must
leave to his countrymen."[115] In June 1853, delegates from across the South

met in Memphis, Tennessee. There they approved of Maury's proposal for a mail steamship line between the United States and Brazil and sent Congress a memorial praying for the same.[116] In Washington, a group of slaveholders even approached the Brazilian minister to the United States "with a proposal to settle with one thousand slaves in the Amazon Valley."[117]

Not everyone was as taken with the expedition as the enslavers who had crowded into the Brazilian embassy. The *New-Englander* wondered where proslavery expansion would end: the Union, it wrote, "requires so many safety-valves that we begin to fear the demand will become greater than the supply."[118] Maury even confronted opposition within his own family. When a relative and antislavery advocate, Mary B. Blackford, read about his plans for the Amazon, her spirits sank. "When I came to the part about perpetuating Slavery," she wrote him, "of opening a new and lucrative trade in human beings with all the separation of husbands and wives, mother and child, all the numberless ills that flow from Slavery; and the Slave trade, my heart sickened, yes! If a heart could bleed, mine did when I thought that one so near me had proposed this mighty wrong, the greatest of all wrongs, the degredation [*sic*] of the Human Soul."[119]

Other Black and white antislavery activists were as disturbed as Blackford. In 1854, the Boston-based champion of freedom, William Lloyd Garrison, praised and reprinted a fellow abolitionist's strident criticism. "Brother [Wendell] Phillips was right," Garrison claimed: "the future seems to unfold a vast slave empire united with Brazil, and darkening the whole west."[120] Garrison's former mentee, Frederick Douglass, believed that US expansion into Brazil posed a greater threat to the antislavery cause than the annexation of Cuba.[121] J. H. Banks, a free Black leader in the North, meanwhile, comprehended that the Amazon Expedition was a plot "to unite with Brazil and extend the disunion of slavery to the Pacific."[122] And in Canada, the Black newspaper *Provincial Freeman* thought Maury's plans posed a grave threat to the international antislavery campaign. The writer concurred with Maury's basic assumption that the "surplus slave population" of the South was "now staring [slaveholders] in the face like doom." If, however, white Southerners "could but get a foothold in that rich tropical valley . . . a great slaveholding empire would arise," he warned, "fortifying the system at home and removing for centuries the only danger which threatened it."[123]

The *Provincial Freeman* need not have worried; Brazilians were too wise. While they had granted permission for Herndon and Gibbon to explore their territories, they strongly suspected what the explorers were really after.[124] Upon learning of the expedition, Rio immediately dispatched diplomats to conclude exclusive navigation treaties with its Spanish-speaking neighbors. These agreements were designed to block the United States from gaining access to the Amazon through treaties with neighboring nations.[125] In Cochabamba, Bolivia, for example, Gibbon reported that the Brazilian minister gave an impassioned speech to Bolivia's president and his cabinet at dinner, urging them to give Brazil the sole right to navigate foreign ships on Bolivian waters. When a friend of the president opined that Bolivia's economic development would be better served by letting the United States have that right, the Brazilian minister reminded him that the "North Americans had already annexed a large territory from Mexico, and he considered such a proposition an invitation for them to come to South America."[126]

Maury soon justified the Brazilian minister's concern. One of his articles, "The Amazon and the Atlantic Slopes of South America," proved so popular that he published it as a pamphlet in 1853. When translated and reprinted in the Rio press, this overtly imperialist pamphlet caused a sensation in Brazil. When Brazilians later heard rumors of a filibustering expedition assembling at New York "to force the opening" of the Amazon, they panicked.[127] In a spirit of crisis, patriotic Brazilians picked up their pens. In late 1853, the Brazilian minister to Peru composed a booklet assailing Maury's plans and pledging to resist US annexationism.[128] The following year, a member of Dom Pedro II's royal court, Pedro de Ángelis, published a refutation of Maury's writing in French. Citing US filibustering operations against Spanish Cuba, de Ángelis accused Maury of stirring up "that fever of expansion, of which the unfortunate expeditions against Cuba are the most recent examples."[129] "The Valley of the Amazon," he continued, "appears to him more worthy than Texas of the honor of an annexation to the United States."[130] Another Brazilian writer agreed: "This nation of pirates," he wrote, "wish[es] to displace all the people of America who are not Anglo Saxons."[131]

Brazilian resistance frustrated Maury to no end. He had orchestrated a plot designed to appeal to their interests, only to be discovered as a wolf in sheep's clothing. In desperation, he assailed Brazil as another Japan, which the Fillmore administration had already committed to opening with a fleet of modern warships under Commodore Matthew Calbraith Perry in March 1852.[132] Brazilians stood their ground; they would not open their empire's freshwaters to international shipping until September 1867.[133] By then, the question of whether or not US slavery could be expanded into Amazonia had been rendered mute by the carnage of the US Civil War and the passage of the Thirteenth Amendment.

THE RÍO DE LA PLATA EXPEDITION, 1853–1860

Although Maury and Herndon had failed to open Brazil to Southern settlers, they had been successful at amassing considerable federal and public support behind them. By the start of the Franklin Pierce administration in March 1853, prospects for the further exploration and colonization of South America looked as bright as ever. There were several reasons for this: first, proslavery expansionists had strong allies in the White House in Pierce and his successor, James Buchanan. Both Pierce and Buchanan were "doughfaces" who won the presidency by promising to lead an aggressive foreign policy. Secondly (and perhaps most important), the focus of proslavery exploration shifted south after the Amazon Expedition, toward the fertile watershed of the Río de la Plata. Here, naval personnel encountered creole leaders who admired the United States and wanted to attract white immigrants. If proslavery expansionists were ever to establish slaveholding colonies in South America, the period from 1853 to 1860 represented their greatest opportunity.

Like the Amazon Expedition, the Río de la Plata mission was born Whig. It was the brainchild of Millard Fillmore's Secretary of the Navy, John P. Kennedy. Kennedy was an accomplished fiction writer and a prominent Whig from Maryland.[134] While a slaveholder himself at times, Kennedy does not appear to have ranked slavery as the primary reason for organizing the La Plata expedition.[135] As an Upper South Whig from Baltimore, Kennedy sought to transcend sectionalism in his politics. He believed slavery to be morally wrong but could suffer neither proslavery fire-eaters nor abolitionists, both of whom he saw as extremists.[136] As an antebellum nationalist, however, he recognized that slavery was deeply engrained in the nation's laws, society, and economy. Thus, Kennedy may have been willing to extend the institution alongside other commercial and scientific pursuits. In this context, he likely saw the La Plata expedition as a perfect marriage of both Northern and Southern interests as well as an opportunity to advance Whiggish notions of science and progress.[137] He was certainly excited about it, planning in his journal "with obvious zest" and skirting around Congress to set aside $220,000 of the navy's operational budget to the expedition.[138]

Kennedy was well aware that the expedition had significant backing by Northern commercial interests. Indeed, much of the popular impetus for the mission can be credited to Northern businessmen. Most prominent among them was a Rhode Island native named Edward Hopkins. Hopkins was a failed naval officer and diplomat whose past assignments had caused him to spend time in South America. During his brief tenure as James K.

Polk's special agent to Paraguay in the mid-1840s, he became a born-again believer in Paraguay's economic opportunities.[139] In New York, he won over the American Geographical and Statistical Society in New York, which sent a memorial to Washington urging the federal government to send the navy to reconnoiter the La Plata and its tributaries.[140] Alongside Hopkins, other Northern businessmen also supported the La Plata expedition in word and deed. In 1857, after diplomatic difficulties with Paraguay had interrupted the navy's cartographic work in the Platine region, the Boston Board of Trade sent a petition to Washington urging the completion of the survey.[141] George W. Blunt of New York and Robert Bennet Forbes of Boston were avid supporters as well; Forbes, a China trader and shipwright, even made two new steamers for the Platine survey in the late 1850s.[142] He personally delivered the second steamship to Montevideo from Boston in January 1859.[143]

The precise relationship between these Northern merchants and the proslavery dimension of the navy's missions in South America is unclear. Hopkins, at least, was antislavery enough to hope that a white Platine republic would take shape in Paraguay on the backs of European immigrants. This would ensure that the region would be free of slavery, which he called "the only plague-spot to be found upon our own incomparable body-politic."[144] With the onset of the US Civil War, Forbes would be a fierce supporter of the Union, dedicating his shipyard to producing vessels for the navy.[145] On the other hand, Boston and other industrial and shipping centers in New England profited enormously from slavery. With the notable exception of Hopkins, it is therefore possible that the merchants who backed the La Plata expedition were Northern "cotton Whigs" who foresaw an opportunity to benefit from the extension of slavery as well as US commerce in general.[146]

Whatever Yankee merchants thought, Kennedy's choice to lead the expedition speaks volumes. Lieutenant Thomas Jefferson Page was a Virginian who would later serve the Confederacy as a naval officer and diplomat.[147] Crucially, he was also a mentee of Maury's, with whom he had worked at the Naval Observatory. In that capacity, Page would have been abundantly familiar with Maury's plans for the Amazon, as well as his published statements regarding the fertility of La Plata.[148] Maury even advised Page on scientific instruments and "several" unnamed "important portions of our work"—perhaps slavery.[149] Regardless of Maury's precise advice, Page's later writings would strongly suggest that he envisioned an extension of his mentor's original Amazon scheme into the La Plata region.[150]

As before, South American politics played an important role in the genesis of the Platine expedition. In 1853, the Argentine Confederation was emerging from an era of brutal authoritarian rule under Juan Manuel de Rosas. In 1851, Rosas had been deposed by an alliance comprising Brazil, Uruguay, and two breakaway Argentine provinces. One of Rosas's own generals, Justo José de Urquiza, took his place at the head of the Argentine Confederation.[151] Kennedy saw Urquiza's ascension to power as a major opportunity for US commercial expansion. Whereas Rosas had barred foreign vessels from the Río de la Plata and the Paraná (one of its major tributaries), Urquiza threw the great river open to international shipping.[152] "The seal of many navigable waters," Page would later write, "was thus broken."[153] In December 1852, Kennedy reported to Congress that the La Plata expedition had "grown out of the recent decree of the Provisional Director of the Argentine Confederation," which had opened "a vast territory of boundless resource." Argentines and their neighbors, he promised, were "ready to welcome the first messenger of commerce and throw their treasures into his hands."[154]

Kennedy was right that many elites in the confederation would celebrate an influx of US nationals. Liberal Argentines aspired to French and US models of development and hoped that Urquiza would modernize Argentina along similar lines. One of the future presidents of modern Argentina, for example, Domingo Sarmiento, believed that the United States formed the preeminent template for Argentina's development. He especially praised US immigration policy, writing wistfully of the "human torrents . . . pouring into the primitive forests" in what he called the "newest," "youngest," and "most daring republic on the face of the earth."[155] One of Sarmiento's intellectual and political rivals, Juan Alberdi, also had high encomiums for the United States. Like Sarmiento, he believed that South America's "chief foe" was the "vast, unpopulated territory, which [kept] the scattered inhabitants isolated and unsuccessful."[156] He argued that Argentines should "yield to the foreigner" and witness "what intelligent immigration can do in promoting the civilization of the country."[157]

Pierce's election in November 1852 cut Kennedy's tenure at the Navy Department short, but it may have actually accelerated the United States' plans for La Plata. The incoming Democrats of the Pierce administration harbored little of that party's moral misgivings about militant foreign policies. To many white Southerners, in fact, Pierce's election in 1852 seemed a godsend. When the results of the election became known, slaveholders feted his election "with bonfires and torchlight parades."[158] In his inaugural address on March 4, the new president thrilled proslavery imperialists by pledging not to "be controlled by any timid forebodings of evil from expansion."[159] Furthermore, Pierce was a major supporter of Maury's plans for opening the Amazon; in his first annual message, Pierce urged Brazil to join its Spanish-speaking neighbors and open the "great natural highway" of the Amazon River to foreign navigation.[160] In December 1854, Pierce returned to the Amazon in his second annual message. While crowing about new commercial treaties with Paraguay, Uruguay, and the Argentine Confederation, he admitted that "the same success has not attended our endeavors to open the Amazon," and pledged to continue negotiations.[161]

Yet for all the promises, sectional animosity crippled both Pierce's and Buchanan's efforts to extend slave territory. Above all, the Kansas–Nebraska Act of 1854 hamstrung Pierce's expansionist agenda. By opening the Kansas and Nebraska Territories to slavery through popular sovereignty, the act repealed the Missouri Compromise line, which had previously prevented the extension of slavery above the 36° 30′ parallel.[162] Northern backlash convinced Pierce to abandon the pro-Southern foreign policies that he had earlier supported.[163] For example, while he had previously encouraged the filibustering plans of former Mississippi Governor John Quitman, he did an abrupt about-face in May 1854. If Quitman sailed, Pierce warned, he would use federal neutrality laws to stop him.[164] Pierce's sudden change of tack was too little, too late: the Democratic Party bore deep losses in the midterm elections. In late November, the publication of the Ostend Manifesto further embarrassed the administration. Composed by the US ministers to Great Britain, France, and Spain, the Ostend Manifesto declared that the US had the right to seize Cuba if Spain refused to sell her.[165] Outraged, Northerners pounced. Their resistance ensured that the only territory either Pierce or Buchanan acquired was the meager Gadsden Purchase from Mexico in 1853.[166]

With intransigent Yankees blocking forceful diplomacy in Central America, expansionists had to look for alternative ways to extend slavery. One such method was filibustering, which achieved some notable successes in the middle of the 1850s with William Walker's subjugation of Nicaragua and reinstallation of slavery in 1856.[167] In spite of popular support for Walker and his comrades, filibustering never overcame the stigma of its illicit nature among elected officials.[168] For some Southern Democrats, such a supposedly civilized institution as slavery could be extended only through noble and lawful means.[169] In 1858, for example, Congressman Lucius Quintus Cincinnatus Lamar of Mississippi claimed that he not would let slavery be expanded by "the hands of marauding bands, or violate [its] sanctity by identifying [its] progress with the success of unlawful expeditions."[170] Page agreed, arguing that filibustering would neither "promote our commercial interests nor advance civilization."[171]

The solution was exploration. Naval reconnaissance offered a legal alternative to the brash violence of filibustering, especially if exploration resulted in treaties favorable for US immigration and colonization. Even better, it promised to promote science and commerce—thereby appealing to transnational ideals of progress in the nineteenth century. Proponents therefore emphasized the scientific and commercial goals of the expedition over its proslavery agenda. When Page finally reached Asunción on October 1, 1853, and held an interview with Carlos Antonio López, Paraguay's dictatorial president, he explained that his goals were to negotiate a treaty of friendship and commerce and "to extend and enlarge the bounderies [*sic*] of Science."[172] On learning that the US chargé d'affaires to the Argentine Confederation had already negotiated a commercial treaty, Page flattered López as an enlightened patron of natural history and claimed that Paraguay was too remote for the United States to have any interests in it besides science.[173] Humbly, he asked the president's permission to explore the Paraguayan tributaries of the La Plata.[174]

López was inclined to gratify Page. Like his South American neighbors, López desired to modernize along Western lines. He had come to power following the isolationist regime of a brutal doctor-turned-dictator named José Gaspar Rodríguez de Francia. Francia was censured time and again in the court of global opinion, and López desired a different reputation—even if his own suppressive policies did not depart significantly from Francia's.[175] Promoting scientific discovery, he believed, would increase Paraguay's cultural clout in the eyes of foreign governments.

López also probably thought that the United States' survey would bolster Paraguay's defensive capabilities. In 1853, Paraguay was a nation surrounded by enemies. The Argentine Confederation had long refused to recognize Paraguayan independence, viewing the country as a rebellious province. The Empire of Brazil, meanwhile, seemed eager to expand westward into Paraguayan territory. As a result, López concluded that he had to jumpstart the nation's military arsenal by investing in European arms, equipment, warships, and especially training.[176] Thus, López may have viewed Page's expedition as an opportunity to learn more about the strategic contours of his riparian country and to forge closer ties with a nation capable of providing military training and technology. In fact, Pierce tried to capitalize on this interest directly by instructing Page to give López "howitzers and boxes containing Shrapnell Shells and canisters."[177] Finally, López hoped that the United States would become a main trading partner. For all these reasons, he assented to Page's mission in and around Paraguay.[178]

As the *Water Witch* trudged up the La Plata and its tributaries, Page found himself overawed by the region's agricultural promise. "Nature," he wrote, "seems to have exhausted her bounty upon these Argentine States."[179] The fertility of Platine soil was such that, with proper equipment, the "labor of one man would be equal to that of ten in regions less favored."[180] Best of all, the soil and climate appeared well adapted to traditional Southern crops like cotton, tobacco, rice, sugarcane, and indigo, but they could also produce wheat and corn. Its Chaco grasslands, meanwhile, made for fine grazing land for cattle and sheep.[181] Such findings confirmed the predictions of Page's mentor Maury, who claimed that the La Plata region "has all the agricultural capacities . . . of India."[182] Just as important, the Río de la Plata and its tributaries would allow steamboats to bear agricultural products to market.

Through his publications and official correspondence with the Navy Department, Page argued that South Americans were ill equipped to take full advantage of this bounty. "The people of the Country are not at this time prepared to encounter labor," he told the secretary of the navy, adding that "energy and enterprise form no part of their Character."[183] In March 1854, he predicted that "until immigration shall have reached such a point as to produce an agricultural population," the Paraguayan cotton industry would continue to languish.[184] From the Argentine state of Corrientes in August 1854, Page again commented that "the Soil is not cultivated because laboring men are not to be had," and bemoaned the "natural apathy and want of energy of the landholders."[185]

As Page's use of the term *natural* suggests, the solution to unlocking La Plata's commercial promise was a racial one. Like many whites in the mid-nineteenth century, Page believed that race was an inherent biological category that shaped a person's physical and mental capacities. In this context, the creole elites and mixed-race farmhands who managed landed estates would have to be joined by Anglo-Saxon landowners who had the ambition and determination to cultivate La Plata's rich soil. "Until the introduction of a foreign, laboring population," Page assured the Navy Department, "the resources of the country must remain dormant."[186] La Plata may have been "blessed by nature," but only an "agricultural population" could reap Heaven's reward.[187]

Intriguingly, Page did not discuss slavery openly, either in his correspondence or publications. The closest he came to directly broaching the subject were those occasions when he mused that Indigenous locals might form "a useful population."[188] Yet while he appears to have contemplated some form of coerced Indigenous labor, Page anticipated that most of the manpower in La Plata would come from Black slaves. He knew, however, that he had to keep his proslavery ambitions quiet in order to curry favor with Northern commercial allies and South American creoles. Page's silence on slavery was therefore strategic. He had learned from Maury's mistakes regarding Brazil.

Despite his caution, Page's vision for La Plata surfaces when contextual-
ized in a larger body of proslavery thought. Like other Anglo-Saxonists,
Page believed that Blacks were far better equipped than whites for agricultural labor in warmer climates. The proslavery apologist Estes expressed
this theory perfectly in his *Defence of Negro Slavery* in 1846. "The genuine
Caucasian race has never pursued agricultural labor successfully in very
hot climates," he wrote. "Wherever this race has flourished in hot countries, they have had the African to till the soil."[189] In his *Sociology for the
South*, George Fitzhugh, one of slavery's greatest champions, declared that
Blacks were "admirably fitted for farming."[190] When Mississippi secessionists sought to justify their parting from the Union in 1861, they portrayed
secession as an attempt to protect slavery's agricultural productivity, writing, "By an imperious law of nature, none but the black race can bear exposure to the tropical sun."[191] Familiarity with the ideology of environmental
racism reveals Page's true intentions: when he wrote about La Plata's need
for importing "laboring hands" and an "agricultural population," he meant
enslaved Blacks and their white masters.[192]

Indeed, the aggregate of Page's writings during and after the expedition
reveals that he envisioned La Plata as the future scene of Southern colonialism. His letters to the Navy Department, his official report, and his final
published narrative in 1859 read as booster literature for enterprising merchants and slaveholders. After climbing the Pan de Azúcar (present-day
Fuerte Olimpo, Paraguay) in November 1853, Page gazed out from its summit upon the steamy jungle and imagined a "great predestined future" for
what he called the "fairest unbroken extent of cultivable land in the world"
outside the Mississippi River Valley.[193] If only Bolivia, Paraguay, the Argentine Confederation, and Buenos Aires could unite under a federal government, guarantee religious liberty for Protestant Christians, and invite "new
populations—above all, to cultivators and artisans," the result would be a
"South American Republic, which would advance to a zenith of unprecedented power."[194] Neither filibustering nor violent revolutions would be
required to "place the inhabitants of these regions under the beneficent
influences of a great republican civilization."[195] Instead, white immigrants
and their slaves would gradually transform the landscape, people, and institutions of this imagined nation until US annexation.[196]

Like Page, Argentine officials also understood that the establishment of
US colonies within their nation's borders would fulfill their progressive visions and facilitate the development of the Platine watershed. When Page
first arrived at Buenos Aires in May 1853, for instance, Urquiza ordered all
Argentine officials to aid the expedition.[197] Later, the governor of Corrientes told Page he believed that white immigration was the "only remedy

for the existing evil" of laggard economic development.[198] He hoped Page's surveys "would stimulate immigration and commercial enterprise toward La Plata."[199] Similarly, the governor of Santa Fe claimed that the "resources of this productive Country can be developed only by the introduction of a foreign population." He informed Page that he was prepared to offer immigrants the "most liberal inducements."[200]

Page's arrogance soon spoiled that invitation. At the time of Page's visit, López was facing steep boundary disputes with Brazil. He was determined to enforce territorial control over Paraguayan rivers; accordingly, he asked Page not to extend his surveys beyond the country's territory during his journey up the Paraguay River in the fall of 1853. When Page ignored these directives and sailed as far as Corumbá, Brazil, López fumed that it had set a dangerous precedent that Brazil could use against him.[201] Later, when Page intervened in a feud between López and a US businessman-turned-consul, the dictator exploded in rage. In response, Page ushered the consul and other US nationals to the *Water Witch* and fell back downriver to the Argentine Confederation. Relieved, López forbade all foreign warships from entering Paraguayan waters.[202]

Once again, Page disregarded the president's edict. He directed Lieutenant William Jeffers to take the *Water Witch* and complete the survey of the Paraná River, which formed Paraguay's southeastern border, while he explored another tributary of La Plata in Argentina. Jeffers's exploration would have to pass by the Paraguayan fort of Itapirú on its way upriver. On February 1, 1855, while looking for a safe channel, the *Water Witch* brazenly crossed into the Paraguayan side of the river right under the guns of Itapirú while looking for a safe channel. Paraguayan defense forces hailed the *Water Witch* repeatedly, but Jeffers ignored them.[203] Itapirú opened fire. The shots blasted the ship's wheel and mortally wounded a quartermaster.[204] As the *Water Witch* beat a hasty retreat, Jeffers fired back. He later estimated that his cannons killed as many as fifteen Paraguayan soldiers.[205]

The United States' immediate response to Itapirú was mixed. Page, of course, was outraged, but the commanding officer of the Brazil squadron refused Page's pleas to grant him additional guns and men to "knock down Itapirú" and make independent war on Paraguay.[206] Pierce's secretary of state, William Marcy, may have been convinced by the testimony of Edward Palmer, a tar who had been on the *Water Witch* at Itapirú. The "conduct of the W. Wich [sic] was wrong," Palmer admitted to Marcy, calling "the attack upon her . . . justifiable."[207] Pierce, for his part, was feeling increasingly paralyzed by the nation's growing rift over Kansas. Thus, while US newspapers carried headlines like "A SPECK OF WAR," no storm clouds seemed imminent in the affair's immediate aftermath.[208]

ATTACK UPON THE WATER WITCH.

Figure 5.3 *Attack upon the* Water Witch, from Thomas Jefferson Page, *La Plata, the Argentine Confederation, and Paraguay* (New York: Harper & Brothers, 1859, 306). (Courtesy of Library Company of Philadelphia)

James Buchanan set a different course. In December 1857, he told Congress he would dispatch a special commissioner to Paraguay and asked for congressional authorization for a fleet of warships to accompany him.[209] In October 1858, a massive US armada consisting of nineteen vessels, almost 2,500 men, and more than two hundred guns sailed south for the Río de la Plata. It was, noted *Harper's Magazine*, "the largest naval force which our Government has as yet fitted out"—larger even than Commodore Perry's famous mission to Japan.[210] Page sailed as its flag captain. In the winter of 1859, Buchanan's special commissioner persuaded López to apologize for the Itapirú affair, provide $10,000 to the family of the slain quartermaster, and sign a new commercial treaty.[211] The restoration of diplomatic relations reopened the rich inland nation to reconnaissance. Page returned to La Plata, and, between March 1859 and March 1860, completed his survey.[212]

The Paraguay Expedition of 1858 showed how proslavery expansionists had come to view naval exploration as a potent tool. Given the federal government's extended interest in opening the La Plata region to Southern settlement, it seems likely that Buchanan hoped to unfreeze the process of exploration and colonization. The naval composition of the expedition itself shows that it was more for show than actual force. Most of the fleet's guns were mounted on deep-draft warships, which would have been un-able to reach Asunción if diplomacy failed. Only a handful of the armada's vessels, totaling about twenty to twenty-five guns, could actually sail into Paraguayan waters. Such a force would have been greatly outmatched by Paraguay's navy and river fortifications.[213] Even Buchanan's cabinet was pessimistic about the expedition's chances if it came to war; they privately admitted that "the Expedition will be defeated, should President López de-termine to fight."[214] But López was not the audience—white Southerners were. Buchanan's massive armada may have sought to reunite a fracturing nation, as Gene Smith and Larry Bartlett have suggested. However, it was also meant to reassure white slaveholders that Buchanan, despite his fail-ures to acquire new slave territory, still had their interests at heart.[215]

FALLOUT

As this chapter has sought to argue, the 1850s witnessed the genesis of a third, previously unrecognized method of proslavery expansionism. With further conquests in Latin America unpalatable and the diplomatic pur-chase of Cuba unlikely, proslavery elites in the executive branch sought creative means of expanding the "Slave South." Domestic affairs, including Northern obstruction to slavery's extension in the North American West and fears of racial warfare at home, heightened their sense of urgency. In this context, naval exploration emerged as a viable method of expanding the boundaries of US slavery. Part of its viability was that naval surveyors appeared poised to meet a warm reception in South America. Many South American creoles and governing elites in the nineteenth century sought to develop their nations along European lines, especially through white im-migration and colonization. Expansionists like Maury, Kennedy, and Page knew this; their goal was to hijack South American ambitions.

They sold their program better at home than abroad. The proslavery surveys of South America opened white Southerners' eyes to the benefits of naval exploration. This realization came on the back of an earlier one: in the 1840s, some Southern Whigs, fearful of British imperial abolition-ism, had become navalists. It had been their hope that in the event of a war between the United States and Great Britain, "wooden walls" would block the Royal Navy from unleashing abolitionism by the sword in the slave-holding South.[216] Now, in the 1850s, they had a further epiphany: the navy could actively work to extend, not just defend, slavery. Like many other white constituencies in the early US republic, slaveholders realized that state-sponsored voyages of discovery were a means of promoting their own interests. Because the white South controlled much of the key branches of the federal government in the late antebellum period, it is hard to overstate the significance of this development for the explorationist coalition.[217]

Nonetheless, there were costs for the coalition as well. Abolitionists like Frederick Douglass, Mary Blackford, and William Lloyd Garrison were alarmed by what one Black Canadian called a "stupendous scheme of the Slave Power."[218] And while neither the Amazon nor the La Plata expeditions aroused anything close to the antislavery hysteria provoked by the Kansas–Nebraska Act, the Ostend Manifesto, or the Dred Scott decision, they certainly did not help the growing sectional divide of the 1850s. For those who knew the evil that was "the demon Slavery"—whether in their own bones or through the experience of others—the proslavery missions in the Southern Hemisphere must have bestirred great anxiety and trepidation.[219] Like Maury, they saw the possible extension of US slavery into South America as a game changer.

Proslavery exploration also summoned significant opposition from South Americans themselves, especially in Brazil and Paraguay. While the Amazon expedition may have influenced the emigration of defeated Confederates to Brazil, these exhausted, war-weary immigrants were a far cry from the confident masses of slaveholding families and enslaved persons that Maury had foreseen subduing the Amazonian jungle.[220] Similarly, the one watershed most thoroughly mapped by the United States outside its own borders—the Río de la Plata and its tributaries—never became the system of arteries of the "South American Republic" that Page had envisioned from the top of Brazil's Pan de Azúcar.[221] The failure of US colonialism in South America owes much to the disruption of the US Civil War, yet South American resistance also stymied Maury's dreams of extending the Empire of Slavery from Kansas to Tierra del Fuego. Writing of the postbellum white South, W. E. B. Du Bois once observed that "it is a hard thing to live haunted by the ghost of an untrue dream; to see the wide vision of empire fade into real ashes and dirt."[222] Such was to be Maury's fate—there would be no "universal Yankee Nation" after all.[223]

Lastly, the navy's proslavery labors in South America had powerful implications for the United States' old quest for European esteem. Nowhere was this the case more than in Great Britain. Once the world's greatest slave traders, Britons had begun tilting toward antislavery in the late eighteenth century. That process accelerated with the end of the Napoleonic Wars.[224] After Waterloo, British subjects could rally around antislavery as a new cause célèbre that promised to unite their diverse ethnic nation and broad empire.[225] After Parliament's establishment of a gradual abolition program in the British West Indies in 1833, the United Kingdom could assume a higher moral ground than the United States on the global stage. Britons made good use of it, often pointing to slavery whenever white US citizens crowed too loudly about their nation's commitment to freedom.[226] And like Brazilians, they saw right through the veil that Maury had sought to spin in the Amazon; as one London reviewer of Herndon and Gibbon's *Narrative* put it, "Something very like Texan annexation peep[ed] out" of Herndon's orders. "Slavery," he noted, "improved and *enlarged*, forms a part of the gallant traveller's [*sic*] notions for civilizing South America."[227]

For white US citizens who sought the respect of the United Kingdom and other "Great Powers," slavery was a problem. "Slavery, in this age," opined the London *Times*, "is a deep blot upon any country."[228] The budding naturalist Charles Darwin agreed. When he visited Brazil in 1832 during his famous cruise on the HMS *Beagle*, he was disgusted with the horrors of human bondage. When the *Beagle* finally quit Brazilian waters, Darwin thanked God and pledged "never again [to] visit a slave-country." "It makes one's blood boil," he penned in his journal, "to think that we Englishmen and our American descendants, with their boastful cry of liberty, have been and are so guilty."[229] As Darwin knew, great nations were supposed to be just as well as mighty. If the United States was to ever approach that status in British perception, it had to prove that it could be both.[230] With slavery the law of the land in the early republic, white US citizens had to find a national claim to moral righteousness somewhere else.

CHAPTER 6

Arctic Exploration and US–UK Rapprochement

For those living in southern England in 1849, April must have been a disappointment. Late that month, a great blizzard waded through, burying everything in its path. In County Kent, southeast of London, the high snow drifts even swallowed a carriage.[1] The change in weather could not have helped Lady Jane Franklin's spirits. Holed up in her large, five-story terrace house at Bedford Place, London, Franklin suffered frequent bouts of fear, anxiety, and depression.[2] The reason was simple enough: her husband had been gone for far too long. In May 1845, Sir John Franklin and 138 officers and crew had sailed from England aboard the HMS *Terror* and *Erebus*. Their mission: to pursue Arctic science and discovery.[3] They were relatively well provisioned, with supplies for three years. But now it was nearly four years later, and there had been no word from Sir John or his men. In 1848, the Admiralty had sent out a rescue operation "in three divisions"; however, these had all stalled for various reasons. Lady Franklin was desperate. She ached to know John's whereabouts, his health, whether he was even alive. Any "survivors of so many winters in the ice," she reasoned, "must be at the last extremity."[4]

Determined to seize any last chance of rescuing her husband and his comrades, she turned abroad for assistance. Moved by her entreaties, Tsar Nicholas I pledged to search the Russian portions of the Bering Strait. Lady Franklin next penned a letter to Zachary Taylor, president of the United States. She knew from a visit in 1846 that US citizens admired Sir John and his many contributions to Arctic geography.[5] Given the porous boundary between the US and the UK press, she likely knew that her husband's fate was a major subject of speculation among white US citizens.[6]

On April 4, 1849, Lady Franklin put the finishing touches on her letter to Taylor. She crafted her message carefully, appealing to US national pride and to white citizens' desires for international prestige: "I address myself to you at the head of a great nation," she began, "whose power to help me I cannot doubt." After summarizing the shortcomings of the three

British expeditions dispatched in the summer of 1848, Lady Franklin asked for his help. "I am not without hope," she told Taylor, "that you will deem it not unworthy of a great and kindred nation to take up the cause of humanity, which I plead in a national spirit, and thus generously make it your own." Noting the tsar's promises, Lady Franklin anticipated the "noble spectacle . . . if three great nations, possessed of the widest empires on the face of the globe, were thus to unite their efforts in the truly christian [*sic*] work of saving their perishing fellow men from destruction." She closed her letter with a gendered appeal to chivalry: only the "intense anxieties of a wife" had inspired "the fearlessness with which I have thrown myself on your generosity."[7]

Secretary of State John M. Clayton responded to Lady Franklin in a reassuring and sympathetic public letter on April 25, 1849. He portrayed the United States as a civilized, generous, and compassionate nation that had been deeply moved by her plight. Lady Franklin's appeal, Clayton wrote, was "such as would strongly enlist the sympathy of the rulers of the people of any portion of the civilized world." He praised John Franklin's "heroic virtues" and his willingness to endure "sufferings and sacrifices . . . for the benefit of mankind." The chief US diplomat reproduced the gendered and ethnic themes of Lady Franklin's letter, writing that "the appeal of [Sir John's] wife and daughter in their distress has been borne across the waters, asking the assistance of a kindred people." Clayton promised to encourage Yankee whalers to help, and that he would give them the most up to date information on the Franklin search. Lastly, he pledged that the president would do all he could "to meet this requisition on American enterprise, skill, and bravery."[8]

Thus began the United States' participation in what Jane Franklin and her family called "the Search," an international quest to either rescue Franklin and his men from the Arctic or uncover their fate.[9] In all, thirty-six expeditions sought to resolve the mystery of Franklin's disappearance in the mid-nineteenth century. Most were British, either public or private, but several came from the United States. None saved Franklin or any of his missing sailors, and some of their members even died. Only one expedition found any evidence of the lost Britons—and that was bare enough, raising more questions than answers. And then there was the fact that all of these missions were too late: unbeknown to all but a few Inuits, the early autumn ice had seized Franklin and his crew off Prince of Wales Island, Canada, in September 1846.[10] Arctic scurvy snuck aboard, striking the icebound men.[11] Franklin died of the disease on June 15, 1847.[12] With provisions dwindling, his second-in-command, Captain Francis Crozier, ordered the expedition to embark on an impossible journey: they would attempt to reach the outposts of the Hudson's Bay Company, well over a thousand miles away. It was a desperate measure, undertaken, perhaps, only to preserve morale in the face of certain death.[13] Just as Crozier feared, not a soul would make it. As the march deteriorated, cannibalism helped some stagger on for a few more days.[14]

From the humanitarian perspective, therefore, the US Arctic missions were complete failures: there was no dramatic rescue, no material assistance given to Franklin or his men. From a diplomatic and imperial perspective, however, they could not have been more successful. The US participants of the Franklin search sincerely wanted to find the famed British explorer and his men, but they also wanted more: they wanted British respect. Having consolidated white support at home, explorationists now circled back to their original purpose of cultural admission into the ranks of the leading European powers. Their final goal was to convince the British to buy into the explorationist vision of a great and civilized United States. As this chapter shows, they succeeded beyond their wildest imaginations.

Historians of US–UK relations have generally missed the crucial role of Arctic exploration in US–UK rapprochement.[15] The scholarly literature recounts a series of thaws and freezes from the late eighteenth century through the twenty-first, with "the first rapprochement" occurring as early as the period from 1795 to 1805.[16] The more common understanding, however, has been that the modern foundations of the US–British "special relationship" were laid in twentieth century, over the course of two world wars and the Cold War. What historians of US–UK relations have failed to recognize is that one of the early eras of rapprochement occurred in the 1850s as a result of Lady Franklin's letter. The willingness of US citizens to risk life, limb, and expense in uncovering Franklin symbolized, in US and European eyes, that the United States possessed the genteel mores of a great and generous nation. Before the United States and Britain faced Germany in 1917–1919 and 1941–1945, or stood shoulder to shoulder against Stalin in the Cold War, they fought the Arctic.

The polar rapprochement of the 1850s had significant racial underpinnings.[17] Indeed, US and British actors saw US–UK cooperation in the Arctic as a saga of Anglo-Saxonhood in which "kindred" peoples had united together against nature in "the cause of humanity."[18] Though not in the least successful as search and rescue operations, US and British crews had nonetheless stood side by side as brothers and had persevered in the harsh Arctic environment. The publications, speeches, and press reports that flowed from that racial unity fed into a larger current of Anglo-Saxonism in Britain and the United States. What happened in the

Arctic—or, more accurately, what was said about what happened in the Arctic—supported white supremacy in both imperial nations. Rapprochement in the Arctic was therefore similar to the ways in which white Unionists and ex-Confederates would later find reconciliation along racial lines in the late nineteenth century.[19]

There were also powerful, gendered, and medievalist elements to this Arctic rapprochement.[20] Sir John was a knight—literally—and his distraught, bereaved wife was the picture of ladylike devotion in the Victorian Age. Lady Franklin used the ethos of chivalry to magnificent effect, attracting powerful, ambitious, and dedicated men to her side. Some died while pursuing her aims, while others, like US Navy surgeon Elisha Kent Kane, returned home in broken, worn-out bodies.[21] At least they achieved fame; hundreds of other, less-powerful men found their lives and health jeopardized by the international effort to rescue Lady Franklin's husband or discover his doom. Among them was the Arctic sailor William Godfrey, who accused US leaders of abandoning their masculine rationality in the face of Franklin's feminine emotionality. For Godfrey, at least, the whole thing was a farce, an upper-class chivalric sham.[22]

US elites saw things differently. They supported Arctic exploration not only because of cultural notions, but also because they saw the tangible benefit in doing so. The bitterness that beset the US–UK relationship in the 1850s has largely been forgotten by the larger public. The US predation of northern Mexico scared Britons as well as Brazilians. The British Empire continued to hold on to colonies and protectorates in Central America and the Caribbean, and many white US citizens viewed these as roadblocks to their "manifest destiny" in the Western Hemisphere. Indeed, tensions over the terms of US territorial expansion led to numerous US–UK war scares throughout the 1850s. In this context, the US and British mercantile community saw the Franklin search as an peaceful influence: comity would protect commerce from the ravages of war.[23] For those had deep business interests in the entangled mercantile community of the Atlantic World, this was a worthwhile investment.

It paid off. By the end of 1856, British plaudits for the United States, its citizens, and its Arctic men were positively gushing. Never before had the white citizens of the United States received so much flattering praise from Europe. They relished it; they had finally achieved the respect accorded to the great European powers without any of the diplomatic responsibilities in Europe and the Ottoman Empire. And perhaps best of all, in 1856 the British bowed to them as the dominant power of the Western Hemisphere, at least for a while. With the exception of strained relations during the US

Civil War, Great Britain would largely acknowledge US supremacy in the Americas until the Venezuelan boundary crisis of 1895. For a campaign of informal diplomacy, it was a remarkable achievement.

THE CULTURAL WORLD OF DIPLOMATIC CHIVALRY

Lady Jane Franklin has never received her due as one of the greatest private diplomats of the Victorian Age. She was not an elite by birth—her father was a middle-class silk weaver—but her family had had good fortune in business.[24] And in marrying Sir John Franklin in 1828, she had chosen well.[25] By all accounts, Franklin adored her husband and was devoted to him and his career.[26] She genuinely seemed to enjoy the social clout that came with her status as the wife of a great explorer.[27] As an adventurous soul herself, moreover, she relished the opportunities for foreign travel that had come through her husband's political appointments and long absences at sea.[28]

Most important for this chapter, Jane Franklin understood the role of gender in elite culture and how it might be used to advance her goals. As Lady Franklin knew, middle- and upper-class culture in the Western world believed that men had a social duty to assist supposedly helpless, emotional women. She loved her husband, but it is also equally clear that she carefully crafted a public image of a devoted, anxious, and afflicted wife—a "rare and admirable Penelope," as one US sailor called her.[29] This, she rightly believed, was the mechanism by which she could intrude on powerful men and storm the traditionally male sphere of politics and diplomacy. It certainly helped that Lady Franklin's physical and emotional presence coincided with cultural expectations of what women should look, sound, and act like in nineteenth-century Britain and the United States: she was slight, quiet voiced, and charming—"so gentle & such a lady," as Alfred, Lord Tennyson, once described her.[30]

Beneath that soft exterior, however, was an iron woman. She knew what she wanted and she knew how to get it. Like Queen Victoria herself, Lady Franklin was a master of public relations, a shrewd politician, and an adroit diplomat. In the rapidly expanding world of print of the mid-nineteenth century, she comprehended that the public press was not merely "a reality behind diplomacy," in David Brown's words, "but also a reality of diplomacy."[31] To bear maximum pressure on public officials, she ensured that her letters to great men—and their responses—were published in the newspapers. And she leveled so many letters at the Admiralty from her London apartment that her family called it "the Battery."[32] Finally, she enlisted her niece, Sophia Cracroft, to serve as her personal bulldog with officials and the press. Cracroft could roar so that Lady Franklin did not have to.[33] No wonder, then, that her contemporaries compared her to Elizabeth I, or that a modern biographer has even confessed to fearing her.[34]

For all that, it is important to note that Lady Franklin was no countercultural feminist. Her political and social views were thoroughly mainstream.[35] Moreover, her transimperial celebrity status was a double-edged sword for women's equality in the Atlantic World. On the one hand, she demonstrated that, in certain conditions, women could turn social restrictions in a potent weapon. In that sense, her story parallels those of colonial English women who found that the brutal, unusual circumstances of the frontier sometimes allowed them to become violent avengers without shedding their femininity.[36] On the other hand, this strategy worked to entrench the very same, limited social roles that Franklin used to such great effect. "Convention protected her," Alison Alexander, writes, but Lady Franklin also protected convention.[37] Indeed, she became the epitome of female virtue, lauded on both sides of the Atlantic as "that admirable woman," "whose devotion to her gallant husband has made her name a household word in two continents."[38] Later writers, Alexander notes, would use her as "an example of indefatigable wifely fidelity in an instructive book for young ladies."[39] Nor was Lady Franklin's celebration restricted to elite or middle-class circles; working-class sailors, too, feted her in such popular ballads as "Lady Franklin's Lament."[40] Here was a feminine role model for all classes in the English-speaking world.

The Victorian era's obsession with chivalry and the Middle Ages also had an important part to play in Lady Franklin's public campaign to locate her lost husband. While US medievalism is more commonly thought of as a Gilded Age phenomenon, its roots are actually much deeper. English medievalism dates back to the early modern era, and colonists in British North America inherited that tradition.[41] Thomas Jefferson, for example, was an early Anglo-Saxonist who believed that the Revolution would restore liberty to an Anglo-Saxon people whose rights had been quashed by a corrupt, Norman ascendancy.[42] Emergent theories of racial science were a key part of early US medievalism: blood was destiny, and Anglo-Saxon blood was understood to be naturally freedom-loving, brave, hardy, and virtuous.[43] Inspired by such notions, British Romantic writers like Sir Walter Scott, Lord Tennyson, and Lord Byron poured out heroic narratives of Christian, Anglo-Saxon knights striving for noble goals. Their works were enormously popular in Britain and the United States and contributed to a kind of gendered, medievalist ethics across the English-speaking (indeed, Western) world.[44]

Medievalism informed and justified US expansionism and empire. While this is a dynamic that is much better understood by scholars of the North American West, medievalism also romanticized global and oceanic expansion in the early US republic.[45] Melville compared the rankings of whalemen to knights and squires, and suggested that the historical St. George was actually a whaler.[46] William Francis Lynch drew on crusader history to make sense of his time in Ottoman Palestine, seeing in himself "the pure, disinterested aspirations of the Crusader."[47] In Nicaragua, meanwhile, the proslavery filibuster William Walker extolled the "gallantry" of his comrades, which appeared to him "like that of the knights of feudal times."[48] Walker's compatriot in proslavery crusades, Matthew Fontaine Maury, similarly described his Amazon expedition as one of many "beautiful castles" for his brother-in-law to "to figure in."[49] US citizens and Britons alike perceived Arctic exploration through the prism of this gendered, medievalist mystique. Franklin was a lady in pain; she needed male champions and knights to aid her in what one naval officer called her "crusade of rescue."[50]

It initially seemed that US chivalry was not up to the task. Indeed, for all its future successes, the United States' Arctic diplomacy had a disastrous start. President Taylor's optimistic promises turned out empty—but not before they had already won significant praise across the Atlantic. By mid-May 1849, rumors that the president would dispatch two naval vessels to the Arctic to search for Franklin had begun circulating in the US and the British press.[51] The news was warmly hailed in the British Isles. On June 15, the US minister to Great Britain, George Bancroft, wrote Clayton to report that he had "heard Sir Robert Inglis, Lord Palmerston, and Mr. D'Israeli speak upon it in the handsomest manner" in the House of Commons. Clayton himself wrote a friend that when Parliament and the Royal Society learned of Taylor's intentions, they broke out in spontaneous applause.[52] The Royal Society passed a resolution of thanks and presented it to Bancroft on June 9. They explicitly tied US participation in the Franklin quest to the nation's civilizational maturity, hoping that the United States would "continue to progress with the same Extraordinary rapidity in the arts of Peace and civilization, and to hold the same high place, in the science and literature of the World."[53] This was precisely the kind of praise that so many white US citizens craved.

The transatlantic honeymoon was not to last; constitutional scruples intervened. On receiving Lady Franklin's letter, Taylor had directed his secretary of the navy, William Preston, to convene a board of navy captains and to report on the practicability and constitutionality of ordering warships to the Arctic.[54] Preston was a Virginia Whig with a strict constructionist streak. He had supported the initial organization of the Amazon expedition without congressional approval because it promised to advance proslavery expansion. However, he got cold feet when it came to sanctioning an Arctic foray. It reminded him too much of the Holy Land expedition, which many Whigs had opposed as unconstitutional.[55] His disapproval may have influenced the board's final report, which came back negative in mid-June. The board had two major points: first, the navy had no available vessels that would be strong enough to endure the rigors of the Arctic. It recommended that the government purchase "two coasting vessels of about 200 tons burthen" and use the fall and winter to ready them for a spring sailing date. Second, having studied the most recent naval appropriations bill and previous legislation, they concluded that it did not authorize the executive branch to buy those vessels on its own.[56] If he was to respond positively to Lady Franklin's entreaty, Taylor would need Congress's help.

This false start was a severe embarrassment for the United States. A republican system of government had hobbled the nation's ability to respond swiftly and positively to an international exigency. In New York, the *Weekly Herald* ran the headline "ABANDONMENT OF THE SEARCH FOR SIR JOHN FRANKLIN BY THE UNITED STATES GOVERNMENT." Clayton wrote a friend in July 1949 that his "mortification [had] been extreme. . . . It was a pretty feather in the president's cap, and *lost* by the opposition of the navy."[57] Britons were also crestfallen. As before, Lady Franklin summoned the power of gender and the press. In a public letter to a US friend that achieved wide circulation in US and UK newspapers, she bemoaned the United States' missed opportunity: "O that they could cover themselves with glory by putting in execution their generous intentions of last year!"[58] Bitterly recounting the premature return of one of the search parties under Sir James Clark Ross, Lady Franklin clung to the hope that the United States would yet come round.[59] "The field is now open before her," she wrote. "How anxiously I still look to them for aid in the time of my greatest need[!]"[60]

The moral necessity of coming to Lady Franklin's aid inspired others to join the fray. If President Taylor would not be her knight, then others would. Proposals for private expeditions soon filled the newspapers. In Washington, Charles Wilkes took a break from publishing the Ex Ex volumes and managing the National Gallery to promote his own. Anticipating the navy's constitutional and logistical hurdles, he put forward a plan to send several hardy fishing vessels from Maine to the Arctic at private expense.[61] Lynch, enchanted with chivalry and always eager to lead any US exploring expedition no matter where or why, also published his own scheme.[62] Bostonians, meanwhile, began talking of shipping out their own private voyage to find Franklin. One advocate hoped that Massachusetts "vessels may sail out of the harbor in this holy cause before three weeks are passed."[63]

As this phraseology suggests, many white US citizens felt passionately, even religiously, about the need to answer Lady Franklin's appeal. The chivalric honor of the nation, after all, was at stake. It bears reminding that elite US citizens in the first half of the nineteenth century still worried about their country's cultural inferiority in comparison to Great Britain and the Great Powers of Europe. Indeed, they writhed under any British criticism whatsoever.[64] In the arts and literature, US citizens were barely beginning to find authentic national expressions. In 1837, Ralph Waldo Emerson famously fretted that national culture "cannot always be fed on the sere remains of foreign harvests."[65] US science, meanwhile, though it had begun to gain momentum and international prestige, still trailed far behind that of European nations. On the eve of an international exhibition of the products of industrial nations in London in 1851, the US minister to the Court of St. James, Abbott Lawrence, fretted that the United States would embarrass itself: "I look forward to the Exhibition with deep interest," he wrote the State Department, "and not without fear, lest our Country should do itself injustice."[66]

One bright spot for the United States' national reputation in the first half of the nineteenth century was in the maritime realm. White US citizens looked upon their globe-spanning merchant marine and fisheries with great pride.[67] They took tremendous satisfaction from their reputation as great sailors, shipwrights, and naval engineers. In August 1851, the United States defeated the British in the first America's Cup, the transatlantic yacht race.[68] That same year, a wealthy Philadelphian noted how US clipper ships had come to dominate the route between Hong Kong and London. "We can beat John Bull in any thing we please," he crowed.[69] After the repeal of Britain's Corn Laws in November 1849, even the trepidatious diplomat Abbott spouted that "the United States will soon possess a full share of the commerce of the World."[70] In short, using Arctic exploration as a vehicle for national prominence appealed to many US nationals because they were confident of a good showing.

Among these nationals was a New York City merchant and shipping tycoon named Henry Grinnell. Grinnell had been born and educated in New Bedford, Massachusetts, but as a young man he settled in New York and became a shipping clerk. In 1825, he partnered with two brothers, Joseph and Moses Hicks, and formed a new corporation, Fish, Grinnell & Company, to distribute the thousands of barrels of whale oil brought in by the nation's gargantuan whaling fleet every year.[71] The brothers' success in this endeavor inspired them to diversify their holdings. They established a packet service between Liverpool and New York and then gradually added other vessels to their commercial empire; they were the owners of the *Flying Cloud*, for instance, one of the country's most famous clipper ships.[72] In 1850, Grinnell retired as one of New York City's wealthiest men—just in time to devote his wealth and attention to the Franklin quest. In early 1850, he stepped forward and offered to partner with the federal government in an Arctic search. The navy could use two of his own ships, he declared, so long as Congress assigned them officers, men, and supplies.

Grinnell had both cultural and pragmatic reasons for making his offer. Like many other men of prominence, he adored Lady Franklin. He addressed her as "my dear Lady" and was eager to please her.[73] At the same time, Grinnell wished to cultivate US–UK affinity in order to avoid war. The early to mid-1850s were especially fraught years between the United States and Great Britain (and oftentimes France and Spain as well) as they jockeyed to determine the future of Central America and the Caribbean. The British were especially fearful that further US expansion would jeopardize their holdings in Central America and their naval supremacy in the Western Hemisphere. Naval bases in the West Indies and free transit across the Isthmus of Darien (now Panama) in Central America were crucial links in upholding British mastery of the oceans on both sides of the Americas; they were desperate to preserve them.[74] The United States, meanwhile, had important commercial interests in Central America, including slavery and transportation to and from the gold fields of California. Even as Grinnell was offering his ships, diplomats were busy negotiating a resolution to the crisis, though none was assured. The maintenance of peace, as it seemed to some observers in early 1850, was in the balance. Grinnell reasoned that Arctic exploration could be a safety valve.

Race was central to Grinnell's calculations. More than anything, he appeared to abhor the prospect of a war between nations that were predominantly Anglo-Saxon. After all, he had spent three decades cultivating a complex web of transatlantic friendships and business relationships. That world encompassed New York City merchants—many of whom were also invested in the packet lines that tied Great Britain to the United States—as well as New Bedford whaling barons, British East India Company officials, and the London merchants who would purchase the China cargoes of his clipper ships. The possibility that a transatlantic war would destroy this entangled mercantile community weighed heavily on him.[75] In February 1856, US–UK saber-rattling over Central America prompted Grinnell to pledge, in a letter to Lady Franklin, that "there never can be any war between" the United States and Great Britain. "As I have before stated to you, the *people* of the *two countries* would never consent to anything of the kind, let [Prime Minister] Lord Palmerston and President Pierce act as they may."[76] A fanciful thought, perhaps, but a telling one.

What is further revealing is that Grinnell's opposition to white-on-white warfare applied at home, too. Grinnell was a nativist who desired peace over justice—at least, regarding Black Americans held in slavery. When ex-president Millard Fillmore ran on the American Party ticket in 1856, Grinnell attended the convention as one of the state electors from New York. He could live with a Democratic president if need be, but what he feared most was a victory by John C. Frémont, the former explorer and Republican Party candidate: "If Fremont is elected President," he wrote Lady Franklin before the election, "I really fear that something much worse will follow, all occasioned simply on the question whether slavery shall be allowed in [the] territories."[77] When James Buchanan won and Frémont lost, Grinnell breathed a sigh of relief. "This country is safe for years to come," he told Franklin.[78]

Grinnell's white supremacism points to the dark underbelly of Arctic exploration. If the United States was so eager for a "philanthropic adventure," as one statesmen claimed, why not look closer to home?[79] It is worth noting that at a time when close to four million Black Americans were suffering the hell that was slavery, leading white citizens invested enormous amounts of blood and treasure to rescue foreign white men in a distant, dangerous clime. Of course, they did not think of it quite in the same terms as we do today. For Wilkes, "the Slave question" was an inconvenience, sucking up valuable oxygen in Congress when he needed appropriations for the Ex Ex publications.[80] While wintering in the Arctic from 1853 to 1855, US officers and sailors joked at African Americans' expense.[81] William Francis Lynch seemed to be one of the few naval explorers who was genuinely concerned about slavery and the toxicity of racism. His solution, however, was to send US Blacks to Africa through colonization—something that most of the Black community in the United States did not want.[82] Until that happened, Lynch reasoned, Christian slaves and antislavery activists had to practice "submissive piety," and "[bow] to the dispensation of Providence." Slavery, in his mind, had divine sanction.[83]

White contemporaries in the United States and Great Britain ignored such paradoxes. Instead, Grinnell's liberality met with widespread praise on both sides of the Atlantic. In Alabama, newspaper editors called his plan a "praiseworthy enterprise."[84] In March 1850, the *Hudson River Chronicle* went further. "In such noble and benevolent enterprises as this lies the true use of wealth," it opined. "Mr. Grinnell has shown an example of what a merchant prince should be, which will win the admiration of the world."[85] And indeed it did. On March 25, 1850, the London *Times* found itself tongue-tied when trying to laud Grinnell for his generosity. "We fall short of words to express our feelings towards Mr. Grinnell," it wrote, "who has himself alone contributed no less a sum than $30,000, or upwards of £5,000." The paper hoped that US and British search parties would "go forward heart and soul together in this sacred cause of humanity, and . . . leave no effort untried to restore to us our lost countrymen."[86]

In the United States, the public rhetoric in favor of Grinnell's offer signaled that the nation's character was at stake. In New York, the *Weekly Herald* prayed that members of Congress would act in a way that would be "equal to the character of a generous and enlightened government."[87] When Senator Henry Clay of Kentucky laid a petition from Grinnell before the Senate on April 5, 1850, he expressed misgivings that Franklin and his party would be found alive, if at all. Even so, "the attempt to do so," he told his colleagues, "will be gratifying to the whole world."[88] In the House on April 22, Congressman Samuel Finley Vinton of Massachusetts declared that "the discovery and assistance of the gallant officer who has hazarded his life in the prosecution of scientific discovery" would be "among the noblest victories which could crown the brow of any nation." He urged his colleagues to approve "an expedition so creditable to the country and the service."[89] In the Senate, Jacob Miller, a Whig senator from New Jersey, emphasized the international dishonor that the nation would accrue if it failed to help Grinnell. "If we refuse these ships," he pleaded, "we will defeat the whole enterprise, and lose all opportunity of participation in a work of humanity which now commands the attention of the world."[90]

Even many of those who argued against the bill in Congress invoked the explorationist vision of a great and powerful United States. Democratic Senator William King of North Carolina argued that it was demeaning to let a private merchant like Grinnell take the lead in what should have been a national expedition.[91] Another Southern Democrat, Henry Foote of Mississippi, agreed. Slamming the Taylor administration for the previous years' aborted promises to Lady Franklin, Foote proclaimed that the federal government would make itself even more despicable by joining with Grinnell. "The Government cannot engage in this enterprise without a serious loss of dignity at least," he warned. "I am not willing that this Government should play second fiddle to Mr. Grinnell or anybody else."[92] When pressed, Foote stayed the course, arguing passionately that "we should go into it, as a great and magnanimous nation, acting in a 'national spirit'—making all the glory of the undertaking our own."[93]

Much of this was partisan maneuvering, but it had a kernel of truth. Foote was right that the expedition would be a joint public-private venture. But while he was inclined to view this as a weakness, it was actually a strength. Historians and political scientists have recently demonstrated that US governance was and remains highly flexible and nimble. Government power could be exerted in numerous ways, one of which was to empower private enterprise and voluntarism to govern on its behalf.[94] Strong malpractice laws, for instance, encouraged lawyers and their injured clients to police that field of business themselves.[95] Similarly, much early road, bridge, and canal construction was the result of states providing charters to businesses to complete those projects.[96] Arctic exploration was similar; Grinnell's offer permitted the United States to save face abroad, and it allowed the government to pursue a voyage of high diplomatic value at minimal cost. It also made perfect logistical sense. The navy was right that its ships were not designed to endure the rigors of Arctic exploration—in the Antarctic portions of the voyage of the United States Exploring Expedition, the *Vincennes* and other vessels had nearly courted disaster.[97]

As a whole, Congress saw the advantages of Grinnell's proposal. They passed a bill authorizing the president to receive Grinnell's vessels, to man them with naval personnel, and to provide three years' worth of rations.[98] Taylor signed it on May 2, 1850.[99] Lady Franklin was thrilled; she thanked Grinnell for his "spirit of generous philanthropy" and hoped that God would "reward this self-sacrificing and noble devotion."[100] Whether He would or not remained to be seen.

THE FIRST GRINNELL EXPEDITION

On May 22, 1850, Grinnell's two ships, the *Advance* and the *Rescue*, finally inched out of the Brooklyn Navy Yard and sailed down the East River to the sea. In command was Lieutenant Edwin Jesse De Haven, a veteran of the Ex Ex.[101] As De Haven's small squadron passed Manhattan Island, the national feeling manifested itself from crowded docks and quays. "Cheers and hurras followed us till we had passed the Battery," a navy surgeon later remembered, while "ferry-boats and steamers came out of their track to salute us in the bay."[102] Grinnell found it hard to say farewell; he stayed with them in the pilot boat for three days before finally taking his leave.[103]

Grinnell may have lingered because he knew that Arctic navigation was hard. Of all the planet's regions, the poles possessed the greatest obstacles to human exploration and physical survival. Extreme temperatures, the total darkness of winter, malnutrition and Arctic scurvy, the risk of slipping into an unfathomable crevice on the ice, falling into the frigid water, or having one's vessel crunched to splinters posed a severe threat to the life of any polar navigator.[104] Mid-nineteenth-century observers likened the Arctic to a kind of natural battlefield. They frequently anthropomorphized its forces, fashioning up "Arctic Queens" or even a "King Death," who, "with hoary beard and glistening spears and crunching ice-batteries," bid defiance to any intruder foolish enough to enter his domain.[105] Such dangers made the Arctic a "field of toil"[106] and a "martial plain."[107] It was a place where heroic navigators fought to "break the frost-friend's spell" and "to grapple with the grim enemy, Cold."[108] Even the animals were dangerous: walruses were "sphinx-faced monsters" that were notoriously hazardous to hunt, while polar bears were "tigers of the ice" that provided both a means of sustenance and a constant danger.[109]

Ironic enough, it was precisely these perils that made Arctic exploration so attractive to white US citizens. They craved European respect, and the Arctic was the perfect place to get it. As one writer described it, a polar voyage was "the test of physical endurance, as well as the trial of character."[110] By traveling and persevering in the Arctic, these men would reveal what they were made of. They didn't even have to find Franklin; they had just to survive. After all, only truly hardy, technologically sophisticated, and well-organized expeditions could endure the harsh environment.

Grinnell ensured that the expedition combined the best practices of past English voyagers and contemporary private enterprise. His ships reflected this understanding: the *Advance* and the *Rescue* were much smaller than the *Erebus* and *Terror*. Their diminutive size, noted one naval officer, made the venture "something like a return to the dimensions of our predecessors of the olden time," and he compared them to the discovery ships of Martin Frobisher and William Baffin.[111] More than these, however, the *Advance* and the *Rescue* were built to endure the rigors of the Arctic; in the event that they were frozen in, their wedge-shaped hulls would help the ice lift them out of harm's way.[112] And in case this didn't happen, the hulls were doubled, "a brig within a brig," with "strips of heavy sheet-iron extended from the bows to the beam, as a shield against the cutting action of the new ice." To repair the iron strips and the expedition's ice anchors, Grinnell had installed "an armorer's forge."[113] These precautions made the ships into floating castles—small ones, but strong.

Onboard were knights—or, at least, so they fancied themselves. And no one did more fancying in this regard than Passed Navy Surgeon Elisha Kent Kane. At age thirty, Kane was the eldest son of a distinguished Philadelphia family. His romance with medievalism went back to his boyhood, when he would sketch "exciting scenes of battle and heroism—soldiers fighting with drawn swords and exotic turban-clad warriors galloping on horseback."[114] His brother compared him to "our very lovable Don Quixote."[115] As a gesture of affection, Kane once gave his secret love a copy of Friedrich de la

Motte Fouqué's *Undine*, a tale about the romance between a water sprite and an errant knight.[116] Though Kane suffered from a weak heart and frequent bouts of rheumatic fever, his deep desire for adventure and heroic service had long since overridden any concerns about his health. As he wrote his mother, it was "better die in the bloody struggle . . . better be lance struck or fever smitten than expire in a white washed chamber."[117]

Concern for his masculinity had its effect as well. Kane was small and sickly. His acquaintances often compared him—favorably, at least—to girls. "So pretty," a housemaid remembered, "with his sweet young face and lovely complexion like a girl's."[118] In contrast, his father, John Kintzing Kane, was a large, powerfully built man. He had been a fireman in his youth, and an imposing judge in professional life.[119] He struggled to be compassionate during his son's frequent illnesses. Once, while Elisha was recuperating from a particularly rough affliction of rheumatism, his father decided that he had had enough. "If you must die," he told Elisha, then "die in the harness."[120] Kane took the harsh advice to heart; before he requested Arctic service, he had traveled the world as a diplomat's physician. He had descended into a volcano in the Philippines, explored the ruins of ancient Egypt, hunted elephants with British officers in Ceylon, and been wounded in the US–Mexican War. He was, in short, the perfect romantic hero to serve Lady Franklin and win British esteem.[121]

There would be much of it to win. The US records of the First Grinnell Expedition read like an international bromance, a celebration of common Anglo-Saxon heritage and masculinity. When the *Advance* and the *Rescue* arrived off of St. John's, Newfoundland, Kane recounted how "six brawny Saxon men rowed out nine miles to meet us." They were disappointed not to be able to serve as pilots, "but their hearty countenances brightened into a glow when we added, 'in search of Sir John Franklin.'"[122] The same might be said when Kane looked on Sir John; he had a portrait of the explorer mounted in his bunk, where he would sit and admire this "good, genuine, hearty representative of English flesh and blood."[123]

Kane would soon see other representatives of the Anglo-Saxon race. Because the US expedition joined and encountered two other search parties, one private and one public, there were plenty of other opportunities for ethnic backslapping. While approaching Lancaster Sound in August 1850, for instance, the expedition suddenly encountered the *Lady Franklin*, a vessel in Captain William Penny's private squadron. In his published account, Kane described the rousing cheers that the US and British crews gave each other, delighting in the sound of "that good old English hurra, which we inherit on our side [of] the water." The British welcome was "as much of brotherhood as sympathy," Kane claimed. In his account, US and

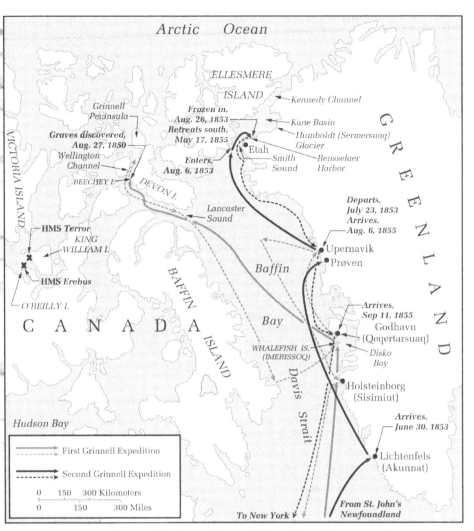

Figure 6.1 Routes of the First and Second Grinnell Expeditions, 1851–1855.
(Created by Chris Robinson)

UK seamen were brothers sailing under "sister flags," allied together on an "errand of mercy."[124] Indeed, the phrase "our English brethren" shows up twice in Kane's narrative.[125] Arctic exploration was a family union.

That spirit of ethnic, masculine comity persisted. Two days later, in the bright early morning of the Arctic summer, the *Advance* caught up with the Royal Navy schooner *Felix*, captained by "that practical Arctic veteran, Sir John Ross." The sea was heavy, every wave "shipping seas," but nonetheless the two parties could hear each other over the din. When the US party asked where the rest of the British vessels were, Ross roared back, "You and I are ahead of them all." "It was so indeed," Kane gleefully recorded: "The Felix and the Advance were on the lead." "I shall never forget the heartiness with which [Ross] sang out," he wrote. Kane's admiration for "brave old Sir John" seemed to know no bounds; he was a "manly old seaman" who had "embarked himself in the crusade of search for a lost comrade."[126] The young doctor was thrilled to be a fellow crusader.

The amity was mutual. In late August, the expeditions found themselves frozen in together in a cove off Beechey Point. Commodore Sir Horatio Thomas Austin, commanding the British rescue squadron, fittingly named it "Union Bay."[127] Solid ice allowed Kane to visit the various British ships. Between their wooden walls, he enjoyed conversations with the accomplished polar explorer Sir James Clark Ross, was welcomed by the officers of the HMS *Resolute* "with the cordiality of recognized brotherhood," identified one of *Resolute*'s lieutenants as an old acquaintance from his adventures in the Philippines, and became fast friends with the ship's surgeon.[128] British gratitude during the First Grinnell Expedition was so great that while passing through Baffin Bay in July 1851, the English whalers gave them much-needed fresh provisions free of charge. In contrast, a US whaleship demanded payment for similar victuals.[129]

Cooperation between the US and British expeditions went hand in hand with the camaraderie. On July 1, 1850, De Haven reported on the progress of the US and British search squadrons to the British Admiralty itself, asking if they would forward the intelligence to Lady Franklin.[130] When "a strong current and the dropping tide" grounded the *Advance*, the British offered to tow them off.[131] US and British naval officers conferred several times in order to coordinate the search, often at the invitation of Austin.[132] De Haven was generally receptive to Austin's proposals, though he was also clear when the Commodore's plans went against his orders.[133] On August 27, 1850, US and British seamen conducted a joint search of the coastline of Beechy Island. When one of the British searchers sent word that he had discovered several graves, members of both nationalities hurried to the scene. There they found conclusive proof that the dead men were from Franklin's expedition.[134] They made quick plans to continue the search overland. Ross suggested they leave behind a small boat he had towed from England in case the search mission had to fall back. De Haven concurred, contributing several barrels of food to the vessel.[135]

Such US–UK collaboration did not mean that national rivalries had disappeared, however.[136] In London, Lady Franklin realized that her interest was actually best served *through* nationalistic competition. Thus, she regularly pitted US commitments against those of the Admiralty, hoping to embarrass them into further action. Her niece, Sophia Cracroft, wrote undercover letters to precisely this effect. In a letter to the editor of the London *Times* in January 1850, for example, she affected the position of a Briton concerned that the US sailors would beat them to Franklin: "Let 1850 be the year to redeem our tottering honour," her anonymous letter read, "and let not the United States snatch from us the glory of rescuing the lost expedition."[137]

At times, both De Haven and Kane also portrayed the quest for Franklin as a competitive venture. In early September, the Royal Navy vessels found themselves free of the ice that had seized all the searching vessels. De Haven and his comrades watched enviously as the British ships "steam[ed] away manfully."[138] Earlier, when Kane visited the *Resolute* in late August, he had felt chastened by British technology: "I had to shake off a feeling of almost of despondency when I saw how much better fitted they were to grapple with the grim enemy, Cold. Winter, if we may judge of it by the clothing and warming appliances of the British squadron, must be something beyond our power to cope with; for, in comparison with them, we have nothing, absolutely nothing."[139]

Grinnell's earlier preparations were soon put to the test. The navy had directed De Haven not to winter in the Arctic unless doing so would prove advantageous for continued search in the spring. When the ice around his vessels began weakening, De Haven leaped into action. On September 10, 1850, he ordered the *Advance* and the *Rescue* to begin the long journey home.[140] Thirteen days later, however, they found themselves again held fast in the ice.[141] Winter had come; home would have to wait. For perhaps the first time, US Navy seamen experienced the icebound terrors of an Arctic winter. On numerous occasions, the pressure of the ice around the *Rescue* and the *Advance* appeared to doom their vessels. In late September, the *Advance* found herself "heavily nipped between two floes." The resulting buildup of ice "was piled up so high above the rail on the starboard side as to threaten to come on board and sink us with its weight. All hands," De Haven remembered, "were occupied in keeping it out."[142] To make matters worse, the crews could not set up the ship's heating stoves until late October because they had been buried under provisions in the hold. Ice crept into the interiors of the *Advance* and the *Rescue*.[143] In early December 1850, a massive storm whipped up the surrounding floes and once more threatened to smash the ice-lodged ships.[144] Finally, Kane and his assistant surgeon had to contend with an outbreak of scurvy—the same disease that, unbeknown to them, had already killed Sir John Franklin and his crew. On March 10, 1851, Kane reported to De Haven that scurvy had "embrace[d], with three exceptions the entire Crews under your Command."[145]

Nonetheless, they endured. Kane and his assistant kept their comrades in as good a shape as possible. Freed by the melting ice in June 1851, the First Grinnell Expedition set sights for home. On September 30, 1851, it returned to Manhattan Island. Grinnell was the first to welcome them, standing there on the docks.[146] It was a bittersweet moment. He was glad to have them and his ships back safely, of course; on the other hand, as he observed in a letter to Lady Franklin, "the great object of the Expedition has not been accomplished." "I feel sad, sad," he wrote. "Your husband and your countrymen have not been rescued and restored to their home and country." He was unsure whether the United States would do anything more.[147] Lady Franklin, however, was determined that they would.

ORGANIZING A SECOND VENTURE

The effort to relaunch another US Arctic survey began almost as soon as the first one ended. This time, Lady Franklin had a new ally: Kane. In spite of the dangers, the navy surgeon was captivated by the Arctic and the romantic quest to free Sir John from his icy prison. On November 4, when the British expatriate community in New York honored Grinnell and the officers of the expedition with silver medals and a banquet, Kane took the opportunity to make a toast. He looked forward to meeting Sir John Franklin in person, and he "earnestly" prayed that "the search is not ended."[148] Lady Franklin was pleased. "The sentiments of our own countrymen and allies in America will be reflected here and give new stimulus to our people," she told Grinnell.[149] On November 15, Kane wrote Lady Franklin directly and pledged his "sincere Cooperation" in "the holy enterprise with which you are identified."[150] Like her and Cracroft, he recognized that public sympathy would best be manipulated via the press. He vowed to urge his countrymen to renew their efforts, which would, in turn, "keep the subject sufficiently prominent to sustain the emulative action of your own government."[151] "Your letter has given me great comfort & satisfaction," Lady Franklin responded on December 19, 1851. "I hardly know how to thank you for it sufficiently."[152]

Kane and Franklin quickly grew to admire each other. The courteous, chivalric doctor from Philadelphia and the charming, ambitious noblewoman had complementary personalities. Jefferson's famous observation that John Quincy Adams and James Monroe had been "made for each other" could just as easily have been applied to Franklin and Kane.[153] Lady Franklin "idolised the romantic Kane," according to a biographer, and had "his portrait hung on her drawing room wall in a velvet frame."[154] No doubt their friendship was sincere, but it was also advantageous for both: in Kane,

Franklin found the perfect international hero to increase the pressure on the Admiralty to persist in the search; in Lady Franklin, Kane discovered both a patroness and a means of displaying his highest, noblest, and most masculine properties. His father, already delighted with how his son had turned out, would be made even prouder yet.

Kane's greatest ambition was to the become the American Sir John Franklin. The way seemed clear for the doctor to assume that role. His old Arctic commander, De Haven, was in the best position to do so, but he stepped aside. De Haven's preference was for a quieter life; after submitting his sixteen-page report to the Navy Department in October 1851, he returned to his farm in Pennsylvania.[155] He gave up future Arctic surveys and gave Kane permission to write up a longer narrative of the expedition for publication.[156] He even invited Kane to work at his farmhouse, where De Haven would be available for evening socialization and interviews. "Bring your writing with you," he urged him, "and you employ yourself in quiet whilst I am about the farm."[157] From London, Lady Franklin also encouraged Kane to write his narrative. "You cannot indeed do us a greater service," she wrote, "than by counteracting the desponding and very irrational impression" that her husband and his compatriots were dead.[158] The critics were right, of course, and their conclusions were actually highly rational. Lady Franklin, however, was having none of it; she hoped that Kane's book would help the Admiralty see the light.

Kane acted on Lady Franklin's advice. He focused first on generating public sympathy and interest, drafting his narrative of the First Grinnell Expedition and giving lectures in major northeastern cities like New York and Boston.[159] Societies for distinguished elites and working-class mechanics alike begged him to speak.[160] Kane told them that Franklin and his men might still be alive and well, and that they had likely disappeared up Wellington Channel and into a long-rumored open polar sea. He speculated that an overland sledge journey up the west coast of Greenland would deposit a second US expedition on the shores of that undiscovered ocean. There, they could launch their boats and look for Franklin.[161] When critics pointed out that the *Erebus* and the *Terror* had departed in 1845 with but three years' worth of provisions, Kane countered that the warmer climes of the open polar sea would contain plentiful and nutritious species on which the imprisoned Britons could feast.[162] Sir John and his comrades were not only alive and well—they were probably fat.

To become Sir John, Kane needed ships and funding. Grinnell, whom Kane came to regard as a kind of second father, was initially hesitant to grant them without a federal partnership similar to the first expedition.[163] Taking a lesson from Jeremiah Reynolds's old experience, Grinnell thought the only way to guarantee that a self-funded, private expedition would pursue polar exploration was to "demonstrate for a certainty that the region round the North Pole was covered with fur seals."[164] He again offered his ships to Secretary of the Navy John Pendleton Kennedy, who promised to use them if Congress gave him the authority to do so.[165] Grinnell and his allies spent the winter months of 1852 lobbying members of Congress. In this they were competing against Charles Wilkes, the navy's original polar explorer, who had submitted his own plan for a Franklin mission.[166] Both parties would be disappointed; as the chairman of the Senate Naval Affairs Committee informed Grinnell in March, he had "canvassed the Senate & found a majority against the project."[167]

Discouraged, Grinnell returned home to New York and mulled over his options. As a man of business and a patriot, he was frustrated that Congress had failed to recognize the imperatives of Arctic exploration. Alongside British relations, commerce and manifest destiny were important elements, to his thinking; having overfished much of the world's more temperate oceans, the US whale fishery had now crossed the Arctic Circle in the pursuit of whales. Soon, Grinnell knew, they would need even more whaling grounds. The prospect of a warm polar sea was promising. While explaining why a second Arctic expedition merited federal aid in 1853, Kane declared that polar exploration "ha[d] a direct bearing upon our Whaling interests," and that "the discovery . . . of an Open Polar sea is of the highest utilitarian interest."[168] Finally, Grinnell agreed with Melville that whaling was imperial.[169] He expected that the US would eventually acquire Canada and the Arctic. In a revealing letter in February 1852, he declared that "independent of any further search for Franklin, our Government should send an Exp. Up in the northern regions, they will belong to us in less than 25 years, and we should Know more about them."[170]

Even more ominous was the fact that US–UK relations were looking increasingly unsteady as the election of 1852 approached. While the two nations had sought to clarify Central American affairs through the Clayton–Bulwer Treaty of 1850, Grinnell knew that both powers interpreted the first article of the treaty very differently. In Article I, the parties had pledged not to "occupy, or fortify, or colonize . . . any part of Central America."[171] US officials wanted this to be retroactive. They demanded that the British Empire withdraw from Belize, the Bay of Islands, and their protectorate over the Miskito Nation of Central America. The British, for their part, declared that Article I governed the future, not the past.[172] With the election looming and with most of the leading Democratic presidential candidates being saber-rattling expansionists in the mold of James K. Polk, Grinnell could only wonder how long peace would be maintained.[173] Continued Arctic exploration would promote harmony and commerce in the Atlantic World.

By November 1852, Grinnell decided that the benefits of another Arctic voyage outweighed the price tag. In this he was joined by George Peabody, a wealthy US banker in London who, like Grinnell, had deep interests in stability of US–UK relations. In January 1852, Peabody had pledged $10,000 to any US expedition that would accompany Sir Edward Belcher to the polar north. His goal: to "gratify feelings of international good will and friendship."[174] Grinnell put the funds toward outfitting the *Advance* for another voyage north. Though he did not have congressional support, Kane would at least have his ship.

In the meantime, Kane's publicity efforts had hauled in recruits new and old. Among them was the son of Captain John Symmes, the old War of 1812 veteran and amateur geographer who had first inspired Reynolds to pursue global exploration back in the 1820s.[175] Henry Brooks, an officer in the First Grinnell Expedition, also wrote Kane and asked if he could join him. "As I was with you in the first Expedition," he scrawled, "I would like to be with you in the last."[176] The call of exploration attracted working-class men as well—William Godfrey, a laboring man with no previous experience at sea, attributed his joining to an "unconquerable love of adventure" and "a romantic taste for whatever is strange and marvelous."[177] He gave up a job that was three times as lucrative as the $18 per month he would be paid as an Arctic seaman.[178] It was a decision that he would come to regret.

In Washington, Navy Secretary Kennedy did all he could to assist the expedition. His activities at the Navy Department embodied the new US consensus over exploration as a means of amassing imperial power. Indeed, Kennedy was the most bona fide explorationist to have ever held that position. Between late 1852 and early 1853, he directed William Francis Lynch to search inland Liberia in support of Black colonization, got Perry off to his famous expedition to Japan, organized Page's proslavery expedition to the Río de la Plata, dispatched the USS *Arctic* to sound the bottom of the Atlantic, assigned a party to locate a canal route through the Isthmus of Darien in Central America, and prepared for a massive naval survey of the North Pacific Rim. Like many white US citizens by the early 1850s, Kennedy's sense of nationhood was a highly aggrandized one. The United States, he felt, was large enough to settle South America, bolster colonial protectorates in West Africa and the Sandwich Islands, forge communication links in Central America and the deep Atlantic, pry East Asian nations open to Western trade, advance the interests of polar whalers, and support the humanitarian diplomacy of Arctic exploration. In pursuit of these objectives, old republican concerns about the size, scope, and expenditures of the federal government were sloughed off. They no longer served the "honor" or "the successful adventure of the nation," Kennedy declared.[179] Jeremiah Reynolds's old foe in the Senate, Robert Hayne, had lost, and he had lost big time.

Kennedy's support of the Second Grinnell Expedition made it, at least in part, a public-private enterprise. After all, Kane was a still naval officer, and it was Kennedy who put him on special duty to locate Franklin and the open polar sea.[180] Time and again he gratified Kane's requests to assign willing volunteers from the navy to the *Advance*.[181] The result was that ten of the seventeen members of the expedition came from the navy.[182] He also directed Maury at the Naval Observatory to provide Kane with any navigational or scientific instruments that he could possibly spare.[183] The doctor was as gracious as ever, thanking Kennedy for his "fathering influence towards our little party."[184] By the time the *Advance* set sail for Greenland on May 30, 1853, two portraits hung in her cabin: one was Franklin's, and the other was Kennedy's.[185]

Not all federal officials were as helpful as Kennedy, however. His successor at the Navy Department, James C. Dobbin, refused to follow precedent. While he supported the Río de la Plata expedition and oversaw the launch of some of the navy's most advanced ships, he saw little value in ice-ridden seas.[186] Echoing Hayne, he was especially dismayed by the way Kennedy had aided the Second Grinnell Expedition without the sanction of Congress. Though Dobbin pledged not to roll back the actions that Kennedy had already made, he made it clear that Kane should not expect any more favors from the Navy Department.[187]

Interesting enough, the lack of congressional backing and Dobbin's stonewalling did not halt the growing perception—on both sides of the Atlantic—that the United States might indeed be on the verge of recognition as one of the world's leading powers. At home, newspapers feted the Second Grinnell Expedition as further evidence of national aggrandizement. "It merits and will receive the highest admiration and regard of the world abroad," the *Daily Missouri Republican* proudly proclaimed. "Whatever be the result of their effort . . . their countrymen will welcome them back with open arms and dearly earned plaudits such as [a] Roman conqueror never won."[188] In Boston, the *Daily Atlas* concurred: "The efforts . . . for the recovery of Sir John Franklin, have honored the American flag, and humanity, and when the intrepid Dr. Kane shall again set forth, the heartfelt interest and best wishes of the American people will attend him."[189]

Such statements reveal that while purely public enterprises were ideal, US citizens were perfectly willing to allow a private-public expedition to

represent them on the long road to national equality with European powers. After all, the rabid nationalism of the nineteenth century ensured that
every individual action could be associated with the character of a nation.
This was why even the achievements of nonstate actors, such as scientists,
mariners, and artists, could be invested with national significance. Antebellum citizens may have also instinctively understood the hybrid character of
the United States' governance. In viewing the Second Grinnell Expedition
as a national act, they implicitly acknowledged the country's strong tradition of government-corporate alliances for public ends.[190]

European acclaim kept pace with that of the US press. The British honored Grinnell and Kane by offering the assistance of their most important
Arctic men. On March 16, 1853, the British Consul in New York sent Grinnell a bag from the Admiralty with letters of encouragement and professional advice from Britain's most prominent Arctic explorers, including
Sir Edward Parry, Sir Francis Beaufort, and Sir Edward Sabine.[191] These
were some of the master explorers and scientists of the Victorian Age. Even
Dobbin confessed to feeling "much gratification from the evidences of generous interest displayed by the British Admiralty."[192] Similarly, the king of
Denmark wrote Kane and promised that the Danish colonists of Greenland
would provide him all possible assistance.[193] Support also came from Prus-
sia, where Baron Alexander von Humboldt, that venerable champion of
global scientific exploration and the perpetual inspiration of so many US
and European explorers, wrote Kane and praised his "beautiful and generous Expedition." He wished him "success in the noble enterprise in which
you find yourself nobly engaged."[194] It was the kind of letter than Jeremiah
Reynolds would have craved.

THE SECOND GRINNELL EXPEDITION

The *Advance* left New York on May 30, 1853.[195] As with the First Grinnell
Expedition, the second was a voyage into a white, Christian, and pre-
Christian past. In Greenland, Kane visited Lichtenfels, the home of an
old Moravian mission. From the cool waters of the fjord, Kane's eye was
pleased to land on a "quaint old Silesian mansion . . . crowned with an an-
tique belfry." The "grave ancient men" who greeted him wore skullcaps,
"such as Vandyke or Rembrandt himself might have painted." The interior
of the mansion that they had spotted from the sea, meanwhile, "had the
same time-sobered look."[196]

White pagan history loomed large in Kane's imagination as well. He
named one of his small boats "Eric the Red."[197] Later, when he encountered
a monstrous glacier sliding off the coast of western Greenland, he described

it as the great "crystal bridge," "cementing into one the Greenland of the Scandinavian Vikings and the America of Columbus."[198] Even Greenland's Inuits reminded Kane of white ethnic history. Alongside the almost obligatory analogies to Indigenous Americans, he portrayed them as medieval barbarians.[199] Their governments were "feudal sovereignties," they armed themselves with "unicorn-ivory lances" when hunting walrus, and the pursuit of a bear was "a mad, wild chase, wilder than German legend."[200] The landscape, too, reflected romantic medievalism. In the red sandstones of Dallas Bay, Kane perceived "the dreamy semblance of a castle, flanked with triple towers" and topped with "well-simulated battlements."[201] One particular spire was so distinct and noble that he named it "Tennyson Monument" after one of his favorite Romantic poets.[202]

Like most polar missions, the Second Grinnell Expedition experienced enormous hardship. Intent on locating the long-theorized polar sea and the British sailors it might contain, Kane and his crew sailed up Smith Sound, between Greenland and Ellesmere Island, and into a new Arctic bay that geographers would later name Kane Basin.[203] It was the farthest north that any Western vessel had ever sailed.[204] There they weathered two Arctic winters in a small cove, which Kane named Rensselaer Harbor, after his family's country estate in Pennsylvania.[205] In November 1853, it became so cold that a bottle of whiskey froze solid. Over the course of that first Arctic winter, 127 days would pass without sunlight.[206] The cold even killed one of Kane's childhood friends, Jefferson Baker.[207] It later claimed the life of another crew member, a beloved French volunteer named Pierre.[208] At one point, the party became so desperate for fresh meat that they ate ship rats and their sled dogs' newborn puppies.[209] By August 1854, the privations had become intense enough that nearly half the expedition seceded. Trying to escape another Arctic winter, they bolted for the Danish colonies down south. It was an unsuccessful sprint; by early December the expedition had been reunited, though Kane took time to overcome his bitterness at the secessionists' lack of faith.[210]

He might have charged them with lack of fortitude, too. The expedition, after all, was meant as an exhibition of Anglo-Saxon strength. Wintering in Arctic was a "terrible physical trial," Kane admitted, but it was one he expected his men to endure.[211] He generally praised them for their manliness, especially those who had perished.[212] When a sledge party returned to Rensselaer Harbor, Kane gave them "the good old Anglo-Saxon greeting, 'three cheers!'"[213]

Masculine strength mattered to his sailors, too. William Godfrey had signed aboard the voyage not only because he wanted adventure, but also because he "placed much reliancy on my personal strength and prowess,

Figure 6.2 *Life in the Brig: Second Winter*, from Elisha Kent Kane, *Arctic Explorations: The Second Grinnell Expedition in Search of Sir John Franklin, 1853, '54, '55* (Philadelphia: Childs and Peterson, 1856, 1:442). Note how Kane's brooding masculinity dominates the scene. (Courtesy of Library Company of Philadelphia)

and on my powers of endurance."[214] In his own narrative of the journey, he turned the tables on his commander. He portrayed Kane as cruel, violent, vicious, and, most significant, weak.[215] In one harrowing scene, the party was returning to their sledge when they grew so exhausted and numb with cold that many collapsed into sleep.[216] Kane was awake, but only Godfrey was alert enough to pitch tents to cover the unconscious men. As there was no room for them, Kane suggested to Godfrey that they trudge the nine miles back to their sledge. Godfrey agreed, but Kane was so tired that he had to lean on the larger man's strength. His "constitution was by no means robust," Godfrey explained. The doctor even "swooned away . . . two or three times"; when he did, Godfrey "carried him on my shoulder."[217] For a commander who had carefully crafted an image of himself as the ideal man—sensitive yet strong—it was a devastating portrait.

Kane's obsession with strength and endurance was on full display in his relations with the Inuit. They were often much larger than he was, which, considering his size, should not be so surprising. Kane, however, was very impressed with them, both their physicality and their technology, and he feared for the safety of his party if he did not similarly impress them.[218] He also needed the Inuits to supply fresh meat for the men and dogs.[219] He was therefore determined to prove white superiority in physical as well as technological matters. "I had seen enough of mankind not to know that respect is little else than a tribute to superiority either real or supposed," he explained.[220] During their many hunts together, Kane and his crew took "care to manifest no weariness." At times, they even carried some of the more fatigued Inuits on their backs, much as Godfrey had done for Kane. In this way, the doctor hoped that the Inuit would not see the whites' "rich store of appliances" as a sign of "effeminacy or inferior power."[221]

His strategy appears to have worked. While Kane thought the Inuits "were profoundly impressed with a conviction of our superiority,"[222] it seems more likely that they simply respected them as equals. They probably also recognized that an alliance was profitable for both groups. After several disputes over theft, they drew up a treaty with Kane that mollified both parties.[223] On the US side, Kane and his men became the beneficiaries of Indigenous knowledge. In fact, later biographers contended that that one of the expedition's major contributions to Arctic exploration was in pointing out the value of Inuit knowledge.[224] Accordingly, the US party fashioned the interior of the *Advance* into an igloo, made Inuit-inspired clothing out of animal furs, and even wore Inuit-style wooden goggles carved with slits to blunt the glare of the polar sun.[225] As Kane explained to Dobbin on his return, "We were obliged—as a measure of policy—to live the lives of the Esquimaux."[226] Most critical, they accompanied Inuit hunting parties and enjoyed the seal, bear, walrus steaks, and other fresh game that resulted.[227] The Inuit, for their part, benefited from US guns and gunpowder, which made their hunts far more successful. In at least one case, Kane even saved them from starvation.[228]

Inuit help facilitated geographical discovery. Whether by dogsled, by boat, or on foot, expedition members thoroughly explored Kane Basin and its northern limits. In October 1853, their discovery of a massive glacier sliding off northern Greenland and into Kane Basin nearly scuttled those efforts. Awed, Kane christianized the icy barrier Humboldt Glacier, after his hero.[229] A further expedition in June 1854 managed to bypass Humboldt Glacier and continue the northern trajectory.[230] They found that Kane Basin narrowed into a channel (they named it Kennedy Channel) that in turn led to an extensive sea devoid of ice.[231] It was a shore of the Arctic Ocean, which, technically speaking, the party had already been in for a long time. While it can occasionally appear to be ice free in the right conditions, Kane and his fellows believed they had confirmed the existence of a warm polar sea. Their greatest regret was that the distance and ice-choked condition of Kennedy Channel prevented their search for "traces of the gallant martyrs whose search instigated this Expedition."[232]

Faced with diminishing resources and morale, Kane decided that a third winter would prove fatal. "My party, including myself," he admitted, "were Completely broken—some of them had undergone amputation of toes for frostbite, nearly all were suffering from scurvy."[233] On May 17, 1855, they quit the ice-wallowed *Advance*, tossing their whaleboats onto sledges and packing only the essentials.[234] After a grueling 1,300-mile journey of alternatively towing and rowing their sledges and equipment south, they finally arrived at the northernmost Danish colony of Upernavik on August 6, 1855.[235] From a jolly Danish whaler they heard the latest news: a war in Crimea and the discovery of the remains of Franklin's party, hundreds of miles to the south and west.[236] They had been looking in the wrong place. One can only imagine what went through Kane's mind, or those of his starved, ice-bitten comrades.

A more welcome event awaited them further south, in Godhavn (now Qeqertarsuaq). In September, while in the midst of embarking on a merchant vessel for Denmark, Kane's party spotted a US warship in the distance. It was the war steamer *Release*, commanded by Henry J. Hartstene.[237] As Kane and his men clambered aboard, they learned from the crew that Congress had charged the *Release* with finding and retrieving them from the Arctic. Back in the United States, there had been no news from the expedition since July.[238] By late 1854, Judge Kane, Kennedy, and Grinnell had grown anxious.[239] Together these influential men stirred public concern and sympathy. Petitions begging Congress to dispatch a rescue mission began pouring into Washington from the American Philosophical Society, the New York Chamber of Commerce, the Academy of Natural Sciences, the Boards of Trade of Boston and Philadelphia, and the state governments of New York and New Jersey.[240]

In the winter of 1854–1855, the Pennsylvania congressional delegation took charge of shepherding the bill through Congress. Summoning Kane's heroic status, they warned that abandoning such a citizen would demonstrate that the United States was not a great nation. Rescuing imperiled explorers, Senator Richard Brodhead of Pennsylvania told his colleagues, had become the "duty of a generous Government, representing a generous people."[241] They demanded that the country follow the lead of the British Empire; Kane had become their Franklin. On the wind of such rhetoric, the Kane relief bill easily sailed through Congress in January and February.[242] When a congressman rose to advocate for the measure, a colleague told him to just sit down—"Everybody is in favor of the proposition," he explained.[243]

By the time Hartstene returned to New York with Kane and the crew of the *Advance* on October 11, his countrymen were ecstatic. After all, they had done what the British had not: they had brought back their own missing explorer. Dobbin lavished praise on the commander of the *Release*: "You have discharged the arduous duty which you so nobly volunteered with fidelity, skill, and indomitable energy." He noted that Hartstene had sailed further north than any other explorer aside from Kane, "triumphing over the Shocks of ice bergs & dangers of that inhospitable part of the Globe, and you now return, having accomplished what you had undertaken."[244]

Kane's legend increased even further with his return. By then, his name had become familiar to anyone who followed the national press.[245] "You are now the Lion of the Arctic Regions," Grinnell's son, Cornelius, exclaimed.[246] In Washington, Kane shared tea with the First Lady.[247] He was deluged with requests for lectures, autographs, and artifacts.[248] When, in 1856, publishers released his *Arctic Explorations*, a two-volume account of the Second Grinnell Expedition, they "sold at least 65,000 copies in its first year and 145,000 copies by 1860."[249] Reviewers applauded it on racial grounds. The *North American Review*, for instance, pointed to it as evidence of "the constitution of the Teutonic races." "The Arctic search has served for the test of physical endurance, as well as the trial of character," it boasted.[250]

The British, too, congratulated Kane on his arrival home. The Royal Geographical Society honored him with a gold medal.[251] The British minister to the United States assured Kane of the "sincere regard of the British Government and people for [your] generous exertions."[252] It was Lady Franklin's letter, though, that probably meant the most to Kane. "It is long since I have known any such comfort as that conveyed by your safe return," she wrote him. She praised his "chivalrous devotion" to her cause, and wished that her own countrymen had exhibited the same spirit. She urged him to sail to Great Britain and command her own private search mission to clear up "for ever the mystery which hangs over the fate of my husband's party & obtain their precious records."[253]

Ever attentive to his lady, Kane voyaged to England in October 1856.[254] He knew he could not survive the rigors of another Arctic expedition, but he believed he might help Lady Franklin lobby the British government to assign another vessel for the search. He misjudged his strength. Years of overexertion and exposure on an already frail physiology had taken their toll. Lady Franklin was shocked when she finally met her champion. "He is but a skeleton or the shadow of one," Grinnell had tried to warn her.[255] Still, Lady Franklin hoped he would recover and take to the field once more. But even Kane knew that was no longer possible. "This dream must be over," he wrote his father, for "my health has gone."[256] The Royal Geographical Society held a special meeting in his honor, but Kane was so sick that he had to miss it.[257] He managed to make an interview at Whitehall, where he consulted with the First Lord of the Admiralty, several British admirals and distinguished captains, and the Royal Navy's chief hydrographer. It was his last service to Lady Franklin. In December 1856, he retreated to Cuba. He died in Havana, February 16, 1857, surrounded by his mother, two brothers, and his friend and Arctic comrade William Morton.[258] Lady Franklin was devastated. "I have scarcely the heart to write," she told Grinnell after hearing the news.[259]

In the United States, the national outpouring of grief was enormous. Mourners crowded to pay their respects to Kane as a riverboat and then a locomotive bore his remains to Philadelphia. The historian Mark Sawin estimates that the size of the grieving throngs rivaled those of the funeral trains for Abraham Lincoln and Robert F. Kennedy.[260] They mourned, in part, because Kane had advanced the nation's status abroad. As the *Columbus (GA) Enquirer* opined, Kane's deeds exemplified the kind of "heroism, with all its sacrifices, that exalts nations."[261] When Kane's remains reached Philadelphia, city officials arranged for them to lay in state in Independence Hall. It was a fitting tribute for a man who, white US citizens felt, had helped the nation lay claim to cultural independence and national maturity. Mourners in Philadelphia could advertise their grief by wearing a specially designed black ribbon. "We Mourn the Death of Kane," it said, "Whose Name Adds Lustre to a Mighty Nation."[262] As Kane's fellow citizens watched his slow funeral procession through their towns or filed past his flag-draped coffin in Philadelphia, they may have felt themselves at the crest of a great nation.

THE RETURN OF THE *RESOLUTE*

Participation in the Franklin quest had significantly advanced the US campaign to win recognition from Great Britain as a great Western power. Before 1856, however, slavery and US imperial interests in the Western Hemisphere had held the nation back. So, too, did accusations that British consuls in New York and elsewhere had tried to recruit US citizens to serve in the Crimean War.[263] To white US citizens, such blatant violations of their neutrality laws demonstrated that British officials did not accept the United States as a truly respectable power.

Central America remained a special sore point. US actors were furious that the British continued to hold onto the Bay of Islands in the Caribbean and to shield Indigenous Central Americans with protectorates. In July 1854, their rage turned fiery. Acting on accusations of piracy, the USS *Cyane* shelled Greytown, a British protectorate, on the Nicaraguan coast.[264] While Grinnell and other US merchants feared war, jingoists clashed their swords and shields; they wanted the British to evacuate from the Americas so that they could realize their "manifest destiny." In response, the British press retorted that the United States was a "nation of Pirates" for its own role in producing filibusters.[265] US–UK tensions between 1854 and 1856 were so intense that governing elites on both sides feared the outbreak of hostilities.[266] In late March 1856, Prime Minister Lord Palmerston confessed that the "American dispute" might, and "most likely" would, "end in smoke."[267]

Later that year, however, Palmerston's stance began to soften. The British public, having slogged through Crimea, had little stomach for another war.[268] British merchants—the transatlantic inverts of Grinnell—warned that a military solution would decimate their commerce for a lost cause.[269] Believing that the United States could not be contained, they even suggested that US territorial expansion into Latin America might be good for business.[270] Gradually, Palmerston began to admit his own doubts that the United States could be restricted south of the Rio Grande. By the middle of the twentieth century, he believed, the United States would have settled Cape Horn.[271] He came to agree with economic experts that US growth would benefit British commerce. In October 1856, he opened a new diplomatic overture to settle the dispute over the Clayton–Bulwer Treaty.[272] The British would keep Belize, but, by January 1860, they had abandoned the Mosquito Indians and quit the Bay of Islands.[273] The specter of war dissolved.

Great Britain's retreat from Central America was highly significant. For one, it was a conscious but grudging acknowledgment of US military and economic strength. Nations could achieve greatness in the Western paradigm only if they possessed this bedrock of hard power. Secondly, British acquiescence to US expansion in Central and South America removed the leading external obstacle to the full vision of antebellum US expansion. While the political firestorm over slavery's extension continued, there was now no foreign government powerful enough to keep the US from expanding. Lastly, the recognition of US hard power raised the possibility that the British would also fully acknowledge US advancement in the finer (and final) aspects of national maturity: in culture, science, the arts, and civilization. Of these endeavors, Arctic exploration—far more than any other activity in the decade preceding the US Civil War—had earned the greatest British praise. Even so, the withdrawal from Central America had been a humiliating fallback. Whether or not Britons could overcome their embarrassment and finally acknowledge the United States as one of the greater powers of the world remained uncertain.

The United States still had one more card to play in the game for imperial recognition: they could refurbish and restore the *Resolute*. The HMS *Resolute* had been among those British warships assigned the perennial task of recovering Sir John Franklin or discovering his fate. And, like so many others before, it, too, had gotten fixed in Arctic ice. Abandoned by its captain and crew and lodged firmly in a sheet of ice, the *Resolute* had gradually drifted southward for a thousand miles.[274] A New London whaler discovered the vessel adrift at sea and sailed it back to port. The crew found a ready buyer in the United States Congress, which set aside $40,000 for its purchase and another $40,000 for its restoration.[275]

Supporters in Washington saw the measure as an Arctic peace token over a Central American diplomatic rout. "We have lately wounded the pride of Great Britain," the chairman of the Senate Naval Affairs Committee informed his colleagues. He hoped his countrymen's "true sentiment . . . of high respect and regard for the British people, may be exhibited by promptly restoring a national ship . . . to the possession of Her Majesty."[276] The *Daily Ohio Statesman* agreed; the timing was "most opportune in view of the settlement of the Central American question."[277] In a letter to Grinnell, Secretary of State William Marcy further described the delivery as "one of those international courtesies to be expected from one great nation towards another."[278]

Marcy misspoke. He might have felt like a citizen of a great nation, but only the British could make that assessment.[279] As the *Resolute* rounded the Scilly Islands in December 1856 and rolled toward England, Captain Hartstene pondered what kind of reception he would receive.

The welcome far exceeded his rosiest expectations. The *Resolute* arrived at Spithead in a splitting thunderstorm on December 12.[280] The Royal Navy greeted the *Resolute* handsomely. Acting on a suggestion by Lady Franklin, the queen's warships sounded three royal salutes—a highly unusual honor.[281] Once safely moored, Hartstene took an express to London and began two weeks of visitations and receptions. He and his officers met with the First Sea Lord and attended a banquet in their honor at Plymouth.[282] Back on the *Resolute* on December 22, Hartstene and his officers and crew hosted other British dignitaries. Among them was Lieutenant Bedford Bim, the highest-ranking officer who had abandoned the *Resolute* then in Great Britain. Over drinks that evening in the captain's cabin, Hartstene and his guests agreed on the necessity of another search "to clear up the mystery" of Franklin's disappearance. The following day, a vice admiral accompanied Hartstene to Palmerston's estate for further entertainment.[283] Lady Franklin, dearly hoping she could use Hartstene to convince the Admiralty to send the *Resolute* back to the Arctic once more, hosted the US officers for Christmas supper.[284]

Yet the greatest honor of all came on December 16, when Queen Victoria, Prince Albert, and other members of the royal entourage arrived for a tour of the *Resolute*. When Grinnell's son, Cornelius, received news of the forthcoming visit, he hurried to the ship's new anchorage at Cowes. He was relieved to find the "officers in full uniform, sailors in their best clothes, and the ship exceedingly clean. . . . The royal standard was at the main, ready

Figure 6.3 In *England and America. The Visit of Her Majesty Queen Victoria to the Arctic Ship* Resolute—*December 16th, 1856*, the engraver George Zobel captured the stirring, chivalric sense of US–UK rapprochement contained in the original painting by William Simpson. For explorationists, Queen Victoria's visit to the *Resolute* represented the fulfillment of their aspirations for the United States to be perceived as a cultural equal with the Great Powers of Europe. (Engraving by G. Zobel after the painting by W. Simpson, London: Colnaghi & Co., 1859; courtesy of Library of Congress Prints and Photographs Division, Washington, DC. Control no. 96511945, reproduction nos. LC-DIG-pga-03087, LC-USZC4-4671, https://www.loc.gov/item/96511945/.)

to be unfurled the instant the Queen crossed the gangway. On the fore and mizen [*sic*] masts were the English colors, and at the peak the beautiful spectacle presented itself of our stars and stripes, flowing in graceful harmony with the red cross of St. George."[285]

When the queen reached the gangway, Hartstene offered a short speech, telling Her Majesty that the United States had charged him with returning the *Resolute* "not only as an expression of friendly feeling to your sovereignty, but as a token of love, admiration and respect for your Majesty's person."[286] "The Queen seemed touched by the manly simplicity of this frank and sailor-like address," the London *Times* recorded, "and replied with a gracious smile, 'I thank you, Sir.'"[287]

By bestowing such high honors on the United States, the British came the closest they ever would to recognizing the United States as an equal power in the era of the early US republic. It was a moment that would have made David Porter, Jeremiah Reynolds, John Quincy Adams, or any of the other original explorationists proud. Through a combination of private initiative and public assistance, the United States had earnestly taken up Lady Franklin's invitation in April 1849 to join the ranks of civilized nations. Contemporaries perceived these developments through the lens of gendered medievalism and racial Anglo-Saxonism. Grinnell, De Haven, Kane, and dozens of ordinary sailors had acted gallantly in riding to Lady Franklin's aid. By persevering in the planet's least forgiving environment, they had proven their manly fortitude and racial hardiness. Their exertions thus strengthened domestic and European notions of white supremacy for years to come. Diplomatically, their efforts laid the groundwork for the civilizational component of US national maturity. Once the British Empire had finally come to terms with the juggernaut of US territorial expansion in the Western Hemisphere in 1856, these men had made it all but impossible for the British to withhold recognition of the United States as a fully cultured, imperial nation.

When Hartstene returned to the United States in January 1857, he found a "handsomely mounted Sword of Honor" waiting for him at the Navy Department. It had come from Queen Victoria.[288] Fortunately for both powers, it was a sword of peace.

Epilogue

He must have read it in the paper: Elisha Kent Kane was sailing from England to Cuba to recover his shattered health. South Carolina planter Lewis M. Hatch saw an opportunity; he could be of service to the great man. Knowing that Kane was a Philadelphian and would likely return to that city after a stay in the West Indies, Hatch decided to offer his estate as a way station. "Although I have not the pleasure of a personal acquaintance," he wrote, "I feel in Common with all your Countrymen a deep interest in your welfare." His plantation was four miles outside town, "in a sheltered, sunny spot." "The grounds are dry for walking[,] the pine woods soothing[,] the fields pleasant," he told Kane. Doctors could ride easily in from Charleston if need be, but they likely wouldn't have to: "Many a stranger can bear grateful testimony to the goodness of our ladies as nurses." But of course, he added, "with us . . . you will be no stranger."[1]

Kane never received this letter; it was addressed to Philadelphia and came to his father's hands instead. John Kintzing Kane thought it was notable, and preserved it for future generations. And indeed it is notable. As Hatch made clear in his letter, he knew Kane only through print sources. But that was enough for him to think of Kane as "no stranger." His letter brims with compassion, sympathy, and familiarity. If, by some miracle, Kane had managed to make good on Hatch's offer, it seems clear he would have been well taken care of.

But what did Kane mean to Hatch specifically? We can only conjecture, but his letter suggests a few possible answers. Since Hatch only "knew" Kane through print media, the explorer's portrayal in print would be important. The final chapter of this book has argued that the public press and Kane's own books presented him as the ideal Anglo-Saxon man. As the Philadelphia *Evening Journal* declared after his death, Kane represented "that abstract idea of manly virtue" and one of "the loftiest examples of manhood."[2] As deeply as gender roles were etched in the antebellum North, they were even more so in the white South.[3] Hatch may have admired how Kane's services to Lady Franklin in the Arctic had ennobled patriarchy. He may have further appreciated how Arctic exploration had provided his female relatives ("our ladies") with clear notions of how white men and women should relate to each other. Moreover, as a slaveholder, Hatch could have been tickled to hear so much gushing about Anglo-Saxon endurance and superiority. Perhaps he laughed with Kane and his men, when, in *Arctic Explorations*, a comrade joked about Black men making a feast of beans and pork.[4] He was almost certainly grateful that Kane had not used his celebrity status to join his brother Thomas in militating against slavery.[5] If he had, he surely would not have invited him to his home. In sum, the South Carolina planter may have valued Kane's contributions to a hierarchical society.

Hatch's letter holds other tantalizing clues about the identity of the antebellum US nation. For one, the planter identified with other white US citizens' concerns over Kane's well-being: "I feel in Common with all your Countrymen a deep interest in your welfare." His pledge that Kane would not be a "stranger" in his household suggests he considered him as if he were a friend or a family member. He was far from alone in feeling this way; the Kane family papers at the American Philosophical Society and the Historical Society of Pennsylvania preserve dozens of other condolence letters from US citizens who knew neither Kane nor his family personally. In Cincinnati, Ohio, a young girl named Emma Lou Sprigman wrote Kane's mother, Jane Leiper Kane, and expressed her grief in familial terms. "Long have I loved him as I would a dear brother," she wrote. "I have read of his noble and selfsacrificing [*sic*] deeds, till my heart has overflown with advancing love for him," she explained.[6] "The bereavement that has stricken you," another mourner wrote Mrs. Kane, "lies heavy upon many."[7] In Louisville, Kentucky, the local bar association conveyed its condolences to Kane's father. "A nation claims a participation in your grief," they told him. "The reputation of your son belongs to the American people, and will be cherished as a part of the nation's wealth."[8] Collectively, such letters reveal that white US citizens from every corner of the country believed themselves to be members of a single, almost familial nation before the Civil War.

Naval explorers like Kane had helped to build and strengthen that sense of national identity. They shaped US culture almost as much as they were shaped by it. Edgar Allan Poe based his *Narrative of Arthur Gordon Pym of Nantucket* on Reynolds's obsession with exploring the South Pole.[9] When Poe died of a fever in 1849, he did so with the explorer's name on his lips.[10] Herman Melville, too, was greatly influenced by Reynolds's account of a vengeful white whale in the Pacific named "Mocha Dick." He also owned

a set of Wilkes's five-volume *Narrative*, which he responded to in margi-
nalia.[11] As a young man, Mark Twain consciously tried to replicate his own
Amazon expedition, though not explicitly for slavery.[12] Ralph Waldo Emerson praised Kane and other maritime explorers for increasing the wealth of
Western knowledge and culture.[13] Emerson's rebellious and erstwhile protégé, Henry David Thoreau, loved nothing better than to stretch out and
read a good account of naval exploration.[14] So, too, did his countrymen and
-women. "There is no frigate like a book," the poet Emily Dickinson wrote,
"to take us lands far away."[15]

The white middle and upper classes came to admire naval explorers because such men had helped build a national identity that reflected
what they valued most about themselves: European cultural and racial/
ethnic heritage, liberal capitalism, middle-class character, and conservative evangelical Christianity. In fêting explorers like Kane, white citizens
consistently overlooked the working-class sailors, brown-skinned guides
and porters, Islamic and Inuit allies, South American creoles, and British
noblewomen whose contributions allowed that selective vision of the nation to flourish. When the officers of the Ex Ex decided to raise a monument to commemorate the deaths of Lieutenant Joseph Underwood and
Midshipman Wilkes Henry at Malolo, Fiji, they consciously excluded the
ordinary seamen who had also perished during the expedition. In addition
to Underwood and Henry, the twenty-foot marble obelisk in Mount Auburn Cemetery in Cambridge, Massachusetts, honors two passed midshipmen who had disappeared off Cape Horn with their ship, the *Sea-Gull*, in
1839. It does not list the names of any of the fifteen sailors who drowned
with them.[16] This was a monument for officers, by officers; it reflects the
imperial society that raised it.

Given the national attachment to explorers like Kane, it should come
as no surprise that there was an attempt to memorialize the Arctic hero in
stone. The earliest attempt was Kane's tomb itself, an elegant, Egyptian-
style edifice burrowed into a hill in Laurel Hill Cemetery, Philadelphia.
Overlooking the Schuylkill River and bustling Kelly Drive, it holds the
remains of Kane, his father, mother, and other relatives. It is impressive
but secluded. Kane admirers wanted something more. In June 1859, they
guided a charter for the "Kane Monument Association" through the New
York State legislature. Afterward, members of "Kane Lodge," a newly dedicated Freemason lodge in New York City, began a subscription campaign
to raise funds for a statue.[17]

They ran out of time. In the winter of 1860–1861, the antebellum imperial nation fractured. The explorationist coalition split alongside it. In
South Carolina, Hatch donned the Confederate uniform. In July 1861, he

served as an aide to P. G. T. Beauregard at the Battle of First Bull Run. Afterward, he commanded the 23rd North Carolina regiment, though apparently not without controversy.[18] John Pendleton Kennedy remained loyal, but he and George Bancroft were the only former living secretaries of the navy who did. Isaac Toucey, James Buchanan's secretary of the navy, stayed quietly in the North during the war, but he was strongly suspected of Confederate sympathies. In the waning days of the Buchanan administration, with the nation well into the secession crisis, Toucey spread the navy out across the world's oceans. Critics charged him with aiming to prevent federal warships from being used against the secessionist South. His predecessors, William B. Preston and William A. Graham, both supporters of the Amazon Expedition, passed the war years in Richmond as Confederate politicians.[19]

Matthew Fontaine Maury, Lardner Gibbon, Henry J. Hartstene, and William Francis Lynch also went south. Maury's choice vexed Northern maritime communities. They had been the greatest beneficiaries of his scientific work—far more than slaveholders ever were—and they took the news hard. In 1859, the East India Marine Society in Salem had voted him "their first and only elected honorary member."[20] Two years later, they ejected him. One member pulled his portrait off the wall of the museum and wrote "Lieut/M. P. Maury/Traitor" on its back.[21] Page, the former commander of the La Plata expedition, worked first to strengthen Confederate shore defenses and then to win allies in Europe.[22] Lynch, for his part, spent most of the war on the coast of North Carolina, waging a desperate struggle to hold off a far superior force.[23] His reputation as a naval explorer followed him into Confederate service. Late one evening in February 1862, one of his officers, William Harwar Parker, "found him in his dressing gown sitting quietly in his cabin reading Ivanhoe."[24] It was the night before an anticipated Union assault on Roanoke, and the odds were long. The two officers discussed battle plans, but after a while found themselves circling back to literature. Parker was not entirely surprised: "Lynch was a cultivated man," he explained. "He had made some reputation in the navy by his book upon the Dead Sea exploration," and was "a most agreeable talker."[25] Another secessionist in North Carolina, Catherine Ann Edmonston, also remembered Lynch's expedition to the Holy Land. When Lynch asked to consult her husband on military matters, she wrote in her diary that he "went immediately to see the Dead Sea Explorer."[26]

Other naval explorers stayed loyal. William Reynolds, the midshipman who had kept a secret journal of his thoughts during the Ex Ex, fought with distinction for the North in the Civil War. He became a rear admiral in 1873.[27] His companion on the expedition, the conchologist Joseph B.

Couthoy, commanded a series of Union gunboats in the South and died in battle.[28] Another Ex Ex veteran, Lieutenant James B. Alden, fought in several naval campaigns over the course of the war, including those at New Orleans, Vicksburg, and Fort Fisher.[29] The old commander of the Ex Ex, the cruel and crotchety Charles Wilkes, also had an eventful wartime career. In November 1861, he stopped a British mail steamer named the *Trent* and took two Confederate diplomats into custody. The United Kingdom, outraged by Wilkes's violation of the Union Jack, prepared for war. Secretary of State William H. Seward diffused the situation, but the *Trent* affair was one of the closest moments the British ever came to intervening on behalf of the Confederate cause.[30]

The older generation of explorationists did not have to make the fateful choices that their younger fellows did. David Porter died in Constantinople in 1840 as the resident minister from the United States to the Sublime Porte.[31] He had survived just long enough to see his original proposal from 1815 realized, though we have no record of what he thought about it. John Quincy Adams passed away eight years later, in 1848. Unlike Porter, he had lived to see the return of the Ex Ex and some of its scientific results. On a visit to Wilkes's house in 1842, Adams had marveled at the "great number of the drawings collected during the exploring expedition—portraits of men, women, and children, of the ocean, and Feejee Islands. Fishes, birds, plants, shells, and navigating charts are in great profusion," he wrote in his diary, "more than I had time to examine."[32] His satisfaction must have been supreme. When his fellow explorationist, William Francis Lynch, learned of the former president's death, he was busy charting the Dead Sea. He lowered the flag to half-mast and ordered the expedition's blunderbuss to fire "twenty-one minute-guns . . . in honour of the illustrious dead." "The reports reverberated loudly and strangely amid the cavernous recesses of those lofty and barren mountains," he wrote.[33]

Jeremiah Reynolds never attained the fame he burned for. After the sailing of the Ex Ex, he became a lawyer in New York City, specializing in maritime law.[34] He appears to have written a full account of his travels in South America, but he published only snippets. The full manuscript rotted in his law desk and disappeared with his death in 1858.[35] Reynolds passed at a time when his fellow white citizens, stirred by Kane's exertions in the polar North, began trumpeting his contributions to US global exploration. An early indication of this line of thinking emerged in 1843, when the poet Edgar Allan Poe reviewed Reynolds's *Brief Account of the Discoveries and Results of the United States' Exploring Expedition.* "To him, we say and to him in fact *solely* does the high honor of this triumphant Expedition belong," Poe wrote. "When men, hereafter, shall come to speak of this Expedition, they will speak of it not as the American Expedition nor even as the Poinsett Expedition, nor as the Dickerson Expedition, nor, alas! as the Wilkes Expedition they will speak of it if they speak at all as 'The Expedition of Mr. Reynolds.'"[36] Anna Ella Carroll was another admirer. In an updated edition of her popular *Star of the West; Or, National Men and National Measures* from 1857, she lavished praise on Reynolds as the forgotten founding father of US naval exploration. Reynolds had "conceived and accomplished for his country what the most undaunted navigator had not before imagined, or had the moral courage to propose."[37] Thanks to his pivotal role in the dispatch of the Ex Ex, he had managed "to equalize our condition . . . with every foreign government of the Old World."[38] "All subsequent expeditions and voyages of discovery in this country owe their origin to him," she averred.[39] Whether or not Reynolds saw these lines before his death is unknown. A modern Icarus, he was one of thousands of would-be conquerors and near-great white men in the early US republic. What Scott Sandage once wrote about Henry David Thoreau also applies to Reynolds: "The root of his success—ambition—was also the root of his failure."[40]

Had Reynolds lived through the Civil War years, he would have witnessed the destruction of the global antebellum US empire that he had helped build. The center of that empire had long rested with the Pacific whaling fleet and with the navy's ability to protect and extend it. The conflict of 1861–1865 inflicted deep wounds on both. Off the coast of South Carolina, the Union navy sunk dozens of old whalers in the channels of Charleston harbor. Union strategists hoped that the so-called Stone Fleet would help wall the Confederates in and prevent privateering and blockade running.[41] In England, meanwhile, Maury collaborated with other Confederate agents to purchase and outfit powerful, fast-sailing vessels as commerce raiders.[42] The CSS *Alabama* and *Shenandoah* were two of the most successful incarnations of this strategy. Together, the warships wreaked havoc on Union shipping. The *Shenandoah*'s cruise in the Pacific was particularly ruinous for the US whale fishery; its commander, James Waddell, sailed into the Pacific Ocean and burned twenty-five Yankee whaleships.[43] By war's end, the US whaling fleet was half the size of what it had been in 1860.[44] Overall, the Confederate Navy took three hundred Union prizes and chased a million tons of US shipping from the world's oceans.[45] The redistribution of Union warships from global squadrons to the southern and Gulf coasts made such devastating figures possible. The tentacles had been recalled; for four long years, the kraken fought itself.

The scarred hulk that emerged afterward was different from its antebellum predecessor. Its global maritime presence had been irreparably damaged, for one. While the whaling industry rebounded after the Civil War, its revival was short lived. It had already been under stress as early as the 1840s, when alternative lighting sources became readily available, but the big turning point came in 1859 with the discovery of petroleum deposits in Pennsylvania. Overflowing oil wells made kerosene lanterns much cheaper than those that burned whale oil.[46] In the summers of 1871 and again in 1876, the industry suffered further setbacks when Arctic ice crushed much of the whaling fleet in the Bering Sea.[47] US blue-water shipping also declined in the postwar era. During the Civil War, Northern merchants began registering their ships in foreign ports to protect them from Confederate raiders. They continued the practice after the war. Even today, flying "flags of convenience" remains a major aspect of global shipping.[48] The demographics of the maritime labor force shifted, too. US crews, especially whaleships, had long been international, but they became increasingly so after the Civil War. Nativist white sailors and politicians alike bemoaned the racial and ethnic diversity of postwar shipping lists.[49]

As the number of US citizen-sailors and commercial vessels shrank in the second half of the nineteenth century, the demand for government aid in exploration, charting, and protection also decreased.[50] The postbellum US Navy sent very few exploring expeditions around the world. In 1879, the navy partnered with a New York City newspaper mogul named James Gordon Bennett to send his ship, the USS *Jeannette*, on a scientific expedition to the Arctic. Unlike the Grinnell expeditions, this was not so much a diplomatic thrust as a publicity stunt for Bennett's *New York Herald*. It was thus an Arctic version of Bennett's earlier financing of Henry Morton Stanley's quest for David Livingstone in Africa in 1871–1872. And unlike the Grinnell expeditions, the results, too, were disastrous: all but two of the thirty-three men perished.[51] A much smaller expedition unfolded in the Belgian Congo, where naval Lieutenant Emory Taunt surveyed the Congo River for commercial opportunities between 1885 and 1890. Like his comrades on the *Jeannette*, Taunt also died in the field.[52] Compared to the seventeen antebellum exploring expeditions, these two fatal missions, alongside a few others from the era, come across as paltry and ill designed. National voyages of discovery were no longer the focus of the nation. Shorn of its global empire, the United States had little need for naval exploration.

Foreign relations may have also played a role. Increasing European respect for the United States in the mid-nineteenth century meant that national voyages of discovery were no longer necessary, diplomatically speaking. By 1860, the United States could claim some degree of membership in the exclusive club of the great European nations. While Europeans were not quite ready to raise their US diplomatic missions to embassies and their ministers to ambassadors before the US–Spanish–Cuban–Filipino War, they increasingly used the phrase *great power* to describe the United States as the antebellum era came to a close.[53] In an 1849 letter to the US minister to Great Britain, the UK's foreign secretary, Lord Palmerston, hoped a "union of two great Powers" would result in a transoceanic canal or railway across Central America.[54] Similarly, in 1851 the former French minister to the United States marveled at the growth of the North American republic: "The American nation still exists in all the vigor of early youth," he wrote, "though it has already taken its rank, through its intellectual and material development in the last fifty years, among the most prosperous and civilized nations of the world."[55] In 1859, facing yet another US–UK crisis, the London *Times* sought to explain the bipolar relationship that existed between both nations. They suggested that the United States' antipathy dated back to its colonial founding as a refuge for dissidents, and that this explained why this country, "among all the great Powers of the world," was "the one which is most liable to capricious fluctuations in its friendly affinities to us."[56]

As its utility decreased, US naval exploration sunk from view. Indeed, two of the most public monuments to antebellum naval explorers elide their role in global imperialism. One is the Herndon monument at the US Naval Academy in Annapolis, Maryland. Like Kane or Reynolds, William Lewis Herndon never had to choose sides in the Civil War. In 1855, the leader of the Amazon expedition left the navy and took up the captaincy of the *Central America*, a US mail steamer and transatlantic passenger vessel. In September 1857, an Atlantic hurricane swamped the *Central America* off the coast of North Carolina. More than four hundred passengers and crew lost their lives in the disaster, including Herndon. By all accounts, he acted as a model captain should, prioritizing the lives of his fellow voyagers over his own.[57] In 1860, Herndon's admirers raised an obelisk to his heroism at the Naval Academy. Climbing its greased surface has become an annual tradition for what the academy used to call plebes, or first-year students.[58] The steep surface bears no mention of Herndon's efforts to push the boundaries of the Slave South into the Brazilian Amazon. Until recently, Herndon's brother-in-law Maury had a prominent statue in Richmond, Virginia. Dedicated in 1929, it explicitly celebrates Maury as the "pathfinder of the seas." Its real purpose, however, was to toast another of Virginia's Confederate sons for the twentieth century.[59] The statue was removed as a symbol of white supremacy on July 2, 2020.[60] As with the Herndon monument in Annapolis, it was stonily silent on the subject of Maury's dedication to extending slavery. Perhaps Wilkes's old campaign to make the Ex Ex narrative and scientific volumes the chief "monuments" of his expedition had been all

too successful; Congress, frequently exasperated by the costs of the Ex Ex
volumes, could not conceive of spending any more money on public monuments to naval exploration.[61]

In the present-day United States, perhaps the best physical embodiment
of the subterranean history of US naval exploration is the Smithsonian Institution. Between 1857 and 1858, employees of the National Gallery packed
up the Ex Ex specimens and sent them to the Smithsonian for preserva-
tion and display. They quickly became one of the establishment's core collections.[62] A few are even still visible in the National Museum of Natural
History. Most Smithsonian employees know this history. In the mid-1980s,
Herman J. Viola, Adrienne Kaeppler, and their colleagues staged an elaborate exhibit at the National Museum of Natural History to commemorate
the Ex Ex's contributions to science and the Smithsonian collections.[63] Despite their efforts, the navy's role in this hallmark of national life remains
largely unknown to the general public. Some may know that the name of
the Smithsonian derives from James Smithson, an English chemist whose
generous gift provided the funds for the institution's foundation. His bones
still molder in a public tomb at the very entrance of the Smithsonian Castle;
hundreds of thousands of visitors surge past them every year. Few, however, likely know the full story of how Smithson's institution came to be,
where its oldest collections came from, or who gathered them, and at what
cost. Like so many others across the United States, they know little of the
buried imperial histories over which they walk. And yet, in their curious
footsteps, the empire of knowledge—with all its explorations, commemo-
rations, and forgettings—lives on.

Acknowledgments

Books are intellectual journeys. Like any expedition, they require supplies, guidance, and support. This voyage has been no different. From this book's beginnings during my graduate studies at the University of New Hampshire (UNH), Eliga Gould's insights, encouragement, and scholarly example were indispensable. His hand is very much in this work, as some readers will recognize. Like Lige, W. Jeffrey Bolster has been another crucial adviser and mentor. Both have been my best and most formative intellectual critics. I hope that I have approached their high expectations. I am also grateful to the other members of my dissertation committee, including Kurk Dorsey, Jessica Lepler, Jan Golinski, and Rosemarie Zagarri. All these scholars offered helpful perspectives, suggestions, and motivation. They have since become good friends. I am immensely grateful for their friendship and continued support.

The Department of History at UNH provided not only four years of funding, but also a dynamic and supportive intellectual community that inspired and nourished me. Ellen Fitzpatrick, Gregory McMahon, Cynthia van Zandt, Bill Harris, Jason Sokol, Molly Dorsey, and so many others mentored and buoyed me during my time there. The same can be said for Bill Ross, Roland Goodbody, and the other staff at the Milne Special Collections and Archives at the UNH Library. I am indebted, too, to the UNH Graduate School for numerous travel grants and a crucial Dissertation Year Fellowship. Deans Harry Richards, Cari Moorhead, and the members of Graduate Student Senate kept me rooted, honest, and engaged on campus during the lonely dissertation years.

Many other institutions and organizations provided critical resources along the way. The Naval History and Heritage Command funded my summer 2015 research through a Rear Admiral Ernest M. Eller Graduate Research Grant. A short-term research fellowship at the Massachusetts Historical Society in 2016–2017 permitted me to begin gathering new materials for the book. A fellowship through the Baird Society Resident Scholar

Program at the Smithsonian Libraries allowed me to acquire data for what would become chapter 3. I am especially indebted to Lilla Vekerdy, Leslie Overstreet, Alexandra Alvis, Morgan Aronson, and so many other professionals at the Smithsonian Institution for their warm welcome and assistance. The staff at the Library Company of Philadelphia were just as helpful and hospitable during my residency in 2018 as a National Endowment for the Humanities postdoctoral fellow. I am especially grateful to Jim Green for his assistance and suggestions for chapter 3. As an NEH fellow, I am required to state that any views, findings, conclusions, or recommendations expressed in this publication do not necessarily reflect those of the National Endowment for the Humanities. The archivists and personnel at Princeton University Library, the New Jersey Historical Society, the National Archives and Records Administration (NARA) in Washington, DC, and in Waltham, Massachusetts, the American Philosophical Society, and the Historical Society of Pennsylvania were also enormously helpful in researching this book. Special thanks to Joe Keefe and his colleagues at NARA Boston.

There are many others who deserve my thanks. At the University of Massachusetts Amherst, Heather Cox Richardson and Robert S. Cox were ideal undergraduate mentors. My friends and graduate peers at UNH, especially Amanda Demmer, Patrick LaCroix, Justine Oliva, Sarah Batterson, Matt Smith, Derek Nelson, Sonic Woytonik, and Susannah Deily-Swearingen, were key allies and supporters. John Wilson and Lara Abramowitz graciously opened their home to me during my summer 2014 dissertation research in Washington, DC. My in-laws, Jeff and Ruth Bailey, allowed me to finish the book at their gorgeous seaside home in Carmel, California. Friends and colleagues at the North American Society for Oceanic History, the Society for Historians of the Early American Republic, and the Society for Historians of American Foreign Relations were subjected to many previous incarnations of the chapters that appear here. They bore it well, and I have benefited greatly from their encouragement and scholarly advice. Special thanks to Dane Morrison, Nicole Phelps, Amy Greenberg, and Paul Gilje for their thoughts on chapter 2. Thanks also to Oxford University Press, which published a previous version of chapter 5 under the title "'The Universal Yankee Nation': Proslavery Expeditions to South America, 1850–1860" (*Diplomatic History* 44, no. 2 [April 2020], 337–64). I would also like to thank my colleagues and students at Drury University for their interest in and support of this book project. Among them are Bill Garvin, who supplied the secret library carrel in which I wrote much of my revised chapters, and his colleagues in the Olin Library, who tirelessly and cheerfully processed far too many book orders for a single individual. My chair, Ted

Vaggalis, generously provided department funds for scholarly conferences and for the production of the maps. Thanks especially to my students, who are a constant source of inspiration and energy for my scholarly endeavors.

At the University of Chicago Press, a special thanks to Tim Mennel, Susannah Engstrom, and the American Beginnings series editors for their interest in and patience with this project. I owe a special debt of gratitude to the manuscript's outside readers, Gautham Rao and an anonymous second reader. Their suggestions on the original manuscript pushed me to think far more broadly and deeply about the workers, workings, and meanings of empire than I otherwise would have. Johanna Rosenbohm was an exceptional copy editor. I am grateful for her insights and suggestions.

Lastly, I owe heartfelt thanks to my family. My parents, Steve and Kay Verney, awoke and nourished in me a passion for knowledge and the world. Since my childhood, they have made enormous sacrifices to enable my brother and me to receive the best education possible. They encouraged my passion for history from an early age and supported my first book project with enthusiasm and generosity. Most recently, my mother served as a keen and erudite proofreader, for which I am grateful. Like my parents, my brother, Jon, has been a constant source of inspiration and renewal. To their love and support, and to those of my grandparents, aunts, uncles, cousins, and family friends, I owe so much. Special acknowledgment is due to my grandfather, Frank Reusché, a fellow history lover who took me to Valley Forge and Gettysburg, and my grandmother, Mary Noble, who generously supported my undergraduate education. While neither lived to see this book, both had a hand in shaping it. Above all, I am indebted to my wife and best friend, Blair Bailey Verney. She signed on to this expedition just as it was getting underway, and she has never left my side. She has since recruited two young deckhands, Caroline Grace and Daniel James Verney, who have given this author more pride than any book ever can. Blair's friendship, love, and partnership have meant more to me than I can express. I am infinitely richer for her intellectual companionship, her good humor, and her support of my scholarly endeavors. She is, and always will be, my Abigail.

Notes

INTRODUCTION

1. David F. Long, *"Nothing Too Daring": A Bibliography of Commodore David Porter, 1780–1843* (Annapolis, MD: United States Naval Institute, 1970), 175–76.

2. Historians have narrated Porter's cruise in the Pacific during the War of 1812 in detail. See Long, *Nothing Too Daring*; George C. Daughan, *The Shining Sea: David Porter and the Epic Voyage of the U.S.S. Essex during the War of 1812* (New York: Basic Books, 2013); and Charles Lee Lewis, *David Glasgow Farragut: Admiral in the Making* (Annapolis, MD: United States Naval Institute, 1941). For Porter's own published account of his cruise aboard the *Essex*, see his memoirs, *A Journal of a Cruise Made to the Pacific Ocean* (1815; repr., Philadelphia: Wiley and Halstead, 1822); and *A Voyage in the South Seas* (London: Sir Richard Philips, 1823).

3. David Porter to James Madison, dated October 31, 1815, reprinted in Allan B. Cole, "Captain David Porter's Proposed Expedition to the Pacific and Japan, 1815," *Pacific Historical Review*, March 1940, 61–65.

4. Douglas E. Evelyn, chap. 11, "The National Gallery at the Patent Office," in *Magnificent Voyagers: The U.S. Exploring Expedition, 1838–1842*, ed. Herman J. Viola and Carolyn Margolis (Washington, DC: Smithsonian Institution Press, 1985), 236.

5. For global histories of exploration, see Louise Levathes, *When China Ruled the Seas: The Treasure Fleet of the Dragon Throne, 1405–1433* (Oxford: Oxford University Press, 1994); Felipe Fernández-Armesto, *Pathfinders: A Global History of Exploration* (New York: W. W. Norton, 2006); Giancarlo Casale, *The Ottoman Age of Exploration* (Oxford: Oxford University Press, 2010); and Lincoln Paine, *The Sea and Civilization: A Maritime History of the World* (New York: Knopf, 2013). For the First Age of European Exploration, see titles by Samuel Eliot Morison, as well as the works J. H. Parry, *The Age of Reconnaissance: Discovery, Exploration, and Settlement, 1450–1650* (1963; repr., Berkeley: University of California Press, 1982); Brian Fagan, *Fish on Friday: Feasting, Fasting, and the Discovery of the New World* (New York: Basic Books, 2006); and David Abulafia, *The Discovery of Mankind: Atlantic Encounters in the Age of Columbus* (New Haven, CT: Yale University Press, 2008).

6. Maryland House of Representatives quoted in a letter from Jeremiah Reynolds to the speaker of the US House of Representatives, February 10, 1828, reprinted in "On the expediency of fitting out vessels of the Navy for an exploration of the Pacific Ocean and South Seas. Communicated to the House of Representatives," March 25, 1828, *American State Papers: Naval Affairs*, 3:190.

7. *Cong. Globe*, 34th Cong., 1st Sess., 646 (March 13, 1856).

8. This book uses the phrase *white US citizens* frequently. In general, citizenship was restricted to those deemed white in the early republic. However, there were exceptions, especially in some northern states and in special circumstances at sea. Therefore, though the phrase *white US citizens* may seem redundant, I feel that it is vital to acknowledge both the historical restrictions on US citizenship as well as the ways in which racial minorities have laid claim to—often unsuccessfully, but sometimes successfully—that citizenship. For more on US citizenship at home and abroad in the early US republic, see W. Jeffrey Bolster, *Black Jacks: African American Seamen in the Age of Sail* (Cambridge, Massachusetts: Harvard University Press, 1997); Nathan Perl-Rosenthal, *Citizen Sailors: Becoming American in the Age of Revolution* (Cambridge, MA: Harvard University Press, 2015); Nancy Shoemaker, *Native American Whalemen and the World: Indigenous Encounters and the Contingency of Race* (Chapel Hill: University of North Carolina Press, 2015); and James H. Kettner, *The Development of American Citizenship, 1608–1870* (Chapel Hill: University of North Carolina Press, 1978), esp. 287–333.

9. Brooke Hindle, *The Pursuit of Science in Revolutionary America* (Chapel Hill: University of North Carolina Press, 1956); William E. Burns, *Science and Technology in Colonial America* (Westport, CT: Greenwood Press, 2005); Richard L. Bushman, *The Refinement of America: Persons, Houses, Cities* (New York: Knopf, 1992).

10. Benedict Anderson makes his observation in *Imagined Communities: Reflections on the Origin and Spread of Nationalism* (1983; reprint, London: Verso, 2006), 81.

11. Sam W. Haynes, *Unfinished Revolution: The Early American Republic in a British World* (Charlottesville: University of Virginia Press, 2010); Daniel Kilbride, *Being American in Europe, 1750–1860* (Baltimore: Johns Hopkins University Press, 2013).

12. Eliga H. Gould, *Among the Powers of the Earth: The American Revolution and the Making of a New World Empire* (Cambridge, MA: Harvard University Press, 2012).

13. Kariann Akemi Yokota, *Unbecoming British: How Revolutionary America Became a Postcolonial Nation* (Oxford: Oxford University Press, 2010).

14. Burns, *Science and Technology in Colonial America*, 163.

15. See Christopher McKee, *A Gentlemanly and Honorable Profession: The Creation of the U.S. Navy Officer Corps, 1794–1815* (Annapolis, MD: Naval Institute Press, 1991).

16. Dane Anthony Morrison, *True Yankees: The South Seas and the Discovery of American Identity* (Baltimore: Johns Hopkins University Press, 2014), 91.

17. "Remarks of Mr. Baker, of Illinois, in Favor of the Franklin Expedition, in the House, April 26th," *Daily Atlas* (Boston), May 2, 1850. For more on why explorationists believed that private maritime exploring expeditions could not succeed, see J. N. Reynolds to unknown recipient, February 10, 1828, reprinted in *American State Papers: Naval Affairs*, 4:711; and Benjamin Pendleton to Edmund Fanning, September 15, 1831, reprinted in Edmund Fanning, *Voyages Round the World* (New York: Collins & Hannay, 1833), 486.

18. Ernest R. May discusses this idea in *Imperial Democracy: The Emergence of America as a Great Power* (New York: Harcourt, Brace & World, 1961). See also Haynes, *Unfinished Revolution*; and Gould, *Among the Powers of the Earth*.

19. This definition of what it meant to be a Great Power in the early nineteenth century is an amalgamation of Paul Kennedy's *Rise and Fall of the Great Powers: Economic Change and Military Conflict from 1500–2000* (New York: Random House, 1987); Jack S. Levy's *War in the Modern Great Power System, 1495–1975* (Lexington: University Press

of Kentucky, 1983); and the author's own primary source research in mid-nineteenth-century British newspapers, especially the digital database of the *Times* of London, accessible by subscription at *The Times Digital Archive*, http://gale.cengage.co.uk/times.aspx/.

20. Frederick Merck, "The Genesis of the Oregon Question," *Mississippi Valley Historical Review* 36 (March 1950), 594; Long, *Nothing Too Daring*, 174, and Alexander Slidell Mackenzie, *Commodore Oliver Hazard Perry: Famous American Naval Hero* (1840; New York: D. M. Maclellan, 1910), 320.

21. For opposition even to the establishment of a US naval academy, see William P. Leeman, *The Long Road to Annapolis: The Founding of the Naval Academy and the Emerging American Republic* (Chapel Hill: University of North Carolina Press, 2010).

22. William H. Goetzmann discusses Long's several western expeditions in *Exploration and Empire: The Explorer and the Scientist in the Winning of the American West* (1966; repr., New York: Francis Parkman Prize Edition, History Book Club, 2006), 58–64.

23. A. W. Habersham, *The North Pacific Surveying and Exploring Expedition, Or, My Last Cruise . . .* (Philadelphia: J. B. Lippincott, 1858), 13–14.

24. See, for instance, Andrew Porter, *Religion versus Empire? British Protestant Missionaries and Overseas Expansion, 1700–1914* (Manchester: Manchester University Press, 2004); Jeffrey Cox, *Imperial Fault Lines: Christianity and Colonial Power in India, 1818–1940* (Stanford, CA: Stanford University Press, 2002); Ian Tyrrell, *Reforming the World: The Creation of America's Moral Empire* (Princeton, NJ: Princeton University Press, 2010); and Jay Sexton and Ian Tyrell, eds., *Empire's Twin: U.S. Anti-imperialism from the Founding Era to the Age of Terrorism* (Ithaca, NY: Cornell University Press, 2015).

25. Brandon Mills makes a similar observation in *The World Colonization Made: The Racial Geography of Early American Empire* (Philadelphia: University of Pennsylvania Press, 2020), 4.

26. For more on the term *transimperial*, see Kristin L. Hoganson and Jay Sexton, eds., *Crossing Empires: Taking U.S. History into Transimperial Terrain* (Durham, NC: Duke University Press, 2020), esp. the introduction, 1–22.

27. Neil Asher Silberman, *Digging for God and Country: Exploration, Archeology, and the Secret Struggle of the Holy Land, 1799–1917* (New York: Knopf, 1982), 52–53. See also Barbara Kreiger, *The Dead Sea: Myth, History, and Politics* (Hanover, NH: Published for Brandeis University Press by the University Press of New England, 1997); and Haim Goren, *Dead Sea Level: Science, Exploration, and Imperial Interests in the Near East* (London: I. B. Tauris, 2011).

28. Several scholars have relied on the Hercules analogy in their own works. These include Marcus Rediker and Peter Linebaugh, *The Many-Headed Hydra: Sailors, Slaves, Commoners, and the Hidden World of the Revolutionary Atlantic* (Boston: Beacon Press, 2000); and Max M. Edling, *A Hercules in the Cradle: War, Money, and the American State, 1783–1867* (Chicago: University of Chicago Press, 2014).

29. Anderson, *Imagined Communities*.

30. Quoted in Frances Leigh Williams, *Matthew Fontaine Maury, Scientist of the Sea* (New Brunswick, NJ: Rutgers University Press, 1963), 357.

31. Anderson, *Imagined Communities*.

32. George Rogers Taylor, *The Transportation Revolution, 1815–1860* (New York, 1951); Ronald J. Zboray, *A Fictive People: Antebellum Economic Development and the*

American Reading Public (New York, 1993); Richard R. John, *Spreading the News: The American Postal System from Franklin to Morse* (Cambridge, MA: Harvard University Press, 1995); Daniel Walker Howe, *What Hath God Wrought: The Transformation of America, 1815-1848* (Oxford: Oxford University Press, 2007).

33. Nancy Shoemaker, "The Extraterritorial Nation," in "Forum: Globalizing the Early American Republic," by Konstantin Dierks, Shoemaker, Emily Conroy-Cruz, Rachel Tamar Van, and Courtney Fullilove, *Diplomatic History* 42, no. 1 (January 2018), 17-108.

34. See William F. Lynch, *Naval Life; or, Observations Afloat and On Shore. The Midshipman* (New York: Charles Scribner, 1851), 125-31.

35. D. S. Carr to James Buchanan, August 2, 1848, RG 59, M 46, roll 13, "Despatches from U.S. Ministers to Turkey, 1818-1906," NARA Boston, Waltham, Massachusetts; William F. Lynch, *Narrative of the United States' Expedition to the River Jordan and the Dead Sea* (Philadelphia: Lea & Blanchard, 1849), 76.

36. Lynch compared Arabs to Native Americans in *Narrative*, 142, 182, 220, 394, and esp. 428-32.

37. Col. C. Keeney to Lea & Blanchard, May 4, 1850, box 158, folder 1, "K," Lea & Febiger Records, Historical Society of Pennsylvania, Philadelphia (hereafter cited as HSP).

38. For more on this subject, see David Sehat, *The Myth of American Religious Freedom* (Oxford: Oxford University Press, 2011).

39. The quotation is from a speech by "a New York merchant, Mr. R. Irvin" (William Franklin Rawnsley, ed., *The Life, Diaries and Correspondence of Jane Lady Franklin, 1792-1875* [London: Erskine MacDonald, 1923], 206).

40. Lynch, *Narrative of the Expedition to the River Jordan*, 402.

41. Charles Wilkes, *Narrative of the United States Exploring Expedition. During the Years 1838, 1838, 1840, 1841, 1842*, 5 vols. (Philadelphia: C. Sherman, 1844), 1:xxix.

42. Joseph P. Couthoy to Benjamin Tappan, January 5, 1843, box 17, reel 7, Benjamin Tappan Papers, Manuscript Division, Library of Congress, Washington, DC; *The Baptist Mission in India, Containing a Narrative of Its Rise, Progress, and Present Condition . . .* (Philadelphia: Hellings and Aitken, 1811), iv.

43. Quoted in Paul Frymer, *Building an American Empire: The Era of Territorial and Political Expansion* (Princeton, NJ: Princeton University Press, 2017), 1.

44. For more on entangled histories, see Eliga H. Gould, "Entangled Worlds: The English-Speaking Atlantic as a Spanish Periphery," *American Historical Review* 112, no. 3 (June 2007), 764-86; and Ussama Makdisi, *Artillery of Heaven: American Missionaries and the Failed Conversion of the Middle East* (Ithaca, NY: Cornell University Press, 2008).

CHAPTER 1

1. Jeremiah N. Reynolds, "A Leaf from an Unpublished Manuscript," *Southern Literary Messenger*, June 1839, 408-9.

2. Jeremiah Reynolds to John Quincy Adams, New York, September 3, 1829, P-54, reel 491, Adams Family Papers, Massachusetts Historical Society Boston (hereafter cited as MHS).

3. Pliny A. Durant, ed., *The History of Clinton County* (Chicago: W. H. Beers, 1882), 580.

4. Durant, *History of Clinton County*, 475.

5. Durant, 481–82, 476.

6. Durant, 475.

7. Durant, 482.

8. Durant, *History of Clinton County*, 583; Henry Howe, *Historical Collections of Ohio*, 2 vols. (Columbus, OH: Henry Howe & Son, 1889), 1:432.

9. Jeremiah N. Reynolds, *Pacific and Indian Oceans: Or, The South Sea Surveying and Exploring Expedition: Its Inception, Progress, and Objects* (New York: Harper & Brothers, 1841), first unnumbered dedication page.

10. Jeremiah Reynolds to Samuel Southard, November 12, 1828, box 31, folder 10, Samuel L. Southard Papers, Department of Rare Books and Special Collections, Princeton University Library, Princeton, New Jersey (hereafter cited as Southard Papers).

11. Jeremiah Reynolds to Samuel Southard, Richmond, Virginia, January 2, 1828, box 31, folder 9, Southard Papers.

12. Jeremiah Reynolds to Mahlon Dickerson, August 23, 1837, reprinted in Reynolds, *Exploring Expedition. Correspondence*, 90.

13. Quoted in Durant, *History of Clinton County*, 583.

14. Jane Kamensky, *The Exchange Artist: A Tale of High-Flying Speculation and America's First Banking Collapse* (New York: Viking, 2008), 5.

15. Edward Gray, *The Making of John Ledyard: Empire and Ambition in the Life of an Early American Traveler* (New Haven, CT: Yale University Press, 2007), 190; Joan Shelly Rubin, *The Making of Middlebrow Culture* (Chapel Hill: University of North Carolina Press, 1992), 3.

16. Scott Sandage, *Born Losers: A History of Failure in America* (Cambridge, MA: Harvard University Press, 2005), 13.

17. Sandage, *Born Losers*, 26.

18. Sandage, 5.

19. See Catherine Cangany, *Frontier Seaport: Detroit's Transformation into an Atlantic Entrepôt* (Chicago: University of Chicago Press, 2014).

20. Jeremiah Reynolds to Samuel Southard, c. 1827, box 82, folder 1, Southard Papers.

21. Jeremiah Reynolds to Samuel Southard, December 8, 1828, box 31, folder 10, Southard Papers.

22. Jeremiah Reynolds to Samuel Southard, June 28, 1828, box 31, folder 9, Southard Papers.

23. Reynolds, *Exploring Expedition. Correspondence*, 74.

24. Durant, *History of Clinton County*, 580.

25. Durant, 583.

26. Durant, 579.

27. John Latimer, introduction to *A Life of George Washington, in Latin Prose*, by Francis Glass, ed. Jeremiah Reynolds, 3rd ed. (New York, 1836), 7.

28. Jeremiah Reynolds to an unknown recipient, February 10, 1828, reprinted in *American State Papers: Naval Affairs*, 4:712; Jeremiah Reynolds to Mahlon Dickerson, September 23, 1837, reprinted in Reynolds, *Exploring Expedition. Correspondence*, 100.

29. Mahlon Dickerson to Jeremiah Reynolds, August 10, 1837, reprinted in Reynolds, *Exploring Expedition. Correspondence*, 80. Palinurus was the helmsman of Aeneas's ship in the *Aeneid*.

30. Jeremiah N. Reynolds, *Address on the Subject of a Surveying and Exploring*

Expedition to the Pacific Ocean and South Seas, Delivered in the Hall of Representatives on the Evening of April 3, 1836, with Correspondence and Documents (New York: Harper & Brothers, 1836), 5.

31. Claudia L. Bushman, *America Discovers Columbus: How an Italian Explorer Became an American Hero* (Hanover, NH: University Press of New Hampshire, 1992), 107.

32. Reynolds, *Address on a Surveying Expedition*, 5.

33. Bushman, *America Discovers Columbus*, 107–11.

34. Laura Dassow Walls, *The Passage to Cosmos: Alexander von Humboldt and the Shaping of America* (Chicago: University of Chicago Press, 2009), 5, 121.

35. Walls, *Passage to Cosmos*, 5.

36. Andrea Wulf, *The Invention of Nature: Alexander Von Humboldt's New World* (New York: Vintage Books, 2016), 66. One of Humboldt's disciples, Ernst Haeckel, coined the term *ecology* in 1866 to describe systems of interconnected relationships that Humboldt had witnessed in South America (Wulf, *Invention of Nature*, 362–63).

37. See, for example, Mary Louise Pratt, *Imperial Eyes: Travel Writing and Transculturation*, 2nd ed. (New York: Routledge, 2008); Aaron Sachs, *The Humboldt Currents: Nineteenth-Century Exploration and the Roots of American Environmentalism* (New York: Penguin, 2006); Walls, *Passage to Cosmos*, 2009; and Wulf, *Invention of Nature*, 2016.

38. Walls, *Passage to Cosmos*, 139–40; Sachs, *Humboldt Currents*, 118, 150, 153.

39. Jeremiah N. Reynolds, *Voyage of the United States Frigate* Potomac (New York: Harper & Brothers, 1835), 445.

40. Michael S. Reidy, *Tides of History: Ocean Science and Her Majesty's Navy* (Chicago: University of Chicago Press, 2008), 9.

41. Ohio representatives to Andrew Jackson, July 2, 1836, "Records of the United States Exploring Expedition under the Command of Lieutenant Charles Wilkes, 1838–1842," RG 45, 37, 24, M 75, roll 2, National Archives and Records Administration, Boston, Massachusetts (hereafter cited as NARA Boston); and Jeremiah Reynolds to Samuel Southard, August 5, 1828, box 31, folder 9, Southard Papers.

42. Penelope Hardy, "Matthew Fontaine Maury: Scientist," *International Journal of Maritime History* 28, no. 2 (2016), 404.

43. Andrew J. Lewis, *A Democracy of Facts: Natural History in the Early Republic* (Philadelphia: University of Pennsylvania Press, 2011), 8.

44. See Jason W. Smith, *To Master the Boundless Sea: The U.S. Navy, the Marine Environment, and the Cartography of Empire* (Chapel Hill: University of North Carolina Press, 2018), esp. chap. 1, "Wilderness of Waters," 14–40; Smith, "Matthew Fontaine Maury: Pathfinder," *International Journal of Maritime History* 28, no. 2 (2016), 411–20; Daniel Feller, *The Jacksonian Promise: America, 1815–1840* (Baltimore: Johns Hopkins University Press, 1995), 89–94; Matthew McKenzie, "Salem as Athenaeum: Academic Learning and Vocational Knowledge in the Early Republic," in *Salem: Place, Myth and Memory*, ed. Dane Anthony Morrison and Nancy Lusignan Schultz (Boston: Northeastern University Press, 2004), 91–105; Marcus Rediker, *Between the Devil and the Deep Blue Sea: Merchant Seamen, Pirates, and the Anglo-American Maritime World, 1700–1750* (Cambridge: Cambridge University Press, 1985), 179–86; and D. Graham Burnett, "Hydrographic Discipline among the Navigators: Creating an 'Empire of Commerce and Science' in the Nineteenth-Century Pacific," in *The Imperial Map: Cartography and the Mastery of Empire*, ed. James R. Akerman (Chicago: University of Chicago Press, 2009), 220.

45. Cameron B. Strang, *Frontiers of Science: Imperialism and Natural Knowledge in the Gulf South Borderlands, 1500–1850* (Williamsburg, VA / Chapel Hill: Omohundro Institute of Early American History and Culture / University of North Carolina Press, 2019), 6–7.

46. Dickerson to Reynolds, August 10, 1837, reprinted in Reynolds, *Exploring Expedition. Correspondence*, 81.

47. Sachs, *Humboldt Currents*, 121.

48. John Symmes, letter to the editor, *National Intelligencer* (Washington, DC), reprinted in *City Gazette and Commercial* (Charleston, SC), January 14, 1823. John P. Harrison makes the same point about Reynolds in "Science and Politics: Origins and Objectives of Mid-nineteenth Century Government Expeditions to Latin America," *Hispanic American Historical Review* 35, no. 2 (May 1955), 178. Later, Jules Verne would take Symmes's ideas and spin them into a memorable story, *Journey to the Center of the Earth* (Sachs, *Humboldt Currents*, 124).

49. Sachs, 121. Symmes's wooden globe, complete with polar holes, now resides at the Academy of Natural Sciences in Philadelphia (William H. Goetzmann, *New Lands, New Men: America and the Second Great Age of Discovery* [Austin: Texas State Historical Association, 1995], 259).

50. Sachs, *Humboldt Currents*, 122.

51. Durant, *History of Clinton County*, 419.

52. Jeremiah Reynolds (attributed), "Symmes's Theory of Concentric Spheres," *American Quarterly Review*, March and June 1827 (Philadelphia. Carey, Lea & Carey, 1827), article 11, 253.

53. Stanton, *Great United States Exploring Expedition*, 13; Reynolds, "Symmes's Theory," 241.

54. Sachs, *Humboldt Currents*, 122–23.

55. For more on US nationalism in the early republic, see David Waldstreicher, *In the Midst of Perpetual Fetes: The Making of American Nationalism, 1776–1820* (Chapel Hill: University of North Carolina Press, 1997); Simon P. Newman, *Parades and the Politics of the Street: Festive Culture in the Early American Republic* (Philadelphia: University of Pennsylvania Press, 1997); and Shira Lurie, "Liberty Poles and the Fight for Popular Politics in the Early Republic," *Journal of the Early Republic* 38, no. 4 (Winter 2018), 673–97.

56. Quoted in Haynes, *Unfinished Revolution*, 29–30.

57. Reynolds, *Life of George Washington*, i.

58. Caleb Cushing to Jeremiah Reynolds, June 10, 1836, reprinted in Reynolds, *Pacific and Indian Oceans*, 133–34.

59. Walls, *Passage to Cosmos*, 125.

60. Jimmy L. Bryan, *The American Elsewhere: Adventures and Manliness in the Age of Expansion* (Lawrence: University Press of Kansas, 2017), 87–88.

61. Nathaniel Philbrick, *Sea of Glory: America's Voyage of Discovery, the U.S. Exploring Expedition, 1838–1842* (New York: Viking, 2003), 23.

62. Robert V. Remini, *John Quincy Adams* (New York: Henry Holt, 2002), 3.

63. Charles N. Edel, *Nation Builder: John Quincy Adams and the Grand Strategy of the Republic* (Cambridge, MA: Harvard University Press, 2014).

64. Arthur M. Schlesinger and Fred L. Israel, eds., *My Fellow Citizens: The Inaugural Addresses of the Presidents of the United States* (New York: Checkmark Books, 2005), 62.

65. *Franklin Gazette* (Philadelphia), April 27, 1819.

66. E. F. Rivinus and E. M. Youssef, *Spencer Baird of the Smithsonian* (Washington, DC: Smithsonian Institution Press, 1992), 19.

67. Goetzmann, *Army Exploration in the American West*, 8–9.

68. "North-West Passage," *Daily National Journal* (Washington, DC), June 2, 1827.

69. Andrew F. Rolle, *John Charles Fremont: Character as Destiny* (Norman: University of Oklahoma Press, 1991), 65, 47.

70. Vincent Ponko Jr., *Ships, Seas, and Scientists: U.S. Naval Exploration and Discovery in the Nineteenth Century* (Annapolis, MD: Naval Institute Press, 1974), 12. For another work arguing that the flag simply followed commerce, see John H. Schroeder, *Shaping a Maritime Empire: The Commercial and Diplomatic Role of the American Navy, 1829–1861* (Westport, CT: Greenwood Press, 1985).

71. Daniel A. Baugh, "Seapower and Science: The Motives for Pacific Exploration," in *Background to Discovery: Pacific Exploration from Dampier to Cook*, ed. Derek Howse (Berkeley: University of California Press, 1990), 40, and Helen M. Rozwadowski, *Fathoming the Ocean: The Discovery and Exploration of the Deep Sea* (Cambridge, MA: Belknap Press of Harvard University Press, 2005), 39.

72. Barry Alan Joyce, *The Shaping of American Ethnography: The Wilkes Exploring Expedition, 1838–1842* (Lincoln: University of Nebraska Press, 2001), 12.

73. Fergus Fleming, *Barrow's Boys* (New York: Gove Press, 1998), 1–2.

74. Fleming, *Barrow's Boys*, 7–12.

75. For an overview of these global British exploring expeditions, see the timeline in Fleming, xi–xiv.

76. Robert A. Stafford, "Scientific Exploration and Empire," in *The Oxford History of the British Empire*, vol. 3, *The Nineteenth Century*, ed. Andrew Porter; Alaine Low, assoc. ed. (Oxford: Oxford University Press, 1999), 297.

77. Fred L. Israel, ed., *The State of the Union: Messages of the Presidents, 1790–1966*, 2 vols. (New York: Chelsea House and Robert Hector, 1966), 1:244–45. President James Monroe had proposed a limited naval survey to locate a good site for a coastal fort and naval base in his last annual message to Congress, December 7, 1824 (Israel, *State of the Union*, 1:228).

78. Quoted in William Stanton, *The Great United States Exploring Expedition of 1838–1842* (Berkeley: University of California Press, 1975), 5.

79. "Comments on Certain Parts of the President's Message," *Enquirer* (Richmond, Virginia), December 22, 1825.

80. Matthew Estes, *A Defence of Negro Slavery, As It Exists in the United States* (Montgomery, AL, 1846), Library Company of Philadelphia (hereafter cited as LCP), 181.

81. Register of Debates, House, 19th Cong., 1st Sess., December 16, 1825, 813.

82. Register of Debates, House, 19th Cong., 1st Sess., December 16, 1825, 814–15.

83. "Untitled," *Niles' Weekly Register* (Baltimore), July 20, 1822, 402.

84. Stanton, *Great United States Exploring Expedition*, 11–12.

85. Sachs, *Humboldt Currents*, 123–25.

86. Sachs, 121.

87. William Coyle, ed., *Ohio Authors and Their Books: Biographical Data and Selective Bibliographies for Ohio Authors, Native and Resident, 1796–1950* (Cleveland, OH: World Publishing, 1962), s.v. "Symmes, John Cleves," 616.

88. Sachs, *Humboldt Currents*, 122.

89. David Chapin, *Exploring Other Worlds: Margaret Fox, Elisha Kent Kane, and the Antebellum Culture of Curiosity* (Amherst: University of Massachusetts Press, 2004), 68–69. Belief in an open polar sea, or polynya, goes back at least as far as the quest for a Northwest Passage in the sixteenth century (Goetzmann, *New Lands, New Men*, 324–25).

90. Philbrick, *Sea of Glory*, 3.

91. Dickerson to Reynolds, August 10, 1837, reprinted in Reynolds, *Exploring Expedition. Correspondence*, 74–75. Reynolds expressed a similar goal in a letter to Samuel Southard, May 25, 1827, box 27, folder 7, Southard Papers.

92. Jeremiah Reynolds to Samuel Southard, c. 1827, box 82, folder 1, Southard Papers.

93. Eric Jay Dolin, *When America First Met China: An Exotic History of Tea, Drugs, and Money in the Age of Sail* (New York: W. W. Norton, 2012), 11.

94. Mary Malloy, *"Boston Men" on the Northwest Coast: The American Maritime Fur Trade, 1784–1844* (Kingston, ON: Limestone Press, 1998), 7.

95. Goetzmann, *New Lands, New Men*, 249, 256. In 1828, Reynolds estimated that Americans had sent seven million skins to Canton (Jeremiah Reynolds to Michael Hoffman, chairman of the Committee on Naval Affairs, undated, in "On the Expediency of Fitting Out Vessels of the Navy for an Exploration of the Pacific Ocean and South Seas," *American State Papers: Naval Affairs*, 3:192). This number seems large, but it is possible; between 1792 and 1812, American merchants sold 2.5 million sealskins in China (Dolin, *When America First Met China*, 107). For more on this topic, see David Igler, *The Great Ocean: Pacific Worlds from Captain Cook to the Gold Rush* (New York: Oxford University Press, 2013), esp. chap. 4, "The Great Hunt," 99–128.

96. Thomas Jefferson to Meriwether Lewis, June 20, 1803, available at "Jefferson's Instructions to Meriwether Lewis," Thomas Jefferson Foundation, Monticello (Charlottesville, Virginia), https://www.monticello.org/thomas-jefferson/louisiana-lewis -clark/preparing-for-the-expedition/jefferson-s-instructions-to-lewis/.

97. Eric Jay Dolin, *Leviathan: The History of Whaling in America* (New York: W. W. Norton, 2007), 112–13.

98. Nathaniel Philbrick, *In the Heart of the Sea: The Tragedy of the Whaleship* Essex (New York: Penguin, 2000), 63.

99. Philbrick, *In the Heart of the Sea*, 67, 106.

100. Benjamin W. Labaree, William M. Fowler Jr., John B. Hattendorf, Jeffrey J. Safford, Edward W. Sloan, and Andrew W. German, *America and the Sea: A Maritime History* (Mystic, CT: Mystic Seaport, 1998), 290.

101. Jeremiah Reynolds to Samuel Southard, September 24, 1828, reprinted in "Information Collected by the Navy Department Relating to Islands, Reefs, Shoals, Etc., in the Pacific Ocean and South Seas," January 29, 1835, *American State Papers: Naval Affairs*, 4:700.

102. For more on the masculine, working-class US maritime empire in the early republic, see Hester Blum, *The View from the Masthead: Maritime Imagination and Antebellum American Sea Narratives* (Chapel Hill: University of North Carolina Press, 2008); and Brian Rouleau, *With Sails Whitening Every Sea: Mariners and the Making of an American Maritime Empire* (Ithaca, NY: Cornell University Press, 2014).

103. Reynolds to Hoffman, *American State Papers: Naval Affairs*, 3:192.

104. Bryan, *The American Elsewhere*. Other works that examine sailors' masculinity include Myra C. Glenn, *Jack Tar's Story: The Autobiographies and Memoirs of Sailors in*

Antebellum America (Cambridge: Cambridge University Press, 2010); W. Jeffrey Bol-
ster, "'To Feel like a Man': Black Seamen in the Northern States, 1800–1860," *Journal of
American History* 76, no. 4 (March 1990), 1173–99; and Rouleau, *With Sails Whitening
Every Sea.*

105. Gerald Mcdonald, "Reynolds, Jeremiah N.," in *Ohio Authors and Their Books:
Biographical Data and Selective Bibliographies for Ohio Authors, Native and Resident,
1796–1950,* ed. William Coyle (Cleveland, OH: World Publishing, 1962), 525.

106. Sachs, *Humboldt Currents,* 146.

107. J. N. Reynolds, *Mocha Dick: Or the White Whale of the Pacific* (1839; New York:
Charles Scribner's Sons, 1932), 22.

108. Reynolds, *Mocha Dick,* 17, 12.

109. Reynolds, 22.

110. Reynolds, 44.

111. Reynolds, 86–90.

112. Durant, *History of Clinton County,* 419; Howe, *Historical Collections of Ohio,*
1:432.

113. Israel, *State of the Union,* 1:245; Smith, *To Master the Boundless Sea,* 34; Howe,
What Hath God Wrought, 360.

114. Gray, *Making of John Ledyard.* Jones relied heavily on the patronage of Benjamin Franklin during the heyday of his Revolutionary fame. For an older but thorough
biography of Jones, see Samuel Eliot Morison, *John Paul Jones: A Sailor's Biography*
(Boston: Little, Brown, 1959).

115. Israel, *State of the Union,* 1:244.

116. Jeremiah Reynolds to Samuel Southard, Washington, August 3, 1826, box 23,
folder 13, Southard Papers.

117. Michael Birkner, *Samuel L. Southard, Jeffersonian Whig* (Rutherford, NJ: Fair-
leigh Dickinson University Press, 1984), 90.

118. Birkner, *Samuel L. Southard,* 58–63, 70–71.

119. William Lambert to Samuel Southard on behalf of the Columbian Institute,
May 6, 1828, box 30, folder 12, Southard Papers.

120. Israel, *State of the Union,* 1:261.

121. Gene A. Smith, *Thomas ap Catesby Jones: Commodore of Manifest Destiny* (Annapolis, MD: Naval Institute Press, 2000), 51.

122. Smith, *Thomas ap Catesby Jones,* 47–69.

123. Charles Francis Adams, ed., *Memoirs of John Quincy Adams, Comprising Portions of His Diary From 1795 to 1848,* 12 vols. (Philadelphia, 1874–1877), 7:353.

124. Michael F. Holt, *The Rise and Fall of the American Whig Party: Jacksonian Politics and the Onset of the Civil War* (New York: Oxford University Press, 1999), 5.

125. Remini, *John Quincy Adams,* 69–74.

126. Jackson quoted in Remini, *John Quincy Adams,* 74.

127. Holt, *Rise and Fall of the Whig Party,* 8.

128. John Quincy Adams to Charles Francis Adams, Washington, DC, May 28, 1828,
P-54, reel 485, Adams Family Papers, MHS.

129. Morton J. Horwitz, *The Transformation of American Law, 1780–1860* (Cam-
bridge, MA: Harvard University Press, 1977); John, *Spreading the News*; William
Novak, "The Myth of the Weak American State," *American Historical Review* 113, no. 3
(June 2008), 752–72; Brian Balogh, *A Government Out of Sight: The Mystery of National
Authority in Nineteenth-Century America* (Cambridge: Cambridge University Press,

2009); Gautham Rao, *National Duties: Custom Houses and the Making of the American State* (Chicago: University of Chicago Press, 2016).

130. Jeremiah Reynolds to Samuel Southard, November 14, 1828, box 31, folder 10, Southard Papers.

131. Samuel Southard to Jeremiah Reynolds, Washington, July 11, 1827, box 27, folder 7, Southard Papers.

132. Charles Wilkes, *Autobiography of Rear Admiral Charles Wilkes, U.S. Navy, 1798–1877*, ed. William James Morgan, David B. Tyler, Joye L. Leonhart, and Mary F. Loughlin (Washington, DC: Naval History Division, 1978), 358.

133. Jeremiah Reynolds to Samuel Southard, Boston, November 6, 1827, box 27, folder 7, Southard Papers.

134. Ohio representatives to Andrew Jackson, July 2, 1836.

135. Reynolds to Southard, November 6, 1827.

136. Reynolds to Southard, May 25, 1827.

137. Howe, *Historical Collections of Ohio*, 432.

138. Quoted in Walls, *Passage to Cosmos*, 100.

139. Jeremiah Reynolds to Samuel Southard, October 10 or 11, 1828, box 31, folder 10, Southard Papers.

140. Jeremiah Reynolds to Mahlon Dickerson, June 29, 1837, reprinted in Reynolds, *Exploring Expedition. Correspondence*, 8.

141. Jeremiah Reynolds to Samuel Southard, January 23, 1827, and May 25, 1827, box 27, folder 7, Southard Papers.

142. Jeremiah Reynolds to Samuel Southard, December 22, 1827, box 27, folder 7, Southard Papers.

143. Reynolds to Southard, January 2, 1828.

144. *Patriot & Mercantile Advertiser* (Baltimore), October 18, 1826.

145. Memorial of the citizens of Nantucket, February 1828, in "On the expediency of fitting out vessels of the Navy for an exploration of the Pacific Ocean and South Seas," March 25, 1828, *American State Papers: Naval Affairs*, 3:196–97.

146. For a few examples of the *New-Bedford Mercury* reporting on Reynolds's activism or on the subject of exploring the South Pacific, see issues from April 11, 1828; December 5, 1828; January 23, 1829; and March 6, 1829.

147. These include Massachusetts Congressman Francis Baylies, who made the first motion for an exploring expedition in Congress in December 1825 (*Register of Debates, House*, 19th Cong., 1st Sess., December 16, 1825, 813–15); James Wheelock Ripley, representative of Maine (*House Journal*, 20th Cong., 1st Sess., March 25, 1828), and Massachusetts Congressman John Reed, who introduced the bill that would clear the House on May 21, 1828 (*Register of Debates, House*, 20th Cong., 2nd Sess., May 19, 1828, 2731–32).

148. Christopher McKee, *A Gentlemanly and Honorable Profession: The Creation of the U.S. Navy Officer Corps, 1794–1815* (Annapolis, MD: Naval Institute Press, 1991).

149. Captain George Read to Samuel Southard, Washington, March 12, 1824, box 16, folder 1, Southard Papers.

150. Geoffrey Sutton Smith, "The Navy before Darwinism: Science, Exploration, and Diplomacy in Antebellum America," *American Quarterly* 28 (Spring 1976), 55; David B. Tyler, *The Wilkes Expedition: The First United States Exploring Expedition (1838–1842)* (Philadelphia: American Philosophical Society, 1968), 8.

151. Thomas ap Catesby Jones to Jeremiah Reynolds, February 28, 1828, in "On the

expediency of fitting out vessels of the Navy for an exploration of the Pacific Ocean and South Seas," March 25, 1828, *American State Papers: Naval Affairs*, 3:195.

152. Ferdinand Hassler to Samuel Southard, New York, May 25, 1829, box 34, folder 3, Southard Papers.

153. Stanton, *United States Exploring Expedition*, 31.

154. Jeremiah Reynolds to Samuel Southard, July 15, 1828, box 31, folder 9, Southard Papers.

155. McKee, *A Gentlemanly and Honorable Profession*, chap. 4, "Places Much Sought," 40–53.

156. McKee, 5, 33.

157. Harold D. Langley, *Social Reform in the United States Navy, 1798–1862* (Urbana: University of Illinois Press, 1967), 23.

158. "Monday, Jan. 15," *Courier* (Norwich, Connecticut), January 24, 1827; *Register of Debates, House*, 19th Cong., 2nd Sess., February 5, 1827, 949.

159. "Exploring of the Southern Ocean," *Mirror & Ladies' Literary Gazette* (New York), April 26, 1828, 335.

160. Newburyport (Massachusetts) *Herald*, August 11, 1829.

161. Reynolds to Adams, September 3, 1829.

162. See Herman Melville, *Moby-Dick or the Whale* (1851; repr., Evanston, IL: Northwestern University Press, 2001), 460–62.

163. Jeremiah Reynolds to Michael Hoffman, *American State Papers: Naval Affairs*, 3:192.

164. Jeremiah Reynolds to Samuel Southard, New York, June 11, 1829, box 35, folder 1, Southard Papers.

165. Reynolds quoted in New Bedford (Massachusetts) *Mercury*, April 11, 1828.

166. Quoted in Sachs, *Humboldt Currents*, 135.

167. Sachs, 135.

168. Jeremiah Reynolds to Samuel Southard, Charleston, June 27, 1827, box 27, folder 7, Southard Papers.

169. *Mercury* (Newport, Rhode Island), February 2, 1828.

170. Jeremiah Reynolds to Samuel Southard, New York, October 23, 1827, box 27, folder 7, Southard Papers.

171. Reynolds to Southard, November 6, 1827.

172. *Mercury* (New Bedford, Massachusetts), March 6, 1829.

173. Stanton, *United States Exploring Expedition*, 17.

174. "Exploring Expedition," *Register of Debates, Senate*, 20th Cong., 2nd Sess., February 5, 1829, 51.

175. John Quincy Adams, diary entry, July 14, 1828, microfilm, P-54, reel 39, Adams Family Papers, MHS.

176. Jeremiah Reynolds to Samuel Southard, July 10, 1828, box 31, folder 9, Southard Papers.

177. Jeremiah Reynolds to Samuel Southard, December 3, 1828, box 31, folder 10, Southard Papers.

178. Adams, *Memoirs*, 8:45; "Report on the Polar Expedition," February 13, 1829, *Appendix to Gale & Seaton's Register of Debates in Congress, House of Representatives*, 20th Cong., 2nd Sess., 27–30.

179. John Reed to Samuel Southard, October 11, 1828, RG 45, M 124, Miscellaneous

Letters Received by the Secretary of the Navy, 1801–1884, National Archives and Records Administration, Archives I, Washington, DC (hereafter cited as NARA I).

180. Charles Hay to D. J. Pearce, September 16, 1828, Navy Department, RG 45, M 209, NARA I.

181. Stanton, *United States Exploring Expedition*, 20.

182. Tyler, *Wilkes Expedition*, 12.

183. Stanton, *United States Exploring Expedition*, 20.

184. Wilkes, *Autobiography*, 358.

185. "Voyage of Discovery," *Connecticut Mirror* (Hartford), September 29, 1828; "The Southern Expedition," *Niles' Weekly Register* 11, no. 14 (November 29, 1828), 212; and "United States. Rules and Regulations," *Sailor's Magazine & Naval Journal*, December 1, 1828; quotation from "Naval," *Rhode Island Republican*, December 4, 1828.

186. Wilkes, *Autobiography*, 323.

187. Stanton, *United States Exploring Expedition*, 20.

188. Adams, *Memoirs*, 8:45, June 27, 1828.

189. Jeremiah Reynolds to Samuel Southard, Washington, June 26, 1828, "Letters Received by the Secretary of the Navy: Miscellaneous Letters, 1801–1884," RG 45, M 124, NARA I.

190. Jeremiah Reynolds to Samuel Southard, July 28, 1828, box 31, folder 9, Southard Papers; Jeremiah Reynolds to Samuel Southard, August 12, 1828, RG 45, M 124, NARA I; Samuel Southard to John Quincy Adams, February 13, 1829, reprinted in *American State Papers: Naval Affairs*, 3: 309; Samuel Southard, "Report on the Polar Expedition," February 13, 1829, reprinted in *Appendix to Gale & Seaton's Register of Debates in Congress, House of Representatives*, 20th Cong., 2nd Sess., p. 29.

191. Jeremiah Reynolds to Samuel Southard, July 13, 1828, box 31, folder 9, Princeton; quotation from Jeremiah Reynolds to Samuel Southard, July 30, 1828, RG 45, M 124, NARA I.

192. Tyler, *Wilkes Expedition*, 3; Edmund Fanning, *Voyages Round the World* (New York: Collins & Hannay, 1833), 492.

193. Reynolds to Southard, July 30, 1828.

194. Reynolds to Southard, November 12, 1828; Jeremiah Reynolds to Samuel Southard, November 1, 1828, box 31, folder 10, Southard Papers.

195. Reynolds to Southard, November 1, 1828.

196. John Quincy Adams, diary entry, December 3, 1828, microfilm, P-54, reel 39, Adams Family Papers, MHS.

197. Jeremiah Reynolds to Samuel Southard, November 28, 1828, box 31, folder 10, Southard Papers.

198. Israel, *State of the Union*, 1:289–90; Jeremiah Reynolds to Samuel Southard, November 13 and November 18, 1828, box 31, folder 10, Southard Papers.

199. Jeremiah Reynolds to Samuel Southard, December 10, 1828; box 31, folder 10, Southard Papers; Reynolds to Southard, November 13, 1828; Jeremiah Reynolds to Samuel Southard, December 8, 1828, box 31, folder 10, Southard Papers.

200. *House Journal*, 20th Cong., 2nd Sess., January 15, 1829; "An Act to Provide for an Exploring Expedition to the Pacific Ocean and South Seas," H.R. 240, 20th Cong., 2nd Sess. (January 19, 1829).

201. Irving H. Bartlett, *John C. Calhoun: A Biography* (New York: W. W. Norton, 1993), 140.

202. Bartlett, *John C. Calhoun*, 141.

203. Theodore Jervey, *Robert Y. Hayne and His Times* (New York: MacMillan, 1909), 89.

204. Quoted in Jervey, *Hayne and His Times*, 188.

205. Jervey, 149.

206. Jervey, 187.

207. Howe, *What Hath God Wrought*, 369; *American National Biography Online*, s.v. "Hayne, Robert Young," accessed June 8, 2016.

208. Robert Hayne to Samuel Southard, June 26, 1828, RG 49, M 124, NARA I; Jervey, *Robert Y. Hayne*, 59; Matthew J. Karp, "Slavery and American Sea Power: The Navalist Impulse in the Antebellum South," *Journal of Southern History*, 77 (May 2011), 291; Hayne's article, "Sketches of a Naval History of the United States," appeared in the *Southern Review*, November 1, 1828, 349–83. Hayne references writing the article in Robert Hayne to Samuel Southard, October 30, 1828, box 30, folder 8, Southard Papers.

209. Robert Hayne to Samuel Southard, February 26, March 28, April 7, 1828, box 30, folder 8, Southard Papers.

210. Hayne to Southard, October 30, 1828.

211. John Quincy Adams diary, March 5, 1829, microfilm, P-54, reel 39, Adams Family Papers, MHS.

212. Birkner, *Samuel L. Southard*, 110.

213. Quoted in Harry L. Watson, *Liberty and Power: The Politics of Jacksonian America* (New York: Hill and Wang, 2006), 73.

214. Watson, *Liberty and Power*, 73.

215. John Lauritz Larson, *Internal Improvements: National Public Works and the Promise of Popular Government in the Early United States* (Chapel Hill: University of North Carolina Press, 2001), 177.

216. Howe, *What Hath God Wrought*, 368–72.

217. Register of Debates, Senate, 20th Cong., 2nd Sess., February 5, 1829, 52.

218. "Report on the Polar Expedition," February 13, 1829, *Appendix to Gale & Seaton's Register of Debates in Congress, House of Representatives*, 20th Cong., 2nd Sess., 30.

219. "On the Policy and Objects of the Exploring Expedition to the Pacific Ocean and South Seas, communicated to the Senate," February 23, 1829, ASPS, Senate, 20th Cong., 2nd Sess., vol. 3, p. 336, no. 391, 338.

220. Robert Hayne to Samuel Southard, January 22, 1829, RG 45, M 124, NARA I.

221. Samuel Southard to Robert Hayne, January 29, 1829, contained in "Report on the Polar Expedition," February 13, 1829, *Appendix, Register of Debates, Senate*, 20th Cong., 2nd Sess., 31.

222. "Report of the Senate Committee," February 23, 1829, *Appendix, Register of Debates, Senate*, 20th Cong., 2nd Sess., 35.

223. "Report of the Senate Committee," February 23, 1829, 35.

224. Howe, *What Hath God Wrought*, 367–70.

225. "Report of the Senate Committee," February 23, 1829, 35.

226. "Report of the Senate Committee," February 23, 1829, 35.

227. Hayne's fear of foreign colonization also led him to oppose federal funding for African colonization in 1827 (Mills, *The World Colonization Made*, 85–86).

228. Quoted in Watson, *Liberty and Power*, 62.

229. "On the Policy and Objects of the Exploring Expedition," 3:339; *Senate Journal*, 20th Cong., 2nd Sess., February 23, 1829, 139.

230. *Senate Journal*, 20th Cong., 2nd Sess., March 2, 1829, 176–77.

231. Schlesinger and Israel, *My Fellow Citizens: Inaugural Addresses*, 65–67.

232. Israel, *State of the Union*, 1:310–11.

233. Jeremiah Reynolds to John Branch, April 14, 1829, M 124, NARA I.

234. Reynolds to Southard, June 11, 1829.

235. Reynolds to Adams, September 3, 1829; J. E. De Kay to Samuel Southard, September 23, 1829, New York, box 33, folder 9, Southard Papers.

236. Reynolds, *Address on a Surveying Expedition*, 98.

237. Jeremiah Reynolds to Samuel Southard, October 25, 1830, box 37, folder 2, Southard Papers.

238. Aaron Sachs, *Humboldt Currents*, 138.

239. See Wulf, *Invention of Nature*, 1–5, 98–101.

240. Jeremiah Reynolds to John Quincy Adams, October 26, 1830, P-54, reel 492, Adams Family Papers, MHS.

241. Reynolds, "Leaf from an Unpublished Manuscript," 411–12.

242. Reynolds to Southard, October 25, 1830. In Mark 6:4 of the King James Bible, Jesus says, "A prophet is not without honor but in his own country, among his own kin, and in his own house."

CHAPTER 2

1. John M. Belohlavek, *"Let the Eagle Soar!": The Foreign Policy of Andrew Jackson* (Lincoln: University of Nebraska Press, 1985), 153.

2. Schroeder, *Shaping a Maritime Empire*, 26.

3. Belohlavek, *"Let the Eagle Soar!,"* 153.

4. Reynolds, *Voyage of the* Potomac, 221.

5. Endicott's statement, Levi Woodbury to John Downes, August 9, 1831, RG 45, M 149, NARA I.

6. Endicott's statement, Woodbury to Downes, August 9, 1831.

7. Levi Woodbury gave his original orders in Woodbury to Downes, August 9, 1831. For justifications for ignoring them, see Reynolds, *Voyage of the* Potomac, 95–98; and John Downes to Levi Woodbury, February 17, 1832, RG 45, M 125, NARA I. Benjamin Armstrong gives a detailed and critical examination of Downes's tactical choices at Kuala Batu in chap. 7, "First Sumatran Expedition, 1831–1832," in *Small Boats and Daring Men: Maritime Raiding, Irregular Warfare, and the Early American Navy* (Norman: University of Oklahoma Press, 2019), 150–71. He suggests that diplomacy, rather than force, would have been more effective.

8. Reynolds, *Voyage of the* Potomac, 109.

9. Armstrong, *Small Boats and Daring Men*, 163.

10. Lieutenant Irvine Shubrick to Captain John Downes, February 6, 1832, "Letters Received by the Secretary of the Navy from Captains ["Captain's Letters"], 1805–1861," RG 45, M 125A, NARA I.

11. See, for instance, the early chapters of Walter LaFeber, *The American Age: U.S. Foreign Policy at Home and Abroad*, vol. 1, *To 1920*, 2nd ed. (New York: W. W. Norton, 1994).

12. Philbrick, *Sea of Glory*, xvii.

13. Daniel C. Haskell, *The United States Exploring Expedition, 1838–1842 and Its Publications, 1844–1874* (New York: New York Public Library, 1942), 6.

14. The total increase would be $67,080.76, based on "Report on the Polar Expedition," February 13, 1829, *Appendix to Gale & Seaton's Register of Debates in Congress, House of Representatives*, 20th Cong., 2nd Sess., 28; and "Authorization of the Naval Exploring Expedition in the South Seas and Pacific Ocean, and of the Purchase of and Payment for Astronomical and Other Instruments for the Same," March 17, 1830, House of Representatives, 21st Cong., 1st Sess., *American State Papers: Naval Affairs*, 3:547.

15. There were nineteen scientific volumes prepared for publication, but only fourteen were ever printed (Haskell, *United States Exploring Expedition*, 18–19).

16. Haskell, 16, has a table with all the appropriations for the volumes. Total Ex Ex publication appropriations equaled $359,834.52.

17. Mahlon Dickerson to Jeremiah Reynolds, August 25, 1837, reprinted in Reynolds, *Exploring Expedition. Correspondence*, 88.

18. Richard Hofstadter, chap. 3, "Andrew Jackson and the Rise of Liberal Capitalism," in *The American Political Tradition and the Men Who Made It* (1948; repr., New York: Vintage Books, 1989), 57–86. This chapter defines capitalism as Immanuel Wallerstein did: a system that seeks an ever-increasing amount of capital across geographic space (*The Modern World-System*, vol. 3, *The Second Era of Great Expansion of the Capitalist World-Economy, 1730–1840s* [1989; repr., Berkeley: University of California Press, 2011], xiv, xvii). I am also indebted to the work of Philip E. Steinberg, which portrays how capitalism was an imperialistic force that expanded into new areas—even ocean basins—and arranged their access to resources hierarchically along lines of race and class (*The Social Construction of the Ocean* [Cambridge: Cambridge University Press, 2001], 22). Finally, I have adopted the periodization of Paul A. Gilje, who has argued that the period of the early US republic—circa 1789 to 1861—was the crucial fulcrum of change in the evolution of modern capitalism ("The Rise of Capitalism in the Early Republic," *Journal of the Early Republic* 16, no. 2 [Summer 1996], 160–62).

19. Hofstadter, *American Political Tradition*, 65.

20. For more on Jacksonian economic policy, see Arthur M. Schlesinger Jr., *The Age of Jackson* (Boston: Little, Brown, 1945); Hofstadter, "Andrew Jackson and the Rise of Liberal Capitalism"; George Rogers Taylor, *The Transportation Revolution, 1815–1860* (New York: Rinehart, 1951); Watson, *Liberty and Power*; Charles Sellers, *The Market Revolution: Jacksonian America, 1815–1846* (Oxford: Oxford University Press, 1991); John, *Spreading the News*; Daniel Feller, *The Jacksonian Promise: America, 1815–1840* (Baltimore: Johns Hopkins University Press, 1995); Sean Wilentz, *The Rise of American Democracy: Jefferson to Lincoln* (New York: W. W. Norton, 2005); Howe, *What Hath God Wrought*; Dael A. Norwood, "Trading in Liberty: The Politics of the American China Trade, c. 1784–1862" (PhD diss., Princeton University, 2012); and Jessica M. Lepler, *The Many Panics of 1837: People, Politics, and the Creation of Transatlantic Financial Crisis* (Cambridge: Cambridge University Press, 2013).

21. Howe especially makes the point that Jacksonian democracy was characterized by white supremacist policies (*What Hath God Wrought*, chap. 9, "Andrew Jackson and His Age," 328–66).

22. The new literature on slavery emphasizes how capitalistic it was; in fact, many scholars are even finding slavery the overarching principle of capitalism itself. See, for example, Sven Beckert and Seth Rockman, *Slavery's Capitalism: A New History of American Economic Development* (Philadelphia: University of Pennsylvania Press,

2016). For slavery and the US Postal Service, see John, *Spreading the News*, especially chap. 7, "The Interdiction of Dissent," 257–80; W. Jeffrey Bolster, *Black Jacks: African American Seamen in the Age of Sail* (Cambridge, MA: Harvard University Press, 1997), esp. chap. 7, "Free Sailors and the Struggle with Slavery," 190–214; and Bolster, "'To Feel like a Man': Black Seamen in the Northern States, 1800–1860," *Journal of American History* 76, no. 4 (March 1990), 1192–94; see also Howe, *What Hath God Wrought*, 361.

23. Hofstadter, *American Political Tradition*, 83–86.

24. James R. Gibson, *Otter Skins, Boston Ships, and China Goods: The Maritime Fur Trade of the Northwest Coast, 1785–1841* (Seattle: University of Washington Press, 1992) 27. For the rise and fall of the US otter pelt trade on the Northwest Coast, see Mary Malloy, *"Boston Men" on the Northwest Coast: The American Maritime Fur Trade, 1784–1844* (Kingston, ON: Limestone Press, 1998).

25. Eric Jay Dolin, *When America First Met China: An Exotic History of Tea, Drugs, and Money in the Age of Sail* (New York: W. W. Norton, 2012), 112.

26. Dolin, *When America First Met China*, 161.

27. Dolin, 154.

28. Dolin, 113–14, 126. For more on the US–Fiji trade, see Nancy Shoemaker, *Pursuing Respect in the Cannibal Isles: Americans in Nineteenth-Century Fiji* (Ithaca, NY: Cornell University Press, 2019).

29. Schroeder, *Shaping a Maritime Empire*, 22–23.

30. Andrew Darby, *Harpoon: Into the Heart of Whaling* (Cambridge, MA: De Capo Press, 2008), 87.

31. Labaree et al., *America and the Sea*, 290.

32. Reynolds, *Address on a Surveying Expedition*, 43.

33. Reynolds, 43–44.

34. See, for example, Paul A. Gilje, *Free Trade and Sailors' Rights in the War of 1812* (New York: Cambridge University Press, 2013).

35. William Lewis Herndon and Lardner Gibbon, *Exploration of the Valley of the Amazon: Made Under Direction of the Navy Department*, 2 vols. (Washington, DC: Robert Armstrong, 1854), 1:417.

36. Rouleau, *With Sails Whitening Every Sea*, 1–2.

37. Schlesinger and Israel, *My Fellow Citizens: Inaugural Addresses*, 58.

38. Martin Lynn, "British Policy, Trade, and Informal Empire in the Mid-nineteenth Century," chap. 6 of *The Oxford History of the British Empire*, vol. 3, *The Nineteenth Century*, ed. Andrew Porter; Alaine Low, assoc. ed. (Oxford: Oxford University Press, 1999), 105.

39. Nicole M. Phelps, "One Service, Three Systems, Many Empires: The U.S. Consular Service and the Growth of U.S. Global Power, 1789–1924," in *Crossing Empires: Taking U.S. History into Transimperial Terrain*, ed. Kristin L. Hoganson, and Jay Sexton (Durham, NC: Duke University Press, 2020), 136–58; Belohlavek, *"Let the Eagle Soar!,"* 7–8.

40. Howe, *What Hath God Wrought*, 360.

41. Schroeder, *Shaping a Maritime Empire*, 24.

42. Belohlavek, *"Let the Eagle Soar!,"* 164; Schroeder, *Shaping a Maritime Empire*, 32.

43. See Belohlavek, *"Let the Eagle Soar!,"* chap. 4, "France: Commerce, Claims, and Conflict," esp. 111–26.

44. Howe, *What Hath God Wrought*, 360.

45. Howe, *What Hath God Wrought*, 468; Philbrick, *Sea of Glory*, 23.

46. For more on Native Americans and the Yankee whale fishery, see Nancy Shoe-maker, "Mr. Tashtego: Native American Whalemen in Antebellum New England," *Journal of the Early Republic* 33, no. 1 (Spring 2013), 109–32; and Shoemaker, *Native American Whalemen and the World*.

47. Nicholas Thomas, *Islanders: The Pacific in the Age of Empire* (New Haven, CT: Yale University Press, 2012), 4.

48. Eric Jay Dolin, *Leviathan: The History of Whaling in America* (New York: W. W. Norton, 2007), 430.

49. For more on this, see Rouleau, *With Sails Whitening Every Sea*, esp. chaps. 2, 3, and 4; and Joyce, *Shaping of American Ethnography*.

50. Smith, *To Master the Boundless Sea*, 56.

51. Herman Melville, *Omoo: Adventures in the South Seas* (1847; repr., Mineola, NY: Dover Publications, 2000), 21.

52. Smith, *Thomas ap Catesby Jones*, 54–55.

53. Samuel Eliot Morison, *The Maritime History of Massachusetts, 1784–1860* (1921; repr., Boston: Northeastern University Press, 1979), 324.

54. Gibson, *Otter Skins, Boston Ships, and China Goods*, 165.

55. William Reynolds, *The Private Journal of William Reynolds: The United States Exploring Expedition, 1838–1842*, ed. Nathaniel and Thomas Philbrick (New York: Penguin Books, 2004), 90.

56. Smith, *To Master the Boundless Sea*, 66.

57. Wilkes, *Narrative of the US Exploring Expedition*, 3:244, 260–61; Reynolds, *Private Journal of William Reynolds*, 184–85; Erskine, *Twenty Years before the Mast: With the More Thrilling Scenes and Incidents while Circumnavigating the Globe under the Command of the Late Admiral Charles Wilkes, 1838–1842* (1896; repr., Chicago: Lakeside Press, R. R. Donnelley & Sons, 2006), 194–97, 205.

58. Throughout the Ex Ex narrative, Wilkes repeatedly praised Oceanian watercraft and navigational talent. For examples, see Wilkes, *Narrative of the US Exploring Expedition*, 1:340–41, 2:65–66, 3:19, 54.

59. Claims of Oceanians' interest in acquiring Western goods, and accounts of their propensity to walk away with them if possible, are too numerous to dismiss as mere prejudice in the historical record. For instances when crew members of the Ex Ex accused natives of theft, see Wilkes, *Narrative of the US Exploring Expedition*, 1:132, 3:76; and Reynolds, *Private Journal of William Reynolds*, 85–86, 154.

60. Melville, *Omoo*, 295; Erskine, *Twenty Years before the Mast*, 162.

61. Wilkes, *Autobiography*, 361.

62. Whaling captains to Lieut. John Percival, March 10, 1826, P-157, John Percival Papers, 1826–1841, MHS.

63. Rouleau, *With Sails Whitening Every Sea*, 102–3.

64. Melville, *Omoo*, 1; Richard Henry Dana Jr., *Two Years before the Mast* (1840; repr., New York: Dodd, Mead, 1946), 176.

65. Wilkes, *Narrative of the US Exploring Expedition*, 1:138; Melville, *Omoo*, 1.

66. Morison, *Maritime History of Massachusetts*, 315.

67. Erskine, *Twenty Years before the Mast*, 105.

68. Melville, *Moby-Dick*, 6, 474.

69. Samuel Eliot Morison, *"Old Bruin": Commodore Matthew Calbraith Perry* (Boston: Little, Brown, 1967), 156–57.

70. Undated copy of the deposition of James Cullins, c. 1826, P-157, John Percival Papers, 1826–1841, MHS.

71. Lincoln Paine, *The Sea and Civilization: A Maritime History of the World* (New York: Knopf, 2013), 13.

72. Paine, *Sea and Civilization*, 18–19.

73. Reynolds, *Voyage of the* Potomac, 102.

74. Reynolds, v–vi.

75. Reynolds to Southard, May 25, 1834.

76. Reynolds to Southard, June 11, 1829.

77. Jeremiah Reynolds to Samuel Southard, August 25, 1834, Southard Papers, box 47, folder 10, Southard Papers.

78. Acting Secretary of the Navy John Boyle to Jeremiah Reynolds, August 19, 1834, and September 1, 1834, "Miscellaneous Letters Sent by the Secretary of the Navy, 1798–1886," RG 45, M 209, NARA I.

79. Belohlavek, *"Let the Eagle Soar!,"* 157–62; Reynolds, *Voyage of the* Potomac, vi.

80. See Armstrong, *Small Boats and Daring Men*, esp. chap. 7, "The First Sumatra Expedition, 1831–1832," 150–71, and chap. 8, "Return to Sumatra: The East India Squadron, 1838–1839," 172–90.

81. Reynolds, *Voyage of the* Potomac, 94.

82. Reynolds, 227.

83. Reynolds, 105.

84. Reynolds, ii.

85. For more on how mariners compared Oceanian peoples to Native Americans, see Brian Rouleau, "Maritime Destiny as Manifest Destiny: American Commercial Expansionism and the Idea of the Indian," *Journal of the Early Republic* 30 (Fall 2010), 377–411; and Rouleau, *With Sails Whitening Every Sea*. Nancy Shoemaker has also made a similar observation in *Native American Whalemen and the World*, chap. 4.

86. See Schroeder, *Shaping a Maritime Empire*, esp. chap. 2, "President Andrew Jackson: Advocate of an Expansive Navy," 19–36.

87. Robert V. Remini, *Andrew Jackson and His Indian Wars* (New York: Viking, 2001), 14.

88. Sachs, *Humboldt Currents*, 147–48.

89. Horace Holden, *A Narrative of the Shipwreck, Captivity and Sufferings of Horace Holden and Benj. H. Nute, Who were Cast Away in the American Ship Mentor, on the Pelew Islands, in the Year 1832; and for Two Years Afterwards were Subjected to Unheard of Sufferings Among the Barbarous Inhabitants of Lord North's Island* (Boston: Russell, Shattuck, 1836), 18.

90. Holden, *Narrative of the Shipwreck*, 27–28.

91. Holden, 113–14, 110.

92. Nathan Perl-Rosenthal, *Citizen Sailors: Becoming American in the Age of Revolution* (Cambridge, MA: Belknap Press of Harvard University Press, 2015); Gilje, *Free Trade and Sailors' Rights*.

93. Shoemaker, *Native American Whalemen and the World*, 134, 137.

94. Resolution of the General Assembly of Rhode Island and Providence Plantations, October session 1834, in Samuel Southard, report, March 21, 1836, *American State Papers: Naval Affairs*, 4:869.

95. Dutee J. Pearce, speech, February 7, 1835, *American State Papers: Naval Affairs*, 4:709.

96. Pearce, speech, 4:708.

97. Samuel Southard, speech, March 21, 1836, *American State Papers: Naval Affairs*, 4:868.

98. Philbrick, *Sea of Glory*, 30.

99. Sachs, *Humboldt Currents*, 153.

100. Reynolds, *Address on a Surveying Expedition*, 51.

101. Reynolds, 36.

102. Reynolds, 66–67.

103. Thomas Hamer, speech, May 9, 1836, *Cong. Globe*, 24th Cong., 1st Sess., 338.

104. Hamer, speech, 339.

105. John Reed, speech, May 9, 1836, *Appendix to the Congressional Globe*, 24th Cong., 1st Sess., 571.

106. Reed, speech, 572.

107. Melville, *Moby-Dick*, 270.

108. Benjamin Rodman to Jeremiah Reynolds, June 11, 1836, reprinted in Reynolds, *Pacific and Indian Oceans*, 116.

109. Reynolds, *Voyage of the* Potomac, 470.

110. Contemporaries in the early republic appear rarely to have used the term *white savage* to describe those lower-class whites they disapproved of, calling such individuals "savages" or "vagabonds" instead. *White savage* is instead a phrase concocted by historians who have sought to capture the condescension, disgust, and loathing that middle and upper-class elites felt for impoverished, violent, or drunken whites. See, for example, Fintan O'Toole, *White Savage: William Johnson and the Invention of America* (New York: Farrar, Straus & Giroux, 2005); David Andrew Nichols, *Red Gentlemen and White Savages: Indians, Federalists, and the Search for Order on the American Frontier* (Charlottesville: University of Virginia Press, 2008); Richard Drinnon, *White Savage: The Case of John Dunn Hunter* (New York: Schocken Books, 1972); and Lawrence Jacob Friedman, *The White Savage: Racial Fantasies in the Postbellum South* (Englewood Cliffs, NJ: Prentice-Hall, 1970).

111. Jacksonian reluctance to openly criticize working-class white men was in stark contrast to the governing elites of the revolutionary generation, who fretted about the effects of poor settlers on US expansion (Daniel Immerwahr, chap. 1, "The Fall and Rise of Daniel Boone," in *How to Hide an Empire: A History of the Greater United States* [New York: Farrar, Straus & Giroux, 2019], 25–35).

112. Smith, *Thomas ap Catesby Jones*, 83.

113. Tyler, *The Wilkes Expedition*, 9. The original bill can be found in *United States Statutes at Large*, 24th Cong., 1st Sess., chap. 61, 29.

114. Israel, *State of the Union*, 1:466.

115. Wilkes, *Narrative of the US Exploring Expedition*, 1:xv–xvi.

116. George M. Colvocoresses, *Four Years in a Government's Exploring Expedition* (New York: J. M. Fairchild, 1852), 13.

117. Dickerson's transcribed diary can be found in the Mahlon Dickerson and Philemon Dickerson Papers, box 4, folder 4, New Jersey Historical Society, Newark, New Jersey. It describes in full how much he hated his job. The reference to being a "slave to office" appears in the entry for July 1, 1838.

118. Reynolds, *Pacific and Indian Oceans*.

119. Reynolds, unnumbered dedication pages.

120. Reynolds, *Private Journal of William Reynolds*, 10.

121. John Quincy Adams, diary entry, November 4, 1826, microfilm, P-54, reel 40, Adams Family Papers, MHS.

122. See Rouleau, "Maritime Destiny as Manifest Destiny"; and Rouleau, *With Sails Whitening Every Sea*, esp. chap. 3, "Maritime Destiny as Manifest Destiny," 74–101.

123. Erskine, *Twenty Years before the Mast*, 125.

124. Erskine, 169.

125. Charles Wilkes to James Paulding, Fiji Islands, August 10, 1840 (no. 70), RG 45, 37, 24, M 75, roll 6, NARA Boston.

126. *Catalogue of Boxes, Barrels &c. Shipped on board the American ship Lansamme and consigned to the Navy Agent*, undated, RG 45, 37, 24, M 75, roll 6, NARA Boston.

127. Francis P. Prucha, *The Great Father: The United States Government and the American Indians* (Lincoln: University of Nebraska Press, 1984), 8, 60–61, x.

128. Wilkes, *Narrative of the US Exploring Expedition*, 1:xxviii.

129. Wilkes, 1:xxix.

130. Wilkes, *Narrative of the US Exploring Expedition*, 1:324–25. White US citizens' use of Indigenous people to serve in military and diplomatic roles toward other Indigenous people goes back to colonial days. For a particularly strong analysis of this relationship, see James H. Merrell, *Into the American Woods: Negotiators on the Pennsylvania Frontier* (New York: W. W. Norton, 1999).

131. See Peggy Reeves Sanday, *Divine Hunger: Cannibalism as a Cultural System* (Cambridge: Cambridge University Press, 1986), 152–58.

132. Smith, *To Master the Boundless Sea*, 50.

133. The first case of this reaction to the Ex Ex occurred among the residents of Rio Negro, who believed that the US seamen were French sailors coming to attack them (Reynolds, *Private Journal of William Reynolds*, 22 [February 7, 1839]).

134. Reynolds, *Private Journal of William Reynolds*, 39, 41 (March 12 and March 14, 1839).

135. Wilkes, *Narrative of the US Exploring Expedition*, 1:335.

136. Reynolds, *Private Journal of William Reynolds*, 90.

137. See, for example, Bartholomé de Las Casas's translation and summary of the diary of Christopher Columbus, entry for Sunday, October 14, 1492, reprinted in Howard Zinn and Anthony Arnove, eds., *Voices of a People's History of the United States*, 2nd ed. (New York: Seven Stories Press, 2009), 33–34.

138. Epeli Hau'ofa, "Our Sea of Islands," *Contemporary Pacific* 6, no. 1 (1994), 148–61.

139. Sanday, *Divine Hunger*, 161.

140. Sanday, 152.

141. The scholarly debate over the existence, extent, and meaning of Oceanian cannibalism is an extensive one. In 2005, for example, Gananath Obeyesekere argued that Fijians practiced codified "ritual anthropophagy" instead of the mass cannibalism portrayed in Western accounts, which were largely influenced by colonialist projections and sometimes factually suspect (*Cannibal Talk: The Man-Eating Myth and Human Sacrifice in the South Seas* [Berkeley: University of California Press, 2005]). For the purposes of this chapter, what matters more than the practice's actual verity or extent is the widespread perception among nineteenth-century US citizens that Oceanians were cannibals.

142. Deryck Scarr, *Fiji: A Short History* (Laie, HI: Institute for Polynesian Studies, Brigham Young University–Hawai'i Campus, 1984), 3.

143. Wilkes, *Narrative of the US Exploring Expedition*, 3:239.

144. Reynolds, *Private Journal of William Reynolds*, 143.

145. Wilkes, *Narrative of the US Exploring Expedition*, 3:234–39.

146. David F. Long, *Gold Braid and Foreign Relations: Diplomatic Activities of U.S. Naval Officers, 1798–1883* (Annapolis, MD: Naval Institute Press, 1988), 4, 415.

147. Prucha, *Great Father*, 46.

148. "Feejee Regulations," copy, RG 45, 37, 24, M 75, roll 6, NARA Boston. For more on the Indian Trade and Intercourse Act of 1834, see William E. Unrau, *The Rise and Fall of Indian Country, 1825–1855* (Lawrence: University Press of Kansas, 2007).

149. Prucha, *Great Father*, 42–43.

150. As Ann Fabian notes, "Veidovi" is "a spelling closer to Fijian pronunciation" than "Vendovi," which was the spelling used by Wilkes and other Ex Ex members (*The Skull Collectors: Race, Science, and America's Unburied Dead* [Chicago: University of Chicago Press, 2010], 121).

151. Wilkes, *Narrative of the US Exploring Expedition*, 3:103–5.

152. Reynolds, *Private Journal of William Reynolds*, 156.

153. Wilkes, *Narrative of the US Exploring Expedition*, 3:126–36.

154. Wilkes, 3:160.

155. Reynolds, *Private Journal of William Reynolds*, 159.

156. Prucha, *Great Father*, 63.

157. Fabian, *Skull Collectors*, 121–22.

158. Philbrick, *Sea of Glory*, 300.

159. Fabian, *Skull Collectors*, 125.

160. Fabian, 159.

161. "Extract from Boat Orders, Fiji Islands," May 8, 1840, RG 45, 37, 24, M 75, roll 6, NARA Boston.

162. Reynolds, *Private Journal of William Reynolds*, 165.

163. Reynolds, 144.

164. Taking hostages was actually common practice for Oceanian–European interactions in the Pacific. See, for instance, Igler, *The Great Ocean*, chap. 3, "Hostages and Captives," 73–97.

165. Wilkes, *Narrative of the US Exploring Expedition*, 3:266–71; Philbrick, *Sea of Glory*, 217–20.

166. Lieutenant Alden to Charles Wilkes, Fiji Islands, August 1, 1840, RG 45, 37, 24, M 75, roll 6.

167. As Nicholas Thomas writes in *Islanders*, "If a massacre had taken place, the Fijians, of whom ten had been killed, were more obviously the victims than the Americans" (152).

168. Reynolds, *Private Journal of William Reynolds*, 194.

169. Wilkes, *Narrative of the US Exploring Expedition*, 3:265.

170. Wilkes, 3:274.

171. Wilkes, 3:274.

172. Wilkes, *Narrative*, 3: 274–75; Erskine, *Twenty Years before the Mast*, 211.

173. Erskine, 213.

174. Erskine, 214.

175. Erskine, 215.

176. Erskine, 215.

177. Reynolds, *Private Journal of William Reynolds*, 144.

178. Erskine, *Twenty Years before the Mast*, 217.
179. Wilkes, *Narrative of the US Exploring Expedition*, 3:285.
180. Reynolds, *Private Journal of William Reynolds*, 195.
181. Reynolds, 241.
182. Reynolds, 241.
183. Reynolds, 199.
184. For judicial extension into Indian country as a key element of settler colonialism, see Lisa Ford, *Settler Sovereignty: Jurisdiction and Indigenous People in America and Australia, 1788–1836* (Cambridge, MA: Harvard University Press, 2010). For examples of US missionaries teaching Native Americans how to farm, see Lori J. Daggar, "The Mission Complex: Economic Development, 'Civilization,' and Empire in the Early Republic," *Journal of the Early Republic* 36, no. 3 (Fall 2016), 467–92.
185. Wilkes, *Narrative of the US Exploring Expedition*, 1:339.
186. Herman Melville, *White Jacket, Or, the World on a Man-of-War* (1850; repr., Aegypan), 171.
187. Wilkes, *Narrative of the US Exploring Expedition*, 1:4.
188. Joseph G. Clark, *Lights and Shadows of Sailor Life* (Boston: Benjamin B. Mussey, 1848), ix. Clark's rank is indicated in Wilkes, *Narrative of the US Exploring Expedition*, 1:xli.
189. Clark, *Lights and Shadows*, 236.
190. Reynolds, *Private Journal of William Reynolds*, 95.
191. Erskine, *Twenty Years before the Mast*, 75.
192. Erskine, 102.
193. Wilkes, *Narrative of the US Exploring Expedition*, 2:14.
194. Wilkes, 2:91.
195. Wilkes, 1:238.
196. Philbrick, *Sea of Glory*, 239.
197. Philbrick, 240; Tyler, *Wilkes Expedition*, 194.
198. Philbrick, *Sea of Glory*, 240.
199. Tyler, *Wilkes Expedition*, 194.
200. Philbrick, *Sea of Glory*, 241.
201. Philbrick, 242.
202. Melville, *White Jacket*, 306.
203. Melville, 307.
204. Melville, 306.
205. Melville, 116.
206. Edward P. Montague, ed., *Narrative of the Late Expedition to the Dead Sea. From a Diary By one of the Party* (Philadelphia: Carey and Hart, 1849), 131–32.
207. William C. Godfrey, *Godfrey's Narrative of the Last Grinnell Arctic Exploring Expedition, In Search of Sir John Franklin, 1853–4–5* (Philadelphia: J. T. Lloyd, 1857), 63, LCP.
208. Myra C. Glenn, *Jack Tar's Story: The Autobiographies and Memoirs of Sailors in Antebellum America* (Cambridge: Cambridge University Press, 2010), 113–14.
209. Joyce, *Shaping of American Ethnography*, 144–45.
210. William Stanton, *The Great United States Exploring Expedition of 1838–1842* (Berkeley: University of California Press, 1975), 288.
211. Quoted in Philbrick, *Sea of Glory*, 329.
212. Philbrick, 329–30.

213. Paine, *Sea and Civilization*, 18–19; Steinberg, *Social Construction of the Ocean*, 52–54.

214. J. N. Reynolds to Samuel Southard, September 24, 1828, *American State Papers: Naval Affairs*, 4:688.

215. The practice of using flora and fauna to ascertain position in relation to land masses dates back at least as far as Columbus (Samuel Eliot Morison, *Admiral of the Ocean Sea: A Life of Christopher Columbus* [Boston: Little, Brown, 1946], 201, 202). It was still a common technique in the later years of the Age of Sail, such that Edmund Fanning used it while searching for new sealing islands during his 1829–1830 voyage with Reynolds (Edmund Fanning, *Voyages Round the World* [New York: Collins & Hannay, 1833], 480).

216. Labaree et al., *America and the Sea*, 177.

217. Steven J. Dick, *Sky and Ocean Joined: The U.S. Naval Observatory, 1830–2000* (Cambridge: Cambridge University Press, 2003), 15–16.

218. Dick, *Sky and Ocean Joined*, 17, and Labaree et al., *America and the Sea*, 178.

219. Labaree et al., 179.

220. Wilkes, *Narrative of the US Exploring Expedition*, 3:357.

221. Wilkes, 3:221.

222. Gerard Ward, ed. *American Activities in the Central Pacific, 1790–1870: A History, Geography and Ethnography pertaining to American Involvement and Americans in the Pacific Taken from Contemporary Newspapers, etc.*, 8 vols. (Ridgewood, NJ: Gregg Press, 1966–1967), 2:327.

223. Philbrick, *In the Heart of the Sea*, 14.

224. Daniel Henderson, *The Hidden Coasts: A Biography of Admiral Charles Wilkes* (Westport, CT: Greenwood Press, 1953); Harrison, "Science and Politics: Origins of Government Expeditions," 180; Tyler, *Wilkes Expedition*; Stanton, *Great United States Exploring Expedition*; and, to a lesser extent, even Geoffrey Sutton Smith, "The Navy before Darwinism: Science, Exploration, and Diplomacy in Antebellum America," *American Quarterly* 28 (Spring 1976), 41–55.

225. Harrison, "Science and Politics: Origins of Government Expeditions," 180. In 2001, Bruce A. Harvey made a similar pronouncement about the Ex Ex and Perry missions (*American Geographics: U.S. National Narratives and the Representation of the Non-European World, 1830–1865* [Stanford, CA: Stanford University Press, 2001], 14).

226. Burnett, "Hydrographic Discipline among the Navigators"; Smith, *To Master the Boundless Sea*, chap. 1, "Empire of Commerce and Science," 41–73.

227. Dickerson to Reynolds, August 25, 1837, reprinted in Reynolds, *Exploring Expedition. Correspondence*, 88.

228. Wilkes, *Narrative of the US Exploring Expedition*, 1:xxix.

229. Burnett, "Hydrographic Discipline among the Navigators," 232.

230. Burnett, "Hydrographic Discipline among the Navigators."

231. Charles Wilkes, *Synopsis of the Cruise of the U.S. Exploring Expedition, During the Years 1838, '39, '40, '41, & '42; Delivered Before the National Institute, by its Commander, Charles Wilkes, Esq., on the Twentieth of June, 1842* (Washington, DC: Peter Force, 1842), 29.

232. US Congress, Joint Committee on the Library, *Report by Pearce* (Washington, DC: Ritchie & Heiss, 1846), 2, LCP.

233. Smith, *To Master the Boundless Sea*, 70; Haskell, *United States Exploring Expedition*, 19.

234. George Bancroft to Benjamin Tappan, September 22, 1845, Benjamin Tappan Papers, box 20, reel 8, Manuscript Division, Library of Congress, Washington, DC; "Art. VIII.—United States Exploring Expedition.—," *North American Review*, July 1, 1846, 213.

235. Haskell, *United States Exploring Expedition*, 45; Wilkes, *Synopsis of the U.S. Exploring Expedition*, 41. For examples of Wilkes's recommendations from the *Narrative*, see 1:123, 164; 3:194; 2:395–96.

236. See Haskell, *United States Exploring Expedition*, 19.

237. US Congress, Joint Committee on the Library, *Report by Pearce*, 3.

238. US Congress, Joint Committee on the Library, 3.

239. Horace Galpen to Lea & Blanchard, February 14, 1850, box 157, folder 3 (G—1850), Lea & Febiger Records, HSP.

240. "United States Exploring Expedition," *Times* (London), September 2, 1845.

241. Melville, *Moby-Dick*, 7.

242. Quoted in Shoemaker, *Pursuing Respect in the Cannibal Isles*, 94.

243. Smith, *To Master the Boundless Sea*, 71.

244. Margaret Creighton, *Rites and Passages: The Experience of American Whaling, 1830–1870* (Cambridge: Cambridge University Press, 1995), 36.

245. Creighton, *Rites and Passages*, 16.

246. For more on the North Pacific Exploring Expedition, see Allan B. Cole, "The Ringgold–Rodgers–Brooke Expedition to Japan and the North Pacific, 1853–1859," *Pacific Historical Review* 16, no. 2 (May 1947), 152–62; and Ponko, *Ships, Seas, and Scientists*, chap. 12, "Expedition to the North Pacific, Bering Straits and China Sea, 1852–1863," 206–30.

247. Wilkes, *Narrative of the US Exploring Expedition*, 1:xxix.

248. Wilkes, 5:171.

249. Wilkes, 5:172.

250. Wilkes, 5:172.

251. John Frémont to Col. J. J. Albert, chief of the Corps. of Top. Engineers, March 1, 1845, reprinted in Frémont, *Oregon and California: The Exploring Expedition to the Rocky Mountains, Oregon, and California, by Brevet Col, J. C. Fremont* (Buffalo, NY: Geo. H. Derby, 1849), 123.

252. Charles Wilkes, *Western America, Including California and Oregon, with Maps of Those Regions, and of "The Sacramento Valley"* (Philadelphia: Lea & Blanchard, 1849), viii.

253. Lea & Blanchard, cost book, vol. 54 (1838–1853), p. 141, collection 227B, Lea & Febiger Records, HSP.

254. US Congress, Joint Committee on the Library, *Report by Pearce*, 9.

255. Frederick Merk, ed., *Fur Trade and Empire: George Simpson's Journal, Entitled Remarks Connected with the Fur Trade in the Course of a Voyage from York Factory to Fort George and Back to York Factory 1824–25*, rev. ed. (Cambridge, MA: Belknap Press of Harvard University Press, 1968), xxii.

256. Tyler, *Wilkes Expedition*, 403.

257. Smith, "The Navy before Darwinism," 44–45.

258. US Congress, Joint Committee on the Library, *Report by Pearce*, 86.

259. Tyler, *Wilkes Expedition*, 404.

260. Norman A. Graebner, *Empire on the Pacific: A Study in American Continental Expansion* (New York: Ronald Press Company, 1955).

261. Israel, *State of the Union*, 1:737.

262. Israel, 1:738.

263. The quotation is from William Leggett in 1837, quoted in Feller, *Jacksonian Promise*, 160.

264. Susan Bean, *Yankee India: American Commercial and Cultural Encounters with India in the Age of Sail, 1784–1860* (Salem, MA: Peabody Essex Museum, 2001), 14.

265. Stanton, *Great United States Exploring Expedition*, 3–4.

266. See Jimmy L. Bryan, *The American Elsewhere: Adventures and Manliness in the Age of Expansion* (Lawrence: University Press of Kansas, 2017), especially chap. 2, "The Storyteller Nation," 67–108.

267. Feller, *Jacksonian Promise*, 87–88.

268. Philbrick's *Sea of Glory* carefully charts this change in Wilkes's character.

269. Reynolds, *Private Journal of William Reynolds*, 217.

270. John F. Lee to Samuel Philips Lee, Little Rock, Arkansas, August 11, 1839, box 81, folder 1, Blair and Lee Family Papers, Princeton University Library.

271. Schroeder, *Shaping a Maritime Empire*, 69.

272. Schroeder, 64–67.

273. Schroeder, 69. For a similar observation about the role played by party politics in determining the reception of the Ex Ex, see Philbrick, *Sea of Glory*, 303–4.

274. Andrew C. Jampoler, *Sailors in the Holy Land: The 1848 American Expedition to the Dead Sea and the Search for Sodom and Gomorrah* (Annapolis, MD: Naval Institute Press, 2005), 12; Philbrick, *Sea of Glory*, 329.

275. Wilkes, *Autobiography*, 521–22.

276. Wilkes, 521–22.

CHAPTER 3

1. Charles Wilkes to John W. Davis, January 28, 1845, box 20, reel 8, Benjamin Tappan Papers, Manuscript Division, Library of Congress, Washington, DC (hereafter cited as Tappan Papers).

2. Charles Wilkes to Benjamin Tappan, December 27, 1853, box 22, reel 9, Tappan Papers.

3. Wilkes to Tappan, December 27, 1853; Wilkes to Tappan, November 25, 1850; Wilkes to Tappan, December 27, 1853.

4. The incoming correspondence of the publishing firm Lea & Blanchard of Philadelphia has been preserved from the year 1850 in the Lea & Febiger Records (Collection 227B, boxes 156–63) at the Historical Society of Pennsylvania in Philadelphia. Much of it consists of requests from readers and booksellers for copies of William Francis Lynch's *Narrative of the United States' Expedition to the River Jordan and the Dead Sea* (1849 and 1850). For an example of a book peddler requesting a contract, see George Reynolds to Lea & Blanchard, June 5, 1850, Lea & Febiger Records, box 159, folder 3, "Ra-Ri," HSP.

5. Edwin Wolf II and Marie Elena Korey, eds., *Quarter of a Millennium: The Library Company of Philadelphia, 1731–1981: A Selection of Books, Manuscripts, Maps, Prints, Drawings, and Paintings* (Philadelphia: Library Company of Philadelphia, 1981), 319.

6. Frederick William True, "The United States National Museum," in *The Smithsonian Institution, 1846–1896: The History of Its First Half Century*, ed. George Brown

Goode (Washington, DC: De Vinne Press, 1897), 311, available at Biodiversity Heritage Library, http://www.biodiversitylibrary.org/bibliography/30479.

7. See, for example, Edward W. Said, *Orientalism* (New York: Pantheon Books, 1978); Pratt, *Imperial Eyes*; Edward Said, *Culture and Imperialism* (New York: Vintage Books, 1994); John Carlos Rowe, *Literary Culture and U.S. Imperialism: From the Revolution to World War II* (Oxford: Oxford University Press, 2000); Shelley Streeby, *American Sensations: Class, Empire, and the Production of Popular Culture* (Berkeley: University of California Press, 2002); Amy Kaplan, *Anarchy of Empire in the Making of U.S. Culture* (Cambridge, MA: Harvard University Press, 2002), Kristin Hoganson, *Consumers' Imperium: The Global Production of American Domesticity, 1865–1920* (Chapel Hill: University of North Carolina Press, 2007); and Andy Doolen, *Territories of Empire: U.S. Writing from the Louisiana Purchase to Mexican Independence* (Oxford: Oxford University Press, 2014).

8. Hoganson, *Consumer's Imperium*.

9. M. Birchard to Benjamin Tappan, December 24, 1843, box 18, reel 7, Tappan Papers.

10. [Illegible] to Benjamin Tappan, June 28, 1842, box 17, reel 7, Tappan Papers.

11. McDonald, "Reynolds, Jeremiah N.," 524; J. N. Reynolds to Senator Benjamin Tappan and others, December 25, 1842, box 17, reel 7, Tappan Papers.

12. "United States Exploring Expedition," *Campbell's Foreign Semi-monthly Magazine*, February 1, 1844, 189.

13. Haskell, *United States Exploring Expedition*, 9.

14. First editions of d'Urville's volumes in their original binding are hard to come by. The Library Company of Philadelphia has one of the scientific volumes from 1854 in original binding: Dumoutier, *Voyage au Pole Sud et dans l'Océanie sur les Corvettes l'Astrolabe et la Zélée . . . Anthropologie* (Paris: Gide and Baudry, 1854).

15. John James Abert, *Reply of Col. Abert and Mr. Markoe to the Hon. Mr. Tappan* (Washington, DC: W. Q. Force, 1843), 16, LCP.

16. This recommendation is inferred based on their close relationship at the time. Wilkes's appointment is noted in "Extract from the Minutes of the Joint Library Committee of Congress," August 26, 1842, box 17, reel 7, Tappan Papers; and his subordination to Tappan as a direct supervisor is noted in Wilkes to Davis, January 28, 1845.

17. Wilkes, *Autobiography*, 533.

18. Joan Boudreau, "Publishing the U.S. Exploring Expedition: The Fruits of the Glorious Enterprise," *Printing History*, n.s., no. 3 (January 2008), 25–26; Haskell, *United States Exploring Expedition*, 10.

19. Haskell, *United States Exploring Expedition*, 11.

20. Haskell, 9.

21. Sherman had printed two tomes for the Virginia and New Jersey state geological surveys (Boudreau, "Publishing the U.S. Exploring Expedition," 29).

22. Gaskill was especially famous for fancy embossed bindings, in which the design on the covers of books was raised rather than impressed (Edwin Wolf II, *From Gothic Windows to Peacocks: American Embossed Leather Bindings, 1825–1855* [Philadelphia: The Library Company of Philadelphia, 1990], 25).

23. Benjamin Tappan to James A. Pearce, May 15, 1846, box 21, reel 9, Tappan Papers.

24. Michael Winship, "Manufacturing and Book Production," in *A History of the Book in America*, vol. 3, *The Industrial Book, 1840–1880*, ed. Scott E. Casper, Jeffrey D.

Groves, Stephen W. Nissenbaum, and Michael Winship (Chapel Hill: University of North Carolina Press, 2007), chap. 1, 48.

25. Winship, "Manufacturing and Book Production," 61, 58–59.

26. Boudreau, "Publishing the U.S. Exploring Expedition," 32; John Cassin, *United States Exploring Expedition*, vol. 8, *Mammalogy and Ornithology* (Philadelphia: C. Sherman & Son, 1858), vi, Cullman Library.

27. Joseph Drayton to Benjamin Tappan, July 10, 1855, box 22, reel 9, Tappan Papers. For more on Lavinia and Bowen and Company, see "Bowen, Lavinia," Philadelphia on Stone Biographical Dictionary of Lithographers, n.d., Library Company of Philadelphia, https://digital.librarycompany.org/islandora/object/digitool%3A78899.

28. US Congress, Joint Committee on the Library, *Report by Pearce* (Washington, DC: Ritchie & Heiss, 1846), 9, LCP.

29. Lea & Blanchard, cost book, 54:86, insert, "Specifications of the Manner and Form in Which the Work of the Exploring Expedition is to Be Bound." The conclusion that the d'Urville volumes came out in paperboard is based on my viewing of a copy of Dumoutier's volume on anthropology, published in 1854 in Paris, and housed at the Library Company of Philadelphia (Dumoutier, *Voyage au Pole Sud et dans l'Océanie sur les Corvettes l'Astrolabe et la Zélée . . . Anthropologie* [Paris: Gide and Baudry, 1854]). The claim of the narrative volumes being octavo can be confirmed by examining these volumes on the Biodiversity Heritage Library website, https://www.biodiversitylibrary.org/item/226840#page/21/mode/1up.

30. These figures are from Haskell, *United States Exploring Expedition*, 31–37.

31. The physical description and evaluation of the Ex Ex volumes in this paragraph were the result of close personal investigations of the official Ex Ex volumes preserved in the collections of the Joseph F. Cullman III Library of Natural History, Smithsonian Institution Libraries, Washington, DC. The Cullman Library also has an original copy of Jules-Sébastien-César Dumont d'Urville, *Voyage au Pole Sud et dans l'Océanie sur les Corvettes l'Astrolabe et la Zélée* [. . .], vol. 1 (Paris: Gide, 1841). The date range for the publications of the map and plate volumes comes from Raymond John Howgego, ed., *Encyclopedia of Exploration, 1800 to 1850: A Comprehensive Reference Guide to the History and Literature of Exploration, Travel and Colonization Between the Years 1800 and 1850* (Potts Point, New South Wales, Australia: Hordern House, 2006), s.v. "Dumont D'Urville, Jules Sebastien Cesar, 1837–1840, Antarctica, Pacific, East Indies," 182.

32. US Congress, Joint Committee on the Library, *Report by Pearce*, 8.

33. Haskell, *United States Exploring Expedition*, 9.

34. Haskell, 9; N. P. Trist to W. A. Harris, April 3, 1846, "Diplomatic Instructions of the Department of State, 1801–1906," RG 59, M77, Argentina, roll 10, NARA Boston; Edward Everett to Robert Schenck, February 24, 1853, RG 59, M 77, Brazil, roll 23, NARA Boston, and the inside board of the Cullman Library's copy of John Cassin, *United States Exploring Expedition* [. . .], vol. 8, *Mammalogy and Ornithology* [. . .] (Philadelphia: C. Sherman & Son, 1858), on which is a label with the words, "Presented by the Congress of the United States to the Government of China."

35. Charles Wilkes to Benjamin Tappan, May 28, 1845, Washington, box 20, reel 8, Tappan Papers.

36. William Marcy to William Trousdale, April 26, 1855, RG 59, M 77, Brazil, roll 23, NARA Boston.

37. Robert Owen to Charles Wilkes, July 27, 1853, reel 14, Wilkes Family Papers, Library of Congress, Washington, DC.

38. This term is a combination of Eliga H. Gould's phrase "Europe's diplomatic republic" on page 93 in *Among the Powers of the Earth: The American Revolution and the Making of a New World Empire* (Cambridge, MA: Harvard University Press, 2012), and what the conchologist Joseph Couthoy called in 1843 "the Republic of Science" (Couthoy to Tappan, January 5, 1843).

39. *Captain Cook's Voyages Round the World* (Glasgow: Niven, Napier & Khull, for W. D. & A. Brownlie, 1807), 1:12, Cullman Library.

40. Daniel Henderson, *The Hidden Coasts: A Biography of Admiral Charles Wilkes* (Westport, CT: Greenwood Press, 1953), 214.

41. Howgego, *Encyclopedia of Exploration to 1800*, s.v. "Dumont D'Urville," 177–79; Jeremiah Reynolds to Mahlon Dickerson, January 4, 1838, reprinted in Reynolds, *Exploring Expedition. Correspondence*, 143.

42. Reynolds to Dickerson, January 4, 1838.

43. Lewis Cass to R. K. Meade, December 3, 1857, RG 59, M 77, Brazil, roll 23, NARA Boston.

44. Wilkes to Davis, January 28, 1845.

45. Wilkes, *Autobiography*, 541.

46. Wilkes, 533.

47. As early as December 1844, Sherman had pleaded with Wilkes and Tappan for extra remuneration, claiming that his winning bid had been far too low to cover the costs of publishing the official copies (C. Sherman to Charles Wilkes and Benjamin Tappan, December 6, 1844, box 19, reel 8, Tappan Papers; C. Sherman to Benjamin Tappan, February 17, 1845, Philadelphia, box 20, reel 8, Tappan Papers).

48. Haskell, *United States Exploring Expedition*, 17; Philbrick, *Sea of Glory*, 338. For criticism of Wilkes's copyright, see "United States Exploring Expedition," *Southern Literary Messenger*, May 1, 1845, 316; and "The Narrative of the Exploring Expedition," *Southern Literary Messenger*, June 1, 1845, 389.

49. I am indebted to Mary Louise Pratt (*Imperial Eyes*), Ronald J. Zboray (*A Fictive People*), Jimmy Bryan (*The American Elsewhere*), and Kristin Hoganson (*Consumer's Imperium*, 12) for this concept.

50. For a few examples, see Schlesinger, *Age of Jackson*; Watson, *Liberty and Power*; and Wilentz, *Rise of American Democracy*.

51. See Charles Sellers, *The Market Revolution: Jacksonian America, 1815–1846* (Oxford: Oxford University Press, 1991). The "Age of Clay" reference is from Amy S. Greenberg, *A Wicked War: Polk, Clay, Lincoln, and the 1846 U.S. Invasion of Mexico* (New York: Alfred A. Knopf, 2012), 8.

52. See John, *Spreading the News*; Wilentz, *Rise of American Democracy*; and Howe, *What Hath God Wrought*.

53. The literature on territorial expansion and US foreign relations in the early republic is long; for a fuller historiographical review, see the extensive footnotes in Konstantin Dierks, "Americans Overseas in the Early American Republic," *Diplomatic History* 42, no. 1 (January 2018), 17–35.

54. Rubin, *Making of Middlebrow Culture*, 1–2.

55. For more on this shift, see Sean Wilentz, *Chants Democratic: New York City and the Rise of the American Working Class, 1788–1850* (Oxford: Oxford University Press, 1984).

56. John Lauritz Larson, *The Market Revolution in America: Liberty, Ambition, and the Eclipse of the Common Good* (Cambridge: Cambridge University Press, 2010). For a

particularly fine job of putting the raw and disorienting experience of "panic" back into the historical narrative, see Lepler, *The Many Panics of 1837*.

57. Eric R. Schlereth, "Privileges of Locomotion: Expatriation and the Politics of Southwestern Border Crossing," *Journal of American History* 100, no. 4 (2014), 995–1020; Jimmy L. Bryan, *The American Elsewhere: Adventures and Manliness in the Age of Expansion* (Lawrence: University Press of Kansas, 2017), 13.

58. Rubin, *Making of Middlebrow Culture*, 3; Jennifer L. Goloboy, "The Early American Middle Class," *Journal of the Early Republic* 25 (2005): 537–45.

59. Shoemaker, *Pursuing Respect in the Cannibal Isles*.

60. Reginald Horsman, *Race and Manifest Destiny: The Origins of American Anglo-Saxonism* (Cambridge, MA: Harvard University Press, 1981); Joyce, *Shaping of American Ethnography*; Fabian, *Skull Collectors*.

61. Noel Ignatiev, *How the Irish Became White* (1995; repr., New York: Routledge Classics, 2009).

62. Alexander Saxton, *The Rise and Fall of the White Republic* (1990; repr., London: Verso, 2003).

63. Leon Litwack, *North of Slavery: The Negro in the Free States, 1790–1860* (Chicago: University of Chicago Press, 1961).

64. "Arctic Explorations; The Second Grinnell Expedition in Search of Sir John Franklin, 1853, '54, '55," *Happy Home & Parlor Magazine*, January 1, 1857, xv.

65. Louise Stevenson, chap. 9, "Sites of Reading," in Casper et al., *History of the Book in America*, 324.

66. Melville, *Moby-Dick*, 206.

67. Barbara Sicherman, chap. 8, "Ideologies and Practices of Reading," in Casper et al., *History of the Book in America*, 280.

68. "La Plata, the Argentine Confederation, and Paraguay," *Moore's Rural New-Yorker*, February 26, 1859, 73.

69. William H. Edwards, *A Voyage Up the River Amazon, Including a Residence at Para*, 6th ed. (London: J. Murray, 1847), iii, LCP.

70. Edwards, *Voyage Up the River Amazon*, iii.

71. Zboray, *A Fictive People*, 163.

72. Carl Ostrowski, *Books, Maps and Politics: A Cultural History of the Library of Congress, 1783–1861* (Amherst: University of Massachusetts Press, 2004), 217–18.

73. For more on US curiosity in popular culture, see Chapin, *Exploring Other Worlds*.

74. Alan Taylor, *William Cooper's Town: Power and Persuasion on the Frontier of the Early American Republic* (New York: Knopf, 1995), 24.

75. Alfred Hunter, *A Popular Catalogue of the Extraordinary Curiosities in the National Institute* (Washington, DC: Alfred Hunter, 1855), iii, LCP.

76. Chapin, *Exploring Other Worlds*.

77. Melville, *Moby-Dick*, xiii.

78. Reynolds, *Address on a Surveying Expedition*, 5.

79. Allan Nevins, *Pathmaker of the West* (1928; 3rd ed., Lincoln: University of Nebraska Press, 1992), 617.

80. Nevins discusses Jessie's role, albeit in somewhat dismissive terms in *Frémont*, pages 118, 119, and 191. Andrew F. Rolle gives a far more sympathetic and compelling account of Jessie's contributions in *John Charles Frémont: Character as Destiny* (Norman: University of Oklahoma Press, 1991), pages 44–46.

81. Bryan, *American Elsewhere*, 2.

82. Martin Green, *Dreams of Adventure, Deeds of Empire* (New York, 1979), xi.

83. Richard Henry Dana Jr., *Two Years before the Mast: A Personal Narrative of Life at Sea* (New York: Harper & Brothers, 1840), 460, Dibner Library of the History of Science and Technology, Smithsonian Institution Libraries, Washington, DC (hereafter cited as Dibner).

84. Rolle, *John Charles Frémont*, 44–45.

85. See, for example, the letters of Emma Lou Sprigman to Kane's mother, Jane Leiper Kane, March 12, 1857, May 13, 1857, and April 20, 1858, box 6, folder "Kane, Elisha Kent, Letters of condolence on Kane's death, 1855–1861," Elisha Kent Kane Papers (hereafter cited as Kane Papers), American Philosophical Society, Philadelphia (hereafter cited as APS).

86. For more on how travel accounts could inspire fantasies of male conquest, see Amy Greenberg's *Manifest Manhood and the Antebellum American Empire* (Cambridge: Cambridge University Press, 2005).

87. Benedict Anderson, *Imagined Communities: Reflections on the Origin and Spread of Nationalism* (1983; reprint London: Verso, 2006).

88. Andy Doolen, in *Territories of Empire*, 10, has termed this phenomenon the "continental imaginary." See also Michael F. Robinson, *The Coldest Crucible: Arctic Exploration and American Culture* (Chicago: University of Chicago Press, 2006), 3.

89. Abbott Lawrence to John Clayton, May 31, 1850, "Despatches from United States Ministers to Great Britain," M 30, RG 59, NARA I.

90. Wilkes, *Narrative of the US Exploring Expedition*, 1:3.

91. Like many other chiefs of exploration, Wilkes would frequently conflate I and we throughout his writings, condensing the myriad personal sentiments of the crew into a single, all-sensing, all-feeling narrator. For more on this subject, see Pratt, *Imperial Eyes*, 59; and Ben Maddison, *Class and Colonialism in Antarctic Exploration, 1750–1920* (London: Routledge, 2016), 57.

92. Wilkes, *Narrative of the US Exploring Expedition*, 1:6.

93. Wilkes, 2:129.

94. Wilkes, 2:70.

95. Schroeder, *Shaping a Maritime Empire*.

96. William P. Leeman, *The Long Road to Annapolis: The Founding of the Naval Academy and the Emerging American Republic* (Chapel Hill: University of North Carolina Press, 2010).

97. Wilkes, *Narrative of the US Exploring Expedition*, 2:12, 374, 127.

98. Wilkes, 2:12.

99. Joyce, *Shaping of American Ethnography*, 3.

100. Wilkes, *Narrative of the US Exploring Expedition*, 2:90. Emily Conroy-Krutz has described how US missionaries developed a "hierarchy of heathenism" that helped determine where to focus their evangelist energies (*Christian Imperialism: Converting the World in the Early Republic* [Ithaca, NY: Cornell University Press, 2015], chap. 1, 19–50).

101. Wilkes, *Narrative of the US Exploring Expedition*, 1:339.

102. Wilkes, 1:7.

103. Wilkes, 1:323, 330.

104. See, for example, Wilkes, 1:6.

105. The firm dated back to Matthew Carey, one of Philadelphia's most famous early

printers of the Revolutionary era (*American Dictionary of Printing and Bookmaking* [New York: Howard Lockwood, 1894], s.v. "Matthew Carey," 83).

106. Haskell, *United States Exploring Expedition*, 27.

107. "The Exploring Expedition," *Wiley & Putnam's Literary News Letter*, May 1, 1845.

108. [Illegible] to Lea & Blanchard, March 6, 1850, box 157, folder 1, "D, 1850," Lea & Febiger Records, HSP.

109. Wilkes to Davis, January 28, 1845.

110. Lea & Blanchard, cost book, 54:84–86.

111. Lea & Blanchard, 54:84.

112. Wilkes to Davis, January 28, 1845.

113. Lea & Blanchard, cost book, 54:86; "New Publications," *Banner of the Cross*, May 10, 1845, 150; "The Exploring Expedition," *Wiley & Putnam's Literary News Letter*, May 1, 1845, 319.

114. "Narrative of the United States Exploring Expedition," *Columbian*, June 1, 1845, 284; "The Narrative of the Exploring Expedition," *Southern Literary Messenger*, June 1, 1845.

115. Wilkes, *Autobiography*, 535; the figure of five thousand copies is taken from Lea & Blanchard, cost book, 54:86. Haskell, in *United States Exploring Expedition*, 40, believed that the edition was only three thousand in number, though the cost book includes another two thousand not "yet a/c for."

116. Lea & Blanchard, cost book, 54:84–86.

117. Lea & Blanchard, 54:84, 86.

118. Haskell, *The United States Exploring Expedition*, 41.

119. Rarule, Drinker & Co. to Lea & Blanchard, February 15, 1847, Canton, China, box 159, folder 3, "Ra-Ri," Lea & Febiger Records, HSP.

120. Gray, *Making of John Ledyard*, 76; Howgego, *Encyclopedia of Exploration to 1800*, s.v., "Cook, James, 1768–1771," 255.

121. Edward Belcher, *Narrative of a Voyage Round the World: Performed in Her Majesty's Ship* Sulphur, *During the Years 1836–1842* [. . .], 2 vols. (London: Henry Colburn, 1843), 1:v, Cullman Library.

122. Haskell, *United States Exploring Expedition*, 41.

123. Haskell, 45.

124. Haskell, 44–45, 42.

125. For more on this topic, see Simon Nowell-Smith, *International Copyright Law and the Publisher in the Reign of Queen Victoria* (Oxford: Clarendon Press, 1968); and Eugene Exman, *The Brothers Harper: A Unique Publishing Partnership and Its Impact upon the Cultural Life of America from 1817 to 1853* (New York: Harper and Row, 1965), xiv–xv.

126. "United States Exploring Expedition," *Times* (London), May 15, 1845, 7.

127. "Exploring Expedition of the United States," *Westminster Review*, December 1, 1845, 241.

128. Haynes, *Unfinished Revolution*, 27.

129. "New Publications," *Banner of the Cross*, May 10, 1845, 150.

130. "Notices of New Works," *Southern & Western Literary Messenger*, February 1, 1846, 128.

131. Quoted in Haskell, *United States Exploring Expedition*, 13.

132. "The Exploring Expedition," *Wiley & Putnam's Literary News Letter*, May 1, 1845, 319.

133. Advertisement in Wilkes, *Narrative of the US Exploring Expedition*, vol. 1, back-matter, Cullman Library.

134. "New Publications," *Banner of the Cross*, May 10, 1845, 150.

135. "Narrative of the United States Exploring Expedition," *Columbian*, June 1, 1845, 284.

136. "Art. III—Narrative of the United States Exploring Expedition," *North American Review*, July 1, 1845, 54. Another example of reviewers noting the *Narrative* with "pride" can be found in "Narrative of the United States Exploring Expedition," *Ladies' National Magazine*, January 1, 1845, 36.

137. "Art. III—Narrative of the United States Exploring Expedition," *North American Review*, July 1, 1845, 100, 55.

138. Philbrick, *Sea of Glory*, 338.

139. "Art. III—Narrative of the United States Exploring Expedition," *North American Review*, July 1, 1845, 57.

140. The accusations of plagiarism show up in "United States Exploring Expedition," *Southern Literary Messenger*, May 1, 1845, 316, 320.

141. Wilkes, *Autobiography*, 541.

142. Maddison, *Class and Colonialism in Antarctic Exploration*, 1–2; Gray, *Making of John Ledyard*, 70–71.

143. "New Publications, Etc.," *Spirit of the Times*, June 7, 1845.

144. "11. United States Exploring Expedition," *American Journal of Science & Arts*, October 1, 1844, 212.

145. "11. United States Exploring Expedition," 212.

146. J. Pickering to Charles Wilkes, May 20, 1845, box 20, reel 8, Tappan Papers.

147. Haskell, *United States Exploring Expedition*, 44.

148. Haskell, 44.

149. Haskell, 45.

150. William Reynolds was among those officers who kept a secret journal during the cruise (Reynolds, *Private Journal of William Reynolds*, vi).

151. This data derives from copies available at the Cullman Library, the American Philosophical Society, the Library Company of Philadelphia, and Google Books.

152. Wilkes, *Narrative of the US Exploring Expedition*, 1:xxxvii; George M. Colvocoresses, *Four Years in a Government's Exploring Expedition* (New York: J. M. Fairchild, 1855), 3, APS.

153. Colvocoresses, *Four Years in a Government's Exploring Expedition* (New York: J. M. Fairchild, 1855), APS.

154. George M. Colvocoresses, *Four Years in a Government's Exploring Expedition* (New York: Cornish, Lamport, 1852), Cullman Library.

155. John S. Jenkins, *U.S. Exploring Expeditions* (Peoria, IL: S. H. and G. Burnett, 1852), APS.

156. "Book Notices," *Christian Parlor Book*, March 1, 1855.

157. Colvocoresses, *Four Years*, 26.

158. Colvocoresses, 38.

159. Wilkes, *Narrative of the US Exploring Expedition*, 1:127.

160. Wilkes, 2:408.

161. Wilkes, 1:327, 2:72–73.

162. Wilkes, 1:338, 340–41; 2:65–66, 57, 102.

163. Reynolds, *Private Journal of William Reynolds*, 104.

164. Wilkes, *Narrative of the US Exploring Expedition*, 3:234.

165. Wilkes, 3:101.

166. "United States Exploring Expedition," *Times* (London), May 15, 1845, 7.

167. "Art. III—Narrative of the United States Exploring Expedition," *North American Review*, July 1, 1845, 77.

168. Charles Wilkes, introduction to *Voyage Round the World: Embracing the Principal Events of the Narrative of the United States Exploring Expedition* [. . .] (Philadelphia: Geo. W. Gorton, 1849), Cullman Library.

169. Gananath Obeyesekere, *Cannibal Talk: The Man-Eating Myth and Human Sacrifice in the South Seas* (Berkeley: University of California Press, 2005), 1.

170. "Art. III—Narrative of the United States Exploring Expedition," *North American Review*, July 1, 1845, 85.

171. "United States Exploring Expedition," *Southern Literary Messenger*, May 1, 1845, 315.

172. "Art. VI—Narrative of the United States Exploring Expedition," *Edinburgh Review*, April 1, 1846, 444–45.

173. "Art. VI—Narrative of the United States Exploring Expedition," 440.

174. Shoemaker, *Native American Whalemen and the World*, 140.

175. George Fitzhugh, *Cannibals All! Or, Slaves without Masters* (Richmond, VA: A. Morris, 1857), 27, LCP.

176. Estes, *A Defence of Negro Slavery*, 249.

177. Wilkes, *Narrative of the US Exploring Expedition*, 1:52; Colvocoresses, *Four Years*, 31.

178. Wilkes, *Narrative of the US Exploring Expedition*, 1:64.

179. Wilkes, 1:52.

180. Wilkes, 1:64.

181. Wilkes, 1:64.

182. Evelyn, "National Gallery at the Patent Office," 229–30.

183. Evelyn, 227–29.

184. Evelyn, 232.

185. "Address of the Hon. Joel R. Poinsett before the National Institution, 13th June, 1842," *Southern Patriot* (Charleston, South Carolina), June 21, 1842.

186. Fabian, *Skull Collectors*, 155.

187. Wilkes, *Synopsis of the U.S. Exploring Expedition*, 9.

188. James D. Dana, *United States Exploring Expedition. During the Years 1838, 1838, 1840, 1841, 1842. Under the Command of Charles Wilkes, U.S.N. Crustacea*, part 1 (Philadelphia: C. Sherman, 1852–1855), 2, Cullman Library.

189. Evelyn, "National Gallery at the Patent Office," 236.

190. Evelyn, 229.

191. William M. Morrison, *Morrison's Strangers' Guide to the City of Washington, and its Vicinity*, 2nd ed. (Washington, DC: William M. Morrison, 1844), 40.

192. Wilkes, *Autobiography*, 528.

193. "Visitors Registers of the Smithsonian Institution and the United States National Museum, 1852–1913," vol. 1 (June 19, 1841, to January 1842), record unit 62, Smithsonian Institution Archives, Washington, DC.

194. John Varden, preface to *Synopsis of the Collection in the National Gallery, Patent Office Building; As Originally Arranged by Dr. Chas. Pickering, T. R. Peale, James D. Dana, and Others of the United States Exploring Expedition. Ordered by Charles Mason* (1st ed., Washington: Henry Polkinhorn, 1856), Cullman Library (Varden was the curator and facilities overseer for the National Gallery); Hunter, *Popular Catalogue of Extraordinary Curiosities*, 11.

195. George Brown Goode, "The Founding of the Institution, 1835–1846," in *The Smithsonian Institution, 1846–1896. The History of Its First Half Century*, ed. Goode (Washington, DC: De Vinne Press, 1897), 44–45, available at Biodiversity Heritage Library, http://www.biodiversitylibrary.org/bibliography/30479; Wilkes, *Autobiography*, 528.

196. Evelyn, "National Gallery at the Patent Office," 230, 236.

197. Evelyn, 236.

198. Wilkes, *Autobiography*, 529.

199. Wilkes, 528.

200. Charles Dickens, *American Notes for General Circulation* (Paris: Baudry's European Library, 1842), 142.

201. Edgar Allan Poe, review of *A Brief Account of the Discoveries and Results of the United States' Exploring Expedition*, *Graham's Magazine*, September 1843, 165, available at https://www.eapoe.org/works/criticsm/gm43091.htm; Joyce, *Shaping of American Ethnography*, 146–47.

202. Joyce, 146–47.

203. Varden, preface to *Synopsis of the Collection*; Evelyn, "National Gallery at the Patent Office," 238.

204. "Visitors Registers of the Smithsonian Institution," vol. 2 (January 16, 1842, to April 30, 1845).

205. These cities were taken from "Visitors Registers of the Smithsonian Institution," vol. 2.

206. This data comes from "Visitors Registers of the Smithsonian Institution," vols. 2, 5 (July 8, 1850, to July 6, 1852), and 6 (July 7, 1852, to February 4, 1854).

207. "The Fruits of the Exploring Expedition," *Guardian: Devoted to the Cause of Female Education on Christian Principles*, June 15, 1844, 91.

208. John Kethcum quoted in Evelyn, "National Gallery at the Patent Office," 238.

209. Evelyn, 237.

210. Linnaeus is the Latinized name for Carl Linne. Pratt, *Imperial Eyes*, 38.

211. Pratt, 24–25.

212. Pratt, esp. chap. 2, "Science, Planetary Consciousness, Interiors," 15–36.

213. Hunter, *Popular Catalogue of Extraordinary Curiosities*, iii.

214. Hunter, 50.

215. Hunter, iv.

216. Quoted in Goode, *Smithsonian Institution*, 313.

217. "Address of the Hon. Joel R. Poinsett before the National Institution, 13th June, 1842," *Southern Patriot* (Charleston, South Carolina), June 21, 1842.

218. Augustus Gould to Benjamin Tappan, April 8, 1844, box 19, reel 8, Tappan Papers.

219. Hunter, *Popular Catalogue of Extraordinary Curiosities*, 31; Varden, preface to *Synopsis of the Collection*, 7; Hunter, *Popular Catalogue of Extraordinary Curiosities*, 32.

220. Hunter, 32.

221. Hunter, 23, 62–63, 30.

222. Adrienne Kaeppler, chap. 6, "Anthropology and the U.S. Exploring Expedition," in *Magnificent Voyagers: The U.S. Exploring Expedition, 1838–1842*, ed. Herman J. Viola and Carolyn Margolis (Washington, DC: Smithsonian Institution Press, 1985), 120.

223. Joyce, *Shaping of American Ethnography*, 146.

224. Hunter, *Popular Catalogue of Extraordinary Curiosities*, 11.

225. Varden, preface to *Synopsis of the Collection*, 5.

226. Fabian, *Skull Collectors*, 129.

227. Kaeppler, "Anthropology and the U.S. Exploring Expedition," 123.

228. Hunter, *Popular Catalogue of Extraordinary Curiosities*, 13, 12.

229. Hunter, 14.

230. Wilkes, *Narrative of the US Exploring Expedition*, 3:104–5.

231. Hunter, *Popular Catalogue of Extraordinary Curiosities*, 49.

232. Fabian, *Skull Collectors*, 129.

233. Joyce, *Shaping of American Ethnography*, 153.

234. James Aitken Meigs, "The Cranial Characteristics of the Races of Men," in *Indigenous Races of the Earth*, ed. Josiah C. Nott and George R. Gliddon (Philadelphia: J. B. Lippincott, 1857), 214.

235. Meigs, "Cranial Characteristics," 213.

236. Hunter, *Popular Catalogue of Extraordinary Curiosities*, 25.

237. Jampoler, *Sailors in the Holy Land*, 12; Philbrick, *Sea of Glory*, 329.

238. Wilkes to Tappan, May 28, 1845.

CHAPTER 4

1. Lynch, *Narrative of the Expedition to the River Jordan*, 260.

2. Lynch, *Narrative of the Expedition to the River Jordan*, 262; Montague, *Narrative of the Expedition to the Dead Sea*, 171.

3. Montague, *Narrative of the Expedition to the Dead Sea*, 170–71.

4. John Lloyd Stephens, *Incidents of Travel in Egypt, Arabia, Petraea, and the Holy Land*, 3rd ed., 2 vols. (New York: Harper, 1838), 2:228–29, LCP.

5. Lynch, *Narrative of the Expedition to the River Jordan*, 260–61.

6. Lynch, 260.

7. This description of Lynch's Bedouin companions is taken from page 144 of his *Narrative of the Expedition to the River Jordan*.

8. Lynch, *Narrative of the Expedition to the River Jordan*, 261.

9. Lynch, 263–67.

10. In *Pioneers East: The Early American Experience in the Middle East* (Cambridge, MA: Harvard University Press, 1967), David H. Finnie thought that Lynch had "simply got a bee in his bonnet" and "persuaded the Navy to back him" (269–70). William H. Goetzmann, the don of nineteenth-century US exploration, had little use for the expedition, dismissing it instead as "a wildly impractical junket" (*New Lands, New Men: America and the Second Great Age of Discovery* [New York: Penguin Books, 1986], 332); and Vincent Ponko Jr. described it in passing as a global expression of Manifest Destiny, but stopped short of any deeper analysis (*Ships, Seas, and Scientists*, 60).

11. See, for instance, Robert E. Rook, *The 150th Anniversary of the United States' Expedition to Explore the Dead Sea and the River Jordan* (Amman, Jordan: American

Center of Oriental Research, 1998), 11, 13; and Silberman, *Digging for God and Country*, 52, 54.

12. Bruce A. Harvey and Milette Shamir are among the historians who have recognized this. See Harvey, *American Geographics*, 100; and Shamir, "On the Uselessness of Knowledge: William F. Lynch's 'Interesting' Expedition to the Dead Sea," *Journal of the Early Republic* 38, no. 3 (Fall 2018), 480, 484.

13. Barbara Kreiger situated Lynch's expedition favorably in a longer context of Western exploration of the Dead Sea (*The Dead Sea: Myth, History, and Politics* [Hanover, NH: Published for Brandeis University Press by the University Press of New England, 1997], 58–75). Similarly, John Davis described the Dead Sea mission as "a startling example of government involvement in schemes to explore the Holy Land, lay claim to its promise, and placate religious doubt by locating scripture-affirming evidence" (*The Landscape of Belief: Encountering the Holy Land in Nineteenth-Century American Art and Culture* [Princeton, NJ: Princeton University Press, 1996], 141). Finally, Bruce Harvey acknowledged the mission's contributions to scientific and theological knowledge, and emphasized "hermeneutical desire" as its central theme (*American Geographics*, 113–21; quotation on 104).

14. Shamir, "On the Uselessness of Knowledge," 479, 487.

15. "Then the Lord rained upon Sodom and upon Gomorrah brimstone and fire from the Lord out of heaven; and he overthrew those cities, and all the plain, and all the inhabitants of the cities, and that which grew upon the ground" (Genesis 19:24–25, Authorized [King James] Version).

16. Lynch, *Narrative of the Expedition to the River Jordan*, 288.

17. This perspective could be challenging for some scholars and audiences to comprehend or appreciate. One mechanism for doing so may be to relate it to two of the most evangelical presidents in US history—Jimmy Carter and Ronald Reagan. Though they defined morality differently, both believed that it was a source of national power and prestige. For more, see Gaddis Smith, *Morality, Reason, and Power: American Diplomacy in the Carter Years* (New York: Hill and Wang, 1986); and David T. Byrne, *Ronald Reagan: An Intellectual Biography* (Lincoln, NE: Potomac Books, 2018), esp. chap. 6, "A Moral View of the Cold War," 99–116.

18. For example, Emily Conroy-Krutz, in *Christian Imperialism*, emphasizes how US evangelicals saw themselves as providentially allied with British imperial expansion. Similarly, Walter LaFeber has argued that US missionaries in China in the late nineteenth century helped lay the cultural groundwork for the "new empire" of the turn of the century (*The New Empire: An Interpretation of American Expansion, 1860–1898* [Ithaca, NY: Cornell University Press, 1963]). In European circles, Edward Said, Brian Stanley, and Anna Johnson have been among those who have emphatically come down on the side of missionaries as the quintessential imperial agents. See, for instance, Said, *Orientalism*; Stanley, *The Bible and the Flag: Protestant Missions and British Imperialism in the Nineteenth and Twentieth Centuries* (Leicester: Apollos, 1990); and Johnson, *Missionary Writing and Empire, 1800–1860* (Cambridge: Cambridge University Press, 2001).

19. William R. Hutchison, *Errand to the World: American Protestant Thought and Foreign Missions* (Chicago: University of Chicago Press, 1987); Andrew Porter, *Religion Versus Empire? British Protestant Missionaries and Overseas Expansion, 1700–1914* (Manchester: Manchester University Press, 2004); Jeffrey Cox, *Imperial Fault Lines:*

254 < NOTES TO PAGES 108–112

Christianity and Colonial Power in India, 1818–1940 (Stanford, CA: Stanford University Press, 2002); Tyrrell, *Reforming the World*.

20. Cox, *Imperial Fault Lines*, 27.

21. Porter, *Religion vs. Empire*, 13.

22. Porter, 116.

23. Porter (11, 116) makes this challenge directly.

24. See David Sehat, *The Myth of American Religious Freedom* (Oxford: Oxford University Press, 2011).

25. Lynch, *Narrative of the Expedition to the River Jordan*, 261.

26. This chapter is indebted to the work of Ussama Makdisi, whose *Artillery of Heaven: American Missionaries and the Failed Conversion of the Middle East* (Ithaca, NY: Cornell University Press, 2008) makes a convincing case for the importance of honoring the international as well as North American sides of US expansionism and encounters.

27. Jack P. Lewis, "William Francis Lynch, Explorer of the Dead Sea," Evangelical Theological Society Papers, published in microfilm by the Theological Research Exchange Network (Portland, Oregon, 1993), 1; Rook, *150th Anniversary*, 9.

28. See Jack P. Greene, *Pursuits of Happiness: The Social Development of Early Modern British Colonies and the Formation of American Culture* (Chapel Hill: University of North Carolina Press, 1988).

29. Jon Butler, *Awash in a Sea of Faith: Christianizing the American People* (Cambridge, MA: Harvard University Press, 1990).

30. Sehat, *Myth of American Religious Freedom*, 5–6.

31. Sehat, 51.

32. Denise A. Spellberg, *Thomas Jefferson's Qur'an: Islam and the Founders* (New York: Knopf, 2013).

33. "Treaty of Peace and Friendship, Signed at Tripoli November 4, 1796," article 11, available at https://avalon.law.yale.edu/18th_century/bar1796t.asp. See also Frank Lambert, *The Barbary Wars: American Independence in the Atlantic World* (New York: Hill and Wang, 2005), esp. chap. 4, "The Cultural Construction of the Barbary Pirates," 105–22.

34. Patricia Bonomi, *Under the Cope of Heaven: Religion, Society, and Politics in Colonial America* (New York: Oxford University Press, 1986).

35. Sehat, *Myth of American Religious Freedom*, esp. 1–64.

36. Spellberg, *Thomas Jefferson's Qur'an*, 241.

37. Sehat, *Myth of American Religious Freedom*, 59–64.

38. Sehat, 4.

39. Sehat, 6.

40. William F. Lynch, *Naval Life; or, Observations Afloat and On Shore. The Midshipman* (New York: Charles Scribner, 1851), 9.

41. Lynch, *Naval Life*, 9, 264, 266–67.

42. Rook, *150th Anniversary*, 9.

43. Lynch, *Naval Life*, 104.

44. Lynch, 83–84.

45. Lynch, *Narrative of the Expedition to the River Jordan*, 126.

46. Hutchison, *Errand to the World*, 8; Anders Stephanson, *Manifest Destiny: American Expansion and the Empire of Right* (New York: Hill and Wang, 1995), 5–10.

47. Ira M. Leonard and Robert D. Parmet, *American Nativism, 1830–1860* (New York: Van Nostrand Reinhold, 1971), 4.

48. Melville, *White Jacket*, 124, 123.

49. Ray Allen Billington, *The Protestant Crusade, 1800–1860: A Study of the Origins of American Nativism* (1938; repr., New York: Rinehart, 1952), 240–41.

50. Thomas Pegram, *Battling Demon Rum: The Struggle for a Dry America, 1800–1933* (Chicago: Ivan R. Dee, 1998), 32.

51. Pegram, *Battling Demon Rum*, 33.

52. See Billington, *Protestant Crusade*, chap. 3, "The First Convent is Burned, 1830–1834," and chap. 9, "The Philadelphia Riots of 1844."

53. United States Department of the Interior, National Park Service, "National Register of Historic Places Continuation Sheet for Benton Avenue A.M.E. Church in Greene County, Missouri," April 10, 2001, 14–17.

54. Davis, *Landscape of Belief*, 21–22.

55. Quoted in Davis, 22.

56. See Conroy-Krutz, *Christian Imperialism*, chap. 1, "Hierarchies of Heathenism," 19–50.

57. Billington, *Protestant Crusade*, 239.

58. John O' Sullivan, "An Editor Endorses the Idea of 'Manifest Destiny,' 1845," in *The Early American Republic: A Documentary Reader*, ed. Sean Patrick Adams (Pondicherry, India: Wiley-Blackwell, 2009), 189.

59. Quoted in Richard Lyle Power, "A Crusade to Extend Yankee Culture, 1820–1865," *New England Quarterly* 13, no. 4 (December 1940), 646.

60. Candy Gunther Brown, *The Word in the World: Evangelical Writing, Publishing, and Reading in America, 1789–1880* (Chapel Hill: University of North Carolina Press, 2004), 5; Shamir, "On the Uselessness of Knowledge," 485.

61. Paul C. Gutjahr, *An American Bible: A History of the Good Book in the United States, 1777–1880* (Stanford, CA: Stanford University Press, 1999), 63.

62. Lynch, *Narrative of the Expedition to the River Jordan*, 411.

63. Gutjahr, *American Bible*, 63; Christine Leigh Heyrman, *American Apostles: When Evangelicals Entered the World of Islam* (New York: Hill and Wang, 2015), 36.

64. Power, "Crusade to Extend Yankee Culture," 653.

65. Heyrman, *American Apostles*, 10.

66. Quoted in Power, "Crusade to Extend Yankee Culture," 640.

67. Davis, *Landscape of Belief*, 36.

68. "Political State of Palestine," *Times* (London), March 8, 1842, 8.

69. Royal Geographical Society, "Medals and Awards: Gold Medal Recipients," accessed June 21, 2021, https://www.rgs.org/about/medals-award/history-and-past-recipients/.

70. Lynch, *Narrative of the Expedition to the River Jordan*, 154. See, for instance, page 335 of his *Narrative* and page 31 of his *Official Report of the Expedition to the Dead Sea*; see also Silberman, *Digging for God and Country*, 55.

71. John Young Mason to William Francis Lynch, November 4, 1847, RG 45, M 149, "Letters Sent by the Secretary of the Navy to Officers, 1798–1868," vol. 41, roll 43, NARA I.

72. William Francis Lynch to John Young Mason, Washington, DC, May 8, 1847, "Letters Received by the Secretary of the Navy from Commissioned Officers Below the

Rank of Commander and from Warrant Officers ('Officers' Letters')," RG 45, M 148, NARA I.

73. Finnie, *Pioneers East*, 269–70.

74. Lynch, *Narrative of the Expedition to the River Jordan*, 18.

75. John Young Mason to William Francis Lynch, November 19, 1847, RG 45, M 149, vol. 41, roll 43, NARA I.

76. Lynch, *Naval Life*, 143; Jampoler, *Sailors in the Holy Land*, 13, 259. Ponko offers a summary of this operation in *Ships, Seas, and Scientists*, 199–205.

77. William Francis Lynch to James Dobbin, Washington, May 25, 1853, RG 45, M 147, NARA I, and William Francis Lynch to William Graham, October 16, 1850, RG 45, M 147, NARA I.

78. Lynch frequently made learned references to Humboldt's work throughout his published works. See, for example, Lynch, *Naval Life*, 26, 139; and page 27 of his Dead Sea report.

79. Lynch's article was widely reprinted throughout the United States and beyond in December 1847 (see, for example, "Expedition to the Dead Sea," *American Statesman*, December 4, 1847, 278; and "Expedition to the Dead Sea," *Advent Herald*, December 25, 1847, 167). By December 30, even the *Antigua Observer* had reproduced it.

80. Lynch, *Narrative of the Expedition to the River Jordan*, 153.

81. Lynch, 411, 413.

82. Lynch, *Naval Life*, 104.

83. Goren, *Dead Sea Level*, 126.

84. Stephens, *Incidents*, 2:94–95.

85. Stephens, 2:110–11.

86. Stephens, 2:211.

87. Harvey, *American Geographics*, 115.

88. Lynch, "Scientific Expedition to the Dead Sea. From an American paper," *Antigua Observer*, December 30, 1847.

89. Shamir, "On the Uselessness of Knowledge," 480; Harvey, *American Geographics*, 100.

90. Montague, *Narrative of the Expedition to the Dead Sea*, vii.

91. See William F. Lynch, *Commerce and the Holy Land: A Lecture Delivered by William F. Lynch, U.S.N., before the N. Y. Kane Monument Association* (Philadelphia: King & Baird, 1860); and American Geographical and Statistical Society, *Report and Memorial on Syrian Exploration* (New York: Society's Rooms, 1857).

92. John Young Mason to William Francis Lynch, March 31, 1848, RG 45, T 829, "Miscellaneous Records of the Office of Naval Records and Library," roll 359, NARA I.

93. Jampoler, *Sailors in the Holy Land*, 10.

94. Mason to Lynch, November 11, 1847, quoted in Jampoler, *Sailors in the Holy Land*, 10.

95. For more on this landing, see Gary J. Ohls, chap. 6, "To the Halls of Montezuma," in *American Amphibious Warfare: The Roots of Tradition to 1865* (Annapolis, MD: Naval Institute Press, 2017), 136–53.

96. Lynch, *Narrative of the Expedition to the River Jordan*, 13.

97. LaFeber, *The American Age*, 119.

98. Rook, *150th Anniversary*, 13.

99. Kreiger, *The Dead Sea*, 44–45; Jampoler, *Sailors in the Holy Land*, 167.

100. Kreiger, *The Dead Sea*, 57.

101. A rumor of the expedition reached Lynch in October and threw his plans into disarray. By month's end, however, Mason ordered him to renew his preparations (William Francis Lynch to John Young Mason, October 16, 1847, RG 45, M 148, NARA I; Mason to Lynch, October 18, 1847, RG 45, M 149, NARA I, and Lynch to Mason, October 22, 1847, RG 45, M 148, NARA I).

102. Penelope Hardy, "Matthew Fontaine Maury: Scientist," *International Journal of Maritime History* 28, no. 2 (2016), 407.

103. Frances Leigh Williams, "The Heritage and Preparation of a Statesman, John Young Mason, 1799–1859," *Virginia Magazine of History and Biography*, July 1967, 311.

104. Williams, "Heritage and Preparation," 313.

105. Williams, 317.

106. Quoted in Williams, 328.

107. Williams, 328.

108. Pegram, *Battling Demon Rum*, 36; John C. Pinheiro, *Missionaries of Republicanism: A Religious History of the Mexican–American War* (New York: Oxford University Press, 2014), 7 and throughout.

109. "Strict Constructionist," *State Gazette* (Trenton, NJ), November 29, 1847.

110. "Exploration of the Dead Sea," *Monthly Beacon*, February 1848, 122.

111. D. Millard, "Exploration of the Dead Sea," *Christian Palladium* 16, no. 36 (January 1, 1848), 572.

112. "Expedition to the Dead Sea," *Presbyterian* 17, no. 49 (December 4, 1847), 196.

113. "Expedition to the Dead Sea," 196.

114. "The Dead Sea Expedition," *Gospel Teacher & Sabbath School Contributor* 10, no. 2 (August 1848) 48.

115. Lynch, *Narrative of the Expedition to the River Jordan*, 14.

116. Montague, *Narrative of the Expedition to the Dead Sea*, 132.

117. Lynch to Mason, October 22, 1847.

118. Lynch, *Narrative of the Expedition to the River Jordan*, 13; William Francis Lynch to John Young Mason, New York, August 12, 1847, RG 45, M 148, NARA I.

119. Lynch, *Narrative of the Expedition to the River Jordan*, 19.

120. Lynch, 15.

121. Montague, *Narrative of the Expedition to the Dead Sea*, 120.

122. Montague, 121–22.

123. Montague, 122.

124. Montague, 116.

125. Lynch, *Official Report of the Expedition to the Dead Sea*, 11.

126. Montague, *Narrative of the Expedition to the Dead Sea*, 131.

127. Jampoler, *Sailors in the Holy Land*, 76.

128. Goren, *Dead Sea Level*, 62, 168.

129. Lynch, *Narrative of the Expedition to the River Jordan*, 14.

130. For a summary of Abraham Lincoln's famous "Spot Resolutions," see Amy S. Greenberg, *A Wicked War: Polk, Clay, Lincoln, and the 1846 U.S. Invasion of Mexico* (New York: Alfred A. Knopf, 2012), 248–49.

131. Lynch, *Narrative of the Expedition to the River Jordan*, 16.

132. Lynch, 69–70.

133. Lynch, 24.

134. Lynch, 42–43.

135. Lynch, 36.

136. Lynch, 102.

137. Lynch, 42.

138. Lynch, 42.

139. See Genesis 19:1–12.

140. Colin Spencer, *Homosexuality in History* (New York: Harcourt Brace, 1995), 125; Francis Mark Mondimore, *A Natural History of Homosexuality* (Baltimore: Johns Hopkins University Press, 1996), 21.

141. William Benemann, *Male-Male Intimacy in Early America: Beyond Romantic Friendships* (New York: Harrington Park Press, 2006), x.

142. Benemann, *Male-Male Intimacy*, 71–92. For a critical evaluation of homosexuality among pirates and the Royal Navy, see David Cordingly, *Under the Black Flag: The Romance and the Reality of Life Among the Pirates* (New York: Harcourt Brace, 1997), 100–103.

143. Benemann, *Male-Male Intimacy*, 71–92.

144. Lynch, *Narrative of the Expedition to the River Jordan*, 48; William Francis Lynch to John Young Mason, February 27, 1848, RG 45, T 829, NARA I.

145. Bruce Alan Masters, *The Arabs of the Ottoman Empire, 1516–1918: A Social and Cultural History* (Cambridge: Cambridge University Press, 2013), 157.

146. While the periodizations of Ottoman history has been a subject of scholarly debate, many have seen the late eighteenth and early nineteenth centuries as turning points. For a taste of this scholarship, see Stanford J. Shaw, *Between Old and New: The Ottoman Empire under Sultan Selim III, 1789–1807* (Cambridge, MA: Harvard University Press, 1971); Baki Tezcan, *The Second Ottoman Empire: Political and Social Transformation in the Early Modern World* (Cambridge: Cambridge University Press, 2010); Ali Yaycioglu, *Partners of the Empire: The Crisis of the Ottoman Order in the Age of Revolutions* (Stanford, CA: Stanford University Press, 2016); and Aysel Yildiz, *Crisis and Rebellion in the Ottoman Empire: The Downfall of a Sultan in the Age of Revolution* (London: I. B. Tauri, 2017).

147. Suraiya Faroqhi, *The Ottoman Empire: A Short History*, trans. Shelley Frisch (Princeton, NJ: Markus Wiener, 2009), 22–25, 111.

148. Faroqhi, *Ottoman Empire*, 112.

149. Faroqhi, 114; Masters, *Arabs of the Ottoman Empire*, 144.

150. Masters, *Arabs of the Ottoman Empire*, 157.

151. Lynch, *Narrative of the Expedition to the River Jordan*, 93.

152. D. S. Carr to James Buchanan, June 6, 1847, RG 59, M 46, roll 13, "Despatches from U.S. Ministers to Turkey, 1818–1906," NARA Boston; Lynch, *Narrative of the Expedition to the River Jordan*, 59–60, 64.

153. See, for instance, Jampoler, *Sailors in the Holy Land*, 93; Peter D. Eicher, *Raising the Flag: America's First Envoys in Faraway Lands* (Lincoln: University of Nebraska Press, 2018), 198–201; John Lloyd Stephens, *Incidents of Travel in Greece, Turkey, Russia, and Poland*, 2 vols. (New York: Harper & Brothers, 1838), 1:223–29, LCP; and David Dixon Porter, *Memoir of Commodore David Porter, of the United States Navy* (Albany, NY: J. Munsell, 1875), 403–5.

154. William Francis Lynch to John Young Mason, March 8, 1848, RG 45, T 829, NARA I.

155. Carr to Buchanan, June 6, 1847.

156. Caleb Cushing quoted in Margaret Diamond Benetz, ed., *The Cushing Reports: Ambassador Caleb Cushing's Confidential Diplomatic Reports to the United States Sec-*

retary of State, 1843–1844 (Salisbury, NC: Documentary Publications, 1976), entry for October 3, 1843, Suez, 50.

157. Lynch, *Narrative of the Expedition to the River Jordan*, 415.

158. Lynch, 69–70.

159. Lynch, 94.

160. Lynch, 69.

161. Lynch, 65.

162. Lynch, 73.

163. Lynch, 77.

164. Lynch, 72.

165. Lynch, 74.

166. Lynch, 75.

167. Lynch, 77.

168. Lynch, 77.

169. Lynch, 77.

170. Morison, *"Old Bruin,"* 180.

171. Lynch, *Narrative of the Expedition to the River Jordan*, 91, 428.

172. Carr to Buchanan, June 6, 1847.

173. Carr to Buchanan, June 6, 1847.

174. Carr to Buchanan, August 2, 1848.

175. Lynch, *Narrative of the Expedition to the River Jordan*, 76.

176. Lynch to Mason, March 8, 1848.

177. Lynch, *Narrative of the Expedition to the River Jordan*, 78–79.

178. Masters, *Arabs of the Ottoman Empire*, 149; Faroqhi, *Ottoman Empire*, 115; Carol Lea Clark, *Clash of Eagles: America's Forgotten Expedition to Ottoman Palestine* (Guilford, CT: Lyons Press, 2012), 53; Eicher, *Raising the Flag*, 212.

179. Davis, *Landscape of Belief*, 9.

180. Lynch, *Narrative of the Expedition to the River Jordan*, 260; Montague, *Narrative of the Expedition to the Dead Sea*, 177.

181. As Carr noted to Buchanan, Lynch's meeting with the sultan was "considered a high and very unusual honor, for one of his rank" (Carr to Buchanan, August 2, 1848).

182. Carr to Buchanan, June 6, 1847.

183. Quoted in Michael B. Oren, *Power, Faith, and Fantasy: America in the Middle East, 1776 to the Present* (New York: W. W. Norton, 2007), 115. For more on US–Ottoman relations, see Maureen Santelli's *The Greek Fire: American–Ottoman Relations and Democratic Fervor in the Age of Revolutions* (Ithaca, NY: Cornell University Press, 2020).

184. Lynch, *Official Report of the Expedition to the Dead Sea*, 11.

185. Lynch to Mason, March 8, 1848.

186. Lynch, *Official Report of the Expedition to the Dead Sea*, 11; Lynch, *Narrative of the Expedition to the River Jordan*, 128.

187. Lynch, *Official Report of the Expedition to the Dead Sea*, 12; William Francis Lynch to I. Chasseaud, March 31, 1848, RG 45, T 829, NARA I.

188. Mansour Nasasra, *The Naqab Bedouins: A Century of Politics and Resistance* (New York: Columbia University Press, 2017), 39.

189. Lynch, *Narrative of the Expedition to the River Jordan*, 128–29.

190. Lynch, 129–30.

191. Lynch, 134, 143.

192. Lynch, *Official Report of the Expedition to the Dead Sea*, 12.

193. Lynch, *Narrative of the Expedition to the River Jordan*, 132–33.

194. Clark, *Clash of Eagles*, 191, 61.

195. Lynch, *Narrative of the Expedition to the River Jordan*, 382.

196. Lynch, 133.

197. Lynch, 133.

198. Lynch, 133.

199. Lynch, 431, 292, 334.

200. Lynch, *Official Report of the Expedition to the Dead Sea*, 12.

201. Lynch, *Narrative of the Expedition to the River Jordan*, 359–60.

202. William Francis Lynch to John Young Mason, Tiberias, Galilee, April 7, 1848, RG 45, T 829, NARA I.

203. Masters, *The Arabs of the Ottoman Empire*.

204. Lynch, *Narrative of the Expedition to the River Jordan*, 160.

205. Lynch, 184.

206. Lynch, 145–46.

207. Lynch, 178.

208. Lynch, *Official Report of the Expedition to the Dead Sea*, 19–20.

209. Lynch, 27, 32; Lynch, *Narrative of the Expedition to the River Jordan*, 344–45, 382.

210. Lynch, *Official Report of the Expedition to the Dead Sea*, 15.

211. For Lynch's comparison of Arabs to Oceanians, see *Narrative of the Expedition to the River Jordan*, 117, 295, 357; for his comparisons to Black Americans, see 126, 149, 295, 341; and for his comparisons to Indigenous North Americans, see 142, 182, 220, 394, and esp. 428–32.

212. Karen Ordahl Kupperman, *Settling with the Indians: The Meeting of English and Indian Cultures in America, 1580–1640* (Totowa, NJ: Rowman and Littlefield, 1980), 2. See also David Cannadine, *Ornamentalism: How the British Saw Their Empire* (Oxford: Oxford University Press, 2001).

213. Lynch, *Narrative of the Expedition to the River Jordan*, 195.

214. Lynch, 195.

215. Lynch, 195.

216. Lynch, 347.

217. Lynch, 195.

218. Montague, *Narrative of the Expedition to the Dead Sea*, 184.

219. See Zeynep Çelik, chap. 6, "Dual Settlements," in *About Antiquities: Politics of Archaeology in the Ottoman Empire* (Austin: University of Texas Press, 2016), 175–213.

220. Lynch, *Narrative of the Expedition to the River Jordan*, 115; Montague, *Narrative of the Expedition to the Dead Sea*, 157.

221. For more on Turkish stereotypes in the United States, see Justin McCarthy, *The Turk in America: The Creation of an Enduring Prejudice* (Salt Lake City: University of Utah Press, 2010).

222. Lynch, *Official Report of the Expedition to the Dead Sea*, 30–31.

223. William Francis Lynch to John Young Mason, Engeddi, W. Coast of Dead Sea, April 29, 1848, RG 45, T 829, NARA I.

224. Lynch, *Narrative of the Expedition to the River Jordan*, 268.

225. William Francis Lynch to John Young Mason, April 29, 1848, RG 45, T 829, NARA I.

226. Lynch, *Narrative of the Expedition to the River Jordan*, 269.

227. Lynch, 327.

228. Lynch, 269, 327; Goren, *Dead Sea Level*, 255.

229. Lynch, *Official Report of the Expedition to the Dead Sea*, 32.

230. Lynch, 32.

231. Lynch, 32.

232. Lynch, 37.

233. Lynch to Mason, April 29, 1848.

234. Lynch, *Narrative of the Expedition to the River Jordan*, 14.

235. William Francis Lynch to John Young Mason, June 9, 1848, RG 45, T-829, NARA I.

236. Rook, *150th Anniversary*, 18. Kreiger, in *Dead Sea*, 57, reports that the Jordan is only 130 miles in length.

237. Clark, *Clash of Eagles*, 228–29.

238. Edward Robinson, *Biblical Researches in Palestine, Mount Sinai and Arabia Petraea*, 3 vols. (Boston: Crocker & Brewster, 1841), 2:210, LCP; Lynch, *Official Report of the Expedition to the Dead Sea*, 35; Lynch, *Narrative of the Expedition to the River Jordan*, 304.

239. Lynch, *Narrative of the Expedition to the River Jordan*, 380.

240. Lynch, 330.

241. Lynch, 310.

242. Montague, *Narrative of the Expedition to the Dead Sea*, 151.

243. Lynch, *Narrative of the Expedition to the River Jordan*, 378; Lynch to Mason, April 29, 1848.

244. Genesis 19:26: "But his wife looked back from behind him, and she became a pillar of salt."

245. Clark, *Clash of Eagles*, 163.

246. Rook, *150th Anniversary*, 20.

247. "Scientific Expedition to the Dead Sea. From an American paper," *Antigua Observer* (St. John's, Antigua, and Barbuda), December 30, 1847.

248. Lynch, *Narrative of the Expedition to the River Jordan*, 391.

249. Lynch, *Official Report of the Expedition to the Dead Sea*, 42.

250. Quoted in *Christian Recorder* (Philadelphia), August 17, 1861.

251. Ponko, *Seas, Ships, and Scientists*, 55.

252. See, for example, *New York Herald*, April 11, 1848; *Southern Patriot* (Charleston, South Carolina), April 15, 1848; and *Constitution* (Middletown, Connecticut), April 19, 1848.

253. *New York Herald*, July 29, 1848. The Baltimore *Sun* expressed very similar sentiments on December 14, 1848, as had the *Richmond (VA) Enquirer*, June 9, 1848.

254. "The Dead Sea Expedition," *Christian Ambassador* 1, no. 39 (August 5, 1848) 624.

255. D. M., "The Dead Sea Expedition," *Christian Palladium* 17, no. 24 (October 7, 1848), 376.

256. M. F. Maury, "The Dead Sea Expedition," *Southern Literary Messenger*, September 1848, 553.

257. Maury, "The Dead Sea Expedition," 553.

258. Lynch, *Narrative of the Expedition to the River Jordan*, 14.

259. John Young Mason to William Francis Lynch, August 28, 1848, RG 45, T 829, roll 359, NARA I.

260. John Young Mason to William Francis Lynch, February 10, 1849, RG 45, M 149, NARA I.

261. William Francis Lynch to William Ballard Preston, June 19, 1850, RG 45, M 147, NARA I.

262. "VIII. Official Report of the United States Expedition to the Dead Sea," *Journal of the American Oriental Society* 3 (1853), 496.

263. A fine copy of this work, stamped as the possession of the Naval Observatory, is at the Natural History Library at the National Museum of Natural History, Smithsonian Institution Libraries.

264. See Ponko, *Ships, Seas, and Scientists*, 91.

265. Davis, *Landscape of Belief*, 35; Gutjahr, *American Bible*, 4.

266. American Board of Commissioners for Foreign Missions, *Memorial Volume of the First Fifty Years of the American Board of Commissioners for Foreign Missions* (4th ed., Boston: George C. Rand and Avery, 1861), 76.

267. Julie Roy Jeffrey, *Converting the West: A Biography of Narcissa Whitman* (Norman: University of Oklahoma Press, 1991), 17–20.

268. William Francis Lynch to John Young Mason, February 7, 1849, RG 45, M 148, NARA I.

269. Montague, *Narrative of the Expedition to the Dead Sea*, ix.

270. William Francis Lynch to John Young Mason, February 22, 1849, RG 45, M148, NARA I.

271. Ponko, *Ships, Seas, and Scientists*, 55.

272. Montague, *Narrative of the Expedition to the Dead Sea*, viii.

273. Quoted in Montague, *Narrative of the Expedition to the Dead Sea*, 44; on the flag raisings elsewhere, see 149, 230, 293.

274. Montague, 13.

275. Montague, 121.

276. Montague, 113, 180.

277. Montague, 88, 184.

278. Montague, 183.

279. Montague, 120, 122, 158, 293.

280. Montague, 176.

281. Montague, 241–45.

282. Montague, 226, 228.

283. "Narrative of the United States Expedition to the River Jordan and the Dead Sea / 2. Narrative of an Expedition to the Dead Sea," *Littell's Living Age* 23, no. 281 (October 6, 1849), 3.

284. "Narrative of the Late Expedition to the Dead Sea," *Southern Literary Messenger*, April 1849, 248.

285. "Editor's Book Table—the Late Expedition to the Dead Sea," *Godey's Lady's Book* 38, no. 6 (June 1849), 435.

286. Elisha Kent Kane made this point explicitly in his (noncommander's) account of the First Grinnell Expedition to the Arctic, titled *The U.S. Grinnell Expedition in Search of Sir John Franklin: A Personal Narrative* (New York: Harper and Bros., 1853), 15–16.

287. See Maddison, *Class and Colonialism in Antarctic Exploration*, 60 and through-

out; and Zeynep Çelik, *About Antiquities: Politics of Archaeology in the Ottoman Empire* (Austin: University of Texas Press, 2016), 139.

288. Lynch to Mason, February 7, 1849.

289. Mason to Lynch, February 10, 1849.

290. "The Narrative of the United States Expedition to the River Jordan and the Dead Sea," *Gazette of the Union* 10, no. 25 (June 23, 1849), 401; *Christian Advocate & Journal*, May 30, 1850.

291. Lea & Blanchard, cost book, 54:144.

292. This description of the work is based on examinations of copies in Dibner and the Historical Society of Pennsylvania. The quotations are from Lynch, *Narrative of the Expedition to the River Jordan*, 195.

293. Rook, *150th Anniversary*, 26; *Christian Advocate & Journal*, May 30, 1850.

294. *Sun* (Baltimore), June 12, 1849.

295. Keeney to Lea & Blanchard, May 4, 1850.

296. Reynolds to Lea & Blanchard, June 5, 1850.

297. J. M. Holland to Lea & Blanchard, April 15, 1850, Lea & Febiger Records, box 159, folder 5, "H," HSP.

298. T. B. T., "Lynch's Narrative of the United States Expedition to the River Jordan and the Dead Sea, &c.," *Universalist Quarterly & General Review*, July 1850.

299. "Narrative of the United States Expedition to the River Jordan and the Dead Sea," *Church Review* 2, no. 3 (October 1849), 432.

300. "The Dead Sea," *New-York Organ: A Family Companion; Devoted to Pure Literature, Temperance, Morality, Education & General Intelligence* 9, no. 18 (October 27, 1849), 147.

301. "Exploration of the Dead Sea," *Christian Observatory* 3, no. 6 (September 1849), 438-39.

302. Brown, *Word in the World*, 7.

303. *The Christian Examiner and Religious Miscellany* 53 (4th series, vol. 18 [July, September, November 1852]) (Boston: Crosby, Nichols, 1852), 179.

304. "Descent of the River Jordan," *Sunday School Advocate* 10, no. 4 (January 1851), 42 (in an earlier issue), 62, 69.

305. Edward Thurston Hiscox, *The Baptist Church Directory: A Guide to the Doctrines and Discipline, Officers and Ordinances, Principles and Practices of Baptist Churches* (New York: Sheldon, 1860), 201-2.

306. American Tract Society, *A Dictionary of the Holy Bible, for General Use in the Study of the Scriptures; with Engravings, Maps, and Tables* (New York: American Tract Society, 1859), s.v., "Jordan," 237-38.

307. Fisher Howe cites Lynch as an authority in *Oriental and Sacred Scenes, from Notes of Travel in Greece, Turkey, and Palestine* (New York: M. W. Dodd, 1856), 193, 293, 314, 315, 338, 339, quotation on vii.

308. *Christian Examiner and Religious Miscellany* 53 (4th series, vol. 18 [July, September, November 1852]) (Boston: Crosby, Nichols, 1852), 179.

309. Porter, *Religion vs. Empire*, 65.

310. Erskine, *Twenty Years before the Mast*, 109-11.

311. Wilkes, *Narrative of the United States Exploring Expedition*, 2:161-62. Wilkes notes on page 162 that Oceanians killed Reverend Johnson.

312. Peter Booth Wiley, *Yankees in the Land of the Gods: Commodore Perry and the Opening of Japan* (New York: Penguin, 1991), 168-69.

313. Morrison makes this point about merchant mariners in *True Yankees*, 91. For a similar observation, see Michael A. Verney, "An Eye for Prices, an Eye for Souls: Americans in the Indian Subcontinent, 1784–1840," *Journal of the Early Republic* 33, no. 3 (Fall 2013), 430.

314. Porter, *Religion vs. Empire*, 122.

CHAPTER 5

1. Herndon and Gibbon, *Exploration of the Valley of the Amazon*, 1:32–33, 90–91.

2. Herndon and Gibbon, 2:115.

3. Herndon and Gibbon, 2:115.

4. Herndon and Gibbon, 2:115–16.

5. Ponko, *Ships, Seas, and Scientists*, 92.

6. The centrality of slavery to the Amazon expedition has been a long-established fact among scholars. See, for instance, Whitfield Bell Jr., "The Relation of Herndon and Gibbon's *Exploration of the Amazon* to North American Slavery," *Hispanic American Historical Review* 19, no. 4 (1939): 494–503; Harrison, "Science and Politics: Origins of Government Expeditions"; Ponko, *Ships, Seas, and Scientists*; and Geoffrey Sutton Smith, "The Navy before Darwinism: Science, Exploration, and Diplomacy in Antebellum America," *American Quarterly*, Spring 1976, 49–50. In the twenty-first century, Gerald Horne documented the plan for the Amazon mission carefully in *The Deepest South: The United States, Brazil, and the African Slave Trade* (New York: New York University Press, 2007). John Grady also gives a detailed examination in chap. 13, "Grand Explorations and Manifest Destiny," in *Matthew Fontaine Maury, Father of Oceanography: A Biography, 1806–1873* (Jefferson, NC: McFarland, 2015); as does Laura Dassow Walls in *Passage to Cosmos*, 143–44. Finally, Matthew J. Karp discusses the Amazon expedition briefly in *This Vast Southern Empire: Slaveholders at the Helm of American Foreign Policy* (Cambridge, MA: Harvard University Press, 2016), 144–45.

7. For a recent analysis of the relationship between US colonizationism, race, and empire, see Mills, *The World Colonization Made*.

8. Karp, *Vast Southern Empire*, 4–8 and throughout.

9. Karp, esp. chap. 2, "The Strongest Naval Power on Earth," 32–49, and chap. 9, "The Military South," 199–225.

10. Karp, *Vast Southern Empire*, esp. chap. 1, "Confronting the Great Apostle of Emancipation," 10–31; Edward Bartlett Rugemer, *The Problem of Emancipation: The Caribbean Roots of the American Civil War* (Baton Rouge: Louisiana State University Press, 2008). Rugemer notes the strict limitations on British West Indian emancipation on pp. 2 and 3.

11. Karp, *Vast Southern Empire*, 132–33.

12. James L. Sidbury, *Ploughshares into Swords: Race, Rebellion, and Identity in Gabriel's Virginia, 1730–1810* (Cambridge: Cambridge University Press, 1997).

13. Dale Tomich, *Through the Prism of Slavery: Labor, Capital, and World Economy* (Lanham, MD: Rowman & Littlefield, 2004); Tomich, ed., *The Politics of the Second Slavery* (Albany: State University of New York Press, 2016).

14. Frances Leigh Williams, *Matthew Fontaine Maury, Scientist of the Sea* (New Brunswick, NJ: Rutgers University Press, 1963), 11–15.

15. Norman J. W. Thrower, "Matthew Fontaine Maury," American National Biography, accessed October 6, 2018, www.anb.org.

16. Chester G. Hearn, *Tracks in the Sea: Matthew Fontaine Maury and the Mapping of the Oceans* (Camden, ME: International Marine / Ragged Mountain Press, 2002), 26-27.

17. Thrower, "Matthew Fontaine Maury."

18. Melville, *Moby-Dick*, 182, 199. In his 1851 message to Congress, President Millard Fillmore praised Maury for demonstrating the "advantages of science in nautical affairs" (Israel, *State of the Union*, 1:829).

19. See Williams, *Maury, Scientist of the Sea*; Grady, *Maury, Father of Oceanography*; Penelope Hardy, "Matthew Fontaine Maury: Scientist," *International Journal of Maritime History* 28, no. 2 (2016), 402-10; Jason W. Smith, "Matthew Fontaine Maury: Pathfinder," *International Journal of Maritime History* 28, no. 2 (2016), 411-20; Smith, *To Master the Boundless Sea*, esp. chap. 3, "The Common Highway," 74-106.

20. Margaret Stack, "Matthew Fontaine Maury: Reformer," *International Journal of Maritime History* 28, no. 2 (2016), 397; Williams, *Maury, Scientist of the Sea*, 348.

21. Tim St. Onge, "Scientists of the Seas: The Legacy of Matthew Fontaine Maury," *Worlds Revealed: Geography and Maps at the Library of Congress* (blog), July 25, 2018, Library of Congress, https://blogs.loc.gov/maps/2018/07/scientist-of-the-seas-the-legacy-of-matthew-fontaine-maury/. See also Penelope K. Hardy and Helen Rozwadowski, "Maury for Modern Times: Navigating a Racist Legacy in Ocean Science," *Oceanography* 33, no. 3 (September 2020), 10-15.

22. John Majewski and Todd W. Wahlstrom, "Geography as Power: The Political Economy of Matthew Fontaine Maury," *Virginia Magazine of History and Biography* 120, no. 4 (2012), 343, 350.

23. For more on the United States' reaction to the Haitian Revolution, see Tim Matthewson, *A Proslavery Foreign Policy: Haitian–American Relations during the Early Republic* (Westport, CT: Praeger, 2003); Matthew Pratt Guterl, *American Mediterranean: Southern Slaveholders in the Age of Emancipation* (Cambridge, MA: Harvard University Press, 2008); Ashli White, *Encountering Revolution: Haiti and the Making of the Early Republic* (Baltimore: Johns Hopkins University Press, 2010); Walter Johnson, *River of Dark Dreams: Slavery and Empire in the Cotton Kingdom* (Cambridge, MA: Harvard University Press, 2013); Gerald Horne, *Confronting Black Jacobins: The United States, the Haitian Revolution, and the Origins of the Dominican Republic* (New York: Monthly Review Press, 2015); James Alexander Dun, *Dangerous Neighbors: Making the Haitian Revolution in Early America* (Philadelphia: University of Pennsylvania Press, 2016); and Carl Lawrence Paulus, *The Slaveholding Crisis: Fear of Insurrection and the Coming of the Civil War* (Baton Rouge: Louisiana State University Press, 2017). White US mariners witnessed many scenes of violence during the Haitian Revolution. One such sailor was James Durand, whose *Life and Adventures of James R. Durand* was published in 1820 (repr., 1926; and Sandwich, MA: Chapman Billies, 1995).

24. Samuel Warner, *Authentic and Impartial Narrative of the Tragical Scene which was Witnessed in Southampton County (Virginia) on Monday the 22d of August Last* (New York: Warner & West, 1831), 5, 30, LCP.

25. Matthew Fontaine Maury, *Commercial Conventions, Direct Trade: A Chance for the South* (United States, c. 1852), 25, LCP.

26. Eric Burin, *Slavery and the Peculiar Solution: A History of the American Colonization Society* (Gainesville: University Press of Florida, 2005), 80.

27. Maury, *Commercial Conventions, Direct Trade*, 22.

28. Quoted in Bell, "Relation of Herndon and Gibbon's *Exploration*," 495.

29. Maury, *Commercial Conventions, Direct Trade*, 25.

30. Anonymous "Colored American," *The Late Contemplated Insurrection in Charleston, S.C. with the Execution of Thirty-Six Patriots . . .* (New York, 1850), LCP.

31. Estes, *A Defence of Negro Slavery*, 171–72.

32. Johnson, *River of Dark Dreams*, 307.

33. Guterl, *American Mediterranean*, 24.

34. Maury describes this line of thinking clearly in *Commercial Conventions, Direct Trade*, 22–26.

35. Quoted in Williams, *Maury, Scientist of the Sea*, 357.

36. Majewski and Wahlstrom, "Geography as Power," 349.

37. Matthew Mason, *Slavery and Politics in the Early American Republic* (Chapel Hill: University of North Carolina Press, 2006).

38. LaFeber, *The American Age*, 119–20.

39. James M. McPherson, *Battle Cry of Freedom: The Civil War Era* (Oxford: Oxford University Press, 1988), 59–66.

40. McPherson, *Battle Cry of Freedom*, 69.

41. McPherson, 70–75.

42. Bell, "Relation of Herndon and Gibbon's *Exploration*," 500.

43. Donald Marquand Dozer, "Matthew Fontaine Maury's Letter of Instruction to William Lewis Herndon" (Matthew Fontaine Maury to William Lewis Herndon, April 20, 1850), *Hispanic American Historical Review* 28 (1948), 217.

44. Dozer, "Maury's Letter of Instruction to Herndon," 217–18, 225.

45. Dozer, 217.

46. Dozer, 217.

47. Dozer, 217.

48. See, for example, Michael S. Reidy, *Tides of History: Ocean Science and Her Majesty's Navy* (Chicago: University of Chicago Press, 2008).

49. Maury, *The Amazon and the Atlantic Slopes of South America* (Washington, DC, 1853), 48.

50. William Clark Griggs, *The Elusive Eden: Frank McMullan's Confederate Colony in Brazil* (Austin: University of Texas Press, 1987), 15.

51. See Wilkes, *Narrative of the US Exploring Expedition*, vol. 1.

52. Tomich, *Through the Prism of Slavery*, esp. chap. 3, "The 'Second Slavery': Bonded Labor and the Transformation of the Nineteenth-Century World Economy," 56–71.

53. Leonardo Marques, "The Contraband Slave Trade to Brazil and the Dynamics of U.S. Participation, 1831–1856," *Journal of Latin American Studies* 47 (2015), 663–64.

54. See, for example, W. E. B. Du Bois, *The Suppression of the African Slave-Trade to the United States of America, 1638–1870* (New York: Longmans, Green, 1896); Horne, *Deepest South*; and Marques, "Contraband Slave Trade to Brazil."

55. Jeffrey Lesser, *Immigration, Ethnicity, and National Identity in Brazil, 1808 to the Present* (Cambridge: Cambridge University Press, 2013), 34.

56. Horne, *Deepest South*, 12.

57. Lesser, *Immigration, Ethnicity, and National Identity in Brazil*, 12.

58. Lesser, 29–30.

59. Lesser, 33.

60. Lesser, 27.

61. Lesser, 34.

62. Maury, *Commercial Conventions, Direct Trade*, 19.

63. Herndon and Gibbon, *Exploration of the Valley of the Amazon*, 1:337.

64. Bell, "Relation of Herndon and Gibbon's *Exploration*," 495.

65. Karp, "Slavery and American Sea Power," 319.

66. Karp, 318.

67. Harrison, "Science and Politics: Origins of Government Expeditions," 191.

68. For more on Whig reactions to the US–Mexican War, see Amy S. Greenberg, *A Wicked War: Polk, Clay, Lincoln, and the 1846 U.S. Invasion of Mexico* (New York: Alfred A. Knopf, 2012).

69. Greenberg, *Manifest Manhood*, 182.

70. Maury, *Amazon and Atlantic Slopes*, 63.

71. William Graham to William Lewis Herndon, March 8, 1851, "Letters Sent by the Secretary of the Navy to Officers," RG 45, M 149, roll 47, NARA I.

72. Herndon and Gibbon, *Exploration of the Valley of the Amazon*, 1:406–7.

73. Roderick J. Barman, *Brazil: The Forging of a Nation, 1798–1852* (Stanford, CA: Stanford University Press, 1988), 236–37.

74. Maury to Ann Maury, March 17, 1851, vol. 4, Maury Papers, Manuscript Division, Library of Congress, Washington, DC.

75. Herndon and Gibbon, *Exploration of the Valley of the Amazon*, 1:20.

76. Herndon and Gibbon, 1:21.

77. William Lewis Herndon to William A. Graham, March 8, 1851, "Letters Received by the Secretary of the Navy from Commissioned Officers below the Rank of Commander and from Warrant Officers," RG 45, M 148, roll 201, NARA I; Herndon and Gibbon, *Exploration of the Valley of the Amazon*, 1:90, 2:1.

78. Herndon and Gibbon, *Exploration of the Valley of the Amazon*, 1:146, 160.

79. Herndon and Gibbon, 1:276.

80. Herndon and Gibbon, 1:364.

81. Herndon and Gibbon, 2:170, 205, 303, 313–14.

82. William Lewis Herndon to William Graham, Barra du Rio Negro, January 20, 1852, RG 45, M 148, roll 206, NARA I.

83. Herndon and Gibbon, *Exploration of the Valley of the Amazon*, 1:189. See also Maury, *Amazon and the Atlantic Slopes*, 63.

84. Quoted in Herndon and Gibbon, *Exploration of the Valley of the Amazon*, 1:188.

85. Maury, *Amazon and Atlantic Slopes*, 6.

86. Herndon and Gibbon, *Exploration of the Valley of the Amazon*, 1:281.

87. For more on antebellum Anglo-Saxonism, see Horsman, *Race and Manifest Destiny*.

88. Dozer, "Maury's Letter of Instruction to Herndon," 217.

89. William Lewis Herndon to William Graham, February 8, 1851, RG 45, M 148, roll 200, NARA I.

90. William Lewis Herndon to William Graham, September 26, 1851, RG 45, M 148, roll 204, NARA I.

91. Estes, *A Defence of Negro Slavery*, 159–60.

92. Estes, 160–61.

93. Herndon and Gibbon, *Exploration of the Valley of the Amazon*, 2:183.

94. Herndon and Gibbon, 1:337.

95. Herndon to Graham, March 8, 1851.

96. Johnson, *River of Dark Dreams*, 301.

268   <   NOTES TO PAGES 154–157

97. Herndon and Gibbon, *Exploration of the Valley of the Amazon*, 1:277.
98. Herndon and Gibbon, 1:337.
99. Quoted in Bell, "Relation of Herndon and Gibbon's *Exploration*," 499.
100. Holt, *Rise and Fall of the Whig Party*, 635–36.
101. Daniel Webster to Robert C. Schenck, May 8, 1851, "Diplomatic Instructions of the Department of State, 1801–1906," RG 59, M 77, Brazil, roll 23, NARA I.
102. Maury, *Amazon and Atlantic Slopes*, 58; Herndon and Gibbon, *Exploration of the Valley of the Amazon*, 1:362.
103. Herndon and Gibbon, *Exploration of the Valley of the Amazon*, 1:362.
104. Ponko, *Ships, Seas, and Scientists*, 89; Herndon and Gibbon, *Exploration of the Valley of the Amazon*, 1:351; William Lewis Herndon to John P. Kennedy, January 26, 1853, RG 45, M 148, roll 213, NARA I.
105. Hunter, *Popular Catalogue of Extraordinary Curiosities*, 62.
106. Israel, *State of the Union*, 1:847–48.
107. Ponko, *Ships, Seas, and Scientists*, 91.
108. Maury, *Commercial Conventions, Direct Trade*, 21–26.
109. *Senate Journal*, 32nd Cong., 1st Sess., May 10, 1852, 400; *House Journal*, 33rd Cong., 1st Sess., March 3, 1854, 447, S. 458, *Bills and Resolutions, Senate*, 32nd Cong., 1st Sess., June 15, 1852.
110. "The River Amazon—a Great Project," *Scientific American*, June 5, 1852, 299.
111. Seymour Barofsky, ed., *The Wisdom of Mark Twain* (New York: Citadel Press, 2002), 62.
112. Barofsky, *Wisdom of Mark Twain*, 61–64.
113. "The Navigation of the Amazon," *New York Times*, December 18, 1854.
114. "The River Amazon," *New American Magazine*, September 1852, 85–86.
115. "New Book," *Daily Globe* (Washington, DC), January 30, 1854.
116. Percy Alvin Martin, "The Influence of the United States on the Opening of the Amazon to the World's Commerce," *Hispanic American Historical Review* 1, no. 2 (May 1918), 150; *House Journal*, 33rd Cong., 1st Sess., March 3, 1854, 447.
117. Bell, "Relation of Herndon and Gibbon's *Exploration*," 498.
118. Quoted in Bell, 501.
119. Mary B. Blackford to Matthew Fontaine Maury, January 1851, mss001026, "General Correspondence," box 4, vol. 4, Papers of Matthew Fontaine Maury, Library of Congress, Manuscripts Division, Washington, DC.
120. Quoted in Horne, *Deepest South*, 4.
121. Horne, 124.
122. Quoted in Horne, 5.
123. Quoted in Horne, 123.
124. Graham to Herndon, March 8, 1851.
125. Herndon *Exploration*, 1:352–56; Matthew Fontaine Maury, "Shall the Valleys of the Amazon and the Mississippi Reciprocate Trade?," *De Bow's Review* 14, no. 2 (February 1853), 138–41.
126. Herndon and Gibbon, *Exploration of the Valley of the Amazon*, 2:150.
127. Daniel P. Kidder and J. C. Fletcher, *Brazil and the Brazilians, Portrayed in Historical and Descriptive Sketches* (Philadelphia: Childs & Peterson, 1857), 579, LCP.
128. Martin, "Influence of the United States," 153.
129. Pedro De Angelis, *De La Navigation de L'Amazone. Reponse a un Mémoire de M. Maury, Officier de La Marine des Etats-Unis, Par M. de Angelis* (Montevideo, 1854),

5, Camara dos Deputados, Palácio do Congresso Nacional, Praça dos Três Poderes, Brasília, DF, Brasil, http://bd.camara.gov.br/bd/handle/bdcamara/18162. My thanks to Professor Isadora M. Mota at Princeton University for sharing this source with me.

130. De Angelis, *De La Navigation de L'Amazone*, 5.

131. Quoted in Maury, *Amazon and Atlantic Slopes*, 53.

132. Maury, 21.

133. Martin, "Influence of the United States," 161.

134. For a biography of Kennedy that marries his literary and political histories, see Andrew R. Black, *John Pendleton Kennedy: Early American Novelist, Whig Statesman and Ardent Nationalist* (Baton Rouge: Louisiana State University Press, 2016).

135. Black, *John Pendleton Kennedy*, 72; Henry T. Tuckerman, *The Life of John Pendleton Kennedy* (New York: G. P. Putnam & Sons, 1871), 348.

136. Tuckerman, *Life of Kennedy*, 348.

137. Schroeder, *Shaping a Maritime Empire*, 97; Harrison, "Science and Politics: Origins of Government Expeditions," 192.

138. Tuckerman, *Life of Kennedy*, 223, Harrison, "Science and Politics: Origins of Government Expeditions," 196; John P. Kennedy to Thomas Page, January 31, 1853, RG 45, M 149, roll 50, NARA I.

139. Gene Allen Smith and Larry Bartlett, "'A Most Unprovoked, Unwarrantable, and Dastardly Attack': James Buchanan, Paraguay, and the Water Witch Incident of 1855," *Northern Mariner / Le Marin du Nord*, July 2009, 274–77.

140. Harrison, "Science and Politics: Origins of Government Expeditions," 195.

141. *Senate Journal*, 34th Cong., 3rd Sess., February 7, 1857, 172.

142. Thomas J. Page, *La Plata, The Argentine Confederation, and Paraguay. Being a Narrative of the Exploration of the Tributaries of the River La Plata and Adjacent Countries During the Years 1853, '54, '55, and '56, Under the Orders of the United States Government* (New York: Harper & Brothers, 1859), xxi.

143. Robert B. Forbes, *Personal Reminiscences by Robert B. Forbes* (2nd ed., Boston: Little, Brown, 1882), 224–39.

144. E. A. Hopkins, "The La Plata and the Parana-Paraguay," *De Bow's Review*, March 1853, 249.

145. Finding aid for the Robert Bennet Forbes Papers, Massachusetts Historical Society, Boston, Ms. N-49.70, http://masshist.org/collection-guides/view/fa0039.

146. For more on this subject, see Kinley J. Brauer, *Cotton versus Conscience: Massachusetts Whig Politics and Southwestern Expansion, 1843–48* (Lexington: University Press of Kentucky, 1967); Thomas O'Connor, *Lords of the Loom, the Cotton Whigs and the Coming of the Civil War* (New York: Charles Scribner's Sons, 1968); and Anne Farrow, Joel Lang, and Jennifer Frank, *Complicity: How the North Promoted, Prolonged, and Profited from Slavery* (New York: Ballantine Books, 2005).

147. Ponko, *Ships, Seas, and Scientists*, 133.

148. Maury, *Amazon and Atlantic Slopes*, 11–16.

149. Page, *La Plata, Argentine Confederation, and Paraguay*, xxi.

150. Schroeder, *Shaping a Maritime Empire*, 114.

151. Joseph Criscenti, ed., *Sarmiento and His Argentina* (Boulder, CO: Lynne Rienner Publishers, 1993), 109.

152. Thomas J. Page, *Report of the Exploration and Survey of the River "La Plata" and Tributaries by Thomas J. Page, Commanding United States Steamer* Water Witch*, to the Secretary of the Navy* (Washington, DC: Cornelius Wendell, 1856), 4.

153. Page, *La Plata, Argentine Confederation, and Paraguay*, 25.

154. Page, *La Plata, Argentine Confederation, and Paraguay*, 26; Kennedy, *Political and Official Papers*, 507–8.

155. Domingo F. Sarmiento, *Sarmiento's Travels in the United States in 1847*, ed. and trans. Michael Aaron Rockland (Princeton, NJ: Princeton University Press, 1970), 124.

156. Juan Bautista Alberdi, *The Life and Industrial Labors of William Wheelwright in South America* (Boston: A. Williams, 1877), 208, LCP.

157. Alberdi, *Life and Labors of Wheelwright*, 7, 9.

158. McPherson, *Battle Cry of Freedom*, 107.

159. Schlesinger and Israel, *My Fellow Citizens: Inaugural Addresses*, 123.

160. Israel, *State of the Union*, 1:860.

161. Israel, 1:882.

162. McPherson, *Battle Cry of Freedom*, 121.

163. McPherson, 108–9.

164. McPherson, 108–9.

165. William Earl Weeks, *Building the Continental Empire: American Expansion from the Revolution to the Civil War* (Chicago: Ivan R. Dee, 1996), 151–52; Schroeder, *Shaping a Maritime Empire*, 124–25.

166. McPherson, *Battle Cry of Freedom*, 108.

167. Johnson, *River of Dark Dreams*, 366–70; McPherson, *Battle Cry of Freedom*, 113.

168. Greenberg, *Manifest Manhood*, 165; Robert E. May, *Manifest Destiny's Underworld: Filibustering in Antebellum America* (Chapel Hill: University of North Carolina Press, 2002), 81–116.

169. George Fitzhugh, *Cannibals All! Or, Slaves without Masters* (Richmond, VA: A. Morris, 1857), xiii, LCP.

170. Lucius Quintus Cincinnatus Lamar, *Nicaraguan Affairs and Lecompton Constitution. Speech of Hon. Lucius Q. C. Lamar, Of Mississippi, on Nicaraguan and Kansas Affairs. Delivered in the House of Representatives, January 13, 1858* (Washington, DC: Lemuel Towers, 1858), 2, LCP.

171. Page, *La Plata, Argentine Confederation, and Paraguay*, 287.

172. Page, 114; Thomas Page to Carlos López, October 1, 1853, Miscellaneous Records of the Office of Naval Records and Library, RG 45, T 829, roll 445, NARA I.

173. Page to López, October 1, 1853; Page, *La Plata, Argentine Confederation, and Paraguay*, 118–19.

174. Page to López, October 1, 1853; Thomas Page to Carlos López, October 13, 1853, Miscellaneous Records of the Office of Naval Records and Library, RG 45, T 829, roll 445, NARA I.

175. E. Shippen, "Recollections of the Paraguay Expedition," *United Services: A Quarterly Review of Military and Naval Affairs* 2 (March 1880), 333; James Schofield Saeger, *Francisco Solano López and the Ruination of Paraguay: Honor and Egocentrism* (Lanham, MD: Rowman & Littlefield, 2007), 41.

176. *López and the Ruination of Paraguay*, Saeger's biography of Carlos López's son and heir, Francisco Solano López, describes how father and son imported European war technology and expertise in the 1850s and 1860s.

177. Thomas Page to Carlos López, October 12, 1853, Miscellaneous Records of the Office of Naval Records and Library, RG 45, T 829, roll 445, NARA I.

178. Page, *La Plata, Argentine Confederation, and Paraguay*, 119.

179. Page, 97.

180. Page, 98.

181. Page, *Report of the River "La Plata,"* 12.

182. Maury, *Amazon and Atlantic Slopes*, 11.

183. Thomas Page to James Dobbin, March 10, 1854, "Miscellaneous Records of the Office of Naval Records and Library," RG 45, T 829, roll 445, NARA I.

184. Page to Dobbin, March 10, 1854.

185. Thomas Page to James Dobbin, August 13, 1854, "Miscellaneous Records of the Office of Naval Records and Library," RG 45, T 829, roll 445, NARA I.

186. Page to Dobbin, August 13, 1854.

187. Page, *Report of the River "La Plata,"* 23.

188. Page, *La Plata, Argentine Confederation, and Paraguay*, 85.

189. Estes, *A Defence of Negro Slavery*, 159.

190. George Fitzhugh, *Sociology for the South, or the Failure of Free Society* (Richmond, VA: A. Morris, 1854), 149.

191. "A Declaration of the Immediate Causes which Induce and Justify the Secession of the State of Mississippi from the Federal Union," *The Avalon Project: Documents in Law, History, and Diplomacy*, 2008, Lillian Goldman Law Library, Yale Law School, http://avalon.law.yale.edu/19th_century/csa_missec.asp.

192. Page, *Report of the River "La Plata,"* 23.

193. Page, *La Plata, Argentine Confederation, and Paraguay*, 164.

194. Page, 165.

195. Page, 165.

196. Page, 165.

197. Thomas Page to John P. Kennedy, May 21, 1853, Miscellaneous Records of the Office of Naval Records and Library, RG 45, T 829, roll 445, NARA I.

198. Page to Dobbin, August 13, 1854.

199. Page, *La Plata, Argentine Confederation, and Paraguay*, 100.

200. Thomas Page to James Dobbin, Steamer Yerba, Santa Fe, August 7, 1855, Miscellaneous Records of the Office of Naval Records and Library, RG 45, T 829, roll 445, NARA I.

201. Page, *La Plata, Argentine Confederation, and Paraguay*, 200.

202. Page, 281.

203. William Jeffers to Thomas Page, February 2, 1855, "Miscellaneous Records of the Office of Naval Records and Library," RG 45, T 829, roll 445, NARA I.

204. Jeffers to Page, February 2, 1855; Thomas Page to James Dobbin, February 5, 1855, "Miscellaneous Records of the Office of Naval Records and Library," RG 45, T 829, roll 445, NARA I.

205. Page, *La Plata, Argentine Confederation, and Paraguay*, 307.

206. Page, 314; Thomas Page to William Salter, April 1, 1855, Miscellaneous Records of the Office of Naval Records and Library, RG 45, T 829, roll 445, NARA I; Thomas Page to James Dobbin, April 16, 1855, Miscellaneous Records of the Office of Naval Records and Library, RG 45, T 829, roll 445, NARA I.

207. Testimony of Edward Palmer, dated June 20, and enclosed with José Falcón's letter to the US minister of foreign affairs, Asunción, Paraguay, February 5, 1855, "Notes from the Paraguayan Legation in the United States to the Department of State, 1853–1906," RG 45, M 350, roll 1, NARA I.

208. "A Speck of War," *New Hampshire Patriot & State Gazette* (Concord, New Hampshire) April 18, 1855.

209. Israel, *State of the Union*, 1:954–55.

210. "La Plata," *Harper's New Monthly Magazine*, February 1859, 327.

211. Smith and Bartlett, "'Unprovoked, Unwarrantable, and Dastardly Attack,'" 286–87.

212. Ponko, *Ships, Seas, and Scientists*, 130–31.

213. "The Paraguay Expedition," *New York Times*, November 3, 1858.

214. "The Paraguay Expedition," *New York Times*, November 18, 1858.

215. Smith and Bartlett, "'Unprovoked, Unwarrantable, and Dastardly Attack.'"

216. See Karp, "Slavery and Sea Power"; and Karp, *This Vast Southern Empire*, esp. chap. 2, "The Strongest Naval Power on Earth," 32–49.

217. See Karp, *This Vast Southern Empire*, 4, 5, 199; and Schroeder, *Shaping a Maritime Empire*, 59.

218. Quoted in Horne, *Deepest South*, 123. Horne notes Douglass's fears of the Amazon mission on 124.

219. Harriet Jacobs, *Incidents in the Life of a Slave Girl, Written by Herself, with Related Documents*, ed. Jennifer Fleischner (Boston: Bedford / St. Martin's, 2010), 106.

220. Bell, "Relation of Herndon and Gibbon's *Exploration*," 503. For more on the post–Civil War Confederate exodus to Brazil, see Eugene C. Harter, *The Lost Colony of the Confederacy* (Jackson: University Press of Mississippi, 1985); Frank J. Merli, ed., "Alternative to Appomattox: A Virginian's Vision of an Anglo-Confederate Colony on the Amazon, May 1865," *Virginia Magazine of History and Biography*, April 1986, 210–19; and Griggs, *The Elusive Eden*.

221. Page, *La Plata, Argentine Confederation, and Paraguay*, 165.

222. W. E. B. Du Bois, *The Souls of Black Folk* (1903; repr., Mineola, NY: Dover Publications, 1994), 47–48.

223. Dozer, "Maury's Letter of Instruction to Herndon," 217.

224. English antislavery had deep roots, going back to the early modern period. For legal opposition to slavery in Britain, however, most scholars look back to the decision in the James Somerset case in 1772 (Eliga H. Gould, *Among the Powers of the Earth: The American Revolution and the Making of a New World Empire* [Cambridge, MA: Harvard University Press, 2012], 49–50).

225. Linda Colley describes how antislavery became a new national rallying cry for Britons after Napoleon's defeat at Waterloo (*Britons: Forging the Nation, 1707–1837* [New Haven, CT: Yale University Press, 1992], 357–68).

226. Colley, *Britons: Forging the Nation*, 361.

227. Quoted in Bell, "Relation of Herndon and Gibbon's *Exploration*," 501.

228. "The Slavery Question Is the Great Difficulty of the United States," *Times* (London), June 27, 1856, 9.

229. Charles Darwin, *Journal of Researches into the Natural History and Geology of the Countries Visited during the Voyage of H.M.S. Beagle Round the World* [. . .], 2nd ed. (London: John Murray, 1845), 499–500, Dibner.

230. It was partly for this reason that, as Charles Edel argues, John Quincy Adams embraced antislavery as part of his grand strategy for national grandeur in the last phase of his political life (*Nation Builder: John Quincy Adams and the Grand Strategy of the Republic* [Cambridge, MA: Harvard University Press, 2014], esp. chap. 5, "A Stain upon the Character of the Nation: The Fight against Slavery," 249–89).

CHAPTER 6

1. Pascal Bonenfant, "British Weather from 1700 to 1849," 2015, https://www
.pascalbonenfant.com/18c/geography/weather.html; Charles Stephen Dessain, *The
Letters and Diaries of John Henry Newman*, 31 vols. (London: Thomas Nelson and Sons,
1963–1984), 12:117–18.

2. This description of 21 Bedford Place comes from Rawnsley, *The Life, Diaries
and Correspondence of Lady Franklin*, 10; and Alison Alexander, *The Ambitions of Jane
Franklin: Victorian Lady Adventurer* (Sydney: Allen & Unwin, 2016), 7–8.

3. Andrew Lambert has argued that Franklin's expedition was set forth in order to
conduct geomagnetic research, not the North West Passage, as is commonly believed
(*The Gates of Hell: Sir John Franklin's Tragic Quest for the North West Passage* [New
Haven, CT: Yale University Press, 2009]).

4. Jane Franklin to Zachary Taylor, April 4, 1849, reprinted in *Daily Picayune* (New
Orleans), May 10, 1849.

5. *Daily Picayune* (New Orleans), May 10, 1849.

6. For two examples of this interest, see *New Hampshire Sentinel* (Keene, New
Hampshire); and *Daily Picayune* (New Orleans), both March 29, 1849.

7. Jane Franklin to Zachary Taylor, April 4, 1849, reprinted in *Daily Picayune* (New
Orleans), May 10, 1849.

8. John M. Clayton to Jane Franklin, April 25, 1849, reprinted in *Daily Picayune*
(New Orleans), May 10, 1849.

9. Alexander, *Ambitions of Jane Franklin*, 207.

10. Lambert, *Gates of Hell*, 337.

11. Lambert, 339.

12. Lambert, 280, 287.

13. Lambert, 341–42.

14. Lambert, 1, 345–48.

15. There are exceptions. David Chapin, for instance, notes the diplomatic angle to
Arctic exploration (*Exploring Other Worlds*, 61), as does Michael F. Robinson in chap.
1, "Building an Arctic Tradition," in *The Coldest Crucible: Arctic Exploration and American Culture* (Chicago: University of Chicago Press, 2006), 15–29. Neither historian,
however, frames it in the larger historiography of US–UK relations.

16. Bradford Perkins, *The First Rapprochement: England and the United States, 1795–
1805* (Philadelphia: University of Pennsylvania Press, 1955). Haynes, in *Unfinished Revolution*, approaches a kind of rapprochement with the end of the US–Mexican War (see
chap. 12, "Brother Jonathan Is Somebody," 274–96). See also Ronald Angelo Johnson,
*Diplomacy in Black and White: John Adams, Toussaint Louverture, and Their Atlantic
World Alliance* (Athens: University of Georgia Press, 2014); Alan Taylor, *The Civil War
of 1812: American Citizens, British Subjects, Irish Rebels, and Indian Allies* (New York:
Alfred A. Knopf, 2010); and Patrick Lacroix, "Choosing Peace and Order: National
Security and Sovereignty in a North American Borderland, 1837–1842," *International
History Review* 38, no. 5 (2016), 943–60.

17. For another study that examines Anglo-Saxonism and the warming of relations
between Britons and white US citizens, see Daniel Kilbride, *Being American in Europe,
1750–1860* (Baltimore: Johns Hopkins University Press, 2013), esp. chap. 4, "'The mani-
fold advantages resulting from our glorious Union,' 1840s–1861," 124–66.

18. Franklin to Taylor, April 4, 1849.

19. David W. Blight, *Race and Reunion: The Civil War in American Memory* (Cambridge, MA: Harvard University Press, 2001).

20. For more on masculinity and US Arctic exploration, see Robinson, *Coldest Crucible*; and Lisa Bloom, *Gender on Ice: American Ideologies of Polar Exploration* (Minneapolis: University of Minnesota Press, 1995).

21. Joseph Bellot, a French naval officer, perished in the Franklin search (Alexander, *Ambitions of Jane Franklin*, 220).

22. William C. Godfrey, *Godfrey's Narrative of the Last Grinnell Arctic Exploring Expedition, In Search of Sir John Franklin, 1853–4–5* (Philadelphia: J. T. Lloyd, 1857), 28. Felipe Fernández-Armesto discusses how chivalry influenced Christopher Columbus and other early modern European explorers ("The Sea and Chivalry in Late Medieval Spain," in *Maritime History*, vol. 1, *The Age of Discovery*, ed. John B. Hattendorf [Malabar, FL: Krieger, 1996]).

23. This approach mirrors the way Marc C. Hunter has portrayed US–UK naval relations in the equatorial Atlantic: as "a safety-valve" and "a way to avoid conflict" (*Policing the Seas: Anglo-U.S. Relations and the Equatorial Atlantic, 1819–1865*, Research in Maritime History 36 [St. John's, NL: International Maritime Economic History Association, 2008], 1, 3).

24. Rawnsley, *Life, Diaries and Correspondence of Lady Franklin*, 9.

25. Rawnsley, 10.

26. Alexander, *Ambitions of Jane Franklin*, 222.

27. Lambert, *Gates of Hell*, 55.

28. Alison Alexander, in *Ambitions of Jane Franklin*, effectively portrays Franklin as a "Victorian lady adventurer."

29. Godfrey, *Godfrey's Narrative*, 28.

30. Quoted in Alexander, *Ambitions of Jane Franklin*, 223.

31. David Brown, chap. 2, "Diplomacy and the Fourth Estate: The Role of the Press in British Foreign Policy in the Age of Palmerston," in *On the Fringes of Diplomacy: Influences on British Foreign Policy, 1800–1945*, ed. John Fisher and Anthony Best (New York: Routledge, 2011), 51.

32. Alexander, *Ambitions of Jane Franklin*, 223.

33. Alexander, 212.

34. Alexander, x, 211.

35. Alexander, 223, 247.

36. For an English colonial example of how women could break into supposedly masculine social roles in the right circumstances, see Laurel Thatcher Ulrich, *Goodwives: Images and Reality in the Lives of Women in Northern New England, 1650–1750* (New York: Alfred A. Knopf, 1982), esp. part 3, "Jael," 165–235.

37. Alexander, *Ambitions of Jane Franklin*, 223.

38. Elisha Kent Kane, *The U.S. Grinnell Expedition in Search of Sir John Franklin. A Personal Narrative* (New York: Harper & Brothers, 1853), 15; contemporary writer quoted in Alexander, *Ambitions of Jane Franklin*, 227.

39. Alexander, *Ambitions of Jane Franklin*, 244.

40. Alexander, 244.

41. Eric P. Kaufmann, *The Rise and Fall of Anglo-America* (Cambridge, MA: Harvard University Press, 2004), 16.

42. Horsman, *Race and Manifest Destiny*, 18–23.

43. See Horsman, *Race and Manifest Destiny*.

44. Horsman, 38–41, 160–64.

45. As early as the 1930s, Albert Weinberg identified Anglo-Saxonist thought as contributing to westward expansion (*Manifest Destiny: A Study of Nationalist Expansionism in American History* [1935; repr., Chicago: Quadrangle Books, 1963]). Weinberg did not emphasize this heavily, however, leaving Reginald Horsman to investigate the subject thoroughly in his *Race and Manifest Destiny*, published in 1981. Jimmy Bryan has revealed how western adventurers leaned hard on the works of Sir Walter Scott in fashioning themselves (*The American Elsewhere: Adventures and Manliness in the Age of Expansion* [Lawrence: University Press of Kansas, 2017], 74).

46. Melville, *Moby-Dick*, 115–21, 362.

47. Lynch, *Narrative of the Expedition to the River Jordan*, 236–37, 276–77, 279, 291; quotation on 323.

48. William Walker, *The War in Nicaragua* (Mobile, AL: S. H. Goftzel, 1860), 201.

49. Dozer, "Maury's Letter of Instruction to Herndon," 216.

50. Kane, *U.S. Grinnell Expedition*, 15.

51. *Weekly Herald* (New York), May 19, 1849.

52. John M. Clayton to J. J. Crittenden, July 11, 1849, reprinted in Mrs. Chapman Coleman, *The Life of John J. Crittenden, with Selections from His Correspondence and Speeches*, 2 vols. (Philadelphia: J. B. Lippincott, 1873), 1:344.

53. Earl of Rosse to George Bancroft, June 9, 1849, enclosed in George Bancroft to John M. Clayton, June 15, 1849, "Despatches from U.S. Ministers to Great Britain, 1791–1906," RG 59, M 30, vol. 59, roll 55, NARA Boston.

54. *Senate Journal*, 31st Cong., 1st Sess., January 4, 1850, 55.

55. Clayton to Crittenden, July 11, 1849, 1:344.

56. "Abandonment of the Search for Sir John Franklin by the United States Government," *Weekly Herald* (New York), June 23, 1849.

57. Clayton to Crittenden, July 11, 1849, 1:344.

58. *Sun* (Baltimore), May 19, 1849.

59. Lambert believes that Lady Franklin's accusation against Ross and the public censure that followed his return was unjustified, and that Ross had tried to penetrate the Arctic ice as far as he could during a particularly cold year (Lambert, *Gates of Hell*, 186–89).

60. Jane Franklin to unknown, November 17, 1849, reprinted in *Daily Missouri Republican* (St. Louis), December 28, 1849.

61. *Sun* (Baltimore), May 19, 1849.

62. In December 1849, Lynch declined the services of Elisha Kent Kane, the future Arctic explorer, who had written to offer himself for his proposed adventure (William Francis Lynch to Elisha Kent Kane, December 6, 1849, box 9, "Folder Lynch, William, 1849–1852," Kane Papers, APS).

63. *Sun* (Baltimore), June 25, 1849.

64. Sam W. Haynes, *Unfinished Revolution: The Early American Republic in a British World* (Charlottesville: University of Virginia Press, 2010), esp. chap. 2, "What Do You Think of Our Country?," 24–50.

65. Ralph Waldo Emerson, "The American Scholar," 1837, at "Digital Emerson: A Collective Archive," http://digitalemerson.wsulibs.wsu.edu/exhibits/show/text/the-american-scholar.

66. Abbott Lawrence to John Clayton, March 7, 1851, RG 59, M 30, vol. 62, roll 58, NARA Boston.

67. Rouleau, *With Sails Whitening Every Sea*, 1–2.

68. Haynes, *Unfinished Revolution*, 285–86.

69. John Kintzing Kane to Elisha Kent Kane, April 21, 1851, box 8, folder "Kane, John Kintzing," folder 3, 1850–1852, Kane Papers, APS.

70. Abbott Lawrence to John M. Clayton, November 2, 1849, RG 59, M 30, vol. 60, roll 56, NARA Boston.

71. *American National Biography Online*, s.v. "Grinnell, Henry," accessed February 15, 2016.

72. Robert G. Albion, *The Rise of New York Port, 1815–1860* (1939; New York: Charles Scribner's Sons, 1970), 247–48.

73. Henry Grinnell to Jane Franklin, October 7, 1851, reprinted in Rawnsley, *Life, Diaries and Correspondence of Lady Franklin*, 205.

74. Kenneth Bourne, *Britain and the Balance of Power in North America, 1815–1908* (Berkeley: University of California Press, 1967), 171.

75. For the idea of entangled communities mattering to historical actors, see Eliga H. Gould, "Entangled Worlds: The English-Speaking Atlantic as a Spanish Periphery," in *American Historical Review* 112, no. 3 (June 2007), 764–86.

76. Henry Grinnell to Jane Franklin, February 19, 1856, reprinted in Rawnsley, *Life, Diaries and Correspondence of Lady Franklin*, 218.

77. Henry Grinnell to Jane Franklin, September 3, 1856, reprinted in Rawnsley, 220–21.

78. Henry Grinnell to Jane Franklin, November 11, 1856, reprinted in Rawnsley, 223.

79. James Dobbin to Henry J. Hartstene, October 13, 1855, RG 45, M149, NARA I.

80. Wilkes to Tappan, November 25, 1850.

81. Elisha Kent Kane, *Arctic Explorations: The Second Grinnell Expedition in Search of Sir John Franklin, 1853, '54, '55*, 2 vols. (Philadelphia: Childs and Peterson, 1856), 1:446.

82. For an account of Lynch's Liberian reconnaissance, see Ponko, *Ships, Seas, and Scientists*, 199–205. For Black opposition to colonization, see Leon F. Litwack, *North of Slavery: The Negro in the Free States, 1790–1860* (Chicago: University of Chicago Press, 1961), 259; and Eric Burin, *Slavery and the Peculiar Solution: A History of the American Colonization Society* (Gainesville: University Press of Florida, 2005), 82–83.

83. William F. Lynch, *Naval Life; or, Observations Afloat and On Shore. The Midshipman* (New York: Charles Scribner, 1851), 28.

84. *Daily Alabama Journal*, March 5, 1850.

85. *Hudson River Chronicle* (Ossining, New York), March 5, 1850.

86. "Sir John Franklin's Expedition," *Times* (London), March 25, 1850, 3. In New Jersey, the *Trenton State Gazette* reprinted the article on May 1, 1850.

87. "Abandonment of the Search for Sir John Franklin by the United States Government," *Weekly Herald* (New York), June 23, 1849.

88. *Cong. Globe*, 31st Cong., 1st Sess., April 5, 1850, 644.

89. "From Washington—Correspondence of the Republican," *Daily Missouri Republican* (St. Louis), April 22, 1850.

90. *Cong. Globe*, 31st Cong., 1st Sess., May 1, 1850, 844.

91. *Cong. Globe*, May 1, 1850, 884.

92. *Cong. Globe*, May 1, 1850, 885.

93. *Cong. Globe*, May 1, 1850, 888.

94. For more on this concept in US history, see Morton J. Horwitz, *The Transforma-

tion of American Law, 1780–1860 (Cambridge, MA: Harvard University Press, 1977); William J. Novak, "The Myth of the Weak American State," *American Historical Review* 113, no. 3 (June 2008), 752–72; Novak, chap. 1, "Public-Private Governance: A Historical Introduction," in *Government by Contract: Outsourcing and American Democracy*, ed. Jody Freeman and Martha Minow (Cambridge, MA: Harvard University Press, 2009), 23–40; and Balogh, *A Government Out of Sight*.

95. Novak, "Public-Private Governance," 31.

96. Novak, 30.

97. Ponko, *Ships, Seas, and Scientists*, 21–26.

98. *House Journal*, 31st Cong., 1st Sess., April 26, 1850, 1623–1624.

99. *Senate Journal*, 31st Cong., 1st Sess., May 1, 1850, 317, and *House Journal*, 31st Cong., 1st Sess., May 6, 1850, 879.

100. Franklin to Grinnell, April 19, 1850, reprinted in Rawnsley, *Life, Diaries and Correspondence of Lady Franklin*, 201.

101. George W. Corner, *Doctor Kane of the Arctic Seas* (Philadelphia: Temple University Press, 1972), 77.

102. Kane, *U.S. Grinnell Expedition*, 24.

103. Elisha Kent Kane to "home people," May 25, 1850, box 8, folder "Kane Family, 1850–1853," Kane Papers, APS.

104. Joseph-Louis Bellot, a French naval officer who had volunteered in a private British expedition to locate Franklin, disappeared into an icy crevice (Corner, *Doctor Kane*, 101). Likewise, August Sontagg, one of the scientists aboard the Second Grinnell Expedition, also perished in this manner during a later Arctic mission (Corner, *Doctor Kane*, 273).

105. Anonymous author, *The Arctic Queen*, poem dedicated to Elisha Kent Kane, commander of the Grinnell expedition in search of Sir John Franklin, c. 1850s, HSP; Kane, *Arctic Explorations*, 2:22; Daniel P. Kidder and J. C. Fletcher, *Brazil and the Brazilians, Portrayed in Historical and Descriptive Sketches* (Philadelphia: Childs & Peterson, 1857), 432, LCP.

106. Kane, *U.S. Grinnell Expedition*, 14.

107. Margaret E. Wilmer, "Lines to the Memory of Dr. E. K. Kane; Who Died at Havana, Cuba," reprinted in Godfrey, *Godfrey's Narrative*, 265.

108. Wilmer, "Lines," in Godfrey, *Godfrey's Narrative*, 265, and Kane, *U.S. Grinnell Expedition*, 171.

109. Kane, *Arctic Explorations*, 1:69, 416, 276.

110. "Art. V.—1. Arctic Explorations: The Second Grinnell Expedition in Search of Sir John Franklin, During the Years 1853, '54, '55/2. The Last of the Arctic Voyages; Being a Narrative of the Expedition in H.M.S. *Assistance*, under the Command of Sir Edward Belcher, C.B., in Search of Sir John Franklin, During the Years 1852, '53, '54," *North American Review*, January 1, 1857, 119.

111. Kane, *U.S. Grinnell Expedition*, 19.

112. Godfrey, *Godfrey's Narrative*, 35.

113. Kane, *U.S. Grinnell Expedition*, 19.

114. Mark Metzler Sawin, *Raising Kane: Elisha Kent Kane and the Culture of Fame in Antebellum America* (Philadelphia: American Philosophical Society, 2008), 11.

115. R. P. Kane to C. Grinnell, February 13, 1854, box 3, folder "Grinnell, Cornelius, folder 2, 1853–1857," Kane Papers, APS.

116. Corner, *Doctor Kane*, 116.

117. Sawin, *Raising Kane*, 56.

118. Quoted in Corner, *Doctor Kane*, 27.

119. Sawin, *Raising Kane*, 13.

120. Sawin, 13.

121. Corner, *Doctor Kane*, 36. For more on this period of Kane's life, see Corner, esp. chap. 3, "Navy Doctor at Large," 32–48, and chap. 4, "Coast Fever and War Fever," 49–70.

122. Kane, *U.S. Grinnell Expedition*, 27.

123. Kane, 245.

124. Kane, 152.

125. See Kane, 247, 350.

126. Kane, 153.

127. Kane, 172.

128. Kane, 171–72.

129. Kane, 436; Edwin De Haven, *Lieut. De Haven's Official Report of the American Arctic Expedition*, October 4, 1851, reprinted in Kane, *U.S. Grinnell Expedition*, 506–7.

130. Edwin De Haven to Hamilton, secretary of the Admiralty, July 1, 1850, contained in Edwin De Haven to William Graham, October 31, 1851, RG 45, M 148, NARA I.

131. De Haven, *Official Report of the American Arctic Expedition*, 494.

132. One of the early records of this kind of activity is taken from De Haven's reply, dated August 11, 1851, to a circular from Austin. While the circular does not appear to have survived, De Haven copied his reply in a letter to Graham (De Haven to Graham, October 31, 1851).

133. De Haven to Austin, August 11, 1850, contained in De Haven to Graham, October 31, 1851.

134. De Haven, *Official Report of the American Arctic Expedition*, 495.

135. De Haven, 496.

136. David Chapin has noticed a similar trend (*Exploring Other Worlds: Margaret Fox, Elisha Kent Kane, and the Antebellum Culture of Curiosity* [Amherst: University of Massachusetts Press, 2004], 65–66).

137. "To The Editor of the Times." *Times* (London), January 9, 1850, 5. I am indebted to Alison Alexander for making this connection (*Ambitions of Jane Franklin*, 215).

138. Kane, *U.S. Grinnell Expedition*, 179.

139. Kane, 171.

140. De Haven, *Official Report of the American Arctic Expedition*, 497.

141. De Haven, 499.

142. De Haven, 499.

143. De Haven, 500.

144. De Haven, 501–2.

145. Elisha Kent Kane to Edwin De Haven, March 10, 1851, box 1, folder "E. J. DeHaven," Kane Papers, APS.

146. Kane, *U.S. Grinnell Expedition*, 487.

147. Grinnell to Franklin, October 7, 1851, reprinted in Rawnsley, *Life, Diaries and Correspondence of Lady Franklin*, 204–5.

148. Quoted in Rawnsley, 206.

149. Jane Franklin to Henry Grinnell, November 21, 1851, reprinted in Rawnsley, 207.

150. Elisha Kent Kane to Jane Franklin, November 15, 1851, box 3, folder "Lady Jane Franklin, Folder 1, 1849–1852," Kane Papers, APS.

151. Kane to Franklin, November 15, 1851.

152. Jane Franklin to Elisha Kent Kane, December 19, 1851, folder "Lady Jane Franklin, Folder 1, 1849–1852," APS.

153. Quoted in Remini, *John Quincy Adams*, 51.

154. Lambert, *Gates of Hell*, 265.

155. Edwin De Haven to William Graham, October 4, 1851, and October 11, 1855, both RG 45, M 148, NARA I.

156. Edwin De Haven to James Dobbin, November 14, 1853, RG 45, M 148, NARA I, and Kane, *U.S. Grinnell Expedition*, 15–16.

157. Edwin De Haven to Elisha Kent Kane, April 29, 1852, box 1, folder "E. J. DeHaven," Kane Papers, APS.

158. Franklin to Kane, December 19, 1851.

159. In a letter to Lady Franklin on October 24, 1852, Kane confirmed that the reason for publishing a narrative of the First Grinnell Expedition was to increase public interest and raise funds for a second mission (box 3, folder "Lady Jane Franklin, folder 1, 1849–1852," Kane Papers, APS); Henry Grinnell to Elisha Kent Kane, January 22, 1852, box 3, "Grinnell, Henry, Folder 1, 1851–1852," Kane Papers, APS; Cornelius Grinnell to Elisha Kent Kane, New York, February 11, 1853, box 3, folder "Grinnell, Cornelius, Folder 2, 1853–1857," Kane Papers, APS.

160. Edward Everett, Rufus Choate, William H. Prescott, Samuel Elliot, and Robert S. Shaw, to Elisha Kent Kane, Boston, March 19, 1852, box 2, folder "Everett, Edward," Kane Papers, APS; G. W. Reynolds of the Providence Association of Mechanics & Manufacturers to Elisha Kent Kane, October 2, 1852, box 10, folder "Reynolds, G. W., Jr.," Kane Papers, APS.

161. *Georgia Telegraph*, January 4, 1853; Kane, *U.S. Grinnell Expedition*, 549–51.

162. Corner, *Doctor Kane*, 103.

163. "I cannot agree with you," he wrote Kane in early 1852, "that a private Expedition would more likely be successful" on account of the difficulty of recruiting officers and men (Henry Grinnell to Elisha Kent Kane, February 1, 1852, box 3, "Grinnell, Henry, Folder 1, 1851–1852," Kane Papers, APS).

164. Grinnell to Kane, February 1, 1852.

165. Henry Grinnell to Elisha Kent Kane, November 28, 1851, box 3, "Grinnell, Henry, Folder 1, 1851–1852," Kane Papers, APS.

166. Henry Grinnell to Elisha Kent Kane, February 11, 1852, and March 16, 1852, box 3, "Grinnell, Henry, Folder 1, 1851–1852," Kane Papers, APS.

167. The financial cost of Wilkes's proposal, especially, seems to have been too much for many congressmen to bear (Grinnell to Kane, March 16, 1852).

168. Elisha Kent Kane to Thomas Dobbin, April 11, 1853, "Letters Received by the Secretary of the Navy from Commissioned Officers below the Rank of Commander and from Warrant Officers ('Officers' Letters')," NARA I.

169. See Melville, *Moby-Dick*, 111.

170. Grinnell to Kane, February 1, 1852.

171. "The Clayton-Bulwer Treaty," April 19, 1850, available at Avalon Project: Docu-

ments in Law, History and Diplomacy, accessed February 23, 2016, http://avalon.law
.yale.edu/19th_century/br1850.asp.

172. Bourne, *Britain and the Balance of Power*, 178.

173. Before Franklin Pierce won the Democratic nomination in June 1852, the leading contenders were Lewis Cass, James Buchanan, and Stephen Douglas (Schlesinger
and Israel, *My Fellow Citizens: Inaugural Addresses*, 120).

174. *Sun* (Baltimore), February 2, 1853; Elisha Kent Kane to Jane Franklin, January 14, 1853, copy, box 3, folder "Lady Jane Franklin, Folder 2, 1849–1852," Kane
Papers, APS.

175. John C. Symmes to Elisha Kent Kane, October 20, 1851, box 10, folder
"Symmes, John C.," Kane Papers, APS. Symmes never did sail on the Second Grinnell
Expedition (Kane, *Arctic Explorations*, 1:18).

176. Henry Brooks to Elisha Kent Kane, January 7, 1853, copied and enclosed in a
letter from Elisha Kent Kane to John P. Kennedy, Philadelphia, January 8, 1853, RG 45,
M 148, NARA I.

177. Godfrey, *Godfrey's Narrative*, 19.

178. Godfrey, 18.

179. John Pendleton Kennedy, *Political and Official Papers* (New York: G. P. Putnam
& Sons, 1872), 535.

180. John P. Kennedy to Elisha Kent Kane, November 27, 1852, box 8, folder "Kennedy, John P.," Kane Papers, APS.

181. Kane to Kennedy, January 8, 1853; Elisha Kent Kane to John P. Kennedy, Philadelphia, January 11, 1853, RG 45, M 148, NARA I; Elisha Kent Kane to John P. Kennedy,
Philadelphia, January 26, 1853, RG 45, M 148, NARA I.

182. Kane, *Arctic Explorations*, 1:16.

183. Elisha Kent Kane to John P. Kennedy, January 29, 1853, box 8, folder "Kennedy,
John P.," Kane Papers, APS.

184. Elisha Kent Kane to John P. Kennedy, June 18, 1853, Elisha Kent Kane Letters,
1853–1857, Mss.Film.1296, APS.

185. Ponko, *Ships, Seas, and Scientists*, 189; Kane to Kennedy, June 18, 1853.

186. "Dobbin," *Naval History and Heritage Command*, accessed February 15, 2016,
http://www.history.navy.mil/research/histories/ship-histories/danfs/d/dobbin.html.

187. Elisha Kent Kane to John P. Kennedy, May 17, 1853, Kane Letters, Mss.
Film.1296, APS, and James Dobbin to Elisha Kent Kane, April 11, 1853, RG 45, M 149,
NARA I.

188. "Search for Sir John Franklin—Dr. Kane's Expedition," *Daily Missouri Republican* (St. Louis), April 24, 1853.

189. "Kane's Arctic Expedition," *Daily Atlas* (Boston), May 21, 1853.

190. Horwitz, *Transformation of American Law*; Novak, "The Myth of the Weak
American State"; Novak, "Public-Private Governance"; Balogh, *A Government Out of
Sight*.

191. Grinnell to Kane, March 16, 1853; "Search for Sir John Franklin—Dr. Kane's
Expedition," *Daily Missouri Republican* (St. Louis), April 24, 1853.

192. James Dobbin to Elisha Kent Kane, March 21, 1853, RG 45, M 149, NARA I.

193. "Untitled," *Daily Atlas* (Boston), May 25, 1853.

194. Alexander von Humboldt to Elisha Kent Kane, March 8, 1853, box 3, folder
"Humboldt, Alexander von," Kane Papers, APS.

195. Kane, *Arctic Explorations*, 1:20.

196. Kane, 1:25.

197. Kane, 1:67.

198. Kane, 1:225, 2:153.

199. See, for example, Kane, 1:24, 384, 386, 392; 2:123, 209.

200. Kane, 2:124, 141, 144.

201. Kane, 1:223–24.

202. Kane, 1:224.

203. Corner, *Doctor Kane*, 138.

204. Dobbin to Hartstene, October 13, 1855.

205. This can be put together based on the data in Corner, *Doctor Kane*, 136, 258.

206. Elisha Kent Kane to James Dobbin, New York, October 11, 1855, RG 45, M 148, NARA I.

207. Kane, *Arctic Explorations*, 1:201.

208. Kane, 1:239–40.

209. Corner, *Doctor Kane*, 185.

210. This episode is thoroughly described in Corner, *Doctor Kane*, chap. 10, "Secession," 169–91.

211. Kane, *Arctic Explorations*, 2:86.

212. Kane, 1:240, 2:240.

213. Kane, 1:131.

214. Godfrey, *Godfrey's Narrative*, 19.

215. Godfrey, 5–6, 181.

216. Godfrey, 130–33.

217. Godfrey, 133–34.

218. See, for example, Kane, *Arctic Explorations*, 2:203. Godfrey also thought they were well suited for the polar regions (*Godfrey's Narrative*, 24).

219. Kane, *Arctic Explorations*, 1:211, 364.

220. Kane, 1:441.

221. Kane, 1:383.

222. Kane, 1:383.

223. Ponko, *Ships, Seas, and Scientists*, 193; Corner, *Doctor Kane*, 182–83.

224. Jeannette Mirsky, *Elisha Kent Kane and the Seafaring Frontier* (Boston: Little, Brown, 1954), 185–87; Corner, *Doctor Kane*, 263.

225. Corner, *Doctor Kane*, 153, 209.

226. Kane to Dobbin, October 11, 1855.

227. Mirsky, *Elisha Kent Kane*, 160, 185.

228. Kane, *Arctic Explorations*, 2:64–66.

229. Kane, 1:225.

230. Corner, *Doctor Kane*, 143.

231. Corner, 165–66.

232. Kane to Dobbin, October 11, 1855.

233. Kane to Dobbin, October 11, 1855.

234. Corner, *Doctor Kane*, 207.

235. Elisha Kent Kane to James Dobbin, Godhavn, September 10, 1855, RG 45, M 148, NARA I; Corner, *Doctor Kane*, 219.

236. Kane, *Arctic Explorations*, 2:291–93.

237. Corner, *Doctor Kane*, 219–23.

238. Kane's last letter home appears to have been the one that he sent to his father

from Upernavik, July 23, 1853, box 8, "Kane, John Kintzing, Folder 4, 1852–1853," Kane Papers, APS.

239. John Kane to John P. Kennedy, November 20, 1854, Mss.Film.1296, Kane Papers, APS; John P. Kennedy to John Kintzing Kane, Baltimore, November 23, 1854, box 8, folder "Kennedy, John P.," Kane Papers, APS; Grinnell to John Kintzing Kane, December 4, 1854, box 3, "Grinnell, Henry, Folder 3, 1854–1857," Kane Papers, APS.

240. See *House Journal*, 33rd Cong., 2nd Sess., December 12, 1854, 59; *Cong. Globe*, 33rd Cong., 2nd Sess., December 14, 1854, 54; *House Journal*, 33rd Cong., 2nd Sess., January 6, 1855, 155; *Senate Journal*, 33rd Cong., 2nd Sess., December 26, 1854, 67; *Senate Journal*, 33rd Cong., 2nd Sess., January 5, 1855, 97; *House Journal*, 33rd Cong., 2nd Sess., January 19, 1855, 201; and *Cong. Globe*, 33rd Cong., 2nd Sess., January 22, 1855, 352.

241. *Cong. Globe*, 33rd Cong., 2nd Sess., December 19, 1854, 83.

242. Corner, *Doctor Kane*, 221.

243. *Cong. Globe*, 33rd Cong., 2nd Sess., January 29, 1855, 444.

244. Dobbin to Hartstene, October 13, 1855.

245. Chapin, *Exploring Other Worlds*, 12.

246. Cornelius Grinnell to Elisha Kent Kane, June 2, 1855, box 3, "Grinnell, Cornelius, Folder 2, 1853–1857," Kane Papers, APS.

247. Elisha Kent Kane to John Kintzing Kane, November 21, 1855, box 8, "Kane, John Kintzing, Folder 4, 1852–1853," Kane Papers, APS.

248. Benson J. Lossing to Elisha Kent Kane, July 10, 1856, box 9, folder "Lossing, Benson J.," Kane Papers, APS; Fannie Holmes to Elisha Kent Kane, January 19, 1857, collection no. 1851, box "Correspondence, 1826–1860, John Kent Kane Correspondence, 1842–1857," D-47, folder "Letters mainly addressed to members of the family of John K. Kane. Letters concerning Kane Lodge F + AM New York, and proposed monument to Elisha Kent Kane," John Kintzing Kane Papers, 1714–1946, HSP.

249. Sawin, *Raising Kane*, 334.

250. "Art. V.—1. Arctic Explorations: The Second Grinnell Expedition in Search of Sir John Franklin, During the Years 1853, '54, '55/2. The Last of the Arctic Voyages; Being a Narrative of the Expedition in H.M.S. *Assistance*, under the Command of Sir Edward Belcher, C.B., in Search of Sir John Franklin, During the Years 1852, '53, '54," *North American Review*, January 1, 1857, 97, 119.

251. Corner, *Doctor Kane*, 240.

252. John F. Crampton to Elisha Kent Kane, Washington, December 8, 1855, reprinted in "Sir John Franklin's Expedition," *Times* (London), January 9, 1856, 10.

253. Jane Franklin to Elisha Kent Kane, London, November 2, 1855, box 3, "Franklin, Jane, Folder 2, 1853–1857," Kane Papers, APS.

254. Corner, *Doctor Kane*, 245.

255. Grinnell to Franklin, NY, July 19, 1856, reprinted in Rawnsley, *Life, Diaries and Correspondence of Lady Franklin*, 218.

256. Elisha Kent Kane to John Kintzing Kane, likely May 31, 1856, box 8, "Kane, John Kintzing, Folder 4, 1852–1853," Kane Papers, APS.

257. *New York Herald*, November 26, 1856.

258. Corner, *Doctor Kane*, 248–49.

259. Jane Franklin to Mr. Grinnell, March 5, 1857, box 3, folder "Lady Jane Franklin, Folder 2, 1849–1852," Kane Papers, APS.

260. Sawin, *Raising Kane*, 2; Corner, *Doctor Kane*, 254.

261. *Columbus (GA) Enquirer*, February 24, 1857.

262. Mourning ribbon for Elisha Kent Kane, John A. McAllister Ribbons & Textiles Collection, 1832–1896 (McA 10090.F), box 1, folder 26, LCP.

263. Bourne, *Britain and the Balance of Power*, 185.

264. Bourne, 182.

265. Lord Clarendon's phrase, quoted in Bourne, 195.

266. "The American Question," *Times* (London), May 29, 1856, 8.

267. Bourne, *Britain and the Balance of Power*, 194.

268. Bourne, 203.

269. Bourne, 198–200.

270. Bourne, 201.

271. Bourne, 203.

272. Bourne, 201.

273. Bourne, 204.

274. *New Hampshire Patriot & State Gazette* (Concord), January 16, 1856.

275. Corner, *Doctor Kane*, 240; "America," *Times* (London), July 7, 1856, 10.

276. "A Courteous ACT of the United States," *Times* (London), July 14, 1856, 6.

277. *Daily Ohio Statesman* (Columbus), November 14, 1856.

278. Thomas to Henry Grinnell, September 25, 1856, box 3, "Grinnell, Henry, Folder 3, 1854–1857," Kane Papers, APS.

279. I am not the first to make this observation. Ernest R. May discussed this idea in *Imperial Democracy: The Emergence of America as a Great Power* (New York: Harcourt, Brace & World, 1961). More recently, Sam W. Haynes and Eliga H. Gould have drawn similar conclusions (Haynes, *Unfinished Revolution*; Gould, *Among the Powers of the Earth: The American Revolution and the Making of a New World Empire* [Cambridge, MA: Harvard University Press, 2012]).

280. "One Relic of the Many Expeditions Which Have," *Times* (London) December 15, 1856, 6.

281. Corner, *Doctor Kane*, 240; C. Grinnell to H. Grinnell, December 16, 1856, reprinted in *Times-Picayune* (New Orleans), January 10, 1857.

282. *Daily Atlas* (Boston), January 9, 1857.

283. "The Arctic Ship Resolute," *Times* (London), December 23, 1856, 7.

284. Alexander, *Ambitions of Jane Franklin*, 241. Her hope was in vain; the Admiralty was sick of the quest and wanted to move on (Rawnsley, *Life, Diaries and Correspondence of Lady Franklin*, 104; Lambert, *Gates of Hell*, 260).

285. C. Grinnell to H. Grinnell, December 16, 1856.

286. *Times-Picayune* (New Orleans), January 10, 1857.

287. "Her Majesty's Visit to the Resolute," *Times* (London), December 17, 1856, 7.

288. George M. Dallas to William Marcy, January 23, 1857, RG 59, M 30, vol. 70, roll 66, NARA Boston.

EPILOGUE

1. Lewis M. Hatch to Elisha Kent Kane, January 18, 1857, "Correspondence, 1826–1860, John Kent Kane Correspondence, 1842–1857" (box D-47), folder 14, "Letters Addressed to Dr. Elisha Kent Kane, 1842–1857," John Kintzing Kane Papers, HSP.

2. Quoted in Mark Metzler Sawin, *Raising Kane: Elisha Kent Kane and the Culture of Fame in Antebellum America* (Philadelphia: American Philosophical Society, 2008), 329.

3. See, for example, Drew Gilpin Faust, *Mothers of Invention: Women of the Slave-*

holding South in the American Civil War (Chapel Hill: University of North Carolina Press, 1996), esp. "Introduction: All the Relations of Life," 3–8; and Bertram Wyatt-Brown, *Southern Honor: Ethics and Behavior in the Old South* (Oxford: Oxford University Press, 1982).

4. Kane, *Arctic Explorations*, 1:446.

5. See Corner, *Doctor Kane*.

6. Sprigman to J. L. Kane, March 12, 1857.

7. M. E. Amidou to Jane Leiper Kane, May 31, 1857, box 6, folder "Kane, Elisha Kent, Letters of condolence on Kane's death, 1855–1861," Kane Papers, APS.

8. Henry Pirtle and others to John Kintzing Kane, February 28, 1857, "Correspondence, 1826–1860, John Kent Kane Correspondence, 1842–1857" (box D-47), folder "Correspondence, Contains Letters of Sympathy on Death of Dr. Elisha Kent Kane, 1820–1857," John Kintzing Kane Papers, HSP.

9. See Sachs, *Humboldt Currents*, chap. 5, "'Mocha Dick': The Value of Mental Expansion," 143–76.

10. Aubrey Starke, "Poe's friend Reynolds," *American Literature* 11, no. 2 (May 1939), 152.

11. William H. Goetzmann, *New Lands, New Men: America and the Second Great Age of Discovery* (1986; repr., Austin: Texas State Historical Association, 1995), 287.

12. Seymour Barofsky, ed., *The Wisdom of Mark Twain* (New York: Citadel Press, 2002), 61–64.

13. Ralph Waldo Emerson, "Wealth," from *Conduct of Life*, reprinted in *The Complete Essays and Other Writings of Ralph Waldo Emerson* (New York: Modern Library, 1940), 699–700.

14. Goetzmann, *New Lands, New Men*, 229–31.

15. Emily Dickinson, "There Is No Frigate Like a Book," in *Selections from American Literature*, ed. Leonidas Warren Payne Jr. (Chicago: Rand McNally, 1927), 762.

16. Wilkes, *Narrative of the US Exploring Expedition*, 3:310–12; "Naval Monument," Mount Auburn Cemetery, accessed July 18, 2020, https://mountauburn.org/naval-monument/. The number of the unknown sailors who perished on the *Sea-Gull* is taken from Wilkes, *Narrative of the United States Exploring Expedition*, 1:212. Their names are given in the personnel lists of Wilke's *Narrative*, 1:xxxviii–lxii.

17. Sidney Kopman to Robert P. Kane, June 10, 1859, "Correspondence, 1826–1860, John Kent Kane Correspondence, 1842–1857" (box D-47), folder "Letters mainly addressed to members of the family of John K. Kane. Letters concerning Kane Lodge F + AM New York, and proposed monument to Elisha Kent Kane," John Kintzing Kane Papers, HSP.

18. "Col Lewis Melvin Hatch," *Find a Grave*, accessed July 18, 2020, https://www.findagrave.com/memorial/32139194/lewis-melvin-hatch.

19. "Secretaries of the Navy," Naval History and Heritage Command, accessed July 18, 2020, https://www.history.navy.mil/content/history/nhhc/research/library/research-guides/lists-of-senior-officers-and-civilian-officials-of-the-us-navy/secretaries-of-the-navy.html. William M. Fowler Jr., in *Under Two Flags: The American Navy in the Civil War* (Annapolis, MD: Naval Institute Press, 1990), thinks Toucey was less a "knave" than a "fool" (34).

20. George H. Schwartz, *Collecting the Globe: The Salem East India Marine Society Museum* (Amherst: University of Massachusetts Press, 2020), 161.

21. Schwartz, *Collecting the Globe*, 162.

22. Williams, *Maury, Scientist of the Sea*, 369–70; Ponko, *Ships, Seas, and Scientists*, 133.

23. Rook, *150th Anniversary*, 28.

24. William Harwar Parker, *Recollections of a Naval Officer, 1841–1865* (New York: Charles Scribner's Sons, 1883), 228.

25. Parker, *Recollections of a Naval Officer*, 228.

26. Catherine Ann Devereux, *Journal of a Secesh Lady: The Diary of Catherine Ann Devereux, 1860–1866*, ed. Beth G. Crabtree and James W. Patton (Raleigh: North Carolina Division of Archives and History, 1979) 444.

27. William Stanton, *The Great United States Exploring Expedition of 1838–1842* (Berkeley: University of California Press, 1975), 380.

28. Stanton, *United States Exploring Expedition*, 379.

29. Stanton, 379.

30. LaFeber, *The American Age*, 151.

31. Eicher, *Raising the Flag*, 211.

32. Charles Francis Adams, ed., *Memoirs of John Quincy Adams, Comprising Portions of His Diary From 1795 to 1848*, 12 vols. (Philadelphia: J. B. Lippincott, 1874–1877), 11:202.

33. Lynch, *Narrative of the Expedition to the River Jordan*, 321–28.

34. Pliny A. Durant, ed., *The History of Clinton County* (Chicago: W. H. Beers, 1882), 585; McDonald, "Reynolds, Jeremiah N.," 524.

35. McDonald, 525.

36. Edgar Allan Poe, review of *A Brief Account of the Discoveries and Results of the United States' Exploring Expedition*, *Graham's Magazine*, September 1843, 165, available at Edgar Allan Poe Society of Baltimore, https://www.eapoe.org/works/criticsm/gm43091.htm.

37. Anna Ella Carroll, *The Star of the West; Or, National Men and National Measures* (3rd ed., New York: Miller, Orton, 1857), 16, LCP.

38. Carroll, *Star of the West*, 15.

39. Carroll, 136.

40. Sandage, *Born Losers*, 35.

41. Eric Jay Dolin, *Leviathan: The History of Whaling in America* (New York: W. W. Norton, 2007), 310–16.

42. For a thorough account of Maury's Confederate service, see Williams, *Maury, Scientist of the Sea*, chaps. 19 and 20, 365–420.

43. Dolin, *Leviathan*, 332.

44. Dolin, 310.

45. Fowler, *Under Two Flags*, 298.

46. Dolin, *Leviathan*, "Chapter 18: From the Earth," 336–41.

47. Dolin, "Chapter 19: Ice Crush," 342–32.

48. Fowler, *Under Two Flags*, 298–99.

49. Rouleau, epilogue to *With Sails Whitening Every Sea*, 195–207.

50. For more on the decline of the US whaling industry and the blue-water merchant marine as well as the expansion of new maritime industries in the postwar years, see Labaree et al., *America and the Sea*, esp. chap. 10, "The Sea and Post-Civil-War America," 365–435.

51. Hampton Sides, *In the Kingdom of Ice: The Grand and Terrible Polar Voyage of the USS Jeannette* (New York: Doubleday, 2014).

52. Andrew C. A. Jampoler, *Congo: The Miserable Expeditions and Dreadful Death of Lt. Emory Taunt, USN* (Annapolis, MD: Naval Institute Press, 2013).

53. Ernest R. May, *Imperial Democracy: The Emergence of America as a Great Power* (New York: Harcourt, Brace & World, 1961).

54. Viscount Palmerston to Abbott Laurence [*sic*], Foreign Office, November 13, 1849, reprinted in *Correspondence with the United States Respecting Central America. Presented to both Houses of Parliament by Command of Her Majesty, 1856* (London: Harrison and Sons, 1856), 7.

55. Guillaume Tell Poussin, *The United States; Its Power and Progress*, trans. Edmund L. Du Barry, American 1st ed., from French 3rd ed. (Philadelphia: Lippincott, Grambo, 1851), 485.

56. "Anniversary of the Foundation of the Australian Colonies," *Times* (London,), January 27, 1859, 7.

57. Williams, *Maury, Scientist of the Sea*, 296, 335; Ponko, *Ships, Seas, and Scientists*, 92.

58. Owen M. Taylor, *The History of Annapolis, with a Full History and Description of the United States Naval Academy* (1872; repr., Bedford, MA: Applewood Books, 2009), 37–38; United States Naval Academy, "History and Traditions of the Herndon Monument Climb," accessed August 1, 2020, https://www.usna.edu/PAO/faq_pages/herndon.php.

59. The statue exists in large part due to the fundraising efforts of the United Daughters of the Confederacy (Hildegarde Hawthorne, *Matthew Fontaine Maury: Trail Maker of the Seas* [New York: Longmans, Green, 1943], 224). See also Penelope Hardy and Helen M. Rozwadowski, "Reckoning with a Racist Legacy in Ocean Science," *History of Oceanography*, International Commission of the History of Oceanography, June 16, 2020, https://oceansciencehistory.wordpress.com/2020/06/16/reckoning -with-a-racist-legacy-in-ocean-science/#_edn3. For an alternative perspective on the Maury monument, see Matthew Mace Barbee, "Matthew Fontaine Maury and the Evolution of Southern Memory," *Virginia Magazine of History and Biography* 120, no. 4 (2012), 372–93.

60. Aimee Ortiz, "Richmond Removes Confederate Statues from Monument Avenue," *New York Times*, July 2, 2020, https://www.nytimes.com/2020/07/02/us/ stonewall-jackson-statue-richmond.html.

61. Wilkes, *Autobiography*, 533, 541. Daniel C. Haskell discusses Congress's discontent with the expense of publishing the Ex Ex's scientific volumes in *United States Exploring Expedition*, 12–16.

62. For a full account of this history, see Evelyn, chap. 11, "National Gallery at the Patent Office"; and Nathan Reingold and Marc Rothenberg, chap. 12, "The Exploring Expedition and the Smithsonian Institution" in *Magnificent Voyagers: The U.S. Exploring Expedition, 1838–1842*, ed. Herman J. Viola and Carolyn Margolis (Washington, DC: Smithsonian Institution Press, 1985). See also Stanton, *United States Exploring Expedition*, 358–59; Philbrick, *Sea of Glory*, 333–51; and Nina Burleigh, *The Stranger and the Statesman: James Smithson, John Quincy Adams, and the Making of America's Greatest Museum: The Smithsonian* (New York: HarperCollins, 2003).

63. The exhibit ran from November 19, 1985, to November 9, 1986, before being passed along to other institutions across the country ("Magnificent Voyagers: The U.S. Exploring Expedition, 1838–1842 [Wilkes Expedition]," Smithsonian Institution, accessed August 1, 2020, https://www.si.edu/exhibitions/magnificent-voyagers-us -exploring-expedition-1838-1842-wilkes-expedition-event-exhib-2215).

Index

Page numbers in italics refer to figures.